Is the Good Book Good Enough?

Is the Good Book Good Enough?

Evangelical Perspectives on Public Policy

Edited by David K. Ryden

LEXINGTON BOOKS

Lanham • Boulder • New York • Toronto • Plymouth, UK

Published by Lexington Books
A wholly owned subsidiary of The Rowman & Littlefield Publishing Group, Inc.
4501 Forbes Boulevard, Suite 200, Lanham, Maryland 20706
www.rowman.com

10 Thornbury Road, Plymouth PL6 7PP, United Kingdom

Copyright © 2011 by Lexington Books
First paperback edition 2012

British Library Cataloguing in Publication Information Available

Library of Congress Cataloging-in-Publication Data
This book was previously cataloged by the Library of Congress as follows:

Is the good book good enough? : evangelical perspectives on public policy / edited by David K.
Ryden
p. cm.
Includes index.
ISBN 978-0-7391-5059-7(cloth : alk. paper) -- ISBN 978-0-7391-7707-5 (pbk. : alk. paper) -- ISBN
978-0-7391-5061-0 (electronic)
1. Evangelicalism—United States. 2. Christianity and politics—United States. 3. Public policy. I.
Ryden, David K.
BR517.18 2011
261.7--dc22

2010039528

Contents

Introduction: The Evolving Policy Agenda of Evangelical Christians

David K. Ryden

We call for an expansion of our concern beyond single-issue politics, such as abortion and marriage, and a fuller recognition of the comprehensive causes and concerns of the Gospel. . . . Although we cannot back away from our biblically rooted commitment to the sanctity of every human life, including those unborn, nor can we deny the holiness of marriage as instituted by God between one man and one woman, we must . . . [engage] the global giants of conflict, racism, corruption, poverty, pandemic diseases, illiteracy, ignorance, and spiritual emptiness, by promoting reconciliation, encouraging ethical servant leadership, assisting the poor, caring for the sick, and educating the next generation.

"An Evangelical Manifesto," Summer 2008

The scene of the first joint appearance by the presidential candidates in the 2008 general election was a striking one, for reasons obvious and subtle. On August 15, Barack Obama and John McCain appeared on the same stage for back-to-back interviews with Rick Warren, California megachurch pastor and author of *The Purpose-Driven Life*. The event drew broad national coverage, suggesting that perhaps the political obituaries of those values-driven, religiously conservative voters of 2004 might have been premature. But while the politics of the event were not lost on anyone, the more interesting and potentially significant developments involved policy, and were to be found in what Warren and the candidates actually talked about.

Warren didn't shy away from the hot-button issues with which religious conservatives have been closely associated. He peppered the candidates with pointed questions on their faith commitments and moral failings, and on their stands on abortion and same-sex marriage. But the far-ranging discussions went well beyond those topics, encompassing such domestic policy subjects as education, poverty reduction, taxes, and faith-based initiatives. The candidates' responses ranged far and wide, touching on Katrina, energy policy, climate change, and more. At Warren's prompting, McCain and Obama weighed in on American international obligations with respect to AIDS and orphans, genocide and humanitarian crises, human trafficking and religious persecution abroad. In addition to matters of war and peace, the candidates talked about public service and the greater good. In short, the interviews spanned the full spectrum of the contemporary domestic and global policy agenda in America.

Too much can be made of a single campaign event.[1] Yet perhaps no one personifies the evolving face of evangelical public policy engagement like Rick Warren. For this reason, the Saddleback church interviews illustrated a key development that is occurring at the intersection of faith and contemporary politics—namely, the expanding policy agenda of evangelical Christians. With relatively little fanfare, evangelical Christianity is being employed as a lens through which to view an ever-broadening range of contemporary public policy issues. This change carries with it real implications for the future of American politics and policy debates.

The robust political engagement by evangelical Christians has been a signal development in American politics in the past quarter century. As their political involvement has risen, so too has their public profile. But while their role in electoral politics has been much scrutinized, evangelical approaches to public policy have largely been neglected. There is a paucity of serious systematic study of evangelicalism as a perspective for viewing the gamut of policy matters. Hence evangelical policy attitudes are poorly understood and oft mischaracterized.

Popular perceptions of evangelicalism are mostly impressionistic, sometimes bordering on caricature. They're seen as anti-intellectual Bible thumpers whose policy positions are derived from chapter and verse of scripture and devoid of reasoned analysis, logic, empirical evidence, or other bases of policy analysis. They're lemming-like, susceptible to group think and prone to follow the cues of high-profile leaders like James Dobson and Pat Robertson. They march in lockstep with the Republican party and are uniformly conservative on the "wedge" issues of gay rights, abortion, the death penalty, and guns.

These caricatures persist, even in the midst of a prodigious amount of scholarly and popular writing that has been published in recent years on Christianity in the public realm, much of it aimed at evangelicals. But while the political activism of evangelical Christians has been a popular target, there has been little serious attention devoted to the undercurrents of evangelical engagement in the public policy context.

On the broadest level, a spate of virulently antireligious books launched a robust assault on faith itself, and certainly on its public manifestations. Richard Dawkins' *The God Delusion*, Sam Harris's *Letter to a Christian Nation*, and Christopher Hitchens' *God Is Not Great: How Religion Poisons Everything*—each made its way onto the *New York Times* bestseller lists by demonizing religion and its presence in the public and political spheres. In a different vein, a number of other books took up the politicization of faith, in particular the close association of religious conservatives with the Republican Party. Illustrative of this genre were Garry Wills' *Under God: Religion and American Politics*, Kevin Phillips' *American Theocracy: The Peril and Politics of Radical Religion, Oil, and Borrowed Money in the 21st Century*, New York Times correspondent Chris Hedges' *American Fascists: The Christian Right and the War on America*, and *Faith and Politics* by former U.S. senator John Danforth.

A related line of attacks came from within, launched by self-declared evangelicals who bemoaned the unhealthy nexus between the Christian right and the Republican Party. Those included *Thy Kingdom Come: An Evangelical's Lament* (Randall Balmer), former president Jimmy Carter's *Our Endangered Values: America's Moral Crisis*, and Jim Wallis' *God's Politics: Why the Right Gets It Wrong and the Left Doesn't Get It*. Some issued a plea for evangelicals to retreat from political activism, in the vein of Minneapolis pastor and theologian Greg Boyd's *The Myth of a Christian Nation: How the Quest for Political Power Is Destroying the Church*. Others sought to advance a new political engagement on the left that might answer the influence of evangelicals on the right (Amy Sullivan, *The Party Faithful: How and Why Democrats Are Closing the God Gap*; Michael Lerner, *The Left Hand of God*; Jim Wallis, *The Great Awakening: Reviving Faith and Politics in a Post-Religious Right America*).

Many of these works offered valuable insights into the dynamic interplay between faith and politics, as they convincingly delineated real weaknesses in evangelical policy activism. But they by and large failed to capture the richer, more diverse reality of evangelicalism in the public policy realm that has sprouted in recent years. As such, it is debatable how much they have done to clarify the current state of evangelicalism as a policy influence. Indeed, they may only have obfuscated genuine developments in the attitudes of evangelicals relative to public policy, in particular the notable expansion of the issues and questions in which evangelicals are now showing an interest. This book offers a corrective, examining not only the *what* of contemporary evangelical public policy perspectives, but also the *why* and the *what next*.

RELIGION AND PUBLIC POLICY: BRINGING EVANGELICALS INTO FOCUS

This project has two foundational purposes, both of which are prompted by an unease over the treatment of evangelicals in the recent literature. The first purpose is simply to provide a more sophisticated and nuanced portrait of evangelicalism in the public square. Much of the criticism of evangelicalism as a policy force sweeps with too broad a brush. The critics often rely upon a sketchy, crabbed understanding of evangelicalism, and are either ignorant or dismissive of the dynamic changes occurring within evangelicalism. The writers frequently miss what is an increasingly vibrant and vigorous debate among evangelicals over the implications that their faith holds for their public policy views. One aim, then, is to provide a more systematic and comprehensive description of evangelical attitudes on American public policy and the theological underpinnings for those attitudes.

The neglect of evangelical policy attitudes is inexcusable, given their size and the unsettled nature of their policy views. Evangelicals comprise a big slice of the American public, representing somewhere from a quarter to over a third of the adult population.[2] In short, they make up the single largest identifiable religious bloc in the United States. Moreover, their evangelical identity is especially salient in relation to their political and policy views. This is because evangelicalism tends to be the central formative influence in shaping the thinking and action in the political realm of those who adhere to it. More than any other religious group, evangelicals are inclined to attune their politics with their faith. According to the U.S. Religious Landscape Survey, evangelicals are easily the most apt to conclude that their religious views influence their thinking on politics.[3] By virtue of their size *and* the political impact of their religious views and traditions, this highly influential subset of the American polity is deserving of a much more sophisticated and accurate rendering than it has received to date.

Given their sheer numbers, it is easy to understand why evangelicals have never quite fit the common perception of a monolithic, uniformly conservative religious bloc. Evangelical historian Mark Noll has noted the "surprising spectrum of economic, political, and social viewpoints [that] can be found in evangelical communities" (Noll 2000, 25). Not only has there been more diversity of thought and belief than we are typically led to believe, but that diversity is also steadily growing. One need only have kept a casual eye on the news headlines of recent years to realize that evangelicals are engaging the public policy arena in new and expansive ways.

Indeed, evangelical attitudes on public policy are unsettled and evolving. A new breed of evangelical leaders has taken public stances on issues such as the environment, immigration, and poverty that do not fit the profile of the conventional religious conservative. The rank and file, especially younger college-age evangelicals, see their faith as relevant to a broader swath of issues than just abortion and gay marriage. Evangelicals with the same view of scriptural authority diverge in applying that religious authority to the range of policy issues. A distinctive (albeit smaller) evangelical left mirrors the religious right, and an emerging evangelical center seeks a broader policy framework around which evangelicals might coalesce.

David Gushee comes the closest to capturing this new reality of evangelical political involvement in his book, *The Future of Faith in American Politics: The Public Witness of the Evangelical Center*. Gushee explores in detail the rise of a new policy-based evangelicalism, one that is broadening its policy range to include a host of issues, including social justice, environmentalism, and more. While evangelicals have not abandoned traditional issues such as abortion and marriage, there has been a serious movement on their part toward a broad and holistic moral agenda (Gushee 2008).

This is one of the most interesting and potentially significant developments of late to have occurred at the intersection of faith and politics. It has, however, been obscured by overwrought cries of theocracy and the zeal among many to read believers out of public life. Nor have the voices of more progressive evangelical Christians necessarily clarified the picture. Theologian Charles Marsh, in observing the emergence of a stronger left leaning presence in the debates on faith and politics, wonders whether it "seems to be producing as much cacophony as clarity" (Marsh 2008, 5).

This book is an effort to dampen the cacophony and sharpen the clarity around the evolving evangelical thinking on public policy. It aims for a more carefully modulated and complex view of evangelicalism as a formative public policy influence. It gently pushes back against indictments of theocracy that urge the diminishment or outright removal of the faithful in policy debates. It aims to capture as precisely and accurately as possible the changing nature of evangelicalism as a prism for viewing a broad range of public policy questions. It seeks a fully multidimensional portrait of evangelicalism relative to public policy, even as that portrait seems to be in the midst of taking on a different face.

EVANGELICALS AND THE INDICTMENT OF UNREFLECTIVE ACTIVISM

> All too often we have disobeyed the great command to love the Lord our God with our hearts, souls, strength, and minds, and have fallen into an unbecoming anti-intellectualism that is a dire cultural handicap as well as a sin. ("An Evangelical Manifesto," 12)

The second, and related, aim of this book is to present a serious intellectual critique of evangelicalism as a distinctive policy perspective. The attacks on evangelicalism certainly carry enough truth to suggest deeply ingrained weaknesses in evangelical policy involvement. The animated critiques of evangelicalism are attributable at least in part to the intellectual shallowness and overbearing self-righteousness that pervades much of the activism that evangelical Christians bring into the public realm (Marsh 2008, 4). One senses a far-reaching faith-fatigue, a tiring of the cuckolding by religious conservatives toward the rest of society.

It is important to note that the critiques of Christian political activism are hardly confined to secular voices or those outside the evangelical camp. Indeed, some of the most searing criticism has been internal, castigating evangelicals for their failure to reflect in a more sophisticated and thoughtful way upon what their faith means for their politics.

In his classic mid-1990s book, *The Scandal of the Evangelical Mind*, historian Mark Noll took his fellow evangelicals to task for their inability to sustain serious intellectual life. He characterized modern evangelicals as failing to have "pursued comprehensive thinking under God or [to have] sought a mind shaped to its furthest reaches by Christian perspectives" (Noll 1994, 3–4). For Noll, an evangelical then teaching at evangelical Wheaton College, the scandal of the evangelical mind was that there really was not much of an evangelical mind. While Noll was speaking more to the deeper philosophical and intellectual underpinnings of evangelicalism, his indictment of modern evangelicalism as intellectually vacuous could just as easily have been applied to their shortcomings in applying their substantive theological traditions to public policy.

Indeed, Noll's critique of evangelicalism aptly fits their policy behavior. Evangelical participation in political and policy debates has lacked a genuine theologically informed approach to public policy. Even as evangelicals have expanded their policy awareness, their approach to public policy has been mostly untethered from a serious or well-developed theological framework. As a result, evangelicals have lacked a coherent or integrated vision that might guide their participation in public policy debates.

This is attributable in part to the nature of evangelicalism as a faith tradition, and in part to those circumstances that drew evangelicals into the political world in large numbers in the past three decades. On one hand, the emphasis placed on one's personal relationship with Christ renders the evangelical faith highly personal, experiential, and individualistic. The political behavior that it produces tends toward the impulsive, visceral, reactive, and emotional, rather than the more rational and intellectual. Evangelical political reflection has

> drawn upon intuitive conceptions of justice because evangelicals in general
> have trusted their sanctified common sense more than formal theology, [or]
> systematic study . . . the most visible forms of political reflection have [been]
> carried on without serious recourse to self-conscious theological construction,
> systematic moral philosophy, thorough historical analysis, or careful social
> scientific research. (Noll 1994, 169)

Evangelicals tend to be "intuitionists" who trust their "sanctified common sense" for their political and policy views (Ibid.). But being fully human, their common sense may not be all that sanctified, and indeed it too often does not reflect much common sense. In short, "orderly political reflection has not yet risen to its task" among evangelicals (Budziszewski 2006, 18).

Moreover, the historical and contextual influences on modern evangelical political activism reinforced their intuitive inclinations. The developments that drove religious conservatives into politics were more cultural than intellectual in origin. Evangelicals' political posture from the outset has been essentially defensive, stemming from their perception of themselves as the protectors of traditional values in the culture wars. Their politics has been more reactive than proactive, in response to the tenor of the 1960s, abortion and *Roe v. Wade*, the stripping of prayer and bible reading from the schools, and the like. These cultural prompts played a greater role in motivating evangelicals to political action than did seriously grounded theological justifications, which tended to spring up after the fact. To this day, one senses that the intellectual bases for evangelical policy activism are "constantly evolving and still being framed from election to election and issue by issue" (Cromartie 2001, 132).

But absent the anchor of well-articulated theological principles, evangelicals inevitably fall back on other, non-scriptural influences—ideological commitment, partisan attachment, cultural cues, or basic intuition—in staking out positions on complex policy questions. This undermines the integrity of consistent application of religious belief to political thought and action. Evangelicals run the risk of appearing to adapt their theological views to fit preconceived ideological or partisan attachments, rather than the other way around. This is an obvious problem for those who by definition are supposed to take principled policy positions based upon transcendent truth revealed in the form of biblical text (Buzzard 1989, 143).

The result is a compromised faith, one that takes a backseat to party, power, and politics. It makes it difficult, if not impossible, to "look upon the political sphere as a realm of creation ordained by God for serious Christian involvement" (Noll 1994, 174). It also increases the chances that evangelicals will be unable to make what in theory should be their unique contribution to ongoing policy debates—namely, to provide an alternative, transcendent reference point for policy decisions.

The corollary objective of this book is to provide a clear-eyed and chastened view of evangelical policy activism, by illustrating just how far short of a principled evangelical policy framework actual evangelical policy participation has fallen. The contributors to this volume seek to demonstrate what an intellectually richer and rhetorically more nuanced application of the evangelical religious tradition to ongoing policy debates might look like. In that sense, this is a book *about* evangelicalism that also ought to be of interest *to* evangelicals. It is intended as something of a primer for those genuinely interested in acquiring a genuine understanding of evangelicalism as a formative influence on public policy views. At the same time, it provides a mirror by which evangelicals might examine their effectiveness, or lack thereof, as active participants in the contemporary public policy arena.

DEFINING EVANGELICALISM: WHO AND WHAT ARE WE TALKING ABOUT?

Before we delve too deeply into the pool of policy analysis, we need to clarify who is at the center of this discussion. Genuine understanding of evangelical political behavior has been impeded by misuse and abuse of the evangelicalism label, which is bandied about carelessly by those with little understanding of it.[4] A central underlying premise of this book is the notion that there is a substantive core of evangelical beliefs that has clear implications for the resolution of contemporary policy questions. If indeed this book seeks to identify and explain an evangelical policy perspective—to the extent that there is one—that effort will locate that perspective in the essential theological beliefs, doctrines, and traditions that make up evangelicalism. Hence we need to articulate and describe those key substantive principles of evangelical Christianity.[5]

The doctrinal substance of evangelical Christianity is for the most part held in common by most protestant Christians. It includes belief in the Trinitarian nature of God, the reality of His revelation in word and deed, the fall of man and the hope for redemption through the incarnation of God in Christ, atonement through Christ's death and resurrection, the importance of a personal faith commitment, and a faith in the life of the world to come (Budziszewski 2006, 19).

The distinctive nature of evangelicalism rests more in its emphasis on particular aspects of the Protestant Christian faith and the blend of four primary components around which there is general consensus. Those are biblicism, Christ-centeredness, conversion, and evangelism. *Biblicism* simply refers to the belief in the Bible as divinely inspired and containing God's revealed truth. It is inerrant truth and constitutes specific revelation of the creative design of God. Scripture represents the ultimate authority for evangelicals, and hence they put greater emphasis on scriptural authority—both in general and literal form—as the guide for all things. In other words, at the heart of the evangelical faith is an elevated, exalted view of scripture that sets them apart from other Protestant traditions. Second, evangelicals believe in the *centrality of Christ*; He is the Son of God and the exclusive path to salvation. The forgiveness of sins and the redemption of humanity are available only through Christ, his death on the cross, and His resurrection. Likewise, Christ's words and actions are the main guide for what Christians ought to believe and how they should live. *Conversion* emphasizes the absolute necessity of a personal acceptance of and commitment to Christ, what is colloquially referred to as having a "born again" experience. Moreover, at the center of one's faith experience is an ongoing personal relationship with Christ. Finally, evangelicals put great emphasis on *evangelism*, on the sharing of their faith with the world. Evangelicals take to heart the great commission to go forth to all corners of the world to share the Gospel of Christ and win converts to Him (Noll 2000, 140). Evangelicals are bound by a common belief in

> salvation by grace through faith in Jesus Christ, emphasis on a personal and vibrant religious experience through the transforming work of the Holy Spirit, the supreme authority of the Bible for Christian faith and practice, and a fierce commitment to the spread of the gospel through evangelism, missions, and social reform. (Gushee and Hollinger 2005, 118)

Three additional observations might help to begin the task of shaping an evangelical methodology relative to public policy. First, the evangelical faith tradition views the sovereignty of God as all-encompassing; it is the foundation for everything—law, morality, human rights, and human institutions such as civil government. In this way, evangelicalism is an "engaged orthodoxy," whereby believers bring their faith to bear on all aspects of their lives, including their surrounding culture and the political realm (Gushee 2008, 18). This leads to the view of government as a God-ordained enterprise, and a legitimate avenue for pursuing God's ends of justice and righteousness. In this light, government and politics demand one's obedience, attention, and involvement. Christians cannot ignore politics or public policy; it is their sacred duty to serve God through civil authority and to pursue His purposes of justice through policy-making institutions and processes.

Second, for evangelicals the Bible is God's revelation and the source of authority trumping all else. Evangelicals accept the historic teachings of Christianity in a more literal sense. Moreover, the tenets of the faith as revealed in scripture require more than intellectual assent. Rather they are to be heartfelt and life changing. That is, theological truth should mold the actions of the believer in fundamentally important ways. Hence evangelicals are likely to examine scripture on multiple levels; they read scripture for broad ethical or moral principles while at the same time combing the text for particular commands and instructions (including public policy). Ethical and political cues are to be found both in the general and in the special revelation of scripture.

Finally, Christ represents the embodiment of all truth; Christ's words and deeds are the ultimate guide for evangelical behavior in the policy realm. Again, Christ's example has multiple implications for evangelical involvement in the policy arena. On one hand, He offers wisdom and guidance as to substantive policy prescriptions on specific issues. On the other hand, the example of Christ likewise ought to shape how we are to conduct ourselves in the political realm. Thus scripture and Christlikeness apply not only to the substance of policy positions but also to how we are to do politics. In the same way, the call to evangelize likewise holds out ramifications for the style and tone that mark evangelicals' political presence and participation.

THE EXPANDING EVANGELICAL PUBLIC POLICY AGENDA

Precisely what the elements of evangelicalism enumerated above mean in specific policy contexts is a primary focus of the chapters that follow. But as we turn our attention to the question of how evangelical doctrine translates into particular policy positions, one thing is clear. Those policy orientations of evangelical Christians are becoming less predictable or likely to simply align with traditionally conservative viewpoints.

Clearly something is afoot with respect to evangelical sentiments on public policy questions. Increasingly, evangelicals are becoming more sophisticated policy actors who do not neatly fit the monolithic mold of the religious right. Consider some of the actions taken in the past decade by the National Association of Evangelicals (NAE), the major organizational voice for evangelical individuals, churches, and denominations in the United States

- In 1996, the NAE issued a Statement of Conscience raising awareness of religious persecution around the world. The statement became a rallying point for evangelical political activism, and helped bring about the passage of the International Religious Freedom Act in 1998. It was significant in elevating religious freedom as a core objective of U.S. foreign policy. In the intervening years, that policy has grown to include the protection of all faiths and other facets of global human rights (Lindsay 2008, 43).

- In 2004, the NAE released "For the Health of the Nation: An Evangelical Call to Civic Responsibility." The document was a robust call to political activism, laying out an extensive set of issues that warranted the attention of evangelical Christians. Those included poverty and economic justice, peace and nonviolence, preservation of family and life, human rights and liberty, and environmental care.
- In 2006, almost ninety evangelical leaders (including the aforementioned Rick Warren) signed the Evangelical Climate Initiative, asserting that their Christian faith compelled them to proactively work to address the crisis of global warming. The statement did not carry the explicit endorsement of the NAE; however, nearly three dozen of the signatories were members of the organization's board or its executive committee, and the NAE's top leadership indicated strong support for the statement.
- In 2007, the NAE endorsed "An Evangelical Declaration against Torture: Protecting Human Rights in an Age of Terror," in which it denounced the use of torture or other inhumane treatment of detainees as acceptable tools in the war against terror.

A glance at the policy agenda of the NAE in the past five years reveals serious attention to the environment, global warming, human rights, and religious liberty, U.S. detainee policy, democratization, foreign aid, HIV/AIDS, and immigration (Gushee 2008, 95–96).

NAE's actions represent the tip of the evangelical policy iceberg. Other signs of a spreading evangelical activism abound across the policy spectrum. International evangelical NGOs such as World Vision and World Relief are mobilizing evangelicals for a variety of causes—disaster relief, economic development, and campaigns to combat HIV/AIDS. World Vision is the largest handler of food in the world, most of it donated by the U.S. government. The synergy between evangelical groups like World Vision and the federal government has led to a dramatic increase in evangelical involvement in AIDS treatment and prevention, famine and poverty reduction, and other global concerns. Those actions have been reinforced by the efforts of high-profile evangelical leaders such as Warren, Bishop T. D. Jakes, and others to promote evangelical activism to fight global poverty and international HIV/AIDS. Evangelical nongovernmental organizations have similarly been on the forefront of international human rights issues, often with the tangible support and involvement of the U.S. government.[6]

Nor is this newfound activism limited to global issues. Numerous evangelical associations—Ron Sider's Evangelicals for Social Action, John Perkins' The Christian Community Development Association, and Tony Compolo's Evangelical Association for the Promotion of Education, to name a few—are active domestically on issues of poverty and economic justice. The Evangelical Covenant Church made the cause of the poor a moral imperative when it established a department of compassion, mercy, and justice, which lobbied the Bush administration on the reauthorization of the State Children's Health Insurance Program (SCHIP). In the summer of 2008, high-profile evangelicals issued "An Evangelical Manifesto," exhorting evangelicals to engage the full range of issues implicated by the Gospel. The document addressed abortion and marriage, but also extended to education, global conflict, racism, corruption, poverty, pandemic diseases, illiteracy, ignorance, and racial reconciliation. Other examples abound. Taken together, they suggest a roiling of the waters of evangelical activism on a slew of topics that extend well beyond the wedge issues of abortion, school prayer, and homosexuality that launched conservative Christians into the political arena in the first place.[7]

The actions of evangelical associations and organizations clearly have grown to encapsulate a host of issues not typically associated with Christians in politics. More difficult to discern is the extent to which this broadened policy agenda has trickled down to rank-and-file evangelical Christians. Nevertheless, here too are signs that evangelicals are less monolithic and uniformly conservative than they typically are portrayed. They do not accept wholesale the economic conservatism of the Republican Party, if in fact they ever did. A recent Pew poll revealed large majorities of evangelicals in favor of a minimum wage increase and greater health care for all citizens, while opposing huge profits and the concentration of power of corporate America. Other polls have shown majorities of self-declared evangelicals as supporting greater governmental intervention on behalf of the poor, even if it means higher taxes (Monsma 2008).

Evidence of this emerging populist evangelical agenda could be seen on the 2008 presidential campaign trail, especially in the Republican primary success of Mike Huckabee. Huckabee, a former governor of Arkansas and one-time Baptist minister, staked out policy positions on a number of questions that seemed to put him closer to the Democratic Party than Republican orthodoxy. On the one hand, Huckabee maintained traditionally conservative views on abortion, same-sex marriage, and other social issues. But he also advocated for increased funding of the arts, governmental action to protect the environment, poverty reduction, and health care reform. He adopted a relatively forgiving stance on immigration (Grainger 2008). In short, he adopted numerous policy stances that diverged from the dominant perceptions of Republican-affiliated religious conservatives. Moreover, he was unapologetic in running as an evangelical Christian, explicitly linking his policy views to his religiosity.

While Huckabee's populist melding of positions opened him up to harsh attacks by the business wing and other elites within the Republican Party, it clearly resonated with rank-and-file evangelicals. He opened the 2008 presidential nomination contest with a stunning victory in the Iowa caucuses, despite being outspent ten to one by Mitt Romney. Huckabee's outspoken evangelicalism (and his natural political talent) continued to earn him deep support among evangelical voters and kept him in the top tier of Republican contenders.[8]

Huckabee's surprisingly competitive campaign for the Republican nomination revealed another important facet of the changing face of evangelical public policy activism—its relative youthfulness. Simply put, much of the evolution in evangelical policy engagement is occurring along generational lines, among both evangelical leadership and those in the pews. Waves of young evangelicals were drawn to Huckabee, both for his fresh blend of conservative and progressive positions and for the culturally attractive style of his presentation (Kirkpatrick 2008). Huckabee liked to describe himself as conservative, but not angry about it. He did not hesitate to leaven his policy stances with a quick wit and sharp sense of humor. His comfort with the popular culture showed in his willingness to crack jokes on Jon Stewart's *The Daily Show* or to take the stage to hammer out classic rock tunes on his bass guitar.

The generational divide with respect to policy orientations is likely apparent to anyone who has spent much time in recent years on the campuses of evangelical colleges. Among college-age Christians there is a growing social conscience on matters of poverty, race, the environment, and a broader slate of issues. Much of the interest in climate change, global hunger, human rights, and other "social justice" issues is being driven by these college students and other younger evangelicals.[9] Repelled by the partisan dogmatism of their elders, they are less inclined to mix it up over abortion, gay marriage, and other cultural bellwether issues, even as their positions on those issues are just as conservative as those of older evangelicals.

A third measure of the policy change in evangelical circles is the extent to which it has been embraced by high-profile evangelical pastors, media figures, or other public evangelicals who claim to speak for evangelical Christians. Here too a generational shift appears to be taking place. The 2008 Republican presidential primaries left the old guard of evangelical leadership appearing to be out of touch, if not downright irrelevant. Jerry Falwell and James Kennedy were gone. Evangelicals could no longer be relied upon to take their cues from James Dobson or Pat Robertson, who, despite Huckabee's impressive evangelical bona fides, hardly queued up behind him. Robertson endorsed Rudy Giuliani, touting his national security credentials while ignoring his mess of a personal life. Dobson vowed to sit on his hands in November if John McCain were the Republican nominee; he bypassed Huckabee in favor of Mitt Romney. Only when McCain had secured the nomination did Dobson offer Huckabee his tepid support.

Meanwhile, a new breed of evangelical leaders—Rick Warren, Rick Osteen, Bill Hybels, Joel Hunter, and others like them—have begun to push the evangelical movement in different directions. They eschew the confrontational style of Dobson and his ilk, opting instead for a broader and more bipartisan approach to their policy involvement. They deserve significant credit for the new interest in public policies that address problems of peace, health, and poverty.

It should not have been surprising, then, that Rick Warren sat center stage at Saddleback Church conducting interviews with candidates McCain and Obama. His is a broad-based, holistic public-policy agenda that is pro-life and pro-family while also being pro-foreign aid, pro-debt relief, and pro-AIDS funding in Africa. As Warren himself has said, "Jesus' agenda is far bigger than just one or two issues. . . . We have to care about poverty, we have to care about disease, we have to care about illiteracy, we have to care about corruption in government, sex trafficking" (Dionne 2008). Thus is Warren's church heavily invested in African ministries that include the combating of poverty, disease, AIDS, and illiteracy (Gushee 2008, 113).

This is the preliminary snapshot of evangelicals engaging the policy arena in new ways. While not ready to jettison core issues like abortion and same-sex marriage, neither are they preoccupied with them. The new evangelicalism is marked by an active embrace of a policy agenda that includes climate change and environmentalism, domestic and global poverty, HIV/AIDS, human trafficking and torture, and racial reconciliation (Lampman 2008).

This emerging set of evangelical attitudes on public policy clearly deserves a far more careful parsing than it has received. The flurry of books, the often contradictory actions of evangelical leadership, the efforts of political candidates to appeal to the religious, and the changing attitudes of evangelicals themselves all have done little to elucidate these shifts in evangelical policy views. If anything, there may be greater uncertainty and confusion than ever, both within evangelical circles and among outside observers.

Nor has the journalistic coverage of evangelicals done much to enlighten. It has shed little light on the underlying reasons for the evolving evangelical policy agenda, or what it means for the future of policy debates. Instead, it invariably is reduced to electoral and voting behavior. A journalistic profession with a rather attenuated understanding of what drives evangelicals simply is not in the best position to help us process and deconstruct the hodge-podge of religious developments on the public policy front.

LOOKING AHEAD: PUBLIC POLICY THROUGH AN EVANGELICAL LENS

The shifting policy terrain for evangelicals and the potential political implications heighten the need for a deeper understanding of evangelical policy perspectives. The chapters that follow seek to bring the phenomenon of evangelical policy engagement into clearer focus by examining evangelical Christianity as a determinative influence in specific policy contexts. The contributors include a diverse group of writers, each of whom is analyzing a particular issue through an intentionally evangelical lens. The chapters reflect the considerable variety of perspectives that characterize modern evangelicalism. There is no dominant ideological slant, some authors leaning right, others left, and yet others striking a middle ground. The chapters are informed by multiple disciplines, including political science, law, economics, and social work. Likewise, the authors employ a variety of methodologies—empirical, historical, philosophical, and conventional policy analysis. Notwithstanding the points of divergence across the chapters, there also are common themes and questions that run through them.

- *How does the evangelical faith tradition shape or inform analysis of the policy issue at hand?* Is there a discernible or distinctive evangelical approach to the issue? Does it incorporate principles of social science? Are there tensions between conventional policy analysis and a faith-informed analysis? What are the weaknesses or shortcomings in evangelical policy approaches? Are there unique contributions the evangelical tradition brings to the specific policy debate?
- *How does evangelicalism compare to other faith traditions in its stance on this policy issue?* How do evangelical modes of policy analysis compare to those of Catholics, mainline Protestants, Jews, or other faith traditions. What are the points of divergence and commonality? What are the implications of these similarities and differences?
- *How might evangelicals pursue the same policy outcome using alternative, nonreligious language or arguments?* Pragmatically, how do evangelicals effectively engage those who do not share their theological sources of authority? Are evangelicals obligated to employ rhetoric not bounded by religious foundations? If so, how might they invoke nonreligious language for those operating outside the evangelical point of view?

The first section explores the application of evangelical principles to a series of domestic policy questions. In the first chapter, Noah Toly considers evangelical participation in debates on environmental issues. He finds evangelicals to have been inaccurately caricatured as ignorant or callous toward the environment; rather, they have taken positions on the environment that are more diverse than popular reports suggest. However, increasing evangelical environmental activism has not reflected much intellectual coherence. As he surveys the variety of evangelical voices, Toly considers the limits of translating evangelical positions into a more broadly accessible secular discourse, concluding that a transcendent point of reference may be the one truly distinctive contribution evangelicals can make to policy debates on environmental issues.

Steve Monsma in chapter 2 explores a similar gap between image and reality in evangelical antipoverty efforts in the United States. Contrary to popular perceptions, evangelicals have shown a deep concern for the poor that is grounded in scriptural mandate. They tend to act on that concern through free market and family-oriented approaches that accept a government role in poverty reduction while emphasizing corresponding obligations on the part of the poor.

In the third chapter, Jennifer Walsh examines evangelical policy perspectives on the American criminal justice system. After reviewing historical trends in criminal justice and the competing theoretical models of modern criminology, Walsh lays down a set of philosophical and pragmatic arguments grounded in evangelical theology that might assist policymakers in better understanding the underlying origins of crime and considering possible solutions.

In the fourth chapter, Timothy Barnett turns his attention to economic and fiscal issues, assailing evangelicals for lacking anything resembling a coherent position on political economy. He castigates evangelicals for relying too heavily on simplistic slogans and absolutist principles of limited government in the area of economics. He demonstrates how Christians might look to scriptural authority to better inform their perspectives on fiscal and monetary policy. He suggests that doing so compels an updated understanding of economic principles in a modern era of finance capitalism and globalized central banking.

In the fifth chapter, Ruth Melkonian-Hoover examines the biblical and theological underpinnings of evangelical perspectives on U.S. immigration policy. While evangelical leaders were slow to enter the debate around immigration policy, many are now speaking out the issue. The author suggests that evangelicalism may offer a distinctive approach that recognizes the social justice tensions inherent in the issue. Evangelicals tend to stake out a position that upholds the rule of law, pursues justice for American citizens, *and* adheres to the biblical injunctions to welcome the stranger and treat all people with dignity as beings made in the image of God.

The second section of the book explores evangelical views on foreign relations and global issues. In chapter 6, Mark Amstutz reviews the historical roots of evangelical humanitarianism and international political advocacy, which date back to the missionary movement of the late nineteenth and early twentieth centuries, with notable contributions to the development of civil society and human dignity. Only in the mid-twentieth century did evangelicals become more proactive in political affairs, as the emergence of their domestic political activism of the 1990s was coupled with a heightened interest in global affairs and U.S. foreign policy.

In chapter 7, Eric Patterson and Jacob Lenerville provide a complement to Amtutz's historical overview by surveying the existing empirical evidence on evangelical attitudes on foreign policy questions. The authors find that evangelical interest in a variety of foreign policy issues does not, for the most part, vary significantly from mainstream attitudes on those questions.

In chapter 8, Zachary Calo looks at evangelical attitudes on human rights. Calling them the "new internationals," Calo identifies a distinct evangelical voice in recent human rights debates, analyzing the strengths and limits of evangelical political theology in this regard and comparing it to the Catholic intellectual tradition. He ends with a reflection on how evangelical voices might shape and challenge the mainstream human rights agenda of the future.

In chapter 9, Ron Kirkemo examines the acute tensions that national security issues present for evangelical Christians. Kirkemo draws upon biblical narratives and biographies as scriptural sources that evangelical Christians can draw upon in the national security realm as they attempt to negotiate their way through a complex and dangerous set of earthly circumstances, where discerning the hand of God at work can appear exceedingly difficult.

The final section of the book reflects on evangelical engagement of the broader secular culture across several important public policy fronts—family and marriage, racial reconciliation, education, and stem cell research and the culture wars. In chapter 10, David Ryden and Jeffrey Polet find a distinctive evangelical perspective on family and marriage policy (including gay marriage) in the view of scripture as God's revealed creative design for humanity. They find evangelical marriage policies to be consonant with the general good of society and supported by alternative secular claims. But they also caution evangelicals to be as attuned to the tone, style, and spirit of their politics as to the substance, and to avoid the harsh language of condemnation, demonization, and isolation in favor of Christ-like traits of love, compassion, and human dignity.

In chapter 11, David Ryden explores the largely unsuccessful efforts of white and black evangelicals to achieve lasting racial reconciliation. He contends that those efforts have been undone by ideological predispositions among white evangelicals that emphasize individual effort and personal relationship building to the neglect of collective and societal causes of persistent racial inequities. He then identifies several contemporary policy areas that hold out the potential to promote racial healing within evangelical churches and in society at large.

In chapter 12, Francis Beckwith focuses on the "culture wars" in which evangelicals have become vibrant participants. He invokes the philosophical subdiscipline of metaphysics to defend evangelicals' reliance upon particular readings of scripture and moral theology for their policy views. He critiques those who contend that such scripturally informed views are irrational or inappropriate for public argumentation, and finds the entire "secular" versus "religious" dualism to be contrived. Rather, it is a matter of evangelical Christians and their political adversaries offering conflicting understandings of human nature.

The final chapter draws upon the previous chapters to explore important themes regarding evangelicalism in the public policy arena. It is ambivalent on whether the expanding evangelical issue agenda is in fact religiously and theologically motivated, positing instead that it may be one more instance of evangelicals taking their cues from the broader secular culture. The chapters reveal the need for a far more mature evangelical policy framework, one supported by a richer set of intellectual and theological foundations. At the same time, they provide a portrait of a fresh model of evangelical engagement, where core evangelical principles are combined with serious, in-depth intellectual ideas and applied to a broad range of policy questions.

It remains to be seen whether there is indeed a distinctive evangelical approach to public policy—a biblically derived set of values, aims, or ends that can shape and drive evangelical positions and participation across the board. Is there an identifiable set of theologically generated values—justice, righteousness, the punishment of evil, the maintenance of peace, the preservation of order—that can provide common ground even as evangelicals find much to disagree about over what policy prescriptions best achieve those agreed-upon aims? I close by sketching out an analytical framework that all evangelicals—from the left, right, and center—might be able to agree on, using the health care issue as a context for demonstrating how that distinctive evangelical perspective might inform debate. In so doing, the hope is that evangelicalism can positively contribute to ongoing public policy debates while maintaining its integrity to the substance and principles of that faith tradition.

NOTES

1. One commentator on the pages of the *Washington Post* went so far as to declare Rick Warren the true winner of the event, and credited him with changing overnight "the face of evangelicals in this country from the cartoon caricature of rigid, rightwing fundamentalists to one of open-minded, intelligent, concerned citizens" (Quinn 2008).

2. Gallup polls put those who identify themselves with evangelical Christianity at anywhere from 33 percent (in 1987) to 47 percent (1998). According to Wheaton College's Institute for the Study of American Evangelicals, the nation's evangelical population is between 30 and 35 percent of the population, or about one hundred million Americans (http://www.wheaton.edu/isae/defining_evangelicalism.html). According to the latest survey by the Pew Forum on Religion and Public Life, evangelical Protestants make up 26 percent of Americans. Self-declared evangelicals comprised 26 percent of the 2008 electorate.

3. 28 percent of evangelicals say that their religion influences their politics, twice the number in the overall population, three times that of Catholics, and 3.5 times that of liberal Protestants.

4. This confusion was implicit in the release in the summer of 2008 of "An Evangelical Manifesto: A Declaration of Evangelical Identity and Public Commitment." The document, the drafting of which was led by such evangelical luminaries as Os Guinness and Richard Mouw, sought to clarify the identity of evangelicals—who they are and what they stand for. A central purpose of the manifesto was to "address the confusions and corruptions that attend the term *Evangelical* in the United States" ("An Evangelical Manifesto," 2).

5. There are a variety of ways to define evangelicalism. One approach is to use self-declaration as a measure of evangelicalism, that is, to identify and quantify evangelicals based upon their willingness to describe themselves as such. A second method is to define evangelicalism denominationally, categorizing evangelicals by their affiliation with those protestant denominations that are typically classified as evangelical in belief and tradition. A third approach is to define evangelicals by the central theological ideas and beliefs to which they ascribe. Since this book explores how specific theological beliefs and convictions might lead to specific policy prescriptions or positions, we adopt the third approach, and define evangelicals by the beliefs they hold.

6. The administration of George W. Bush, himself an evangelical Christian, committed an unprecedented $15 billion to combat AIDS in Africa. Likewise, the administration redoubled its foreign aid contributions to African countries in an effort to relieve global poverty and hunger.

7. All of this activity prompted a meeting of evangelical intellectuals in Boston in the fall of 2007. The two-day conference examined the subject of "An Emerging Evangelical Intelligentsia: How the Evangelical Mind Is Opening and Why It Matters."

8. Huckabee's fellow Republican presidential candidate, Kansas senator Sam Brownback, while not an evangelical, offered a similarly expansive policy platform. The staunchly pro-life Catholic Brownback embodied the growing range of issues to which heartfelt religious conviction could apply. Describing his pro-life commitment as of a piece with a "whole-life" approach to issues, Brownback advocated concern not only for the unborn but also for poverty and hunger at home and abroad, care for the sick and poor, openness to the immigrant, and compassion for the prisoner (Brownback 2007).

9. To illustrate the point, environmental initiatives can be found at about half of those institutions belonging to the Council for Christian Colleges and Universities (Feder 2008).

Part I

Engaging America: Evangelical Approaches to Domestic Policy Questions

Chapter One

Evangelicals and the Environment: From Political Realism to a Politics of Freedom

Noah J. Toly[1]

On March 10, 2008, I suspended a book project in a rare and awkwardly gratifying moment of simultaneous discouragement and encouragement. While nowhere near the project's completion, I had poured considerable energy into *Some Like It Hot: Evangelicals and Global Warming*, and was selfishly discouraged to take a hiatus, especially one that might have been the end of the project. The book was intended to be not merely an insider's look at evangelicalism's environmental failures. The goal had been change, however small; the objective had been to join a refrain calling for more careful consideration of gospel-centered political engagement with environmental issues. Too much evangelical political engagement with environmental concerns had lacked thoughtful articulation of evangelical foundations. Too many leading evangelicals and evangelical institutions expressed unqualified and ill-considered reservations about environmentalism, and recent intramural debates about climate change and climate politics seemed idiosyncratically ill-tempered.

In the summer of 2007, the Southern Baptist Convention (SBC), the largest Protestant denomination in North America, affirmed a statement casting doubt upon climate science and expressing dismay at possible harmful effects of supposedly unwarranted regulation. But on March 10, 2008, several high-profile members of the SBC shifted positions on climate change, giving me pause in my project and reinforcing prior reservations about caricaturing evangelical political engagement (Banerjee 2008; Southern Baptist Environment and Climate Initiative 2008; "Southern Baptist Leaders Shift Position on Climate Change" 2008; Zoll 2008). Just one year after the 2007 statement by the Convention, the authors and signatories of "A Southern Baptist Declaration on the Environment and Climate Change" admitted to past recalcitrance: "We believe our current denominational resolutions and engagement with these issues have often been too timid. Our cautious response to these issues in the face of mounting evidence may be seen by the world as uncaring, reckless and ill-informed. We can do better" (Southern Baptist Environment and Climate Initiative 2008). The "declaration" elaborated upon four statements:

- "Humans must care for creation and take responsibility for our contributions to environmental degradation";
- "It is prudent to address global climate change";
- "Christian moral convictions and our Southern Baptist Doctrines demand our environmental stewardship"; and
- "It is time for individuals, churches, communities, *and governments* to act" (Southern Baptist Environment and Climate Initiative 2008, emphasis added).

Not only are humans obligated to act, but Christians, especially, are also obligated to act; we should repent from "reckless, preventable, and sinful" environmental degradation, individually and in concert—that is, *politically*—and care for the environment.

While the document was not an official statement of the denomination—and many who refrained from signing it have taken great pains to make that clear—it marked significant movement on the part of an important constituency. And in calling for political engagement, the authors and signatories of this document joined a larger chorus of voices bringing environmental policy into the fold along with several other issues with which Southern Baptists, along with evangelicals from various traditions, have long been engaged. Framing environmental stewardship, including efforts to achieve a climate-stable future, as a matter of the "common good," the declaration echoes several other such statements, saying "*action by government* is often needed to assure the health and well-being of all people. We pledge, therefore, to give serious consideration to responsible policies that acceptably address the conditions set forth in this declaration" (Southern Baptist Environment and Climate Initiative 2008, emphasis added). Whether by means of a Southern Baptist declaration or a more ecumenical assertion, many Christians now demonstrate a ready commitment to political action. Even those who dissent from such "calls" and "declarations" often assent to the necessity of some measure of government regulation of environmental quality.

Yet while this political engagement is encouraging, the terms of such engagement are rarely articulated, in spite of their importance. As with the other contributions to this volume, this chapter contributes to that articulation, answering the following questions:

- What are the weaknesses, shortcomings, or inadequacies in the ways in which evangelicals have approached the issue?
- What tensions exist between conventional policy analysis and a faith-informed analysis?
- How might evangelical faith and tradition inform an approach to this policy issue?
- What, if anything, can the evangelical tradition bring to the issue that is fresh, unique, or otherwise might be missing from the policy debate?

This chapter first briefly explores the contemporary moment in environmental politics and policy before interpreting the state (not the history) of evangelical political engagement with environmental issues. Climate change and climate policy serve as appropriate proxies for environmental policy issues writ large. And climate change has occasioned the most robust evangelical political engagement with environmental issues. This engagement is briefly narrated (and hopefully accurately represented, despite necessary selectivity) here for the purposes of assessing broader contours of evangelical political engagement.

Drawing upon the contributions of French social theorist and theologian, Jacques Ellul, I argue that a pathological political realism pervades evangelical policy engagement with climate change. Following this interpretation, I articulate ways in which an ethic of freedom might inform the substance *and* style of evangelical political engagement with environmental issues.

One possible departure from other chapters in this volume concerns evangelical pursuit of desired policy outcomes by using alternative or nonreligious language, arguments, or persuasion. This is a crucial pragmatic issue facing evangelicals: How do we connect most effectively with those who do not share or accept the theological or scriptural sources of authority from which our policy stances are derived? Some assert that evangelicals are obliged to state their policy positions in a rhetoric that is not bounded or limited by theological foundations. This position might be tenable if policy were a strictly technical endeavor (yet, even in this case, the position would remain unattractive if technique were regarded as having a politics). But policy has a politics and policy preferences originate to some extent (and more or less transparently) in basic moral obligations. Because there is no common, neutral, or universally accessible vantage point from which to discern such moral obligations,[2] evangelicals are obliged to *articulate*, but *not to translate*, such views.

While cognate language for secondary goods may approximate common cause, distinctly evangelical foundations for policy preferences must be articulated in idiosyncratic terms. I argue that evangelicals should make such foundations transparent. To do so, we need to be comfortable invoking theological language and arguments that may seem incredible to those operating from other points of view. Unfortunately, this chapter leaves little room to develop that argument beyond a few brief concluding thoughts. I am thankful for the opportunity to anticipate a line of reasoning that I hope to develop elsewhere.

A SPIRITUAL MOMENT IN ENVIRONMENTAL POLITICS

Environmental issues have been at the forefront of the policy domain, both domestically and internationally, for almost half a century. At least since Rachel Carson's *Silent Spring* (1962) spurred both a policy prohibiting the domestic use of DDT and the eventual formation of the Environmental Protection Agency, nature-society relations have been critical to domestic political consciousness. Internationally, such issues have been among leading political concerns since before the 1972 United Nations Conference on the Human Environment in Stockholm, which was the first international gathering to juxtapose development and environmental quality, though it did not resolve tensions between them. That task was left to the World Commission on Environment and Development, or Brundtland Commission, which first articulated the principle of sustainable development, meeting the needs of the present generation without compromising the ability of future generations to meet their own needs.

Sustainable development has been the hallmark of environmental politics and the chief goal of environmental policy since the WCED's report, *Our Common Future*, and especially since the 1992 United Nations Conference on Environment and Development, the Rio de Janeiro "Earth Summit." After all, few in the policy community would doubt the importance of development, especially for the poorest among us, or question commitments to long-term viability of an environment suitable for human life and livelihood. Thus, sustainable development has leveraged an intersection of important issues and focused environmental policy on the long-term viability of producing and distributing opportunities for the good life.

Nevertheless, whether in spite of this focus or because of its multi-valence, the compass of environmental policy issues can be bewilderingly broad. Michael Kraft writes that "environmental policy comprises a diversity of governmental actions [or deliberate inactions] that affect or attempt to affect environmental quality or the use of natural resources" (2004, 12). In an age of public-private partnerships, intentionally diffuse governance capacity, and neoliberal governance-by-market, even Kraft's broad definition is effectively inadequate. More suitable is the still more expansive description offered by Noel Castree in his article, "Environmental Issues: From Policy to Political Economy."

> Environmental policy can demonstrably ameliorate or even eradicate ecologically destructive practices. . . . [It] is not always and everywhere associated with the state, regulatory authorities or quasi-state agencies . . . takes places in and through grass-roots organizations, community groups, charities, and non-governmental bodies . . . [and is also] an essential instrument for achieving a more [environmentally] just and sustainable future. (Castree 2002, 358)

Notable here is Castree's connection between policy and governance, which is effective, rather than formal, authority; policy not only includes mechanisms of formal governmental authority but also emerges from various and diffuse formal and informal governance mechanisms, which constitute effective authority. Also important is the instrumentality of environmental policy: it is a means of achieving both equity and sustainability. In other words, environmental policy attempts to achieve an equitable distribution of goods and ills, risks and opportunities, both intragenerationally and intergenerationally.

Such risks and opportunities are extremely inequitably distributed. Environmental inequities further marginalize already vulnerable subpopulations according to class, gender, and race, while future generations will bear the brunt of our environmental recklessness. Those who benefit most from industrial and postindustrial lifestyles internalize goods and opportunities and externalize risks generated in the creation and sustenance of such lifestyles. Those who benefit least absorb the greatest risks. Environmental policy seeks to ameliorate these inequitable temporal and spatial distributions.

Most environmental policy has advanced toward these goals in issue-specific fashion—domestically with the Clean Air Act, the Clean Water Act, the Endangered Species Act, and so on; internationally with the Convention on Biological Diversity, the Convention on International Trade in Endangered Species, the Montreal Protocol, and others. In the short run, such fragmentation can make for the implementation of apparently successful environmental policies. In the long run, it can represent the greatest potential threat to the successful development of coherent policy regimes establishing sustainability and equity. In their now-infamous 2004 essay, "The Death of Environmentalism," Michael Shellenberger and Ted Nordhaus made precisely this case. Environmentalism suffers, they wrote, not only from issue-based fragmentation, but above all from the suggestion of any such discrete concern as "environmental" policy. Environmental policy is deeply and permanently intertwined with other policy domains. Such breadth frustrates the often narrowly technocratic sensibilities of policy analysis as well as the disciplinary proclivities of the academy. Yet understanding this breadth has become even more critical given the exigencies of anthropogenic climate change.

Recently, climate change has demonstrated the capacity to serve as a sort of meta-issue in environmental politics. Al Gore, in his award-winning documentary, *An Inconvenient Truth*, noted that issue-specific policy interventions have successfully addressed previous environmental issues, such as ozone depletion, but, with regard to climate change, "we have to have a different perspective. . . . It is different than any problem we have faced before" (Guggenheim 2006). The potential impacts of global warming are so severe as to threaten human survival; the causes and consequences of this phenomenon are so pervasive and ubiquitous as to make climate change a meta-, or at least meso-, hazard, one with a wide range of origins in and implications for human concerns, from biological diversity to war.

Climate change highlights the need for an environmental politics that recognizes what Castree has called "the ontological promiscuity of nature" (2002). Nature partners indiscriminately with everything: it "is inextricably *a part of* those things we conventionally call 'economic,' 'cultural,' 'social,' or 'political' entities" (Castree 2002, 358, emphasis in original). At the same time, as John Byrne, Leigh Glover, and Cecilia Martinez note, "nature is undergoing a process of social capture which eventually may make it in effect a social sub-system subject to political attitudes and ideology, and a functioning part of the world political economy" (2002, 262). In a material sense, there is nothing "social" or "political" which is not also environmental. No action of any material consequence is without environmental implications.[3]

The once unfathomable, but now unavoidable, consequence of climate change is that planetary and systemic environmental conditions are now co-produced by human behavior, accidentally, incidentally, and purposefully. While the impacts will not be evenly distributed across subpopulations, they will be ubiquitous. So we must now manage planetary systems in such a way as might require significant changes to our lifestyles and reconsideration of our values, of what we take for the good life. Shellenberger and Nordhaus argue that, in this moment of environmentalism, we "need a set of new institutions founded around a more expansive vision and set of values" (2004, 34), an environmental politics less fragmented and issue-specific— indeed, an environmental politics that is considerably more than simply environmental.

Recently, this theme has been elaborated by James Gustave Speth, Sara Shallenberger Brown Professor in the Practice of Environmental Policy and dean of the School of Forestry and Environmental Studies at Yale University. In his 2008 book, *The Bridge at the End of the World: Capitalism, the Environment, and Crossing from Crisis to Sustainability*, Speth notes that

> today's environmental reality is linked powerfully with other realities, includ-
> ing growing social inequality and neglect and the erosion of democratic
> governance and popular control. . . . [T]hese three seemingly separate areas of
> public concern come together and . . . we as citizens must now mobilize our
> spiritual and political resources for transformative change on all three fronts.
> (Speth 2008, xi)

Speth suggests not only that effectively addressing environmental issues will require a comprehensive and coherent approach to economic, political, and environmental realities, but that this approach will require the mobilization of "spiritual resources."

This explicit re-enchantment of what had (only) seemed for a long time an exclusively technical policy domain has been an obvious theme of environmental concern for the past decade. The early years of the new millennium have been marked by the effort to reach out to various spiritual resources for potential environmental effectiveness. Paul Hawken, in his 2007 bestseller, *Blessed Unrest: How the Largest Movement in the World Came into Being and Why No One Saw It Coming*, writes:

> It has been said that we cannot save our planet unless humankind undergoes a
> widespread spiritual and religious awakening. In other words, fixes won't fix
> unless we fix our souls, as well. . . . To salve the world's wounds demands a
> response from the heart. . . . [S]piritual deeds and acts of moral imagination lay
> the groundwork for the great work that is ahead. (Hawken 2007, 184–85)

Make no mistake: Hawken believes that a spiritual awakening is the "groundwork" and that environmental sustainability and justice are the "great work." A nonspecific spiritual awakening is, for Hawken, instrumental to the larger purpose of saving the planet. He relativizes whatever spiritual resources might serve the grander, more absolute project of material—human and otherwise—well-being. He wants a generic spiritual awakening; any spiritual awakening will do, so long as the gravity of our environmental and social condition is met by a resilient, resourceful, and resolute human nature. In this, Hawken echoes Peter Teague, who has suggested that "it isn't God we need to be addressing our concerns to—it's us" (2004). Ultimately, the spiritual awakening Hawken, Speth, Teague, and others hope for is an immanent and humanistic one.

THE EVANGELICAL RESPONSE

Despite the instrumentalization, relativization, and humanism of spirituality by many prominent and influential members of the environmental movement, the current moment in environmentalism and environmental politics is an opportune one for evangelicals. The discursive context for environmental politics welcomes the religious element. And in the United States, many environmentalists are seeking out evangelicals, in particular, for their political clout.

A few scattered evangelical voices have been present in the discourse at all times. But evangelicals have been much maligned and broadly caricatured, sometimes deservedly so, for anemic, laggardly, and occasionally inane responses to environmental issues. Now, evangelicals have joined the discussion in earnest, largely through engagement with climate change, the world's unavoidable issue—it's an inconvenient truth.[4]

Constructive Engagement

Until the recent declaration by members of the SBC, two ecumenical statements had been the focus of attention regarding constructive evangelical engagement with environmental politics. In the winter of 2006, more than eighty evangelical leaders—theologians, pastors, educators, and others—signed "Climate Change: An Evangelical Call to Action" (Evangelical Climate Initiative 2006), a document of the Evangelical Climate Initiative (ECI). The "Call to Action" was more than two years in the making, with retreats and other events serving as precursors to a February 2006 press conference in Washington, D.C. The "Call to Action" made four claims, focusing on (1) the reality of climate change, (2) its consequences for the poor and other vulnerable populations, (3) the consistency of concern with Christian moral convictions, and (4) the urgency of action in public and private sectors.

The ECI document prompted a number of responses. Among these was "A Call to Truth, Prudence, and Protection of the Poor: An Evangelical Response to Global Warming," composed by the Interfaith Stewardship Alliance (ISA) and signed by more than fifty natural and social scientists. The "Call to Truth" was presented to the ECI signatories with an open letter, urging them to remove their signatures from the ECI "Call to Action" and to sign the ISA document (Beisner, Driessen, McKitrick, and Spencer 2006; Interfaith Stewardship Alliance 2006).

These two statements represented constructive evangelical engagement with climate politics, evincing common interest in and motivation by sustainability and equity and forming the basis for a significant, if strained, dialogue. Both statements shared a concern for the marginalized and vulnerable, whether of this generation or the next, recognizing as important the material well-being with which Hawken and others are preoccupied. And while a few evangelicals have publicly and mistakenly set in permanent opposition care for human and nonhuman parts of the created order, most have recognized the Christian call to care for both. Furthermore, most now recognize the profound social dimensions of climate change, climate change policy, and other aspects of environmental policy.

Despite these similarities, the two "calls" highlighted important intramural differences. For example, the ISA "call" claimed that the kind of action advocated by the ECI would hurt the poor more than the ill effects of climate change would, while the ECI was concerned that the poor would be victimized by the ill effects of global warming. Both agree that climate change is a social issue that will impact the marginalized and vulnerable. But some believe that regulating greenhouse gas emissions is inefficient interference with economic activity that otherwise would result in the gently rising tide of economic growth, floating yachts and lifeboats, alike, lifting many out of poverty, and providing the financial means for adaptation to the ill effects of climate change, should it prove to be as burdensome as many predict. Others believe that regulating greenhouse gas emissions will serve the planet and the poor. They argue that violently rising seas of climate change will swamp lifeboats first and yachts later, that already-vulnerable populations will suffer "first and worst" from the ill effects of anthropogenic climate change, and that it will serve their interests to mitigate those effects by stunting increases in atmospheric concentrations of greenhouse gases.

Such disagreements are largely framed by a debate around regulation, economics, and the welfare of poor and vulnerable people on the margins of the global political economy.[5] Other contentions concern risk management, the ways in which we act—in this case, collectively—under conditions of relative uncertainty. The full extent of global warming's ill effects are not yet known, despite the fact that our certainty regarding its origins and implications increases immensely each year. Under conditions of uncertainty, even slight uncertainty, we must decide what option values to preserve: those associated with the capital investment necessary to reduce greenhouse gas emissions or those associated with the integrity of the global environment.

Such discussions are by no means simple; they are important, complex, and potentially constructive. While disagreement remains, and while some suggest that others do not understand the pathological anti-poor bent of their positions, evangelical responses on both sides of the issue have been built upon explicit concern for both sustainability and intragenerational equity, common causes with many who are not evangelical and the basis for ecumenical partnerships. These common causes are grounded in biblical and theological calls to stewardship and justice,[6] which animate evangelicals of various bents to engage climate change.

Paths of Disengagement[7]

But not all evangelical responses to climate change have been so constructive. In fact, the past few years have seen intramural squabbles in which both
sides have called into question the evangelical credentials of the other and in
which some have called for systematic disengagement from the issue. For
example, while the organizers of the ECI deliberately sought the signatures
of high-profile evangelical leaders known to be theologically conservative,
many questioned the conservative credentials of those leaders once they had
signified their support for the Initiative.

Some evangelicals have accused the ECI of making alliance with an
unsavory cast of characters, including foundations that support international
causes—abortive means of birth control, among others—typically contrary
to the evangelical current. Many evangelicals who disfavor such alliances
prefer modes of political action that at least keep such organizations at arm's
length. However, evangelicals have a long history of such alliances, including anti-pornography and anti-abuse campaigns with pro-choice advocacy
organizations. Among global issues, concerned religious internationalists
have partnered with such organizations to try to stem the tide of human
trafficking related to the sex trade. Why should such partnerships be less
acceptable in stemming the ocean tides associated with climate change? It
appears such critiques may be merely a matter of convenience, appealing to
prior commitments when they suit the interests of the critic and ignoring such
commitments when they do not.

Few public disputes have so clearly evinced this tendency as exchanges in
the spring of 2007 between self-identified conservative evangelicals, the National Association of Evangelicals (NAE), and several progressive evangelicals. In 2007, twenty-five "conservative" evangelical leaders, including Gary
Bauer, James Dobson, and Tony Perkins, coauthored a letter calling for the
resignation of Richard Cizik, vice president for governmental relations of the
NAE (Wildmon et al. 2007). Cizik had become personally activist about
climate change, and those calling for his resignation suggested that Cizik's
concern for climate change was problematic on three counts.

First, Cizik's concern was divisive: The authors suggest that concern for
climate change divides evangelicals. *Second, Cizik's concern was deceitful*:
The authors suggest that Cizik's concern made evangelicals appear monolithically concerned for climate change and, as this was not and is not true, his
concern was misleading. *Finally, Cizik's concern was distracting from the
"important moral issues" of our times*: The authors listed three such issues—
abortion, sex education, and homosexuality—which deserved our political
attention and from which Cizik's activism distracted.

The first two concerns were nothing if not disingenuous.

It takes at least two positions to be divisive: Concern for climate change needs either indifference toward climate change or hostility toward climate concern in order to be divisive. Unless evangelicals were previously monolithic in adopting one or the other of the latter two postures (and the authors of the letter are clear that evangelicals were not monolithic), concern for climate change cannot be any more divisive than lack of concern for climate change.

The critique is selectively applied: Readers have been left to wonder why this group has not called for the resignation of other high-profile evangelicals (themselves included) whose lack of concern for climate change might mislead the world into believing that evangelicals are monolithically indifferent toward global warming or hostile toward climate concern. If Cizik's concern is deceitful, is their indifference or hostility not also?

The third concern was debatable.

Clearly, there are more than three moral issues: Whether there are only three—or more than three—*important moral issues of our time* is obviously moot. Yet this concern motivates intentions to disengage from climate politics. Engagement with climate change threatens to increase the scope of the moral agenda, increase the number and type of agenda setting "public evangelicals," and introduce new fault lines for the distribution of subgroup power. Thoroughgoing evangelical engagement with environmental policy issues might compromise the credibility, authority, and effectiveness of a narrower platform. All of this is problematic for the authors of the letter—problematic enough to write whatever it takes, disingenuous or not, to motivate the desired response.

"REALISTIC POLITICS": THE PATHOLOGY OF EVANGELICAL ENGAGEMENT

Ironically, responses of the sort illustrated above instrumentalize and relativize religious commitments as much as do Hawken and others. Such responses suggest that politics are absolute and theology is relative. Only in this way can famously conservative theologians, pastors, and educators suddenly be regarded as liberal after calling for action on climate change. This can justify the inconsistent deployment of seemingly conflicting prior commitments across various issues. The impulse to relativize the properly absolute and to absolutize the properly relative emerges from what Jacques Ellul has described as "political realism," "in which there is no longer good and evil, just and unjust, legal and illegal, right and wrong. This is a morality of what succeeds and does not succeed, of what is useful and what is not" (Ellul

1997b, 60).[8] The moral infrastructure associated with this politics can be called "the morality of the fact" (Toly 2005a, 29). Whatever works, whatever succeeds, is good.

But an evangelical commitment to Scripture should have taught us otherwise. The Good Book is littered with bad examples, the people of God and others exercising this realism, valuing whatever succeeds. This is the story of 2 Samuel 6 and 1 Chronicles 13, in which King David was returning the Ark of the Covenant to Jerusalem. Leaving the house of Abinadab, David, his men, and Abinadab's sons put the ark on an ox cart to transport it. In his forbearance, God did not strike them immediately for transporting the ark in an unauthorized manner. But later, one of the oxen stumbled, and Uzzah, son of Abinadab, put his hand out to steady the ark and was struck dead.

Upon first reading this story, God may seem cruel. After all, Uzzah was just trying to prevent bad things from happening; the ark most certainly was not meant to spill off of an ox cart and onto the ground. And who knows what might have befallen the whole group if it had hit the ground? And so he reached out to steady the ark.

Uzzah must have been successful. We have no account of the ark falling to the ground. But Uzzah's job was not to keep the ark from touching the ground. Uzzah's job was not to touch the ark. He ought to have obeyed, despite possible failure, and left the results to God. By reaching out and taking things into his own hands—quite literally—Uzzah refused the finitude to which his obedience would have pointed, spurning hope in God despite apparent failure, and trusted in himself instead. By trusting in himself, Uzzah was, in fact, playing God.

And Uzzah's example is not the only one of its sort in Scripture. In Daniel 2 and 3, Nebuchadnezzar grasped at the infinite, symbolizing his own ambitions to a temporally unlimited kingdom with his statue of gold after dreaming of discrete and temporally bounded kingdoms represented by a statue of various materials.[9] Peter embraced political realism when he denied Christ in order to save himself (Mark 14; Luke 22) and then when he refused to continue eating with the Gentiles in Antioch, while being visited by Jewish believers who rejected freedom from ceremonial laws (Galatians 2). If he had eaten with the Gentiles, things might have gone badly. Adam grasped at the infinite, rejecting his finitude—again, quite literally taking things into his own hands—and cast all of creation into bondage to necessity.

And these are the paradigmatic behaviors for much of evangelical engagement with contemporary politics. Many U.S. evangelicals and evangelical institutions have cultivated political realism, among other pragmatic virtues, accommodating themselves to a broader cultural norm regardless of its biblical value (or lack thereof). For many evangelicals, whatever works, whatever succeeds, whatever accomplishes, is good and right. We reach out to steady the ark, hoping to keep bad things from happening, hoping to save the unborn and families from pathologies of progressive politics. And when commitments to stewardship and justice get in the way, when they distract from "important moral issues," we can't bring ourselves to admit that environmental protection, too, is a great moral issue. Instead, we do whatever is necessary. If disingenuousness succeeds, then, by all means, be disingenuous.

The temptation is just as strong for evangelicals of an environmentalist bent; after all, if we don't save the world, who will? To the extent that we are tempted to do whatever it takes, we are tempted to testify that our hope is in ourselves. We are tempted to relativize and instrumentalize religion. We are tempted to undermine the Gospel—the good news that God will make all things right, because God knows we cannot—at every turn. And at that point there would remain nothing uniquely evangelical, but only typically sinful, about our engagement.

ENVIRONMENTAL POLITICS AND THE ETHICS OF FREEDOM: BEYOND STEWARDSHIP AND JUSTICE

A gospel-honoring engagement with environmental politics would certainly embrace both stewardship and justice, but must also reject political realism. Only what Ellul describes as "the ethics of freedom" can rightly center any uniquely Christian environmental politics (Ellul 1976). Ellul writes that the ethics of freedom corresponds to the virtue of hope, "freedom is the ethical aspect of hope" (1976, 12). Importantly, Ellul distinguishes between "freedom defined as freedom of choice" and "freedom viewed as the coming of something new into the world with a creative adherence to an inexhaustible good" (11). This breaking in of a new thing liberates us from acting according to "ineluctable necessity," determination, or fate, according to the demands of political realism (14). Biblical freedom is not libertine; biblical freedom is the freedom for self-giving, self-sacrificing service to God and neighbor, and creation. This ethic must emerge from hope and embrace finitude (and even failure).

Freedom is born of and demonstrates hope: "An ethics of freedom can be founded only on hope and can only try to express hope" (Ellul 1976, 12).

> Hope bears witness to us that there is a future. We can escape destiny. We have scope for life. Life has triumphed over death. . . . This is what opens up for us the path of freedom. Because hope enables us to live by a possible future . . . [w]e are no longer subject to sociological conditioning or individual influences or a simple and incoherent succession of things that just happen. (Ellul 1976, 18)

We do not need to succeed according to necessity, because God already has succeeded. Our hope is in the already accomplished, in our redemption and in creation's release from bondage to corruption through Christ's completed earthly work.

Christians are free to embrace their finitude, rather than to tilt at infinity (Gunton 2002, 47). As Colin Gunton writes:

> It is, or should be, liberating to know that we are able, and are indeed intended, to achieve only so much in one short life. It is also the case that it is an ineluctable part of the human condition as we experience it that all of us in some way or other fail in what we are set or set ourselves to achieve. (Gunton 2002, 48–49)

There are two trajectories, both involving finitude/humility and infinity/glory, available to all people. One may grasp first at the glorious infinite, as did Adam and Nebuchadnezzar, only to be brought low. Or one may follow Christ's trajectory, considering equality with God not something to be grasped, but embracing the humble finite only to be glorified later (Philippians 2:5–9). As Karen Jobes writes in her commentary on 1 Peter, "Christ obeyed, suffered, died, was resurrected, and ascended to eternal glory with the Father. Following in Christ's footsteps, the Christian's life is shaped by the same pattern," and Peter "admonishes his readers . . . to continue to persevere in following Christ by doing the right thing and *leaving the outcome to God*" (2005, 49, emphasis added). Following this trajectory in our political engagement means not taking things into our own hands. It means working toward stewardship and justice and other goods without touching the ark, even when it might touch the ground. It means not doing whatever is perceived as pragmatically necessary, but only whatever is right, even in the face of failure.

I take the plausibility of failure to be a reality of our fallen and cursed world. As Ellul writes, "Perhaps man's problems are so complicated and so badly put that they are in fact [humanly] insoluble" (1976, 373). Perhaps the risk inherent in postlapsarian nature-society relations can only be managed and mitigated; perhaps this management and mitigation, because of our finitude, is sometimes at odds with other good goals. Perhaps we will have to make difficult choices transparently tragic. To the world, this will sound hopeless. But our hope is not in ourselves; it is in God. And in this eschatological perspective, we must point to what is greater than ourselves, even if it seems that our pointing is likely to result in failure. A watching world will wonder why we can do right in the face of failure, and we will point to a hope outside of our own feeble prospects for success.

Does this freedom suggest a disengagement from environmental politics? Not at all. Evangelicals are free to engage in environmental politics, but we must exhibit "a differentiated engagement with society . . . [that involves] neither full assimilation nor complete withdrawal" (Jobes 2005). Does this make success ethically irrelevant? No. It makes success ethically subordinate, considerable only in the context of right substantive commitments *and* right modalities of engagement. *Ceteris paribus*, consequences matter. But this is quite different from the consequentialist paradigm of political realism. Evangelicals should admit to the importance, complexity, and possible insolubility of nature-society relations in a postlapsarian world while still working to improve environmental conditions now and in the future. And where commitments to stewardship and justice may compromise other commitments, we should continue to work toward all of them, explicit about their potential intractability and its source, despite possible failure. This differentiated engagement evinces a radical hope, desacralizes and re-relativizes politics, and re-establishes the normative primacy of theological truths, rather than political necessity, as the source of moral guidance.

And when politics are relative, we are able to demonstrate the truth of the gospel in many ways, not the least of which is reconciliation with other believers. As Ellul noted:

> The role of Christians is to be with other people. That is, it seems important to me that in all parties . . . there should be Christians and that the role of these Christians should be to be well in tune with and serious comrades for those who are in the same party, but that they unceasingly remember, and that is the significance of their political commitment, that they are more united with their brothers in Jesus Christ who belong to the opposite party than with their comrades of the same party. (Ellul 1997a, 179)

An ethics of freedom points to the only true absolute, demonstrating the power of the gospel to reconcile those who are different under that absolute and the promise of the gospel eventually to commensurate seemingly and only temporarily incommensurable ends. This means that it is important for Christians who disagree about climate change and other matters of environmental policy to demonstrate their reconciliation to and love for one another, in spite of their differences. This reconciliation may not advance the interests of a campaign for environmental sustainability and equity. And it may not advance a campaign to limit an evangelical political agenda to just a few moral issues. But it will demonstrate that neither of those goals is ultimate.

FINAL THOUGHTS: ON TRANSLATION/ARTICULACY IN EVANGELICAL ENGAGEMENT WITH ENVIRONMENTAL POLITICS

In this moment in environmental politics, people seek an overarching, even spiritually compelling, truth, one that can oblige us to even difficult choices. Al Gore suggests that this inconvenient truth is climate change. Hawken suggests that environmentalism is the absolute and transcendent issue which must be articulated, while we need a spiritual awakening that is relative and immanent, generic, easily translated and accessible to

> activists, conservationists, biophiles, nuns, immigrants, outsiders, puppeteers, protesters, Christians, biologists, permaculturists, refugees, green architects, doctors without borders, engineers without borders, reformers, healers, poets, environmental educators, organic farmers, Buddhists, rainwater harvesters, meddlers, meditators, mediators, agitators, schoolchildren, ecofeminists, bio-mimics, Muslims, and social entrepreneurs. (Hawken 2007, 187)

Christians should be in this world, working among these others for sustainability and equity. As Jobes writes of social engagement according to Peter's first letter, "Peter's eschatological perspective motivates a Christian life of witness and engagement, not of withdrawal and nonparticipation" (2005, 51). But the basic terms of this engagement are not sustainability and equity, nor even stewardship and justice, as important as these are. Environmental catastrophe (and, make no mistake, climate change of an entirely plausible sort would be catastrophic) is not *our* inconvenient truth.

The world's truly inconvenient truth is the gospel. Its narrative of creation, fall, and redemption suggests that, inconveniently, things are not in our control. Inconveniently, the gospel requires us to embrace finitude and hope not in ourselves. This inconvenient truth compels us to make the most difficult choices, and it is this inconvenient truth that we must articulate.

Translating stewardship and justice into commonly acceptable and universally accessible language is not a uniquely evangelical contribution to environmental politics. Seemingly universally accessible cognate terms may be attractive, but as Stanley Hauerwas argues, the adoption of supposedly universally accessible language is dangerous, "the current emphasis on justice among Christians springs not so much from an effort to locate the Christian contribution to a wider society as to find a way to be societal actors without the action being colored by Christian presupposition" (Hauerwas 1991, 58). Citing Hauerwas, Nicholas Wolterstorff writes:

> The result is that in "the interest of working for justice, contemporary Christians allow their imaginations to be captured by the concepts of justice determined by the presupposition of liberal societies" [63]. But that "larger social

order [does not know] what it is talking about when it calls for justice" [68]. Consequently, in working for justice, Christians "lose the critical ability to stand against the limits of our social orders. [They] forget that the first thing as Christians [they] have to hold before any society is not justice but God" [68]. (Wolterstorff 2008)

Articulating the absolute and transcendent reasons for stewardship and justice would be a uniquely evangelical contribution to environmental politics. Evangelical engagement with environmental politics that recognizes the importance of stewardship and justice, but demonstrates a peculiar foundation in a distinctively evangelical understanding of finitude, freedom, and hope, would be a uniquely evangelical contribution to environmental politics.

In her summary of social engagement according to Peter's first letter, Jobes writes that engagement is "so that 'Gentiles' may be won before the day of judgment" (2005, 51). As Ellul writes, "The important thing is the presence of Christians among other men. The important thing is that witness should be borne to Jesus Christ on the political scene" (1976, 378). It would be a perversion of the good news to witness without acknowledging in word and deed our obligation to stewardship and justice. It is equally a perversion to do so in a way that suggests that stewardship and justice can be disengaged from the gospel of God and translated into universally accessible terms, as if, should we only achieve more sustainable management techniques, we might somehow save ourselves.

All of this is a much grander vision than Hawken and his colleagues have for the place of religion in environmental politics. Rather than religion serving the interests of environmental politics, differentiated evangelical engagement with environmental politics may actually serve the kingdom of God. Evangelical engagement with public policy *on evangelical terms, despite the prospects for futility or, better, precisely because of demonstrated hope in the face of prospects for futility*, is the most significant contribution that can be made. Maybe I should finish writing that book, after all.

NOTES

1. The earliest versions of this argument were presented in "Justice and the Environment" and "How Green Is Your Gospel?" in the Gospel and Culture Project's lecture series, *Understanding Justice*, held at Westminster Theological Seminary in February 2008. Feedback received during and after these lectures has been formative in the development of this chapter. I am grateful for the opportunity provided by the Gospel and Culture Project to share even nascent thoughts on these matters. I would also like to thank Jeff Greenman and Mark Talbot for comments on earlier versions of this manuscript.

2. This is not to say that all such vantage points are morally equivalent.

3. Bruno Latour has explored deeper dimensions of this imbrication, suggesting that false dualisms of "nature" and "culture" (as well as "subject" and "object") are inherent in modernity and, ironically, produce more and more hybrid "nature-cultures" (Latour 1993).

4. Elsewhere, I have written on climate change and climate politics from an evangelical perspective, perhaps never living up to the standards articulated in this chapter. I have described in detail certain aspects of broader evangelical engagements with climate change and climate politics. As this chapter is an evangelical assessment of evangelical engagement, I will limit my comments on climate policy. Interested readers should see Toly 2004, 2005b, 2007, and 2008.

5. For more on evangelical positions on regulation and political economy, see Timothy J. Barnett's chapter "Enlightened Economics and Free Markets" in this volume.

6. Due to constraints on space, I am unable to elaborate upon these principles here. Needless to say, the meanings of stewardship and justice when it comes to the contemporary environmental issues are not uncontested, though a Christian perspective on environmental issues must engage with these two principles. Many resources in biblical and theological studies would be appropriate for further reading. These include, but are not limited to, Toly and Block forthcoming; Scott 2008; Berry 2000, 2006; Bouma-Prediger 1995, 2001; and Northcott 1996.

7. Arguments presented in parts of this section have been adapted and published online at www.gospelandculture.org/2008/11/evangelicalism-realpolitik-gospel/ under the title "Evangelicalism, Realpolitik, and the Gospel," November 3, 2008.

8. The "political realism" described by Ellul is not the same as the "Christian realism" of Reinhold Niebuhr. From the perspective of the former, however, the latter would be regarded as pathologically consequentialist.

9. In Daniel 4, Nebuchadnezzar's second dream is of a tree, the top of which "reached to heaven, and it was visible to the end of the earth. . . . In it was food for all. The beasts of the field found shade under it, and the birds of the heavens lived in its branches, and all flesh was fed from it" (vv. 11–12). This dream reveals Nebuchadnezzar's ambitions to a kingdom that is geographically and temporally unbounded. Both characteristics belong properly only to the kingdom of God, as, of course, does the shelter of all creation and the feeding of all flesh.

Chapter Two

Evangelicals and Poverty

Stephen V. Monsma

Forty years ago President Lyndon B. Johnson launched a "war on poverty," and, as some observed at the time, poverty won. Poverty rates barely budged. It is still true today that in one of the wealthiest countries on earth—where CEOs of major corporations pull down annual salaries in the millions of dollars—there are still many who are poor, even desperately poor.

Using 2008 figures, the U.S. Census Bureau estimates that 13 percent, or almost forty million, Americans are living in poverty, with poverty defined as income of less than $17,163 a year for a family of three (DeNavas-Walt, Proctor, and Smith 2008, 14). The rate of poverty is even higher among some groups of Americans: 19 percent for children under eighteen years of age, 23 percent for Hispanics, and 25 percent for African Americans (DeNavas-Walt, Proctor, and Smith 2008, 14). To put these figures in context, it is important to note that this poverty exists in the midst of unparalleled affluence. The median American household income is just over $50,000 a year, and 21 percent of American households have incomes of over $100,000 a year (De-Navas-Walt, Proctor, and Smith 2008, 6, 31). This juxtaposition of poverty and wealth raises serious questions for thoughtful evangelicals.

In this chapter I consider the question of poverty in the United States and what form a biblically based, evangelical response to it would take. [1] I first consider the basic causes of continuing poverty in the midst of affluence and the public policy alternatives traditionally advocated in response. Next I explore the variety of attitudes that evangelicals have taken on issues of poverty, followed by an examination of the basic principles to which an evangelical theology leads. In the final section I consider some applications of the basic principles discussed in the prior section. In doing so, I hope to demonstrate that evangelicals, at their best, have something distinctive to offer the continuing discussions of reducing the incidence of poverty in the United States.

THE CAUSES OF POVERTY

Any discussion of poverty and the appropriate public policies to deal with it must begin with a consideration of the causes of poverty in the United States today. This is a complex subject upon which entire books have been written. But most causes of poverty that have been advanced fall into three categories. One is poverty that arises out of the cyclical nature of our free market economy. Given the economic upheavals of 2008 and 2009, one hardly need remind anyone of the reality of economic cycles. There are periods of low unemployment and raising wages; there are periods of increased unemployment and stagnant or decreasing wages. Many persons living on the edge of poverty—most of whom are unskilled workers—are in good economic times able to advance above the poverty line, but when unemployment or sharply rising prices hit, they fall below it (Hoynes 2000). As Harry Holzer testified before the Joint Economic Committee of Congress, "[b]etween 2007 and 2008, the beginning of the current recession caused real income to fall and poverty to rise" (Holzer 2008). One group of scholars has written, "The literature on the causes of poverty consistently cites the importance of labor market opportunities . . . [including] poverty rate's cyclical nature" (Hoynes, Page, and Stevens 2006, 53).

A second oft cited cause of poverty consists of certain structural features in the economy or the broader society. These include discriminatory practices that can make securing employment more difficult for certain ethnic or racial groups. William Julius Wilson has argued that poverty among urban African Americans has been fostered by the structural change of both manufacturing jobs and middle-class blacks moving out of inner cities (Wilson 1987). A more recent study found that "the movement of jobs from central cities to suburbs and the rapid expansion of employment outside of central cities in the last quarter of the twentieth century" has negatively impacted the employment prospects of minority workers concentrated in central cities (Cancian and Danziger 2009, 8). This category also includes long-term, permanent shifts in the economy that arise out of technological changes, shifting consumer demands, and changes in patterns of trade. For example, the percentage of the nonagricultural workforce that was in manufacturing in the United States declined from 31 percent in 1970 to only 13 percent in 2005 (West Coast Poverty Center). Recent years have seen a major shift of manufacturing jobs overseas. With the globalization of the economy, American workers compete with workers around the world, many of whom are paid only a fraction of what American workers are paid. Especially in the industrial states of the northeast—sometimes unkindly called the Rust Belt—this has resulted in the displacement of previously well-paid workers and poverty for some (Wilson 2008–2009). As the West Coast Poverty Center of the University of Washington has summarized, "Many researchers would argue that the loss of manufacturing jobs . . . over the past 30 years has contributed to increasing inequality and persistent poverty" (West Coast Poverty Center).

There also are those who are poor because of individual conditions or circumstances that are peculiar to the persons experiencing poverty. This is the third source of poverty in the United States. It might be the person who, due to major health or psychological problems, is unable to hold a job for long or even to work at all. It might be those who have engaged in self-defeating behavior—failing to complete high school, acquiring a criminal record, or having children while young and unmarried. The U.S. Census Bureau statistics tell a story that political liberals sometimes ignore, but which cannot be denied. Of all families composed of a married couple, only 6 percent are in poverty. In contrast, 14 percent of single-parent families headed by a male are in poverty, and 29 percent of single-parent families headed by a female live in poverty (DeNavas-Walt, Proctor, and Smith 2008, 14). Of those with less than a high school education, 24 percent are below the poverty line. That number is cut in half—to 12 percent—for those who have completed high school, even without any college education (U.S. Census Bureau, Factfinder). In the United States, one who completes high school, avoids having children out of wedlock, marries, and remains married is very unlikely to be poor. By saying this, I am not suggesting that most of the poor are poor simply because of their own wrong choices or that the rest of society has no responsibility toward them. Both conclusions are wrong. But it is important to begin our consideration of how to address poverty with a realistic understanding of the facts.

CURRENT PUBLIC POLICY RESPONSES TO POVERTY

We turn next to a consideration of the range of public policy alternatives designed to address poverty. Public policy efforts vary with the three causes of poverty outlined above. For cyclical poverty, the government has a vast array of countercyclical tools that it generally employs in economic downturns. At no time was this more clearly seen than in 2008 and early 2009, with the unraveling of the banking and credit system that we all quickly learned is foundational to the entire free market system. The Federal Reserve System's ability to influence interest rates and thereby the money supply, as well as the spending powers of Congress and the presidency, all were utilized in an extraordinarily vigorous manner. That economic cycles affect not only the poor and near poor but all of society means that cyclical downturns are met with whatever tools the government has in its arsenal. In 2008, even many conservatives—President George W. Bush and treasury secretary Henry W. Paulson, for example—were willing to jettison their small-government philosophy and use government to intervene in the free-market economy when severe cyclical changes posed a major threat (Paulson 2008; Landler and Andrews 2008).

Structural changes in the economy usually affect only certain segments of the population, country, or economy, and thus the government's reaction is usually slower and less vigorous than in the case of cyclical downturns. Laws outlawing discrimination against minorities and women seek to eliminate discriminatory employment practices as a structural cause of poverty. There are programs that target impoverished areas by giving businesses tax breaks and other economic incentives to encourage them to locate there and employ residents. Retraining programs are available for displaced workers. Trade policies also are sometimes altered in efforts to protect American workers displaced by the movement of jobs overseas, although such efforts are usually limited in nature. Debate continues over whether there should be more funding for educational and retraining programs for workers displaced by structural changes in the economy. Similar debates exist around free trade agreements and other trade policies that are crafted to protect American workers and retard structural change due to the shifting of manufacturing activities overseas. Liberals and conservatives sometimes clash on these questions, with liberals more amenable to government action either to protect American workers from overseas competition or, more frequently, to provide retraining programs (Greenhouse 2009; Stolberg 2007).

As to poverty arising from circumstances associated with the individuals who are poor, there are two main national government public policy programs. For those who are permanently disabled due to physical or psychological conditions, there is the Supplemental Security Income (SSI) program. This is a part of the social security system and provides monthly payments on an ongoing basis to those determined to be permanently disabled. The monthly payments alone are not sufficient to lift persons out of poverty, but they provide some help to those unable to work.

The other major government program is Temporary Assistance for Needy Families (TANF). This federal program is administered by the states—and thus it varies somewhat from state to state—and provides cash assistance to families with dependent children. These families usually, but not always, consist of single mothers with young children. In addition to cash assistance, TANF includes job training and child-care components that are designed to enable the recipients to obtain gainful employment so that they no longer need assistance. This program was overhauled in 1996, when a greater emphasis was placed on mandatory training and work requirements. Also, the length of time a person could receive benefits under it was limited to five years (three years in some states). Political liberals tend to favor higher levels of cash assistance, more help with such needs as transportation and child care, and less strict work or training requirements; conservatives fear that if assistance levels are too high and work and training requirements too lax, many will never become economically self-supporting and instead will become indefinitely dependent on a system that leaves them mired in poverty.

EVANGELICAL ATTITUDES TOWARD THE POOR

This section considers the attitudes of evangelical Protestants toward the poor and the public policies described above. There is a widespread image of evangelicals as concerned with only a few limited issues—abortion, same sex marriages, and support for Israel—and having little concern for the poor and public policies that relate to poverty. To some degree this is understandable. Prominent evangelical leaders such as the late Jerry Falwell, Pat Robertson, and James Dobson have had very little to say about the poor. When Joel Hunter was named to head the Christian Coalition in 2005, he expressed a desire to expand its agenda to include a concern for the poor. A board member declared to him that "[t]hose issues are fine, but they are just not what we do" (Hunter 2008, 21). Hunter tactfully withdrew as president before he had formally taken over the leadership position.

However, the old guard evangelical leaders and Hunter's experience with the Christian Coalition are not the whole story in terms of evangelical attitudes toward poverty. In 1972 evangelical sociologist David Moberg wrote a book titled *The Great Reversal* in which he lamented what he saw as twentieth-century evangelicals' departure from their nineteenth-century forebearers' concern for the poor and marginalized of society (Moberg 1972). A year later, a group of evangelicals—including establishment evangelical figures such as Carl H. F. Henry—gathered in Chicago and adopted a declaration that confessed, "Although the Lord calls us to defend the social and economic rights of the poor and oppressed, we have mostly remained silent" ("Chicago Declaration"). Evangelicals for Social Action grew out of this declaration and a few years later the Association for Public Justice (later to be renamed the Center for Public Justice) was formed, both organizations having a concern for the poor as a central goal. Reverend Jim Wallis and the Sojourners Community he founded in Washington, D.C., his many books, and *Sojourners* magazine, all call for a concern for the poor and needy.

The 1990s saw the publication of two thoughtful, scholarly collections of essays by evangelical scholars on poverty and welfare policies in the United States. *Welfare in America: Christian Perspectives on a Policy in Crisis* (Carlson-Thies and Skillen 1996) was published by the Center for Public Justice and *Toward a Just and Caring Society: Christian Responses to Poverty in America* (Gushee 1999) was put out by Evangelicals for Social Action. In 2005 another major work was published by the NAE titled *Toward an Evangelical Public Policy* (Sider and Knippers 2005). It contained thoughtful essays by scholars and activists on key public policy issues, including one on caring for those in need. The NAE's Board of Directors unanimously adopted in 2004 a document titled "For the Health of the Nation: An Evangelical Call to Civic Responsibility." A section titled "We seek justice and compassion for the poor and vulnerable" cited Scripture as condemning "gross disparities in opportunity and outcome that cause suffering and perpetuate poverty, and it calls us to work towards equality of opportunity" ("For the Health of the Nation" 2004, 18). It likewise found that "governmental social welfare must aim to provide opportunity and restore people to self-sufficiency" (Ibid., 19).

My point in citing these persons, books, and declarations is to demonstrate that many evangelicals have for some time been calling for a living out of a concern for the poor and have been giving careful thought to how this should be done. There were other leaders—especially some who were more politically active on behalf of conservative causes and thus able to garner more attention from the secular media due to their outspokenness—who did not demonstrate the same concern. But for many years there has been an undercurrent of evangelical scholars and leaders seeking to draw attention to a biblically rooted concern for the poor and working out just what that means in the present day United States and the public policies it pursues.

In addition, national surveys have found that evangelicals are anything but uniformly conservative on issues of poverty. A major 2007 Pew survey found that 57 percent of white evangelicals agreed with the statement, "Government should do more to help needy Americans, even if it means going deeper into debt" (*U.S. Religious Landscape Survey* 2008). This was only a slightly lower percentage than that for the American population as a whole: 62 percent of all Americans agreed with the statement. Similarly, a 2004 survey by the *Religion and Ethics Newsweekly* found that 65 percent of white evangelicals reported they were either very worried or somewhat worried that "there is a growing inequality between rich and poor in this country" ("America's Evangelicals" 2004). In 2008, the Henry Institute for the Study of Christianity and Politics at Calvin College found that 40 percent of white evangelicals agreed with the statement, "The government should spend more to fight hunger and poverty *even if it means higher taxes on the Middle*

Class" ("Henry Institute National Survey" 2008, emphasis added). All of these percentages are even higher if black and Hispanic evangelicals are taken into account.

In sum, whether it is evangelical leaders or the general evangelical population, there are many who are concerned about poverty in the United States and favor more vigorous governmental action to combat it. Evangelicals are hardly a uniformly conservative group on public policy questions relating to poverty. Majorities or near majorities of evangelicals favor more active public policies to help the poor, and there are evangelical leaders who have for some time been writing and speaking out on how to bring their theological insights to bear on the problem of poverty.

BASIC PERSPECTIVES ON POVERTY ROOTED IN EVANGELICAL BELIEFS

Rooted in an evangelical worldview are four key principles or perspectives that relate to both individuals' and society's responsibility in light of continuing poverty in the midst of a highly affluent society. These stem from evangelicals' high regard for the Bible and their commitment to its being "the inspired, the only infallible, authoritative Word of God," as the statement of faith of the NAE expresses it. These principles are not based on biblical texts or injunctions taken in isolation from the Bible as a whole. Instead, they emerge out of the total witness of the Bible, its truths, and the sense of direction it conveys.

The first biblical truth that is relevant to public policies designed to deal with large numbers of persons and families in desperate poverty is the concept that *God created human beings in his image*. The Genesis creation account says of human beings and human beings alone: "Then God said, 'Let us make man in our image, in our likeness . . .' So God created man in his own image, in the image of God he created him; male and female he created them" (Gen. 1:26–27 NIV). Theologians have differed on exactly what being created in the image of God means, but all are agreed that it signals the great worth of human beings, irrespective of birth, nationality, race, ethnicity, gender, or social class. Most scholars see the creation of men and women in God's image as signaling that they have been given a rational and creative capacity far beyond what animals have. We are not controlled by instincts or our environment, but are choosing, willing, creative beings who are morally responsible for the choices we make. As God's image bearers we have the right, even the duty, to choose our path, develop our talents and gifts, and become all that we can become—and that God intends for us to become.

Growing out of the first basic principle is a second one: it is most assuredly Christians' duty before God to have a deep concern for the poor, a concern that leads to actions designed to help the poor. For the committed Christian, guided by the Bible, this is a requirement, not an option. There are some two thousand references in the Bible to the poor and our obligation to show concern for and to offer help to them. For example, the Old Testament law commanded the ancient Hebrews, "There will always be poor people in the land. Therefore I command you to be open-handed toward your brothers and toward the poor and needy in your land" (Deut. 15:11 NIV). The New Testament is equally clear in its commands in regard to the poor: "Religion that God our Father accepts as pure and faultless is this: to look after orphans and widows in their distress and to keep oneself from being polluted by the world" (James 1:27 NIV). Jesus Christ himself in Matthew 25 makes clear that when one clothes the naked, visits the prisoner, or feeds the hungry, one is doing these acts of mercy to Christ himself, and those who fail to do so are denying him the care he needs: "Truly I tell you, whatever you did for one of the least of these brothers and sisters of mine, you did for me" (Matt. 25:40 TNIV).

A third basic principle underlying an evangelical approach to poverty is that the underlying, God-given purpose of government is to seek justice in our world. This concept both establishes and limits the obligation of government in regard to poverty. The Old Testament is filled with admonitions for the Hebrew rulers to rule with justice. When the Israelites were about to enter the land God had promised them, they were instructed through Moses, "Appoint judges and officials for each of your tribes in every town . . . and they shall judge the people fairly. Do not pervert justice or show partiality. . . . Follow justice and justice alone" (Deut. 16: 18–20 NIV). The prophet Amos condemned those who "deprive the poor of justice in the courts" (Amos 5:12 NIV). In the New Testament, Peter refers to "governors, who are sent by him to punish those who do wrong and to commend those who do right" (I Peter 2:14 NIV).

But what exactly is justice? It traditionally has been defined as ensuring that all persons receive their due. There is much content in that very brief definition. It is rooted in the belief that, as image bearers of God, all human beings possess rights: certain things that are due them. One thinks immediately of the very right to life itself. There is also the right to freedom to worship God as one sees fit, to marry and to raise one's children, and the opportunity to study and learn and to pursue work of one's choosing. As image bearers of almighty God himself, the poor also have a great worth and a right to be able to exercise and to live out—as parents, neighbors, and workers—the creative capacities and abilities with which they are endowed. Yet poverty—when left unaddressed—means limited opportunities and constricted choices. To say that one wishes to contribute to society by the work of one's hands and thereby earn an income with which to support one's self and one's family, but then to be told there is no work available or that the only work available is work with such low wages that they are inadequate to provide for one's family, is to be denied what it means to be God's image bearer.

It also is an injustice: the opportunity to exercise fully what it means to be an image bearer of God is being denied. The concept of justice as the basic God-given duty of government means the government has the right, even the obligation, to come to the assistance of the poor. In doing so it lives up to its role of pursuing a more just order in society.

However, the concept of justice also limits government's role in connection with the poor. It speaks of opportunities, not of guaranteed incomes or a right to the largess of society no matter what one does or fails to do. Justice speaks the language of empowerment, not the language of charity and paternalism. Opportunity and empowerment are rich terms that go beyond the negative freedom of simply an absence of legal restraints. There must be actual, real-life opportunities for such things as a quality education and assistance with transportation or child care when they are essential to obtaining and holding a job, as well as help in overcoming emotional or psychological burdens that life's circumstances may have placed on one. In the latter case, I am thinking of help in overcoming the burdens of growing up in a dysfunctional family, suffering from abusive relationships, and lacking positive social contacts, leading to an absence of what Robert Putman and others have called social capital (Putman 2000, 22–24).

A fourth basic principle based on evangelical thinking is the importance and God-intended nature of civil society. Lying in between the individual and the government are a host of institutions and associations: families, religious congregations, service clubs, nonprofit service organizations, athletic leagues, and much, much more. They grow out of the social nature of human beings that has been an inherent aspect of being human from creation. The Genesis 2 creation story has a moving account of the first man, Adam, living alone and not finding the desired companionship among the animals. It was only when another human being, the woman Eve, was created that Adam's social need was met. We clearly are social beings who need each other to become all that God intends us to become.

Emerging from this basic fact, Christian thought in both the Catholic and evangelical traditions has developed concepts designed to recognize that those social structures lying between the individual and the government are not accidents of history, but have a right to exist and a role to play in society that are given by God himself (Daly 2009; Schindler 2008). The Reformed wing of evangelicalism—especially as developed in the Netherlands by Abraham Kuyper—speaks of *sphere sovereignty*, in which society is divided into certain areas or spheres, such as art, education, economics, family life, and government. The institutions that mark each of these spheres have an inherent right to exist and an inherent role to play; they are "sovereign" in their proper sphere.[2] They do not receive rights or play roles at the sufferance of government.

Similarly, Catholic social thought has developed the concept of *subsidiarity*, which views the various social structures in society as ordered in a hierarchy and asserts that problems ought to be dealt with at the lowest level at which they can be effectively addressed. A religious congregation ought not to do what the individual or the family can do; the nonprofit organization ought not to do what the local congregation can do; the local government ought not to do what the nonprofit service organization can do; and the national government ought not to do what the local government can do.

Sphere sovereignty and subsidiarity hold in common a commitment to the idea that various social structures existing between the individual and the national government have an inherent, God-intended right to exist and a proper role to play in human society; they are neither accidental by-products of random social forces nor mere creatures of the state. They are intentional, rooted in human beings' God-created social nature. Thus governments, in crafting public policies, must not seek to absorb or undercut them, but rather should respect them and their integrity. When policymakers conclude these structures are not up to the task of dealing with a societal problem, it is government's responsibility to work with, supplement, and strengthen them.

This final principle has a special relevance to poverty, since it historically has been families, churches and other religious organizations, along with the nonprofit sector, who have played a huge role in providing for the needy. The public policy-making process needs to sort out the proper roles respectively of government and of civil society structures in such a way that both can play a robust, yet limited role.

APPLYING THE PRINCIPLES

As is often the case, it is easier to articulate basic principles than to apply them in the real world. In that world, lines of responsibility are usually fuzzy and causes and effects rarely clear. Even those who agree on basic principles often end up disagreeing on the application of those principles. This is not the place for a fully developed, well-rounded antipoverty program based on the evangelical, biblical principles just outlined. Nevertheless, some applications are clear, as is the general direction they should take. That is what I seek to do in this section.

First, the basic principles described above lead to a rejection of both a libertarian and a nanny state response to poverty. The libertarian approach says that government has little or no responsibility toward the poor and that anything it does is likely only to make matters worse. But the Christian concept of the justice-promoting role of government affirms that government does indeed have a role to play in working to overcome poverty among its people. Poverty makes it difficult, and for some impossible, to live the lives of freedom and creative purpose God calls his image bearers to live. That is an injustice, and governments are God-intended instruments for combating societal injustices.

Conversely, the principles previously discussed oppose the nanny state, where public policies guarantee to all a continuing income, housing, and other benefits, irrespective of one's willingness to take advantage of the opportunities one has. Such a policy soon degenerates into paternalism, whereby the recipient of the services is rendered wholly dependent on the largess of others and loses independence of action and even of thought and dreams. Life in one sense is made easy, as one's needs are met. But one is reduced to something less than the thinking, willing, contributing being God intends for each of us. Both poverty and paternalism reduce human beings to something less then they were made to be.

But this only eliminates the two extremes. How can one make one's way in the broad center of public policy alternatives that are more than libertarian and less than paternalistic, nanny-state-like in nature? To respond to that question, we first need to consider the role of civil society in reacting to poverty in the midst of affluence. Of special importance are the roles that families, churches,[3] and nonprofit organizations can and should play, consistent with the principles of subsidiarity and sphere sovereignty. Public policy needs to respect the integrity of these actors and look to them first, and not to government. There are two things they can and should offer—even while there is a major factor that limits the good they can do. I examine these three in turn.

First, these civil society structures should offer whatever financial or other material assistance they can. They can be especially effective when the need is for short-term, emergency help resulting from economic cycles or to structural changes in the economy. Family members should, when able, offer financial help, temporary housing, and food when a family member is in need. But often the help that families are in a position to give will not be enough, or there will be persons who are isolated from families or have no family members to whom to turn. Here is where churches should step in. Surely they should offer material assistance to their own members in need. But they also should offer similar aid to others in their neighborhood and the broader community who are in great need. Also, most communities have a wide variety of nonprofit organizations, many of which are faith-based and grow out of churches and others which are secular in background and nature. These too can and should step in, especially when what a local congregation can do is not enough, due either to the overwhelming needs among its members or in its neighborhood or to what may be very limited resources.

A second thing—perhaps even more important than material assistance—that families, churches, and nonprofit organizations can do is to offer emotional support, mentoring, and training to those in great need. Often the poor are socially isolated and lack positive role models in their background. I am primarily thinking here of persons who are poor due to situations peculiar to them and not as a result of cyclical or structural changes in the economy. They often lack social capital of both a *bonding* and a *bridging* nature (Putman 2000, 22–24; Monsma and Soper 2007, 16–17, 107–23). The former consists of ties to family, ethnic, religious, neighborhood, or other in-groups of which one is a part. One who identifies as a member of an in-group gains the emotional and material support that goes with being a member of an in-group. Bridging social capital refers to broader ties to persons and groups in one's community beyond one's immediate neighborhood or social group. Most persons have a reservoir of both types of social capital on which they can call when financial or other stresses envelop them. But those who do not are left to struggle on their own in the face of difficulties and troubles. The result too often is extreme poverty, even homelessness, and despair.

But churches and nonprofit, neighborhood-based organizations can frequently provide the supportive services and emotional support that those in poverty need. They are well situated to provide the social capital that will enable one to get one's life put back together, obtain needed training and employment, and move out of poverty. They can provide mentoring, emergency help, transportation, backup child care, drug counseling, and other such nonmaterial support as may be vital, but which government agencies are ill suited to provide. Those who have been victims of physical and emotional abuse, need to be told—by word and by deed—that God loves them and has good plans for them, that they are in fact of great worth, and that they have much to contribute to others. Some may need positive role models—persons who have gone through similar experiences and have been able to overcome those experiences. Others may simply need a friend to talk to following a day when everything has gone wrong. These are needs that government bureaucracies are poorly constituted to fulfill, in contrast to churches and other faith-based and neighborhood-based programs (Monsma 2005, 2008).

Because of their limited financial resources, however, there is a severe limit to what civil society institutions can accomplish alone. There simply is no way that families, churches, and nonprofit organizations can even begin to meet all of the financial and material needs of the thirty-seven million poor people in the United States. Only the government, with its taxation and borrowing powers, has the requisite financial resources, especially for long-term needs.

In light of this, what is the role that government and its public policies should play in overcoming poverty? And how do they relate to what civil society institutions can and should do? What, in more concrete terms, does it mean for government to seek justice for the poor while respecting the structures of civil society? I suggest that government has a limited, yet very significant, role to play. First, government should provide cash assistance to those in great need; where the need arises from permanent disabilities that cash assistance should be ongoing and indefinite. Where the need arises from economic cycles, structural economic changes, or persons' individual situations, the cash assistance should be temporary in nature. It should be aimed at enabling persons to adjust to changed circumstances and to take actions needed to achieve an economic self-supporting status. Cash assistance should be adequate for persons and their families to live a comfortable, albeit low-income, life. This is a proper role for government, since it alone has the financial resources to provide the needed levels of assistance.

Many of those in need, however, require more than cash assistance. They may need job training, emotional support, help with transportation and child care, or help in overcoming the crises that life often throws down in their paths. This is especially true of those who are experiencing poverty due to their individual situation rather than to economic cycles or structural changes in the economy. This is where churches and both faith-based and secular nonprofit organizations can play a prominent role. They usually do not have the funds to provide ongoing cash assistance and other material help to the poor. However, they do have volunteers and dedicated staff willing and able to come alongside those in need and offer the encouragement, training, and friendship—the social capital—they need. But the work they can do is often limited by the inadequate financial resources they have. This is especially true of organizations located in and largely supported by persons living in high-poverty areas—often the very organizations best situated to relate to those in need and provide them with appropriate help.

In short, government has the financial resources that churches and nonprofits lack; churches and nonprofits have the volunteers and supportive values and services that government does not have. This suggests a "both-and" rather than an "either-or" approach when it comes to parceling out the respective responsibilities of the private, nonprofit sector and the governmental sector. Such an approach is fully in keeping with the principles of subsidiarity and sphere sovereignty discussed earlier. Nevertheless, conservatives usually look primarily and sometimes even exclusively to churches and nonprofit organizations to provide what the poor need (Olasky 1992). Liberals usually look primarily and sometimes even exclusively to government and its agencies to provide what the poor need (Greenberg 2007). The sound approach to antipoverty public policies, based in evangelical thought (as well as Roman Catholic thought) looks to both and assigns each of them a proper, limited role that enables them to work as partners.

A final, crucial point must be made. President George W. Bush created in the White House an Office of Faith-Based and Community Initiatives, charged with making sure that faith-based and small community-based organizations would be able to obtain their fair share of government contracts and grants for the provision of services to the poor and others in need. President Obama has continued this policy with a renamed White House Office of Faith-Based and Neighborhood Partnerships. Partnering with faith-based and other neighborhood nonprofit organizations is an appropriate and needed role for government to play. It is fully in keeping with sphere sovereignty and subsidiarity and their emphasis on civil society and the vital place for its structures in society (Daly 2009). But this will only be the case if the autonomy of churches and other faith-based and community agencies is respected. The goal ought not to be to turn them into arms of the government or convert their programs into government programs. Rather, it should be to empower and expand the work they are already doing, without turning them into clones of the government. For churches and faith-based organizations, this includes the freedom to take religion into account in their hiring decisions, even when they receive government funding for some of their programs. The value-added feature that churches and other faith-based nonprofits bring to the table, above what government agencies typically provide, relates to their sense of values, the volunteers they are able to recruit, and the motivations of their staff members. Yet these, in turn, are rooted in the religious communities from which they come. If religion must be ignored in their staffing as the price of obtaining government funds for the public-serving work they are doing, their very strength will be sapped and the all-too-real tendency will be to turn them into clones of government agencies (Monsma 2005, 188–94). The poor in desperate need of help will be the ultimate losers.

FINAL THOUGHTS ON EVANGELICALS AND POVERTY

Poverty is an ongoing challenge in the United States, a challenge made all the more noteworthy by the affluence of most Americans. Evangelicals have much to offer a society working to address this challenge. Most evangelicals favor doing something to combat poverty. They certainly have the motivation to do so, given their commitment to the Bible as their guide for living. And their leaders are supportive of addressing poverty and have given serious thought on how to do so.

Evangelicals have much to bring to the table. They have numbers (at least a quarter of the voting public), the motivation, and fresh ideas that go beyond the stale liberal-conservative divide. At their best, they bring a theologically rooted concern and respect for those struggling with poverty and a justice-based view of government that assigns it a limited, but significant role in addressing poverty and its underlying causes. By combining the resources of churches and faith-based and neighborhood nonprofit organizations with the financial resources of government, we may yet be able to win the war on poverty and reverse the conclusions of an earlier generation that poverty had won.

NOTES

1. I write this essay as one who considers himself an evangelical Protestant in the Reformed, or Calvinist, wing of evangelicalism. Most of what I write is broadly true of evangelicals. But evangelicals are not monolithic in their views. Many evangelicals undoubtedly would develop their ideas in a slightly different—perhaps even radically different—manner. I do not presume to speak for all evangelicals. I speak here for myself and my views, even though I believe they are shared by increasing numbers of my fellow evangelicals.

2. I put sovereign in quotation marks because it is not a true or absolute sovereignty, but a quasi-sovereignty that recognizes and respects the "sovereignty" of the other spheres. Also, government, in its justice-promoting role, has the right to limit the various spheres if they are seeking to exceed their authority or are themselves acting unjustly.

3. I follow the common practice of using "church" to refer to religious congregations of a variety of religions and religious traditions. I do so because the overwhelming majority of religious congregations in the United States are in the Christian tradition—and, therefore, "churches"—and to avoid awkwardness of language.

Chapter Three

To Do Justly and Love Mercy: Using Scripture to Guide Criminal Justice Policy

Jennifer E. Walsh

The history of American criminal justice is marked by cycles of reform. As with all ongoing social problems, each generation attempts to improve on the efforts of those that have come before it. Often, it is the introduction of new perspectives or values that produces policy innovations that transform our understanding of the problem. In the case of crime and punishment, early Americans, fervent in their Christian faith, rejected European systems of justice that immoderately wielded the death penalty and wantonly imposed cruel corporal punishment in favor of a new penitentiary-based system that encouraged the repentance, salvation, and restoration of offenders. A generation later, reformers sought to save wayward children by exempting them from traditional punishment and creating special institutions to facilitate their educational and moral training. At the dawn of the twentieth century, scientific discoveries in the fields of sociology, psychology, and biology prompted criminologists to view transgression differently. No longer did they consider crime to be a moral failure; instead it was viewed as a dysfunction. With this new perspective, reformers rejected traditional means of punishment in favor of correctional programs designed to treat offenders. Soaring crime rates sixty years later prompted politicians to reject the treatment approach and adopt sentences based upon utilitarian theories of deterrence and incapacitation. Today, with 2.3 million offenders behind bars, Americans are again asking what might be done to solve crime once and for all.

Throughout much of history, the evangelical church was instrumental in shaping the moral debate over crime and punishment. Leaders of the church guided political action so that government policies did not stray far from the teachings of Scripture. Yet, after the 1925 Scopes trial, the evangelical church withdrew from public discourse, leaving a vacuum in its wake. On issues of crime and punishment, that vacuum was filled by social scientists espousing the latest theories on criminal behavior (Tapie 2006). By the 1960s, secular scientists monopolized the marketplace of criminal justice ideas, leaving no room for religious values or influences (Duff 2003). When crime rose again in the 1980s and 1990s, the evangelical church remained on the sidelines as the debate over crime and punishment raged.

Even as crime has recently fallen to historic lows in the last decade—due in part to policies that heavily emphasize incarceration—policymakers have begun to realize that our society can no longer afford to maintain our present policies without compromising the integrity of other vital social services. State legislators have begun debating whether we should release certain groups of offenders from prison early to generate financial savings and relieve overcrowding. Many states have sentenced drug offenders to residential treatment programs instead of prison. Others have trimmed costs by sentencing nonviolent offenders to probation or house arrest. Most recently, voters in California and elsewhere have considered repealing expensive sentencing laws, though they appear to be effective in reducing crime.

With penal reform once again a popular topic in state legislatures across the country, the evangelical church once again has an opportunity—and an obligation—to reinsert itself into the debate. Policies that advance themes of morality and justice have long been ignored in favor of practical solutions that promise only to reduce crime. The result is that many sentencing laws place too much emphasis on the utilitarian benefits of rehabilitation, deterrence, and incapacitation, and too little emphasis on the care of people. As a result, justice has been replaced by expediency, and mercy has been supplanted by apathy.

EVANGELICAL INFLUENCES ON CRIME AND PUNISHMENT CONCERNS

Through much of our nation's history, crime and punishment have been framed by evangelical ideals. American law, for example, defines a crime as an immoral act. It involves a prohibited action (*actus reus*) that is committed with malicious intent (*mens rea*). This definition distinguishes a crime from a tort, which is a legal wrong committed against one person by another. Often, torts occur because of carelessness or negligence—not evil intent. In the case of an accidental injury, such that might occur in a traffic collision, a court assigns fault for the incident and determines whether a civil remedy for the harm, typically financial compensation for the injured party, ought to be imposed. Although paying monetary damages may be financially painful, judgment of this kind is not considered punishment. Rather, in our system of justice, *punishment* is reserved for someone who has been convicted of a crime. This distinction reflects the view that crime is a moral transgression deserving of public condemnation (Garvey 2003).

The concept of punishment is grounded in the Christian belief that civil government is ordained by God for the purpose of preventing anarchy and preserving good. Because of this, directives of the government, unless in conflict with the commands of God, must be obeyed. Evangelicals use Paul's letter to the Christian church in Rome to support this teaching:

> Let every soul be subject to the governing authorities. For there is no authority except from God, and the authorities that exist are appointed by God. Therefore whoever resists the authority resists the ordinance of God, and those who resist will bring judgment on themselves. (Romans 13:1-2, NKJV)

When this epistle was penned, the Christian church was experiencing severe persecution by the Roman government. Despite these difficult circumstances, Paul gave two reasons why Christians should obey. One is practical: believers should obey the law so that they are not punished by the government. The other is moral: believers should obey the law because it is the right thing to do.

Also implicit in Paul's instruction is the understanding that violations of the law will result in two types of punishment. Government officials will punish those who fail to meet the state's legal requirements, and God will judge those who fail to obey His commands. Jesus warned that the two types of punishment are not equivalent in their severity; human punishment is temporal, divine punishment eternal: "And do not fear those who kill the body but cannot kill the soul. But rather fear Him who is able to destroy both soul and body in hell" (Matthew 10:28–29, NKJV). Evangelicals believe that divine punishment for disobedience is certain; only through a saving faith in Christ's substitutionary death and resurrection can one avoid God's wrath.

With this twofold understanding of punishment in mind, early American evangelical Christians sought compassion for those who had received earthly punishment, but who had yet to be saved from the divine judgment to come. To do so, however, they had to completely overhaul the penal system that had been inherited from Britain. Under English common law, corporal punishment was common, and the death penalty was used to punish both minor crimes and serious offenses. Mercy was in short supply, and those in charge of carrying out punishment were rarely interested in the physical or spiritual needs of the offender.

To induce change, pastors and laypeople formed the Philadelphia Society for Alleviating the Miseries of Public Prisons in 1787. This group petitioned authorities for a number of changes to the penal system. First, it urged lawmakers to abolish the death penalty for any crime less than murder. Second, it requested that those convicted of noncapital crimes be sentenced to a new type of imprisonment (McKelvey 1977). Specifically, it recommended that offenders be placed in solitary confinement in a "penitentiary" with no opportunity to engage or interact with others. After a few weeks, they could be given a Bible and other religious literature to read. Eventually they would be allowed to attend church services and engage in religious conversations with pastors, missionaries, and other ministers of the gospel. The isolation was designed to minimize external distractions so that offenders could reflect upon their wrongdoing and repent of their sin. As explained by one warden, "The horrors of his cell are the fruits of sin and transgression, and the only certain relief to be obtained is through his Redeemer" (Pendleton 1948, 392). Following its implementation, the Philadelphia system showed signs of success—with recidivism rates of about 3 percent—and it became a model for the rest of the American states and for many European nations. Although prison overcrowding in the early 1800s forced prison officials to abandon their emphasis on total isolation, the purpose of imprisonment, which was to promote accountability and personal repentance, remained unchanged through much of the nineteenth century.

Evangelical leaders also sought to change the philosophical reasons for imprisonment. Under English common law, prisons were all-purpose institutions. Children who engaged in mischief were incarcerated; vagrants unable to support themselves were placed behind bars. Even debtors who defaulted on small loans were sent to prison. Conditions in these human warehouses were deplorable and American evangelical reformers used their influence to highlight the inmates' plight. Eventually, they were successful. By the mid-1800s, prisons only punished criminals. Debtors were no longer incarcerated for failure to pay minor debts, and misbehaving juveniles were sent to reformatory schools instead of prisons (Pendleton 1948).

Reformers' belief that punishment should only be imposed upon those who commit crimes is often referred to as the *theory of retribution* or the *principle of "just deserts."* Just as the Bible teaches that the wages of sin is death (Romans 6:23), evangelicals asserted that the consequence of criminal transgression is punishment. Governments are only to punish those found guilty of a crime. At the time of this early reform movement, it was routinely believed that imprisonment might accomplish a variety of useful purposes. In addition to punishing criminals, governments also used corporal punishment and imprisonment to persuade citizens to conform to social norms. Executions were staged in public to send a message to the populace at large. Governments also used prisons to house social deviants and to prevent dangerous individuals from harming others. Although evangelical reformers acknowledged that imprisonment might yield useful side benefits—indeed, they hoped that prisoners might find spiritual salvation by experiencing a time of isolated prayer and solitary reflection—they also insisted that the government punish only those who were found guilty of a crime.

Today, the theory of retribution is often mischaracterized as the promotion of vengeance. Yet God declares this responsibility to be His alone: "'Vengeance is Mine, I will repay,' says the Lord" (Romans 12:19, NKJV). Thus evangelicals consider vengeance to be an unfair or unjust retaliatory response. When the state punishes someone for a crime, it is not exacting revenge on behalf of the victim. Instead, it is delivering an earthly payment for a moral debt that is owed. Although some Christians call this "chastisement," it is rejected by most evangelicals. Chastisement, as described in the Bible, is a method by which one is trained or disciplined to do what is good. While one may experience moral training and correction through the penal process (as evangelical reformers in Philadelphia had hoped), it is not the chief end of punishment.

Evangelicals have traditionally insisted that punishment be imposed only for criminal wrongdoing because it is the only response that acknowledges and respects human free will. If government could impinge upon citizens' liberty without establishing a causal link between their actions and its response, then they become nothing more than animals, incapable of acting as free moral agents. According to C. S. Lewis, it is only when one is justly punished because he deserves it that he is "treated as a human person made in God's image" (Lewis 1970, 292). This cause-and-effect relationship between crime and punishment is now a foundational premise for our criminal justice system: most people believe that they should be punished when they commit a crime because this is what they deserve (McCorkle 1993). For evangelical Christians, this remains particularly true. Studies have shown that when compared to those affiliated with other faith traditions, evangelicals still strongly support retributive policies (Grasmick et al. 1992).

Research has also shown that while the public generally believes that some crimes are "more wrong" than others (Garvey 2003), evangelicals do not consider one type of crime to be more sinful than another (Curry 1996). Nonetheless, evangelicals have historically supported the *principle of proportionality*, which ties the severity of the punishment to the gravity of the crime. Under the theory of retribution, there is a sense that lesser crimes should receive less punishment than more serious offenses. The proportionality principle also assumes that similar offenses will be punished similarly. Most evangelicals would argue that it would be unjust for two people convicted of similar crimes to be given dissimilar sentences, just as it would be unfair for grossly dissimilar offenders to receive the same sentence. Retribution necessitates some type of gradated punishment scheme to ensure that sentences are fairly and equitably administered.

Unlike other punishment theories that can be formulated according to objective utilitarian-oriented assessments, a retribution or "just deserts" view of punishment requires the government to make moral judgments based on evaluations of deservedness. Although this can be challenging, lawmakers need not do this on their own. In our democratic system of government, the public is expected to help determine the appropriate balance between crime and punishment (Singer 1979). However, determining the will of the public can be difficult at times. In recent decades, lawmakers have assumed that the public favors harsh sentencing laws. Yet researchers have found that public opinion can be distorted by exaggerated media accounts of criminal events (Roberts 1992). Evangelical Christians are often perceived as favoring punitive policies; however, recent studies have shown that they are much more likely to show compassion and mercy for criminal offenders than those outside their faith tradition (Applegate et al. 2000). Surveys have also shown that Christian believers who embrace the Scriptural tenets of forgiveness are less supportive of capital punishment (Applegate et al. 2000).

MAINLINE PROTESTANT INFLUENCES ON CRIME AND PUNISHMENT CONCERNS

Christians affiliated with mainline and/or progressive Protestant denominations also show great interest in issues of justice. They exhibit concern over the impact of crime on communities, and they express distress over the condition of those who find themselves caught up in a seemingly intractable system. Like evangelicals, they are interested in promoting policies that are right and good, and they encourage members to remain politically active in order to facilitate reform. Where evangelicals and mainline Protestants differ, however, is on their respective views of punishment: while evangelicals are more likely to embrace a theory of retribution and the principle of "just deserts," mainline Protestants believe that the utilitarian theory of rehabilitation is more consistent with New Testament ethics and teaching. They see criminal justice as a societal problem, and they express concern for those inner-city communities especially affected by ongoing cycles of violence. Progressive themes of social justice also have greater resonance in their discussions of crime and punishment (Fraser, Branson, and Williams 1939).

The influence of mainline Protestants increased at the beginning of the twentieth century when rising crime rates, prison overcrowding, and violent behavior within the institutions cast doubt on the effectiveness of early evangelical prison reforms (McKelvey 1977). Mainline Protestants aligned themselves with criminologists who believed that advances in psychology, sociology, and the medical sciences could provide scientific solutions that could reduce—or even eradicate—the problem of crime. At the urging of criminal justice professionals and progressive reformers, lawmakers began to implement these new theories by classifying and segregating inmates according to their potential for rehabilitation and by expanding systems of probation and parole to better facilitate differentiated treatment. Even the prison facilities were modified to accommodate rehabilitative therapies. Psychologists and sociologists, for example, encouraged the development of group counseling sessions; therefore, prisons were reconfigured with this treatment in mind (McKelvey 1977). Furthermore, progressive lobbyists used the slogan "Treat the criminal, not the crime" to remind policymakers that helping the offender was to be the forefront objective of all rehabilitation-based penal reforms (Rothman 1980, 273).

To facilitate the new rehabilitative model, greater discretion was also given to officials within the criminal justice system. Probation officers drafted presentencing reports that predicted the offender's risk of recidivism. Judges had expanded authority to craft individualized sentences based on their assessment of the offender's rehabilitation potential. Parole boards were entrusted with determining when an offender was rehabilitated and ready for release. Within prisons, psychiatrists were given leeway to determine when an offender was mentally ill, and the input of social scientists was valued in formulating institutional rehabilitative programs. The language used within the system was also changed to reflect the new emphasis on treatment and rehabilitation. Prisons were no longer referred to as penitentiaries; in the 1950s, they became known as "correctional institutions," and inmates were referred to as "clients" or "patients" (Singer 1979). Moreover, the focus of these institutional programs reflected a new emphasis on secular rehabilitation. Offenders were not required to attend religious services; instead, they were required to attend individual and group therapy sessions.

Mainline Protestants initially supported these changes, not because they viewed secular programming as superior to spiritual regeneration, but because they placed greater emphasis on the human worth of the offender. These reforms were also championed by political progressives, scientists, educators, and criminal justice professionals. However, three developments in the 1970s brought the rehabilitation era to a halt. First, a number of high-profile analyses of rehabilitation programs revealed that they were largely ineffective in reducing the recidivism rate among their participants. Educational programs, vocational training, and psychological therapy all were deemed expensive failures by taxpayers paying the bills. Using the mantra of "nothing works," lawmakers quickly abandoned rehabilitation programs that had been heavily touted just decades before (Martinson 1974; Wilson 1975).

Second, researchers revealed that judges, in their sentencing discretion, often based their decisions about who would go to prison or who would remain in the community on probation on socioeconomic factors, such as race, ethnicity, and economic status. Wealthy, white, and educated offenders were considered less of a recidivism risk than offenders who were poor, black or Hispanic, and illiterate. Sentencing disparities arose based upon the characteristics of the offender rather than on the nature or severity of the offense (Frankel 1972). Studies found, for example, that when two men—one white and one black—committed the same crime, the first likely would receive probation and the second likely would be sent to prison (Wilson 1975). Third, crime began to spiral out of control in the early 1970s. Political figures ranging from small-town mayors all the way up to the U.S. president pledged to restore law and order to local communities so as to reassure anxious and crime-weary voters (Gatz 1982).

Ironically, it was a progressive Christian group that led the charge to abolish the rehabilitation-oriented indeterminate sentencing system. The American Friends Committee issued a report in 1971 that called on lawmakers to curb the expansive discretion that rested in the hands of those within the system and return to a system of fixed or determinate sentences. They noted that, not only had the system failed in its stated goal of rehabilitation, but the supposedly enlightened system of punishment actually resulted in greater misery for those who could least afford it:

> For those caught in the cycle of arrest, prosecution, and "treatment," and those who share their cultures, the impact of the criminal justice system is profoundly dysfunctional. Instead of encouraging initiative, it compels submissiveness. Instead of strengthening belief in the legitimacy of authority, it generates cynicism and bitterness. . . . Instead of building pride and self-confidence, it tries to persuade its subjects (often all too successfully) that they are sick. (American Friends Service Committee 1971, 9–10)

Furthermore, the Friends Committee noted that prison sentences actually increased under indeterminate sentencing, as parole boards intentionally kept offenders incarcerated longer so they could continue to treat them. This effect was seen most dramatically in California. Under Governor Earl Warren's leadership, the state's remade penal system embraced the rehabilitative ideal. As a result, between 1959 and 1969, the median prison sentence increased from twenty-four months to thirty-six months, and the number of inmates per one hundred thousand doubled (American Friends Service Committee 1971). Instead of producing a promised decrease in the number of people caught up in the criminal justice system, the California model did just the opposite.

Today, mainline and progressive Christians continue to voice concern about the high rate of imprisonment even though the government has abandoned its use of the rehabilitation model in favor of other utilitarian theories, such as deterrence and incapacitation. They note that minority communities disproportionately suffer, both from the violence that plagues their neighborhoods and from punishment policies that impose lengthy sentences for a wide range of crimes. The high rate of imprisonment for the poor and those of color have devastated many urban communities. Furthermore, conditions within prisons have degraded to the point where inmate rape and violence are everyday occurrences (Logan 2008). Some progressive Christian groups believe that, as social institutions, prisons are inherently dysfunctional and thus are incapable of being reformed. Favoring alternative punishments, such as community-based treatment programs and programs that foster restorative justice, advocates of "No More Prisons!" are urging lawmakers to abolish prisons altogether (Taylor 2001).

CATHOLIC INFLUENCES ON CRIME AND PUNISHMENT CONCERNS

In many ways, the Catholic view on crime and punishment straddles the two Protestant perspectives. Catholics generally believe, as do many Protestants, that disobedience of civil law equals a moral transgression. Yet, in deciding whether a violation of the penal code is tantamount to a sin, Catholics allow one's conscience to be the judge. If a person intentionally does something wrong or purposefully fails to do something good, then a sin has been committed. This also means that, if one unintentionally violates the letter of the law, he may not have committed a sin because his conscience does not condemn him. This is similar to the *mens rea* element of criminal intent that American justice typically requires before someone can be punished for wrongdoing (Brennan 2003). Catholic theologians also acknowledge that while human law should serve to restrain all vice and encourage all virtue, it is necessarily constrained to those behaviors that affect the great majority of people. The law simply cannot forbid all that the conscience acknowledges to be wrong; however, what it does require, people must obey.

This understanding of what does or does not constitute sin also affects the Catholic view of just punishment. In *Summa Theologica* Thomas Aquinas noted that punishment is a consequence of sin and that sinners face three types of punishment: punishment of self (by having a guilty conscience), punishment imposed by government or community, and punishment imposed by God (Q. 87, A. 1). Aquinas also noted that the purpose of earthly punishment is to promote the common good. Just as a gangrenous limb may have to be removed to preserve the good of the body, so, too, punishment may have to be inflicted on a moral transgressor for the good of the community. This does not mean, however, that private individuals can pursue the same action under the guise of promoting the common good; rather, this power rests with government authorities alone. Personal retribution is strictly forbidden (Q. 65, A. 1).

Moreover, Catholic theology precludes the use of punishment for strictly utilitarian gains. In this way, Catholics align more with evangelical Protestants who also believe that the purpose of punishment should be anchored only to the concept of desert. Pope Pius XII explains that

> [c]onnected with the concept of the criminal act is the concept that the author of the act becomes deserving of punishment (*reatus poenae*). The problem of punishment has its beginning, in an individual case, at the moment in which a man becomes a criminal. The punishment is the reaction, required by law and justice, to the crime: they are like a blow and a counter-blow. The order violated by the criminal act demands the restoration and re-establishment of the equilibrium which has been disturbed. (Pope Pius XII 1972)

Thus, punishment exists only as a means to correct the disorder caused by criminal wrongdoing; the fact that society might benefit from its imposition, such as when crime is reduced through deterrence or incapacitation, cannot be used to justify its existence. There must be a primary causal connection between the crime and the response.

Modern Catholicism is similar to progressive Protestant thought in its teaching that all human life is sacred and valuable. No person is to be considered worthless or expendable, for even the most heinous of criminals maintains his human value. This does not mean that painful consequences cannot be imposed on criminals. Government may be permitted to inflict punishment upon the guilty to protect the citizenry and to promote the common good. In doing so, however, it must also preserve the human integrity of the individual. For Catholic theologians, this command makes it difficult to justify the death penalty as a legitimate form of punishment. Although the Church acknowledges the right of the government to execute an offender for a grievous offense, it teaches that the cheapening of human life in the modern world, and the availability of other punishment options, precludes the legitimate exercise of that punishment in most circumstances. Moreover, some Catholics believe that the use of violence (e.g., execution) to punish violence (e.g., murder) only perpetuates the cycle of harm, undermining the New Testament teachings of forgiveness and reconciliation (Bernardin 1998).

As one might expect, Catholics in society have views that generally mirror the official teachings of the Church. When compared to evangelical Christians, Catholics register less support for the use of capital punishment (Sandys and McGarrell 1997) and are less likely to cite retribution as a primary justification for punishment (Grasmick et al. 1992). Catholics are also more likely to view rehabilitation as an important aspect of the punishment process. Priests who serve as prison chaplains, for example, express broad support for rehabilitation programs offered to inmates within prison institutions (Sundt and Cullen 2002).

EVANGELICAL INFLUENCE IN THE "GET TOUGH" ERA

After studies in the 1970s raised questions about rehabilitation-oriented sentencing, lawmakers began implementing a series of reforms that would eventually remake the entire justice system. One such reform, introduced in California in 1976, removed much of the sentencing discretion previously held by judges and parole boards and assigned fixed penalties for felony offenses. Sentences were no longer individually crafted with the treatment of the offender in mind. Instead, the legislature resurrected the theory of retribution and the principle of "just deserts" to link criminal punishments to offense type and severity of conduct. This reform ensured that "defendants [would] be punished equally in accordance with the moral and material damage they [had] wrought" (Messinger and Johnson 1978, 55). A few years later, a Minnesota sentencing commission developed a system of gradated punishment to guide judicial sentencing. Using the same principle of just deserts, commission members developed gridlike guidelines that paired the severity of the current offense with the severity of the prior record. Offenders who committed property crimes, for example, received a lesser sentence than offenders who committed violent crimes. Similarly, offenders who had committed fewer crimes in their past received less punishment than did offenders with extensive criminal histories.

Within ten years, nearly all state governments and the federal government had implemented some form of determinate sentencing. However, trust in retribution and the principle of just deserts did not last. As crime arose again in the early 1990s, the public pressured lawmakers to act. Consequently, many states enacted mandatory punishment policies to better deter and/or incapacitate certain types of offenders. Repeat offenders were sentenced to life or given near-life sentences under mandatory three-strikes provisions. Gang members were given punishment enhancements that dramatically increased the lengths of their sentences. Underage felons were exempted from the jurisdiction of juvenile court. In the last several years, voters also have used deterrence and incapacitation to justify additional penalties and parole requirements for sex offenders. Only recently have nonviolent drug users been spared from the harsh punishment invoked by these utilitarian philosophies.

The public's current preference for utilitarian-based crime control theories raises challenges for evangelical participation in the ongoing policy debate. Today, few lawmakers base criminal justice decisions on what is just or right. Instead, they formulate policy according to what costs less or reduces crime the most. This could be attributed to electoral concerns, as many lawmakers favor harsh measures because they fear being labeled as soft on crime. But it could also be attributed to the complexities for lawmakers in engaging debates over moral issues in our postmodern pluralistic society. Nonquantifiable concepts, such as justice and righteousness, are difficult to assess and often vary from group to group. Furthermore, with the exception of the ongoing debate about capital punishment, policymakers have little incentive to consider such things. The public appears generally unconcerned about the moral implications of crime policy, and scholars and experts in the field no longer ponder themes of morality and justice as they once did. Thirty years ago, when the move to determinate sentencing was under way, scholarly discussions over the purpose of punishment were commonplace. Today, these conversations have largely been replaced with less weighty debates over the effectiveness and impact of various crime control policies. Evangelicals, and others concerned with issues of liberty, justice, and mercy, need to initiate those discussions and remind policymakers that philosophical justifications for policies are as important as practical ones.

Although there are many Bible passages to guide evangelicals on issues of criminal justice, the model of a good law offered in Micah 6:8 is perhaps the most instructive. Here the prophet Micah explains: "He has shown you, O man, what is good; And what does the Lord require of you but to do justly, to love mercy, and to walk humbly with your God" (NKJV). For evangelicals seeking to implement crime and punishment laws that are inherently good, the verse in Micah provides two specific maxims. First, a good law is one that moderates our *practice*: people ought to temper justice with mercy. Second, a good law is also one that reframes our *perspective*: people ought to remain dependent on God.

In implementing the Micah 6:8 directive on practice, evangelicals can "do justly" by encouraging policies that safeguard those who are most often victimized by crime. Justice implies fairness or right treatment, and it is only right that a just crime policy endeavors to preserve and protect the innocent in society. In Scripture, God instructs His people to pay special attention to certain groups of people—namely, children, widows, the poor, and the elderly. Not surprisingly, federal crime statistics show that these are the groups in society who are most victimized by crime. In 2004, for example, adolescents between twelve and fifteen years of age were the most frequent victims of violent crime. In fact, they were victimized at more than *twice* the rate of twenty-five- to thirty-four-year-olds and nearly *three times* the rate of middle-aged adults. Women were *ten times* more likely than men to be victims of rape or sexual assault, and those reporting an income of $7,500 or less per year were significantly more likely than those reporting an income of $75,000 per year to be victims of robbery and assault (Bureau of Justice Statistics 2006).

In guiding the debate on crime and punishment issues, evangelicals should be the first to urge lawmakers to enact policies to help protect those who are least able to defend themselves. For example, when lawmakers discuss ways to reduce the threat of violence posed by sexual predators, Christian believers should stress the primary importance of protecting women and children over secondary concerns, such as financial costs. Recent policy innovations such as Meagan's Law, requiring community notification of sex offender movement, and Jessica's Law, enacting enhanced sentencing and monitoring of sex offenders, have been effective in deterring some violent crimes. But gaps remain in the criminal justice system that leave women and children vulnerable to attack. The prevalence of domestic violence, especially in poorer communities, means that women and children are still vulnerable at home, and rising rates of gang violence victimize increasing numbers of juveniles as a result of inner-city warfare.

The verse in Micah also commands believers in their practice "to love mercy." This means that evangelicals must insist upon policies that are just, but not overly punitive. Too often, lawmakers and voters have used the notion of justice as an excuse for vengeance, but excessive punishment violates the commands of Scripture and the principle of just deserts. To be just, the punishment must fit—but not exceed—the crime. While secondary considerations of deterrence and incapacitation may be explored when the type of punishment is debated, offenders should not be arbitrarily or unfairly incarcerated just because lawmakers believe that this is an expedient way to reduce crime. Already, many prison reformers are urging policymakers to adopt alternative sentencing provisions, such as house arrest, community service, or victim restitution, for offenders who do not represent a safety threat to the community.

Nonetheless, in some cases, incarceration remains the only viable option for offenders who are violent in nature or incorrigible in deed. Even then, however, evangelicals must urge lawmakers to practice restraint, lest they view lengthy sentencing laws as an easy way to combat rising crime rates. This occurred in the last wave of sentencing reform, when mandatory sentencing laws were routinely implemented as a way to curb certain types of criminal behaviors. Three-strikes laws for habitual criminals and lengthy sentences for drug users were touted as effective crime-control strategies, yet the policies were often so strict that judges were precluded from considering justice or granting mercy when imposing the sentences. Not all such sentencing laws were like this, however. Despite being heavily criticized for being too broad in its scope, California's three-strikes law is actually more merciful than many of the other more narrowly tailored measures. Under California's law, prosecutors and judges may exclude offenders deemed undeserving of the twenty-five-years-to-life sentence or who do not present significant threats to public safety. Though the law potentially affected thousands of offenders, only about 5 percent of the state's inmate population has actually received the lifetime sentence. Moreover, state prosecutors, who almost universally support the law, credit the policy with preventing hundreds of thousands of crimes over the past fifteen years (Walsh 2007).

To love mercy also means that evangelicals must encourage policies that protect and promote the welfare of the guilty. As the parable of the lost sheep reveals (Luke 15:4-7), God actively seeks to restore those that wander away. Scripture declares that "while we were yet sinners, Christ died for us" (Romans 5:8, NKJV). If God pursues His enemies to restore them to the kingdom, then it is reasonable to expect His children to do the same. Certainly the practice of evangelism does this within the context of salvation, and many prison ministry programs seek to evangelize within the correctional system. But when it comes to the treatment of offenders, evangelicals have been slower than Catholics and mainline Protestants to lobby for those who have been falsely convicted, unjustly sentenced, poorly advised by legal counsel, or who have been raped, assaulted, or seriously injured while in the government's care. Although the courts have done much to expand constitutional protections for inmates, evangelicals should urge lawmakers to examine how the government can better protect inmates from physical abuses committed by others within prison.

Finally, to love mercy means to be generous to those who do not deserve it. In the gospel of Luke, Christians are instructed to love their enemies and to lend freely without expecting repayment. The reason for doing this is so that God's love can be modeled for others to see: "you will be sons of the Most High. For He is kind to the unthankful and evil. Therefore be merciful, just as your Father also is merciful" (Luke 6:35b–36). Evangelicals should support policies that are generous with offenders once their punishment is completed. Too often, offenders are released from the government's care without even the basic provisions—no job, no housing, no clothing, little money, and no one to turn to for help. Unsurprisingly, many will return to prison within their first year of release. Some even admit to committing new crimes just so their physical needs could be met. In light of this problem, secular reformers have encouraged government leaders to expand funding for prisoner re-entry programs. Programs such as those funded by the federal Second Chance Act of 2007 seek to prepare offenders for reintegration into free society by helping them secure housing and employment and by providing them with counseling before they are released. Many faith-based organizations also have been quick to encourage this effort, as their staff members are often the first ones that offenders reach out to when they encounter difficulty on the outside. Scripture supports this approach, too:

> And when you release [your indentured servant], do not send him away empty-handed. Supply him liberally from your flock, your threshing floor and your winepress. Give to him as the Lord your God has blessed you. Remember that you were slaves in Egypt and the LORD your God redeemed you. That is why I give you this command today. (Deuteronomy 15:13–15)

Accordingly, evangelicals should encourage lawmakers to fully fund re-entry services so that offenders leaving prison have access to the basic necessities for successful reintegration into society.

In addition to supporting policies that are good in practice, Micah 6:8 suggests that "walking humbly with God" will give us the proper perspective as we consider what is good. One of the most important ways that evangelicals can help policymakers refocus their perspective is to provide a moral understanding of crime. Scripture reveals that people transgress because they are inherently sinful: the heart is wicked (Jeremiah 17:9); all have sinned and fallen short of God's glory (Romans 3:23); and there is no one that does good (Romans 3:12). Evangelicals acknowledge that free will gives people the option to choose to do good, but most criminal justice professionals and scholars reject the idea that people are free moral agents. Instead, crime is a symptom of a dysfunctional condition. Hence many believe that poor socioeconomic conditions are largely responsible for criminal behavior. Others think psychological illness or biological imbalances may predispose someone to act violently. Still others profess that crime is the by-product of political corruption.

Although the biblical view of crime as sin once infused our political thinking, it is unlikely that policymakers and experts within the field would acknowledge a purely spiritual explanation today. However, they might be more amenable to a spiritual perspective if it was framed in nontheological terms. One strategy would be to explain crime as an outward sign of a flawed personal character. In the early days of the rehabilitation era, this perspective led churches to provide moral training to help inmates improve their personal character (Moore 1924). It was encouraged after studies found that long-term behavioral improvements were sustainable only when prompted by internal changes of morals and character (Thomas and Zaitzow 1930).

More recently, criminal justice practitioners and scholars have established a correlation between religion and criminal inhibition. As might be expected, prison chaplains readily believe that the gospel can aid people in avoiding a life of crime. Some criminal justice experts, as well as a number of lawmakers, are starting to consider this possibility (Sundt and Cullen 2002). In theory, criminologists posit that religion can reduce criminal impulses by promoting greater self-control and accountability for personal behavior. In practice, while initial studies with inmate offenders have been inconclusive (Johnson 1987), studies in the general population have found that religious practices can inhibit criminal behavior (Evans et al. 1995; Baier and Wright 2001).

Some prison ministry programs have demonstrated measurable success in reducing rates of reoffense among former inmates. The best known prison ministry organization is Prison Fellowship Ministries (PFM), established by former Nixon advisor, Charles Colson, in 1976. After thirty years of operation, PFM has more than 22,000 trained volunteers ministering to prison inmates in over 1,800 prison facilities around the country. Each month, more than 120,000 inmates participate in Bible studies and spiritual counseling sponsored by PFM volunteers (Prison Fellowship Ministries 2008). Although criminologists were initially skeptical of the effectiveness of biblically based programming, secular researchers who examined the program found significant reduction in the recidivism rates among former inmates who regularly participated in the PFM ministry program (Johnson 1997).

Similar strategies have been adopted by multifaith organizations. Evaluations of the Life Connections Program, which is housed in federal institutions, recently revealed that inmates who dedicated themselves to the study of Scripture or sacred writings were more likely to complete the eighteen-month program than those who did not (Daggett et al. 2008). Although the impact of Life Connections on recidivism rates is still inconclusive, other studies suggest that inmates who complete a faith-based program are more successful at remaining crime-free after being released into the community than similar offenders who do not.

WILL POLICYMAKERS LISTEN TO EVANGELICALS?

There is no guarantee, of course, that policymakers will listen to evangelicals as they engage in the next round of criminal justice reform. Some contend that the church should stay out of public discourse and be content to exercise influence in what they believe to be its proper private domain. For these individuals, discourse about biblically inspired justice and mercy or even evidence of program effectiveness is irrelevant because morality-based policy represents an establishment of religion. Indeed, despite substantial evidence of effectiveness and widespread support, First Amendment claims have been legally asserted against Prison Fellowship Ministries' Inner-Change gospel-based prison ministry program. At least one federal appellate court found that the PFM program violated the constitutional principle of separation between church and state (*Americans United for Separation of Church and State v. Prison Fellowship Ministries*, 2007). More specifically, the U.S. Court of Appeals for the Eighth Circuit ruled that the InnerChange program operating within the Iowa state prison system used taxpayer funds to promote religious indoctrination. The court also found that the benefits provided by the InnerChange program were neither neutral nor nondiscriminatory. Rather, the court ruled that the exclusive contract negotiated with PFM was coercive because inmates had no other in-prison treatment options (Sullivan 2009).

Despite the judgment, the Eighth Circuit decision did not deliver a fatal blow to faith-based prison programming. On the contrary, the court seemed to indicate that the constitutional flaws identified with InnerChange could be remedied by ensuring that inmates had comparable secular choices available as well. It echoed U.S. Supreme Court jurisprudence conditioning the constitutionality of faith-based programming on the voluntary choice of the participant. Whether a program is explicitly religious appears to be of less concern to the Court now than in the past. Instead, it is more concerned with preserving an individual's freedom to choose (or refuse) such programming without artificial interference from the state.

For evangelicals, what is encouraging is the level of support for faith-based programming among many state correctional officials. The lack of results from traditional behavioral modification programs has created a willingness among state officials to explore more holistic treatment. In the Eighth Circuit case, for example, nine states filed an amicus brief supporting InnerChange. Specifically, they asked the court to refrain from discriminating against an effective program simply because it was founded on religious ideals. The brief noted that all prisoner programs are grounded in some sort of theory about individual behavior; to allow some while forbidding others would be overtly discriminatory and, ultimately, counterproductive. For these state officials, the only criteria that should govern the adoption of such programs is whether or not they are effective. In their evaluation, faith-based programs like InnerChange are among the few that actually work (Sullivan 2009).

These early successes may convince some policymakers to heed evangelicals' call to re-evaluate criminal justice policy according to the principles in Micah 6:8. Evangelicals would be wise to partner with Catholics and mainline Protestants to encourage lawmakers to "do justice" by retaining policies that incarcerate dangerous and violent offenders and by promoting new policies that protect society's most vulnerable—namely, children, women, the poor, and the elderly. Because lives of innocent people are at risk, evangelicals should urge lawmakers to make public safety a high priority, even though it may financially costly.

However, evangelicals should also encourage lawmakers to "love mercy" by implementing policies that protect and preserve offenders in the state's care. Turning a blind eye to inmate violence should no longer be acceptable. Evangelicals should also insist on policies that are only as punitive as they need to be to accomplish a just result. Mandatory sentences should be modified to allow for individual circumstances, and lifetime sentences should be reserved for only the most dangerous or incorrigible offenders. Similarly, offenders with drug addictions should be offered treatment, not mere incarceration, and re-entry services should be fully funded so that parolees returning to the community can have a chance at rebuilding their lives. Lawmakers should be urged to explore other merciful policies, such as the expunging of decades-old criminal records or the restoration of voting rights after a successful probationary period, so that ex-offenders have tangible incentives for pursuing crime-free lives.

Finally, by "walking humbly with their God," evangelicals can remind policymakers of the importance of the moral aspects of crime and punishment and to view offenders as free moral agents and not mere victims of dysfunction or disorder. An evangelically informed perspective on crime and punishment will help lawmakers avoid the "rehabilitation trap" that is promoted by many criminal justice professionals. Although benign in intent, the paternalistic mind-set that undergirds most calls for treatment leads to a lessening of respect for individuals within the criminal justice system and an increasing tendency for governments to treat offenders as something less than fully human. Encouraging partnerships with churches and other faith-based ministry groups can restore a proper perspective about crime and punishment while simultaneously providing offenders with the moral and spiritual guidance to aid them in their pursuit of successful and productive lives.

For too long, evangelicals have relegated themselves to the sidelines of this debate. Consequently, policymakers have forged policies based only upon what is expedient and popular—not necessarily on what is just or right. The fact that our prisons are bulging and our state coffers are nearly dry will force lawmakers to consider a variety of policy options. Not all may be willing to rethink the way we do justice, but by using scriptural principles as a guide, evangelicals can once again lead the way for those who wish to do good.

Chapter Four

Enlightened Economics and Free Markets

Timothy J. Barnett

Evangelicals hold a distinct place in American Christianity due to the premium they put on the literal meaning and authority of the biblical scriptures. Evangelicals believe they must go first and finally to the Bible for truth, leaning only lightly on church authorities or commentators. In addition to believing in the primacy of the scriptures, evangelicals assert that every person is ultimately responsible for his or her own understanding of the Bible. This conviction tends to build into evangelicalism a morally bounded regard for individuality. This spiritualized individuality, somewhat in tension with the communitarian and compliance traditions of the faith, migrates into a political sentiment that helps explain evangelicals' strong preferences for limited government, private property, free markets that facilitate economic growth, states' rights, and meritorious self-responsibility in a charitable private context (Strain 1989, 13–19).[1]

The thread that ties together the economic beliefs of evangelicals is the elevation of free choice. Historically, this notion is rooted in the doctrine that all may come to Christ as an expression of free will. This evangelical theological commitment has for decades bled over into a preference for limited national government and states' rights, the idea being that if states have decision autonomy, national government will have less power to compel or constrain the reasonable choices of individuals. While the hypothetical goal of states' rights is to decentralize decision making, in practice this political system empowers religion to exert more influence on community policy, thus addressing evangelicals' concerns for community as well as individualism.

Of course, evangelical political activism has not consistently fit this model, given their desire to see standards of reproductive morality legislated nationally (Lienesch 1993).

EVANGELICALS AND POLITICAL ECONOMY

In the policy arena, evangelicals often seem preoccupied with issues of abortion, stem cell research, homosexuality, family values, and public schools. Yet, little in the scriptures apart from the central tenets of theology achieves more textual prominence than matters of economic justice (Noell 1993). The attitudes that inform political economy—especially covetousness, greed, and benevolent goodwill—are discussed often in the New Testament, from Jesus' Gospel teachings to the writings of Apostles Peter, Paul, James, and John. Thus, it is unsurprising that the 1990 Oxford Declaration on Christian Faith and Economics called for the reconciliation of global economic norms with the biblical imperatives for justice and love (Schlossberg et al. 1994).

Since the distinguishing belief of evangelicals is that holy scripture is relevant to all aspects of life, it is reasonable to expect that evangelicals will become increasingly vocal on economic justice as financial conditions become more visibly connected with national failures to follow biblical wisdom.[2] The last few years have seen a parade of news headlines concerning public and private debt loads, foreclosures on homes, the redistribution of wealth, a skewing of the sowing and reaping equation, the disproportionate empowerment of elites, economic oppression of poor people, and financial skullduggery by hedge fund managers. These are issues around which evangelicals can be expected to rally if their opinion leaders make clear the connections between biblical insights and current affairs.

If evangelicals stake out increasingly visible positions on the morality of the American political economy, will these opinions appear enlightened to the general public and to secular opinion leaders? What is economic enlightenment, and why does it matter?

Evangelicals possess a rich resource of economic justice and wisdom in the Good Book. Yet the evangelical movement has not fleshed out the book's wisdom adequately regarding governmental regulation of finance capitalism. While evangelicals have examined the biblical concept of economic justice in broad terms—the rule of law combined with limited government and free markets—the lack of creative problem solving has left evangelicals isolated and unable to describe honorable aspects of finance capitalism in contrast with those facets that require strategic reform. Left with traditional slogans instead of tools of evaluation and innovation, evangelicals have fallen prey to the two-party system. Their "conservative votes" on social issues have enabled the Republican Party to gain sufficient electoral success for the agenda of their elite financial constituents—success achieved with the help of many Democrats beholden to Wall Street. Evangelicals have not made headway on an economic agenda that reflects their biblical values soberly considered. Indeed, evangelicals have yet to find a bridge language by which to engage the secular community on issues of finance capitalism.

The problem for evangelicals is that they have not disassociated regulatory burdens on private citizens, small businesses, and general commerce from the ameliorative nature of prudent regulation of paper assets that are furiously traded and sometimes surreptitiously crafted in the temples of Wall Street. Evangelicals tend to generalize their concepts about the regulation of markets rather than craft them for specific situations. Yet evangelicals have no trouble being specific when regulating social mores. Why is it right and prudent to regulate the social morals of individuals but not the business morals of corporations or institutions? It is only rational that, when free market corrections of speculative excess fail to check the abuses, carefully wrought regulation can serve the public interest. This is especially so when prudent regulation prevents the greedy from wrenching capital from the general public.

The general evangelical disposition toward freedom of conscience as a scriptural mandate migrates into a capitalistic ideology of free markets and limited government. That ideology then hardens into a resolute opposition toward rule-making, regulation, and oversight. Evangelicals seem to view big bureaucracy as occupying the high throne reserved for the Almighty. It is easy to forget that the strong hand of government may be needed when, for example, oil prices are soaring out of control as global speculators rotate massive sums of leveraged capital.

Moses taught ancient Israel that a central function of good government, as established in God's covenant, was to prevent evil in society—an idea reinforced in the New Testament (Deuteronomy 17:6–7; 29:14–29; Romans 13:1–7; I Peter 2:13–14). Though government power was abused in both ancient Israel and in Roman application, nearly every good thing can be abused when people are imprudent—food, automobiles, home ownership. Happily, even political conservatives are beginning to realize that government power *per se* is not bad; rather, the abuse of power is (Hay 1989, 173–75).

Fear of government power has been an organizing tool within conservatism for some time. Beginning in the 1970s, conservatives saw government as immersing itself in every part of life—public schools, agriculture, manufacturing, transportation, natural resource development, communications, public safety, and other areas of everyday concern to citizens. Yet national government in the 1970s was small compared to its reach after the World Trade Center attack in 2001. In reality, the regulatory landscape became complicated after Reagan's "New Federalism" of the early 1980s evolved into the "Representational Federalism" of the 1990s. In fact, the U.S. Supreme Court's rethinking of the division of power between states and the national government produced a fractured regulatory landscape. Some sectors became burdened with increased regulation (public safety and education). Other sectors moved toward deregulation, nowhere more so than in the realm of financial services. The result was a dramatic speculative boom in the creation, sales, management, and trading of paper assets and a host of derivatives. This was a time of great economic naiveté. As long as assets prices were booming, deregulated financial services were innocuous to those with a superficial understanding of financial leverage.

Any listener to conservative talk radio from 1990 to 2005 knows that much of the ire of the hosts and their listeners was focused on the regulatory burdens encountered by normal people and small entrepreneurs. It seemed that too many things had to be registered, inspected, reported, modified, or relinquished. When one was allowed to do one's own business, there was Uncle Sam demanding more taxes to support more inept bureaucrats who were good at doing little to nothing. Conservatives and libertarians felt frustrated, and associated their feelings with the frustrations of American patriots leading up to the Revolutionary War. They saw government, then and now, as intent upon fatiguing people into compliance with laws, eating out their substance with taxes, and turning modest, hard-earned estates into social plunder for supporters of social planning and income redistribution. They imagined themselves standing shoulder to shoulder with American colonists in 1776, intent upon stopping Great Britain's king.

Frustrated with big government, grassroots conservatives fought for the redistribution of power back to the states. But for relative novices in the deeper things of power politics, mysteriously guided by the influence of neoconservative infiltrators in the Republican Party, devolution was mostly a meal of bread crumbs. Meanwhile, a laissez-faire feast was laid out for the financial sector. The result was the remarkable expansion of a multi-trillion dollar universe of financial products known as derivatives. Giddy with power, it was Wall Street's "Big Bang II."

WALL STREET AND ECONOMIC JUSTICE

In the late 1990s, Wall Street elevated its powers to compete with the Federal Reserve System in the creation of capital, justifying its imposition by the rationale that power outside government was needed to conquer market imperfections to harmonize capital flows and improve the efficiency of financial markets. The primary instruments for this mission were derivatives—

paper assets whose value depends upon changes in the value of underlying assets (Fleckenstein 2008). Guided by its compass of greed, Wall Street started America down a dangerous road—pitted with hazards for firms betting wrong, but promising incomparable rewards for those betting right. This development only widened the gulf between the haves and have-nots, doing harm to the biblical principle of the laborer benefiting fairly from the harvest.

On the laissez-faire road, the earnings of working-class people worldwide were transferred neatly into the counting houses of elites—people of darkened conscience who hatched plots day and night to pillage the poor. In the words of Micah the prophet, these were like the rebellious of Jacob, "who scheme iniquity, who work out evil on their beds! When morning comes, they do it, for it is in the power of their hands. They covet fields and seize them, and houses and take them away. They rob a man . . . and his inheritance" (Micah 2:1–2, NASV). The laissez-faire road became a freeway for transferring the balance of power in America away from working-class people and into the hands of money-grinding agnostics (Gates 2000).

Empowered by deregulation, the financial industry leaned heavily on the Federal Reserve, borrowed countless billions of dollars to use as collateral, leveraged and releveraged that collateral, and emerged with a multi-trillion dollar paper asset universe that could be managed to capture speculative gains from the portion of the money supply overseen by the Federal Reserve (Fleckenstein 2008). Through the use of derivatives, Wall Street was able to pump up a massive universe of credit by which modest price inflation could be leveraged to great profit in its rollover effects on all categories of financial assets. Thus, the ultra-rich in the financial sector used the structural norm within the political economy (targeted price inflation) to create gains out of money supply dynamics. Congress's ignorance, combined with the blind eye of financial regulators, allowed Wall Street to put hundreds of billions of dollars of bogus money to work, strategically rotated from one sector to another to allow the instigators to be the first in and first out in each new asset bubble—with the public left with the costs of reinflating the bubble in each case. This is the story of the stock market boom (1997–2001) followed by the real estate boom (2003–2007) followed by the multiphase commodities boom (Phillips 2008; Gates 2000).

EVANGELICAL DISCERNMENT DULLED BY IDEOLOGY

Evangelicals were ineffective in stirring government to protect the public from the war against the working man largely because they were hobbled by an intemperate commitment to the ideology of free markets and limited government. Yet could there be a time more important for reasoned evangelical voices to be heard at the gates, judging between righteousness and evil (Jeremiah 7:1–11; Amos 5:10–15)? Sadly for the reputation of Christ's people, most of the light cast upon the excesses was provided by those working from nonbiblical platforms.

The failure of evangelical conservatives to confront serious financial evils reflects what Mark Noll calls the scandal of the evangelical mind; that is, the unwillingness of evangelicals to soberly confront their assumptions in doctrine or practice, and to make discerning and differentiated choices (Noll 1994). The tendency of the evangelical mind has been toward simplifications and moralistic principles, leaving undone the important nitty-gritty of evaluating the actual function and results of financial institutions.

One grave danger of simplifications is that they tend to generalize rather than make nuanced discriminations based upon the merits of individual cases. Anyone in the habit of running on simplifications is vulnerable as prey for another. The financial sector needed the Republican Party as the majority party for long enough so it could build out its strategic agenda under the Republican umbrella of laissez-faire economics. (In the meantime, Wall Street neoliberals were busy hijacking the Democratic Party.) Evangelicals were allowed headroom in the Republican Party to get this done; the values constituency was given as much stage time for as long as secular economic conservatives could tolerate. Two birds were killed with one stone, the so-called prosperity gospel within evangelical ranks serving to further undercut traditional conservative preferences for fiscal restraint, and sanctifying the idea that there is godliness in growth when growth produces prosperity. It did not take Wall Street long to exploit this development as a cover of tolerance for its philosophy that capitalistic greed benefits society.

In exchange for the support by evangelicals for the Republican Party platform—and the stealth economics of neocons that underlay it—evangelicals received lip service in support of Christian symbolism and token support for faith-based initiatives. Financial elites were delighted with the tendency of evangelicals to generalize about the virtues of free markets and limited government, since the disposition undercut evangelical resistance to the speculative games played in financial markets. As a result, hedge funds and sophisticated financial barons were protected from having their deeds exposed to substantial light (or heat) from evangelicals. Meanwhile, despite the rhetoric about free markets and limited government, nonfinancial markets remained heavily regulated for the supposed safety and security of the general public.

In the run-up to these events, evangelicals debated among themselves and with Catholics and mainline Protestants about economic justice and the care of the poor (Bernbaum 1986; Blank and McGurn 2004). Few paid much attention to what was transpiring in the towers on Wall Street—towers rightly associated with the mercenaries of money who erect their fortresses on high then plunder the workers below (Obadiah 1:4; Micah 3:1–5; Habakkuk 2:9–17). Scholars examined the Catholic tradition of communitarianism and compared that inclination with the Protestant tendency toward individualism (Yuengert 2001). But this dialogue existed mainly at the level of theory, since most academics had little experience on the streets of high finance.[3]

This is not to say that scholars did not perform admirable work. But they worked where the light was relatively good for academics, not in the darkened corridors of Wall Street. Scholarly effort has shown that, while the Bible can be read to suggest different notions of proper *administration* of economic justice, most Christian scholars read the Bible to the same ends regarding the core *attitudes* of godly justice. We know the right attitude; we differ over the right tools of design and implementation!

While the Bible may not speak to the issue of speculative bubbles in the way it speaks of adultery, theft, or murder, the underlying principles are the same: the malevolent should not advance their self-interest at the expense of others. The economy does not exist to benefit the duplicitous, the unscrupulous, the dissemblers, and other leeches on the public good. Free markets do not exist in God's economy to shift power from honorable laborers to unprincipled persons in the leisure class. The purpose of freedom, and free markets, is to glorify God and to further goodness on earth for those who are good in God's sight. Those with honorably acquired wealth are to be good stewards of it, maintaining an eye toward the public good (Halteman 2004). When evangelicals discuss economics at this level of generality, there is a healthy amount of agreement, even a "*de facto* consensus" (Strain 1989, 16). It is upon this attitudinal consensus that evangelicals must build in the crucial endeavor of understanding a proper role for government in the financial sector. While evangelicals may want to hold onto their tenets regarding limited government and free markets, a tailoring of those concepts seems warranted.

ECONOMIC ENLIGHTENMENT: THEN AND NOW

Enlightenment is the blossoming of spiritual or intellectual wisdom, especially when it results from a rationally critical examination of previously accepted doctrines or institutions.[4] Economic enlightenment pertains to a keen understanding of the institutions, values, laws, and processes that make for political economy. It refers to a depth of comprehension that, when combined with strategic ingenuity, provides for remedies, marked improvements, and the satisfactory attainment of worthy ends. Enlightenment is not a halfway house. It is sufficient to produce the good fruit sought in a given age or circumstance.

The Bible sets forth general descriptions of the good fruit that God's children are to produce—love, joy, peace, mercy, fairness, and justice. Sufficiently enlightened believers will produce this fruit in the various walks of life, including political economy, when in possession of freedom and power to get the job done. The history of freedom in the United States contains stories of good fruit being produced in varying degrees under changing circumstances. Every emerging generation must seek new enlightenment to meet the challenges of its times. The global economy today is more complex than ever before. Consequently, fresh enlightenment is needed if there is to be sufficient specific understanding of how to produce good fruit. It is not enough to understand the Bible. Competent Bible students do well to understand the evolution of financial institutions—institutions that can be viewed with an eye to biblical wisdom.

When Moses gave instructions concerning money and commerce to Israel—instructions that Christians and Jews read in the books of Leviticus and Deuteronomy—the lawgiver undoubtedly felt he was providing the best enlightenment available at the time. After all, he said to them, "[W]hat great nation is there that has statutes and judgments as righteous as this whole law which I am setting before you today?" (Deuteronomy 4:8, NASV).[5] It is not difficult to imagine the laws of Moses as enlightened for a small nation of relatively illiterate people fresh out of slavery in Egypt. But that was then. How about the here and now? Are the Good Book's teachings on political economy, found mainly in the Old Testament, still relevant to the United States and the world in the twenty-first century? Can we learn what we need to know from the Good Book? Do we need to supplement the Christian scriptures extensively with modern learning? What is to be retained from an ancient storehouse of wisdom? What is to be relinquished?

The tendency of evangelicals is to affirm the insights and principles of economic justice that undergird the laws of Moses as relevant to our lawmaking today (Anderson and Langelett 1996). While some believe the particulars of the Mosaic economic law remain pertinent (e.g., Reconstructionists), most are content to bring the general goals of Moses forward, not the details of an ancient political economy.[6] The difficulty rests in knowing how to translate primitive goals into the complexities of modern finance capitalism with its globally evolving markets.

The challenge is especially large when one considers how Ivy League schools, central bankers, and institutional elites sold most of the developed world on the idea that international economic security and prosperity would result from a new generation of financial and credit instruments. How were legislators, bureaucrats, and voters to know the confidence of the experts was misplaced? How could Americans have anticipated that collateralized debt obligations (CDOs) and credit default swaps (CDSs) would be ruinous to some elites while providing others with unimaginable wealth? Could ancient biblical warnings about debt be extrapolated to paint the future hazards of such tools in laissez-faire environments governed by super-elites?[7]

Historically, Americans have viewed governmental experts as enlightened. Yet the record of the last century, and especially the last twenty years, belies that conclusion. In the George W. Bush era, for example, Federal Reserve Chair Greenspan barely stepped out of his chairmanship before asserting that fed governors did not have satisfactory means of anticipating the 1997–2001 stock market bubble or the 2003–2007 real estate bubble (Fleckenstein 2008). Henry Paulson, President Bush's secretary of the treasury and former CEO of Goldman Sachs, declared in the midst of the spring 2008 credit crisis that hedge funds and investment banks on Wall Street did not need additional regulation—a position he later rescinded. Other examples abound. The world's economic conditions make the case stunningly that vaunted experts have a hard time getting the essentials right, especially when they are committed to models of economics that are built on the type of leverage that the scriptures decry.

If governmental experts struggle, can evangelicals receive sufficient enlightenment through the scriptures? They can, if the enlightenment at issue is justice and righteousness. Upon these pillars a proper system of political economy can be built by those possessing technical expertise. But experts are often employed by elites who want plunder and power, not justice and righteousness. Darkened in their minds, their supporters store up wealth for judgment in the day of the Lord. At least, so declare the holy men of old (Isaiah 3:1–26; James 5:1–7).

The Good Book suggests that God's church should get it right, at least on the level of principle (John 16:7–15). If we move from dependence on milk to the maturity of taking meat, there is hope of excelling in the creation, implementation, and management of sound principle (1 Cor. 3:1–2). We are not excused because reform in the modern world requires specialization. Our specializations ought to be such that we can still make good sense of the political economy as the backbone of justice in society. Christ chastised religious leaders because they did not rightly use the light available from Moses and the prophets (Luke 16:14–21). But Jesus did not end his sermons with his face toward Pharisees. He turned to his budding church, breathing upon it the blessing of Holy Spirit enlightenment. This is not the mere enlightenment of academic debate, but sufficiently deployable enlightenment to make the world a better place.

It is incongruous that God's people should walk in enlightenment concerning family morality while walking in darkness concerning economic morality. If the church is to be God's witness, and if evangelicals with the sword of the Word are to cut through veils of darkness, then evangelicals should set about to understand and proclaim the light of God as touching every relevant field—family, community, and political economy (Barnett 2008, 259–63).

An objection may be raised that, since the Federal Reserve controls the monetary system, Christians cannot do much about this area of the political economy. But the public elects the president, and the president has the power to appoint Fed governors *and* to remove them for cause. Furthermore, Congress has the power to mandate the mission and goals of the Federal Reserve System. Fed governors can be made to pursue whatever form of justice elected officials require. But the last time Congress did this, it sent the Fed down the wrong path.

The Federal Reserve is a quasi-private bank empowered by Congress to serve the central banking interests of the United States. Created in 1913 by the Federal Reserve Act, it has in many respects operated credibly over the years. But recently the Fed's reputation has eroded due to the consequences of its laissez-faire policies and what is widely viewed as a bias in favor of Wall Street. In 1977, Congress amended the 1913 Act, clarifying the Federal Reserve's macroeconomic objectives by mandating that it manage the economy for the primary purpose of economic growth, thereby promoting political goals of maximum employment, so-called stable prices, and moderate long-term interest rates. In essence, Congress tasked the Fed with the responsibility of getting economic growth for capitalists and full employment for the masses while not stimulating the system with so much money as to create destabilizing inflation. Hence, the Fed's *modus operandi* has been to sell the nation on an acceptable level of price inflation, then open the money floodgates for Wall Street without violating that benchmark of acceptable inflation. With productivity gains tending to offset money-supply inflation, this strategy led to massive growth in the value of paper assets with little apparent bleed-over into consumer prices until the excess money began flooding the energy and food commodity markets in 2005.

The craftily worded mandate of Congress was undoubtedly urged upon it by financial experts. While it seemed noble on the surface, beneath lurked the devil in the details. Three decades of mild inflation and fairly steady growth created the ideal climate for wealthy elites to pull away financially from the balance of the population. The result weakened majoritarian politics and gave money a formative role in determining the nation's fate. Sadly, central banking that overstimulates economic growth presents difficult circumstances for an economy to exit safely. Little wonder that God's prophets warned against debt, associating the reliance upon borrowing with impending storms of judgment (Deut. 28:9–15; Prov. 22:7; Ezek. 18:5–9).

While central bankers claimed not to have seen financial storms coming, any biblically grounded expert evaluation of the congressional mandate to the Fed would have foreseen a wealth shift resulting from the implementation of that plan in a laissez-faire environment with low taxes for the rich. Indeed, the tax side of the strategy was accomplished in the early 1980s under the banner of supply-side economics. Unfortunately, our bias in favor of laissez-faire economics, limited government, and largely unregulated private property led to public acceptance of the injustices of this period. During an era of stellar corporate growth brought on by burgeoning technology and business efficiencies, the modest progress in standard of living experienced by the working public was largely attributable to a shift to two-income households and longer hours worked. The rich got ever so much richer off the differential, aided by the expansion of low-wage labor throughout the global economy. This begs the question: Does this circumstance matter to God?

The message of the Bible is antithetical to the exploitation of the bourgeoisie and the poor by the rich. The tragedy is that evangelicals during the Bush, Clinton, and Bush II administrations did not understand the Fed's monetary policies as having this effect. The fact is, evangelicals comprise a sizeable portion of the voting infantry that marched on behalf of that version of capitalism that seized their economic power and gave it to elites. There were efforts by some evangelical scholars to point out the flaws in the evolving economic system (Chewning, Eby, and Roels 1990, 229), and to bridge the gap between secular economics and the Christian vocabulary of the Bible (Stapleford 2002). But the efforts were not equal to the challenge.

REAL BELIEFS AND ECONOMIC REALITIES

In a mere ten year span, Americans have witnessed a massive stock market bubble, an unprecedented housing bubble, a treacherous credit bubble, a seething crude oil bubble, and a food commodity bubble. Each of these has benefitted well-positioned elites while putting the majority of honest working people financially behind on a comparative basis.

Increasingly, Americans believe the working class is getting cheated, the middle-class standard of living is in decline, the greedy dominate society, and too few people are properly committed to thrift and hard work. The real money now is made through speculation or celebrity status, not productive labor. Admittedly speculation has burdened the nation before, most notably in the Roaring Twenties. Even earlier, it was mischief in money-supply management that necessitated the constitutional convention that created our federal government.

Prior to the advent of large corporations and mega-banks, states led the way in the aggregation of faction-based power. Alexander Hamilton observed as much in the *Federalist Papers*, arguing against the hazards of excessively limited national government. His concern was a national government lacking requisite means of protecting the common good from attacks, especially financial assaults stemming from states functioning as vehicles for special interests.

In today's world, mega-corporations and global investment banks produce the type of hazards that Hamilton envisioned being curtailed by a national government armed with sufficient regulatory power. Many corporations today have greater sales revenues or monetary impacts than the GDP of some large states. The 2008 collapse of the investment bank Bear Stearns revealed that it was gambling on the incomprehensible notational value of $2.5 trillion of credit derivatives. This amounts to 80 percent of the annual budget of our federal government, or one-fifth of the national gross domestic product (GDP). How did such leverage exist in a relatively unregulated condition? Should private firms be able to gamble away the national good?

President Theodore Roosevelt built his reputation on the use of government power to confront private sector corruption. He believed government powers could be designed subject to checks and balances, giving government sufficient power in crucial sectors to deal with attacks upon the public good. Oddly, the evangelical movement has been slow to recognize the nuances of this argument. While most evangelicals consider themselves constitutionalists, they seemingly forget that the purpose of the Constitution is to empower government on behalf of the common good and to corral it so that the powers are constructively managed.

The fault in generalizing about limited government is the same fault in generalizing about other things. Are big cars good and small cars bad? Good for what? Small cars are good for running light errands economically; SUVs are good for hauling large loads and big families. Limited government is good if it can accomplish worthy purposes for which it was designed. A large hand for government is good when there are large threats to be stopped. The degree to which government should be limited is conditional upon the circumstances. Government should not be so limited as to allow evil to triumph over the good.

At present there is no area of business activity so desperately in need of insightful regulation as the financial services industry. It creates massive amounts of money invisibly in the background of the system—money that generates gargantuan fortunes for persons of reprehensible character. In essence, Wall Street runs its own monetary system in a universe overlapping the Federal Reserve's. Uncontrolled by an electorate that cannot fathom its operations, Wall Street has the power to damn the world and raise it from the dead again, perhaps similar to St. John's vision (Revelation 13:1–18). This assumes that Wall Street does not miscalculate badly and overreach while trying to capture world wealth—an outcome that seems plausible. Nevertheless, Wall Street has been able to negotiate successfully with government because many of its operations are considered by the Federal Reserve as too essential to be allowed to fail. So to save the global economy, central bankers must now play from the songbook selected by the Street—the songbook of moral hazard and manipulation.

Limited government is good. So are free markets when governed by sane rules. Likewise, *excessively* limited government is a curse in the face of powerful evils that government should arrest. The scope of the limits upon government should be set by the dictates of prudence.

The First Constitutional Convention saw itself tasked with the duty of figuring out how to limit the powers of the central government in some areas while relatively freeing it up in others. Limited government for the framers focused upon degrees of power, not absolutes. Checks and balances were created to fine-tune the new federal system so that it could operate with fewer limitations upon legislative and executive authority than was the case under the flawed Articles of Confederation. Checks and balances coupled with the rule of law in a strategically designed Constitution made it possible for the Framers to give government substantially more power to accomplish good. Thus, the Constitution is as much about scrupled empowerment of government as the sweeping limitation of it. Our constitutional philosophy ought to be more about managing free markets than letting them be run by factions like oil companies and robber barons in their lofty Wall Street towers. The Constitution worked quite marvelously for the first two hundred years, breaking down only when voters put slogans like "limited government" and "free markets" ahead of justice, righteousness, and truth as taught by the Bible. We bowed before golden calves.

THE SCRIPTURAL COUNTERPOINT TO ABSOLUTIST THINKING

The wisdom of avoiding absolutist thinking about limited government and free markets is evidenced everywhere in the Bible by the hermeneutic of good sense that Christians know to employ in other matters. Is there such a thing as biblically justifiable entrance into war? If not, why would God have commended it in multiple instances (Exodus 14:14–16; Jeremiah 51:20; Psalms 144:1)? Yet the Bible also makes the case that freedom from war is a blessing and that war can be both a punishment and a curse (Isaiah 2:4; Jeremiah 6:14–15).

The morality of war is a bounded concept much like the prudence of limited government is bounded. How much war is necessary to stop evil depends upon circumstances. As little war as possible ought to be the goal. To what degree should government intervene in the markets? As little as possible may be the goal, but in some matters it is imperative that the government intervene aggressively. Any shortage of political will in providing needful economic regulation is as dangerous as government not defending its people in times of war.

When global oil traders use speculative tools and propaganda to drive the price of crude from $60 to $147 a barrel, should evangelicals sit on their hands and chant "limited government"? Or should they fight disruptive speculation by supporting the proper use of governmental authority? Biblically, they should fight the temporal evil even while addressing the root evils of not conserving energy resources or developing a sustainable national energy plan. Paul in Romans wrote of government, "for it does not bear the sword for nothing; for it is a minister of God, an avenger who brings wrath upon the one who practices evil" (Romans 13:4).

Are principles and truths generally bounded in scripture? Most careful exegetes would argue that they are. Is the salvation of an individual the result of grace and faith? The answer is a qualified "yes," bounded by the idea that faith without works is dead faith and of no account (James 2:14–26). Is God a god of mercy? He is, but within a set of circumscribed conditions, for as scripture says, "Behold then the kindness and severity of God" (Romans 11:24). Did Isaiah depict the coming Messiah as the Prince of Peace (Isaiah 9:6–7)? Yes, but when Jesus came, he corrected any imbalanced perception about his peacemaker role by saying, "I did not come to bring peace, but a sword" (Matthew 10:43).

What should we say of free markets? Is the principle of freedom absolute? Is it even controlling? Or is freedom an idea that must be tailored? The biblical view advocates a freedom bounded by disciplines that enhance fairness, justice, equitable outcomes, and the sustainable good of the nation. The commandment of Moses was this: "Justice and only justice, you shall pursue, that you may live and possess the land" (Deuteronomy 16:20). Laissez-faire markets are not primarily about justice: they are about the empowerment of money. When Paul wrote that God's children were called to freedom in Christ, he also wrote that people were not to turn freedom into an opportunity for the flesh (Galatians 5:13). So it is with markets: free but not so free as to allow the powerful to abuse the common good. Sadly, the Republican Party has preyed upon Christians' simplifications of theory on free markets (Phillips 2008, 72–73).

The strategy of the rich in societies seduced by covetousness is to lobby legislatures and regulators for laws and administrative rules that can be exploited for unjust gain. Moses warned Israel to nominate "wise, discerning and experienced men," for appointment to high office (Deuteronomy 1:13). The appointees were to be without partiality to the great or to the small— those who could not be corrupted by influence or pressure (Deuteronomy 1:17). Indeed, most of the financial theft that occurs in a developed society does not come from the pickpocket but from crafty legislation and legal loopholes. Little wonder, then, that Jesus became so angry with lawmakers and their conspirators, for laws empowered the covetous to create institutions and operations to fleece the masses and take from them the fruits of their labors (Luke 11:42–52).

It makes little difference whether exploitation is within or outside the law: it violates the Mosaic injunction of to be a brother's keeper (Deuteronomy 22:01). It ignores Moses giving Israel the Sabbath Year and Jubilee Year economic policies to counter exploitation within the law as well as circumstances of misfortune (Anderson 2005; Schaefer and Noell 2005). Those who store up in their banks and stock accounts assets by filching from the poor are guilty of violating the great commandment: love God wholeheartedly and love your neighbor as yourself (James 5:1–5; Matthew 22:34–40). Such considerations point to the importance of initiatives like Jubilee 2000 debt relief for poor countries, though political corruption must be addressed as well.

Pharisees were proud of themselves: they obeyed Moses by not having in their bags "differing weights, a large and a small" (Deuteronomy 25:13). But Jesus knew their real character. He portrayed them as careful to clean the outside of the cup while filling the inside with robbery and self-indulgence (John 8:24; Matthew 23:25–33). Outwardly they appeared moral but inwardly they were tombs filled with their prey's bones (ibid, 23:27). Masters of the art of financial exploitation, they neglected justice, mercy, and faithfulness (ibid, 23:23).

While Christians understand these biblical concepts, they often fail to apply them to political economy. Moses said, "Cursed is he who misleads the blind person on the road" (Deuteronomy 25:18). Who does this today? Wall Street does. It sells to gullible fund managers in Southeast Asia the equivalent of hazardous waste in the form of collateralized debt obligations and other high-risk securities liable to implode. Wall Street gets its fees, even if not all Wall Street players win. In the aggregate, the Street wins and ends up channeling massive amounts to its upper echelon employees.

On the occasions when Wall Street elites miscalculate, they lobby government to have taxpayers bail them out. How is this not the modern equivalent of the ancient sin of misleading the blind on the road? How is this not distorting the justice due an alien, orphan, and widow (Deuteronomy 25:19)? Why is this not the same, in principle, as "striking one's neighbor in secret" (ibid, 25:24), committing aggression under circumstances where there are no witnesses and little potential for lawful punishment? Read fairly, scriptures show us that Christians cannot support insufficiently regulated financial markets when those markets are immoral and reflect cultural decay and plutocratic greed. Then, too, when regulations are in order, it is just as important that Christians keep the regulations in good repair so that they do not become vehicles of injustice (as is often the case when administrative insight is dim). A poorly devised regulatory environment is as dangerous as a laissez-faire context because special interests exploit regulations until constitutional provisions keep them at bay. Unfortunately, our national constitution has little to say about the economic issues of the day.

EVANGELICALS IN THE LEAD?

Evangelicals are uniquely positioned to aid in the reform of our political economy, for they esteem scriptures that show the way to a better world. But they will not succeed in this great mission until they move beyond absolutist slogans, mottos, and simplifications that inhibit them from taking corrective action against abusive capitalistic practices. Evangelicals need to refocus on the spirit of the biblical texts and quit substituting the doctrines of men for the laws of God. After all, this is just what Jesus accused the Pharisees of doing in following their fathers' errors. He invokes Isaiah's words: "This people Honors Me with their lips, but their heart is far away from Me. But in vain do they worship Me, Teaching as their doctrines the precepts of men" (Matthew 15:8–9).

Christian opinion leaders have tended to elevate economic simplifications (e.g., limited government and free markets) above the law of God, thus giving Caesar support for market machinations contrary to God's laws. God-fearing opinion leaders should declare the importance of prudent financial regulations to prevent the rich from hauling into their barns the wages of the poor. But with few exceptions, it is not evangelical leaders who go to pains to point this out.

Edd Noell, an economics professor at Westmont College, has written about the work of some Christian economists on the "applicability of the Mosaic law to modern economics" (1993). Quoting from an unpublished paper by John Mason (presented at a December 1987 Chicago conference for the Association of Christian Economists), he highlights Mason's argument that Christians have an obligation to "grasp the spirit or purposes of Biblical instructions" and then "seek to fulfill those purposes today," doing so without lifting out the exact institutions of the Scriptures.[8]

More than two decades after Mason's argument, evangelicals have yet to find a way to do this in the realm of fiscal and monetary policy. Of course, this supposes the adequacy of the Good Book to enlighten the distracted and indulgent American mind. Whatever the limitations of that supposition, monetary justice in the Bible is not much different than a plausible secular system based upon rational goodwill toward all. If the Bible reasonably interpreted points Christians toward good monetary policy, and if benevolent logic convinces secular minds of the same goodness, then there is harmony and no leap of faith. It is just a matter of different sources for an overlapping wisdom about economic wholeness.

STARTING OVER

Evangelicals believe that the Bible ought to inform the economic views of Christians. Until recently, many evangelicals seem to assume that the American free market version of finance capitalism is the Christian way, suitable for marketing to the rest of the world (Nash 1986). Yet the distressing economic circumstances of recent years may be causing an increasing number of evangelicals to doubt that assumption. Indeed, many evangelical scholars have doubted it for a long time. This is not to say that they prefer socialism, central planning, or a European model. It simply acknowledges that free markets need prudent rules to prevent excess and speculation from working to the public harm (Hay 1989; Halteman 1988; Owensby 1988).

There is little doubt that the Federal Reserve's laissez-faire regulation of financial markets under Alan Greenspan reflected deafness to market morality—an approach only recently modified as the boom in energy prices bled over into food prices, highlighting how leveraged speculation can harm the poor. There is also little doubt that laissez-faire thinking prevailed among the majority of evangelicals during the last several decades.

In fairness, evangelicals should not be singled out for blame. In matters of deficit spending and laissez-faire regulation of the markets, a significant segment of all four quadrants of traditional American religion—mainline Protestants, evangelicals, Catholics, and Jews—leaned away from sobriety and temperance. It oversimplifies recent history to say that evangelicals' reading of scriptures caused their economic outlook. The more complex reality is that a worldwide cultural phenomenon of self-indulgence leads adherents of Western religion to bow at the altar of money. The assumption in the markets is that nothing can solve problems as fast as money, and nothing is capable of generating money as fast as unfettered capital markets working with "growth is good" central banks. Thus, finance capitalism remains the perceived means of delivering the world from its troubles and inequities. Meanwhile, the inequities continue to grow, highlighting the truth that the love of money is a serious root of evil.

When the Iron Curtain fell in 1991, it was left to democratic capitalism to repair the world. America set about the business of making the Middle East capitalistic. Multinational corporations in America shipped jobs and capital to Asia. Communist China hybridized its communism with finance capitalism. It implied that hopelessness could be eradicated if elites could create enough money to trickle down to the poor. In this context the scriptures seemed to lag far behind the times. But reflection suggests the Good Book has it right.

Centuries ago, prophets deputized by God warned about greed, debt, and materialistic excesses. They called for vigilance in guarding the mind, the heart, and the foundations of society. But we did not listen. We allowed ourselves to be beguiled into thinking that it did not matter if hedonists held their church in the stock market or on the silver screen, as long as we held our own in our churches. Now, burdened with problems like ancient Israel, our nation learns painful lessons about letting political and economic institutions become deformed while honorable culture slips away.

George Washington once said that people have to feel before they can see. Now that evangelicals and American Christians of all stripes have felt the effects of free markets gone awry, we are learning that powerful financial markets—to be a gift to humanity—must be regulated with great finesse and expertise. Laissez-faire markets in complex, advanced societies are dangerous, even as regulated markets have the potential to create extensive damage and injustice when mismanaged. As we are learning once again, regulators must also be checked and balanced lest they become a loathsome "free market" of regulatory abuse. Happily, constructive regulation is not as difficult as some laissez-faire advocates suggest, provided the regulatory machinery is well grounded in the national constitution. But since the bureaucratic state is post-constitutional in the United States, it is subject to misconstruction, misdirection, and politics.

There is a silver lining to this cloud. The recent abuses of finance capitalism have been so great that much light has been shed on the entire market system. Once the populace becomes wise to the need for economic prudence, branches bearing bad fruit can be removed, making room for the healthy limbs bearing the fruit of God's kingdom. And what will be the fruit of a good economic tree well-pruned? A virtuous capitalism hedged in by constitutional checks and balances and mechanisms of economic justice. It will be interesting to see what initiative, courage, and insight religiously minded people can show in contributing to such a work.

NOTES

1. I recommend a scholarly survey article on "Economics and the Evangelical Mind" by Anderson and Langelett (1996). The piece reveals the challenge of pinpointing the evangelical position on political economy. Nevertheless, there are basic matters upon which evangelicals have traditionally agreed. Mark Noll (1994) argues that evangelicals have assumed for more than a century that the essentials of good economics are individualism, property rights, and market freedom. Now, due to economic conditions, this consensus may be breaking down.

2. Institute for the Study of American Evangelicals, Wheaton College, "Defining Evangelicalism," www.wheaton.edu/isae/defining_evangelicalism.html, accessed June 23, 2008.

3. My career path includes short stints with two Wall Street firms (off Wall Street), then into the ministry, and finally to academia. For further discussion of honorable capitalism, see www.truthsavvy.com.

4. The definition of enlightenment is my tailored version of the term in *Webster's II New College Dictionary*.

5. Quotations are taken from the New American Standard Version of the Bible (NASV), a fairly literal translation compared to the New International Version (NIV), but easier to read than the King James Version (KJV).

6. The evangelical movement can be explained as the subset of Christians who highly esteem the Bible, believe in its continuing relevance, believe that Jesus Christ plays a central role in God's redemptive plan, and believe God calls his people to engage in spiritually based reform. For further explanation, see www.wheaton.edu/isae/defining_evangelicalism.html.

7. "Laissez-faire" is a French term that means "let do." It is typically understood to mean that private enterprise should be left largely alone by governmental regulators. This autonomy supposedly allows market forces to act as correctives for abuses, reducing the need for penalties (retroactive regulation) or central planning (proactive regulation). Many scholars believe that a laissez-faire approach to economics contributed to the Great Crash of 1929. Laissez-faire has been the reigning economic principle of the 1982–2008 period, and is sometimes (but unnecessarily) called the third ingredient of capitalism (Halteman, 1988). The term is sometimes used as a synonym for limited government but the two concepts are plausibly at odds.

8. These "principles" are examined by Edd Noell (1993), who argues that Christian scholars in the Reformed tradition, especially Reconstructionists, try to ground these ideas in the Mosaic Law. However, an examination of the arguments, especially those of Gary North, may leave one questioning the hermeneutic.

Chapter Five

Better Late Than Never? Evangelicals and Comprehensive Immigration Reform

Ruth Melkonian-Hoover

While it is true that evangelical leaders have been slower than Catholic and mainline Protestant leaders to enter the public debate around immigration policy, many are now speaking out on the issue. Moreover, many (though not all) evangelical leaders are now energetically defending positions on immigration policy that defy hard-line conservative stereotypes of right-wing populism, racism, and nativism. Most of them are gravitating to a more nuanced and syncretic approach, supporting versions of comprehensive immigration reform that attempt to balance moral imperatives of justice and mercy. That is, they seek solutions that show serious respect for the rule of law, while also upholding economic justice for American citizens and other residents, and adhering to the biblical injunctions to welcome the stranger and treat all people with dignity as beings made in the image of God. As such, evangelicals may be able to contribute a distinctive perspective to the contemporary policy debate—a perspective that avoids the extremes of either the political left or right and recognizes the social justice challenges inherent in addressing this complex issue.

In this chapter I examine the underpinnings—biblical, theological, and otherwise—of evangelical perspectives on immigration policy in the United States. I will briefly explore the recent history of evangelicals' involvement (or lack thereof) in advocacy for comprehensive immigration reform. I highlight the main factors that have typically inhibited evangelicals in this policy domain and explain why some evangelical leaders have recently been willing to clear those obstacles and become important players in today's politics of comprehensive immigration reform. In doing so, I draw primarily upon original research I undertook in 2010 (personal interviews with key evangelical leaders on immigration), as well as various secondary sources—including surveys, organizational documents, and scholarship on the issue.[1]

RECENT HISTORY OF ENGAGEMENT

As noted by many contributors to this volume, the range of policy issues on which evangelicals are taking stands has broadened in the last fifteen years or so, as reflected in the National Association of Evangelicals' (NAE) "For the Health of the Nation." Immigration policy, however, has been slow to find a place on this expanded evangelical policy agenda. For instance, during the Bush administration's push for comprehensive immigration reform (CIR)[2] in 2006–2007, white evangelical leaders remained mostly silent on the issue. By contrast, Hispanic evangelical groups, including the National Hispanic Christian Leadership Conference (NHCLC) and Esperanza, have been out-spoken in their support for immigration reform since the early 2000s, and were especially active during the 2006–2007 debate. As Rev. Luis Cortés, president of Esperanza, shared, "We didn't have a choice. Our people suffered it. Our pastors requested it of us . . . the human suffering—that did it" (June 25, 2010, interview).

Both the NHCLC and Esperanza have long been lobbying white evangeli-cal leaders to get on board in support of CIR. They recently have had some success, though the pace of "conversions" has been much slower than they would have liked. George W. Bush—who consistently received very strong support from white evangelicals—had pledged to push some form of CIR when he first ran for the presidency in 2000. But when in 2006 his adminis-tration did put CIR on the front burner, there were only a few expressions of support emanating from white evangelical leadership. For example, the NAE issued a rather vague statement on immigration, calling upon the government to pursue just and reasonable immigration policies and to leave the church free to fulfill its ministry. According to NAE's then–vice president for government affairs, Richard Cizik, the NAE was at that time too internally divided to be more specific (Cooperman 2006). Another example of budding if cautious support for CIR in 2006 came from the Southern Baptist Conven-tion. Richard Land, president the Convention's Ethics and Religious Liberty Commission (ERLC), supported CIR in principle, but was dissatisfied with both the Senate and House approaches that were on the table at the time. In June 2006, the Convention did pass a resolution in favor of a form of CIR, calling for the federal government to provide border security and for churches to encourage immigrants "toward the path of legal status and/or citizenship." Another minor harbinger of change occurred in 2007 with the formation of the group Christians for Comprehensive Immigration Reform (CCIR). Although mainline Protestant[3] and other nonevangelical constituencies were prominent in the creation of CCIR, they joined with two evangelical organizations, Sojourners and Evangelicals for Social Action (both of which are sometimes referred to as representing the "evangelical left") to do so. CCIR's policy resolution was signed by some well-known evangelical leaders as well, including Ronald Sider, Joel Hunter, Noel Castellanos, and Tony Campolo, among others.

However, major conservative evangelical activist organizations, like Focus on the Family and the Family Research Council, kept quiet on the issue of immigration policy. On the whole, Hispanic evangelical leaders were frustrated that there were not more key leaders and groups from the white evangelical tradition getting on board. NHCLC president Samuel Rodriguez stated in 2006, "This is the watershed movement—it's the moment where either we really forge relationships with the white evangelical church that will last for decades, or there is the possibility of a definitive schism here. There will be church ramifications to this, and there will be political ramifications" (Cooperman 2006).

Three years later, immigration reform returned to the foreground of public debate. Barack Obama had pledged to take on immigration reform early in his presidency, and advocates of CIR—now including a larger and more determined group of white evangelical leaders—began to pressure Obama to make good on that promise. Although the NHCLC and other Hispanic evangelical leaders still could not look to groups like Focus on the Family for overt support, there were numerous signs of other white evangelicals getting on board in a more serious way.

One indicator was the release in March 2009 of *Welcoming the Stranger: Justice, Compassion and Truth in the Immigration Debate*, written by Matthew Soerens and Jenny Hwang, both on staff of the NAE's humanitarian arm, World Relief, with a foreword by NAE President Leith Anderson. The book has been used to educate evangelicals on the issue of immigration and immigration policy and to advocate for CIR. Soerens and Hwang have shared their work with numerous congregations, including the influential Willow Creek Community Church outside of Chicago, which bought some ten thousand copies of the book for its members and invited the authors to lead a two-week class on the topic.

The NAE's newly ambitious leadership on the issue was further demonstrated in October of 2009, when it issued a detailed resolution in support of CIR and coordinated events and press coverage around it. The theological and ethical reasoning employed by the NAE and World Relief have solidified the predominant evangelical approach to CIR—namely, to find specific and practical ways to balance justice and mercy, compassion and the rule of law. Galen Carey, the new governmental affairs director at NAE, worked for twenty-five years at World Relief on poverty- and refugee-related issues; his move to NAE signals a prioritizing of those issues. Carey has noted that the passage of a resolution by the NAE board indicates increased organizational emphasis on an issue; he acknowledged that immigration, along with abortion and creation care, comprise NAE's top three priorities (March 26, 2010, interview). In addition to pressing the government on immigration, the NAE has been holding regional forums with church leaders throughout the country to advance understanding, ease the divide between evangelical leadership and laity, and offer resources such as the Soerens/Hwang book and the recent book by Denver Seminary Old Testament scholar Daniel Rodas Carroll, titled *Christians at the Border: Immigration, the Church and the Bible* (2008).

There continue to be other signs of an elevated level of pro-CIR engagement among evangelical leaders and organizations.

- Carroll has been leading workshops and forums on the biblical bases of immigration at key evangelical universities, seminaries, churches, and organizations including the NAE, Willow Creek, and the Christian Community Development Association (CCDA).
- In March 2010, numerous evangelical leaders and activists attended a "Standing with Immigrants" prayer service hosted by Sojourners in Washington, D.C., that immediately preceded a March for America rally on the mall. A number of Hispanic religious leaders commented on the greater diversity of participants than seen in previous efforts.
- On May 13, the NAE took out a full page ad in *Roll Call* urging a bipartisan CIR effort, with top evangelical signatories including Mat Staver (Dean of Liberty Law School), John Perkins (African-American founder of the CCDA), Samuel Rodriguez, and Bill Hybels (senior pastor of Willow Creek).
- Evangelical advocates of CIR are careful to frame their support in a bipartisan manner and have worked collaboratively to make the conservative case for immigration. Throughout 2010, Leith Anderson, Jenny Hwang, Samuel Rodriguez, Noel Castellanos (CEO of CCDA), and others have cooperated with Juan Hernandez' organization, Conservatives for Comprehensive Immigration Reform, on numerous strategy calls for religious, political and business leaders, and the media.
- On July 1, 2010, President Obama invited what CNN's Dan Gilgoff called his "evangelical cabinet on immigration reform" (including Leith Anderson, Bill Hybels, Richard Land, and Samuel Rodriguez) to attend his immigration speech at American University, where he renewed his call for CIR (Gilgoff 2010).

In sum, white evangelical leaders are relative latecomers to the immigration policy debate. However, since 2006—and especially since 2009—an increasing number of them have become serious advocates for reform. By 2010, White House officials like Homeland Security Secretary Janet Napolitano were regularly referencing the NAE's work as representative of faith leaders on the pro-CIR side of the issue. This development brings two questions into relief: What factors explain why it has been a slow process for white evangelical leaders to join their Hispanic evangelical counterparts in backing CIR? And how have the evangelical proponents of CIR worked through or around those inhibiting factors to arrive at their current place in the debate?

BARRIERS TO EVANGELICAL SUPPORT FOR CIR

Grassroots Evangelicalism—Politics and Public Opinion

Like all leaders in public policy debates, evangelical leaders have to be attentive to the opinions of their constituencies. And the simple reality is that significant numbers of evangelicals at the grassroots level are sympathetic to restrictive views on immigration. For example, half of white evangelicals believe *legal* immigration should be decreased, and that illegal immigrants should be deported (Pew 2006; Jones and Cox 2009). Pro-CIR evangelical leaders are aware that they have significant work to do in convincing, not only their government, but their own adherents as well to support CIR.

The partisan context is also significant in this regard. As is well-known, for the last three decades a large majority of the white evangelical population has voted Republican. But the presidency of George W. Bush (himself a white evangelical) demonstrated that CIR is deeply divisive within the Republican Party. Evangelicals' generally strong GOP orientation was not a reliable prompt for them to back Bush on CIR. And after the election of Barack Obama, those GOP evangelicals who were reluctant to support Bush's efforts were likely to be even more resistant to Obama's overtures on immigration. Further complicating the political environment was the shifting posture of Republican John McCain, who had been a Senate champion of CIR in the last go-around, but changed his stance during his bid for the presidency in 2008.

Another concern for pro-CIR evangelical advocates is the recent rise of the Tea Party movement, which has become a major force on the Republican right. Samuel Rodriguez pointed to its growth as a reason for stasis or even slippage in support for CIR:

The hindrance is the Tea Party. The Tea Party movement has the power to galvanize and attract in a good sense those that would like to address issues of government intrusion or overreach or uber-hyper-reach of government. But then in a negative sense, some of the hyperbole, some of the danger we have seen, is a bit scary. To receive a press release that the Tea Party movement will have rallies in support of the AZ law? That is scary. . . . [R]ace is not the only factor, but is a factor and that's embedded in the law verbatim. For Americans to say, "yes this would lead to racial profiling, however we will look the other way," that's just scary. . . . For the Tea Party movement to promote that, in my opinion the Tea Party movement will be promoting and supporting a racist policy. (May 13, 2010, interview)

Daniel Carroll noted a similar concern: "When I was in Cleveland [for a recent presentation] . . . the head of the NAACP in the region was there, and I asked him, 'What are you here for?' And he said, 'You know, I'm starting to see them do to you what they used to do to us'" (April 20, 2010, interview).

Conservative Media Influence

A related factor is the influence of right-wing media in some quarters of American evangelicalism. Advocates of CIR worry that opposition to or silence on CIR is not so often a result of deep scriptural study as it is a result of fear mongering promoted by some contemporary media outlets. As Michael Gerson, former Bush policy advisor and speechwriter and senior fellow at the Institute for Global Engagement, explained, "I would say that maybe among conservative Christians in America, probably the single most important formative institution on their views on immigration is Fox News. And Fox News [has been] deeply anti-immigrant in its coverage" (May 21, 2010, interview). Others have expressed this concern in rather succinct sound bites. Jim Wallis is fond of saying, "It's time to replace the Gospel of Glen, Rush, Sean and Bill with the Gospel of Matthew, Mark, Luke and John" (CCIR conference call to Christian clergy, June 24, 2010). Many advocates fear that evangelicals are informed much more by the media they consume than by their churches; in a recent survey only 16 percent of white evangelical churchgoers said their clergy speak on immigration at least occasionally (Jones and Cox 2010).

Methodological Concerns

Another longstanding tension within evangelicalism is about precisely how religious leaders can or should derive policy positions from scripture—especially when the policy area is complex and there are sharp disagreements among the laity. For instance, Mark Tooley, president of the Institute on Religion and Democracy, has been critical of pro-CIR evangelical leadership, especially the NAE's October 2009 resolution. As he shared, "[The

NAE resolution] had no acknowledgement of the disagreement on immigration policies within the evangelical community and just seemed to make a lot of blanket assumptions about what is virtuous and compassionate, with the implication that those who politically disagree are somehow lacking in those Christian virtues" (February 2, 2010, interview). He is not alone in registering caution, in part because of a concern that churches, denominations, and religious organizations act erroneously when they speak out on issues in which scripture, doctrine, and church history are not clear. As Paul Marshall explained:

> On the political side, my impression, again I stand to be corrected, but on this, and many other things, churches, specifically, denominations, pastors, bishops, clergy tend to speak in platitudes. Jesus said, "welcome the stranger . . . and you took me in"—so we should take in strangers. But now we're talking about the policy of a federal government, a state government . . . which incidentally is not all Christian. It's a question of public policy. People go from fairly abstract morality to public policy without ever questioning what is involved in public policy. . . . Clergy as clergy have no special insight in public policy and are often destructive. (March 22, 2010, interview)

Those wary of the process of religious advocacy on policy are not necessarily opposed to CIR. They do, however, believe some evangelical efforts on this issue are misguided, and the reservations they describe help to explain why some evangelicals have kept silent on this issue.

Rule of Law Concerns

Differing interpretations of what Scripture teaches about the rule of law have led to varying conclusions on immigration and immigration policy. James Hoffmeier, Old Testament scholar at Trinity Evangelical Divinity School, after having studied U.S. immigration law, does not find it to be inherently unjust or in conflict with God's law (although he acknowledges that doesn't preclude the need for some reform). He contends that Christians are "to follow the edicts of the state unless there is a very clear conflict with the teachings of Scripture" (Hoffmeier 2009, 142). As a result, he supports efforts by Christians to abide by and help others comply with the law at this time. Hoffmeier's line of thinking is fairly prevalent among evangelicals. *Christianity Today,* in its coverage of CIR during the last national debate over immigration, found that *almost all* of its reader responses raised concerns regarding the rule of law (Galli 2006).

Economic Justice Concerns

Another argument raised by some evangelical leaders in opposition to CIR is that illegal immigration entails serious violations of economic justice. Hoffmeier points to the injustices that the undocumented and others suffer due to the vast underground economy that the United States has allowed to develop. Drawing on Jeremiah 22, Malachi 3, Leviticus 19, James 5, and similar texts, he highlights the unfair wages that can result: "People of conscience should be able to agree that our legal system should punish those who underpay or deprive of benefits any worker, including the alien, who might be the last one to complain or file a grievance" (Hoffmeier 2009, 121–22). He argues that the vast underground economy of the undocumented should never have been allowed to develop in the first place, as it will by nature be unfair to all workers.

Others believe that scripture compels us to look first to fellow citizens whose needs are not being met before viewing immigration policy as a means to provide for the economic needs of those of other nations. James Edwards of the Mita Group consulting firm writes in *Christianity Today*, "Scripture indicates certain priorities of our obligations. I Timothy 5:8 teaches 'If anyone does not provide for his relatives, and especially for his immediate family, he has denied the faith and is worse than an unbeliever.' Clearly, God organizes society around groups of people: families, clans, communities, tribes, nations. The priorities of allegiance are implied in this verse" (Edwards 2006). According to Edwards:

> God in his providence created civil government for a reason and that is, each civil government's job is to protect a certain group of people, its citizens. That's their job. It's not to take care of people in other lands, even though they may be perfectly deserving as creatures of God [made] in His image, but that's not their job. Now there are other ways we can deal with that, such as, [church missions, etc.]. (February 2, 2010, interview)

Kelly Monroe Kullberg, founder of the Veritas Forum, raises similar scripturally based concerns of responsibility and sustainability. She writes:

> [W]e're called to balance teachings that encourage the welcoming of some (though apparently not all) strangers alongside teachings that encourage cultural and economic stability, the stewardship of resources for sustainable flourishing, and justice not only for the stranger who comes from afar but for the neighbor who already lives amongst us. Those who honor God and his Word will naturally love the foreigner, the fatherless, and the widow. . . . When the United States has paid down our own multi-trillion dollar (and growing) debt, when more of our unemployed are given the dignity of work, when we have

regained cultural stability, strength, and wise leadership, we will be better able to afford an increased rate of immigration. In our present circumstances, however, we are a false hope. (Kullberg 2010)

Former Congressman Tancredo, an outspoken opponent of CIR, also raises issues of sustainability, pushing back against Christian calls for unlimited mercy. He contends that such calls to mercy must be prioritized and qualified.

It is quite impossible for us to operate an immigration system that simply looks at the desire of the person who wants to come into the country, and their economic conditions, as the primary criteria for entry. And so the issue of mercy always gets clouded. Is a poor person in Mexico, desiring a better life in the U.S., desiring a job in the U.S., is that enough to qualify him or her as a refugee? Or is it the person who is being persecuted for his faith or his religion or his political perspective? . . . I think we are very merciful. (April 21, 2010, interview)

EVANGELICAL SUPPORT FOR CIR: OVERCOMING BARRIERS

Given these arguments and obstacles, how is it that some evangelical leaders are now more outspoken than ever in their support of CIR?

New Leadership

Part of the change is a function of a broader shift within evangelicalism, with "Christian Right" leaders receding in prominence while more moderate evangelical leaders are gaining in prominence. In the case of immigration, this can be seen most clearly within the NAE leadership. Around the time of the last immigration debate, the NCHLC became an affiliate member of the NAE. Samuel Rodriguez's presence and advocacy, in conjunction with the work of like-minded executive board members like David Neff (editor in chief of *Christianity Today*), ensured that immigration would be a priority for NAE. Another key factor in the advance of pro-CIR views was the handing over of the NAE presidency in 2006 to Leith Anderson, who is sympathetic to the pro-CIR perspective. As David Neff explained, "From day one, [he's] seen the importance of it, there's never been a problem convincing Leith Anderson. . . . The immigration thing was already on the agenda [prior to Anderson's presidency], but if it had been somebody else other than Anderson, it easily could have just been sidelined" (April 4, 2010, interview).

Having high-profile evangelical organizational leadership in front of the issue helps provide a moral base of support for reform. As Jenny Hwang conveyed, "The NAE has given a lot of cover to denominations and leaders who are speaking out now. . . . Leith Anderson's leadership has been phenomenal on this." What is even more crucial is that "God has broken down a lot of barriers. I feel like this issue is weighing heavily on God's heart and when you have so many leaders who are following after God and pursuing what's on His heart, I think God gives them a heart for this" (March 21, 2010, interview).

Biblical Calls to Combine Justice and Mercy

For many evangelical leaders, mobilization on this issue is part of an expansion of the social concerns on which they feel compelled to engage as a function of a holistic biblical worldview. Many of the biblical arguments in support of CIR center on the scriptural imperative to do both justice *and* mercy (e.g., the welcoming of the stranger, showing mercy to the most vulnerable, offering respect to all of humanity as creatures made in God's image, and pursuing justice for all). As the NAE resolution of October 2009 so clearly states:

> The Bible does not offer a blueprint for modern legislation, but it can serve as a moral compass and shape the attitudes of those who believe in God. An appreciation of the pervasiveness of migration in the Bible must temper the tendency to limit discussions on immigration to Romans 13 and a simplistic defense of "the rule of law." God has established the nations (Deut 32:8, Acts 17:26) and their laws should be respected. Nevertheless, policies must be evaluated to reflect that immigrants are made in the image of God and demonstrate biblical grace to the foreigner.

Jennifer Kottler, director of policy and advocacy at Sojourners, believes evangelicals are engaging on the immigration issue because they now see the biblical nature of the issue: "One of the reasons why I see more and more faith communities coming on . . . is that . . . these are folks in our churches and our communities, and from an evangelical perspective, it's biblical. We have a responsibility to welcome the stranger. [It's] very clear that it's not optional" (February 19, 2010, interview).

Richard Land speaks to the dual citizenship of Christians and their obligation to honor both kingdoms: "As citizens of the US, we have an obligation to support the government and the government's laws for conscience' sake (Romans 13:7). . . . As citizens of the Lord's heavenly kingdom . . . we also have a divine mandate to act redemptively and compassionately toward those who are in need" (Land 2006). Fellow Baptist David Gushee argues that undocumented immigrants are amongst the most vulnerable in our society, due at least in part to the unjust laws in our nation. He contends that Christians are compelled to respond on a number of fronts:

One mark of the reign of God is justice, and one aspect of justice is the inclusion of marginalized people into community. . . . And think about the injustice in the way our enforcement of immigration law has worked, kind of random, sporadic, arbitrary, and when it does happen, breaking up families, kids get left at school while mom and dad get shipped back across the border or put in those horrible immigration prisons in which there is no adequate transparency and oversight. I think Christian people are called to pay attention to those in the shadows, and those in the margins and those who have no status in a society and are therefore by definition the most likely to be abused and mistreated. (March 30, 2010, interview)

Putting the Rule of Law in Perspective

Biblical statements on the rule of law—especially Romans 13—lead many evangelicals to either passively or actively oppose CIR (or at least versions of CIR that lean more toward mercy than law enforcement). Accordingly, supporters of reform have spent much time wrestling with the issue, trying to help evangelicals understand how support for CIR is true to those scriptures. For example, Carroll maintains that current immigration laws are egregiously unjust and that Christians' responses to them should differ. He contends that Romans 13 can be understood only in light of Romans 12. Like Gushee, Carroll argues, "If, on top of these faith convictions, one evaluates the history of immigration law in the US as confused, contradictory, and in some ways unfair to the various effected parties, then that also will affect the perspective on the legality question" (Carroll 2008, 132). As he explains:

This is where I think Christians are beyond excuse, because they want to start at Romans 13, the law, the boundaries, but I think the Christian part is Romans 12. . . . Romans 12 tells me if my enemy is hungry I feed him, if my enemy is thirsty I give him drink. . . . Even if you think they're an enemy of your world, of your country, you have no excuse not to take care of them. You're beyond excuse. Whatever the politics of it, whatever the numbers game is, we have to, as a church, we have no excuse. (April 20, 2010, interview)

Mark Galli of *Christianity Today*, in reflecting on the rule of law concerns, states that

[t]he issue before us is not whether law should be obeyed in normal circumstances. We all agree on that. In addition, everyone agrees that under certain circumstances, laws should be disobeyed. Even normally law-abiding Christians assent to that—or deny the witness of Scripture. The question is: Under what circumstances is it appropriate to disobey a law? And the particular question facing us now is: If a person from another land is suffering economic and political hardship, and if the immigration policies of the U.S. make it nearly impossible for some immigrants to enter this nation, is it legitimate (albeit regrettable) for an immigrant to enter this nation clandestinely to gain those freedoms? (Galli 2006)

As World Relief immigration activist and author Matthew Soerens acknowledges, many undocumented immigrants themselves struggle with the desire to comply with the laws of the land. But this desire is held in tension with other biblical obligations: "Is this situation [like] Acts 5:29, [where] we must obey God rather than men? . . . There's also, I Timothy tells us, if you don't provide for your own family you're worse than an unbeliever. . . . It's not quite as simple as, 'Romans 13—what part of this don't you understand?'" (March 21, 2010, interview). As a pastor, Joel Hunter has faced this question many times. As he shared, "There *is* something to be said that the law is the law, and we need to do something that, both, Jesus words were, I came not to abolish the law, but to fulfill the law. . . . We need to have an approach where the law is respected but it's also fulfilled" (February 22, 2010, interview). Hunter testified before Congress that "[most major religions] see law as not only necessary for restraining evil, but as needed for structuring healthy relationships. It is right that wrongdoers are restrained and/or punished, but it is a better justice when the laws yield correction and the redemption of bad circumstances" (Hunter 2009). Similarly, NAE's Leith Anderson, in congressional testimony given in October 2009 (coinciding with NAE's resolution of October 2009), maintained, "Laws must serve the good of society and create law and order; when they do not, they need to be changed. . . . The process of redemption and restitution is core to Christian beliefs, as we were all once lost and redeemed through the love of Jesus Christ" (Anderson 2009).

Economic Justice Concerns

In addition to rule of law concerns, advocates for CIR have grappled with how immigration—legal and illegal—affects the status of the poor already here, as Christians pursue justice for all residents of this nation. While the scholarship is mixed as to the costs and benefits of immigration for the U.S. economy, most acknowledge some overall gains and some particular losses, and some scholars—George Borjas and Carol Swain, among others—emphasize the adverse implications of increasing the labor supply of low-skilled workers for those already at risk in the United States. Responding to such scholarship, pro-CIR evangelical leader Ronald Sider acknowledged the concerns, but pointed to other structural causes of poverty as paramount:

> I do think that just given our history, our first moral obligation is to continue to right the wrongs we've done with African-Americans. I would want to look at all of that with measures that would, if you can, get rid of the underground economy, and make the minimum wage more livable for everybody. . . . The more it is the case that a certain kind of African-American is hurt by immigrants, the more troubled I am. Another way to work at that is to say that we've got to do what Bush was trying to do, and what Obama is trying to do,

and that is end the scandal of inner-city education. And if more African Americans had quality education and then college, we wouldn't have the problem we're talking about. And it's just unacceptable not to do that. (May 5, 2010, interview)

As Phoenix youth pastor Ian Danley of Neighborhood Ministries stated, "I think in a globalized economy, we've got to get our kids through high school or they're not going to be competitive, whatever our immigration system looks like. Blaming immigration for our high school dropouts not being competitive I think is backwards" (May 6, 2010, interview).

Finally, many advocates argue that such concerns are precisely why CIR is needed. As Matthew Soerens argues, "Part of why legalization is so important for that category of lower skilled workers is that it levels the playing field. And having lawful mechanisms for entry in the future, I'm not going to say it's going to kill illegal immigration . . . but it drastically minimizes illegal immigration" (March 21, 2010, interview). Others call for a different perspective altogether. Concerns about needs and resources stem from a presumption of scarcity, according to Craig Wong of Grace Urban Ministries in San Francisco: "Much of what's at the heart of this crisis is . . . our sense of entitlement combined with limited resources. The question of numbers is very much tied to our own sense of need. So this is where the church comes in, because we really have to live and embody something different" (June 6, 2010, interview).

The U.S. Mission Field

Another reason why many evangelical denominations, churches, and leaders are now acting on immigration is that they, like many Christians of the past, see immigrants as a mission field to whom they are called to minister and to whom they desire to be seen as welcoming (Seager 1959). For example, the final resolution of the 2006 Southern Baptist Convention's statement on CIR states, "Resolved that we make the most of the tremendous opportunity for evangelism . . . among the immigrant population to the end that these individuals might become both legal residents of the United States and loyal citizens of the Kingdom of God." In a similar vein, Galen Carey, government affairs directors for the NAE, offered this remark: "A fundamental concern of our members . . . is that the church's role was to share the good news, and evangelize; and they think God has brought these people here. We've been sending missionaries out for centuries . . . now God has brought people here, and we're supposed to reach them right here" (March 26, 2010, interview). Lynne Hybels, advocate for global engagement at Willow Creek Community Church, expressed a similar sentiment in her recent congressional testimony:

God has entrusted the church with the mission of making disciples of all nations (Matthew 28:19–20). Through immigration, "all nations" have entered our churches and become part of us. Whatever our cultural differences, we are united as one body in Christ. 1 Cor 12:12–26 says that when one part of the body suffers, we all suffer together. As we have listened to our immigrant brothers and sisters in order to understand how our immigrant system is affecting them, we have *heard* their suffering and we must *share* in their suffering. (Hybels 2009)

While many outsiders (and some insiders) are suspicious that pro-CIR evangelical activism on this question is driven by a self-interested desire to grow the church, Center for Immigration Studies executive director Mark Krikorian, a leading voice for restricting immigration, has refused to presume that religious opponents are driven by crass expediency. In response to a similar suspicion of Catholics, he noted the following: "Eighty percent probably of illegal immigrants are at least nominally Roman Catholic. But then you look at the other religious bureaucracies and hierarchies and they take very similar positions . . . [For example], if very few illegal immigrants are Jewish, why are Jewish religious figures backing it?" (CIS 2009).

Rethinking the Role of the Church in Social and Political Engagement

Amongst those interviewees who are sympathetic to CIR, none would deny that Christians are to speak out on the issue of immigration. But a debate is taking place over the appropriate role of the church itself in this arena. The exchange between two pastors of the Boston Chinese Evangelical Church captures much of the deliberation among evangelicals as to what the church should be saying and doing in this regard. Pastor Enoch Liao was hesitant to speak explicitly on behalf of CIR, but not against nativism.

I wouldn't preach any of those [immigration] policies at this point. . . . I would preach against certain fundamental selfishness about how we want to see our country. I could preach against that. I could preach against a sense of ethno-centricity. . . . But to use the pulpit, and it might be my idea of the biblical pulpit, to preach a policy would be akin to preaching a candidate, and I don't know that I would do that either. (May 11, 2010, interview)

But Pastor Thomas Lee of the same congregation differed:

I would, if I could figure out the issue, feel like that it is an extension of our prophetic office. I would say and make it clear that this is not necessarily biblical, these are some biblical principles, and I believe that maybe in this time and space that this is how I understand the situation. . . . Here are some of the reasons why I think this position makes sense. (May 11, 2010, interview)

Michael Gerson is similarly hesitant about the church getting into specific policy recommendations or advocacy, but also troubled if it fails to speak out at all.

> The reality there is that scripture does have a certain set of attitudes toward the stranger, towards the sojourner. . . . [However] there's just an inherent danger in identifying the Gospel too closely with a specific policy agenda. It's alienating to some people who aren't at that point. And it can actually detract from the primary mission of the church. But I think it's a failure if a minister, particularly if you live in a multicultural community, where your people are dealing with others all the time, if you're not giving them guidance on the moral basis to deal with other people of different backgrounds. (May 21, 2010, interview)

Author and *CT* senior editor Andy Crouch also distinguishes between what he believes are appropriate and inappropriate ways for church leaders to speak on public issues. As he explained, "It's risky when church leaders like me, for example, pronounce publicly on things they're not experts on. . . . But should churches be providing opportunities for education for their members and commissioning their members who have some level of expertise to lobby forcefully for this? Yes, absolutely, 100 percent" (March 25, 2010, interview).

Samuel Rodriguez, among others, believes it appropriate that the church speak from a biblical foundation to the pressing issues of the day: poverty, healthcare, education, torture, and human rights. He contends that "the agenda of the evangelical church in America has been two-fold since 1973: It has been sanctity of life and traditional marriage. . . . Now the Hispanic evangelical comes along and says there are other items we need to look at" (Ramirez 2008). Ultimately, as Gushee argues, there has been a desire for a greater breadth of focus by Christians in general, and Hispanic Christians have helped evangelicals see that immigration is an appropriate focus. As he relayed, "[There was] this intuitive sense that evangelicals needed a broader moral agenda . . . and had to have a broad public justice vision, and immigration surfaced, especially as we got to know Latino evangelicals, and got to see how fundamentally important this issue is from their perspective" (March 30, 2010, interview).

At the congregational level, evangelicals do not see it as their job to formulate policy prescriptions themselves. But given the needs of their community, they find themselves in a position where they cannot help but respond. As Heather Larson, director of the Compassion and Justice Ministry of Willow Creek, explained, "We're not looking for some political platform on this. And yet how can we not speak for people in our church and people in our community who are facing these challenges? So please as our politicians, fix this. We're not going to tell you how to do it" (April 7, 2010, interview).

As Daniel Carroll maintains, evangelicals are obliged to respond on this issue. Caring for the sojourner "will entail majority culture Christians and churches opening themselves up and allowing the sojourner admittance to their culture and lives. In addition, if this moral imperative is for all nations, then these Christians have the obligation to be a voice for God's heart in the country at large" (Carroll 2008, 109).

THE EVANGELICAL CONTRIBUTION TO IMMIGRATION REFORM: BALANCING LAW, JUSTICE, AND MERCY

Many evangelical leaders are increasingly engaged on immigration and immigration policy; they feel obliged to speak out, even while aware of the difficulties of doing so appropriately. Evangelicals, along with some other religious voices, are among the most willing to acknowledge the tensions inherent in the debate—between the rule of law, stewardship, sustainability, and justice. Given (a) evangelicals' desire to be as biblically grounded as possible, and (b) the ongoing struggle in their congregations over this issue, many of today's evangelical leaders appear more willing than most polarized immigration activists to wrestle honestly with the need to approach immigration reform from a foundation of mercy *and* justice, grace *and* truth. As Christian ethicist Dana Wilbanks put it in the 1990s in response to that decade's struggles with immigration, "While Christians should advocate vigorously for the needs and rights of migrants, they should not evade the difficult questions of justifiable limits and humane enforcement of the law of these limits" (1996, 209).

Longtime advocates of immigration reform may find evangelicals' recent participation to be too little, too late. They will be quick to remind us that it is only some, and not all, evangelical leaders who have progressed to a pro-CIR position. And most of those leaders have taken concerted action only in the last few years. Indeed, had evangelical supporters of CIR been fully engaged back in 2006–2007 when President Bush and key members of Congress were pushing for reform, a bill might well have passed. Still, there actually may be value added as a result of evangelicals' relatively late arrival on the scene. Their lateness stems in part from their awareness of the complexity and divisions surrounding the issue and a desire to contribute to solutions that reflect the range of legitimate concerns surrounding immigration. Because evangelical constituencies are cross-pressured, and because they are not usually inclined to ignore one ethical principle in favor of another, they likely will not support simplistic policy solutions. The solutions that do emerge with their support may in fact be more workable and sustainable than what otherwise might arise out of a polarized political process. In this respect, we can hope that evangelicals' entry into the debate may indeed be better late than never.

NOTES

1. Recent polling reveals something of a divide between evangelical leadership and the laity on immigration policy overall. While this chapter emphasizes the role of evangelical leaders, this work is part of my larger research project on evangelicals and immigration which includes reasons for and implications of differences amongst evangelical leaders and laity.

2. Comprehensive immigration reform typically refers to legislative efforts to reform immigration law at the national level by linking some combination of security measures, a pathway to legalization for the approximately eleven million undocumented immigrants already here, and a guest worker program, along with other components. It will hereafter be known as CIR.

3. Major African American Protestant denominations did not issue resolutions on CIR, but many are part of the National Council of Churches, which has been outspoken in support of reform. For further information on Christians and immigration policy, see my article, "The Politics of Religion and Immigration," *Review of Faith and International Affairs* 6:3 (Fall 2008), and my guest-edited issue of the *Review of Faith and International Affairs* 9:1 (Spring 2011).

Part II

Engaging the World: Evangelical Views on Global Issues

Chapter Six

The Roots of Evangelical Humanitarianism and International Political Advocacy

Mark R. Amstutz

Are evangelicals concerned with international affairs? If so, do they have a political theory to structure their moral reflections and guide their public policy initiatives? Throughout the Cold War, it was widely believed that U.S. evangelicals were solely concerned with spiritual life and were completely disengaged from political affairs. As the religious right gained influence in the late 1970s, the prevailing perception was that evangelicals were concerned only with domestic issues and unconcerned with global problems. A major aim of this essay is to correct this view.

This chapter makes four broad claims. First, it suggests that evangelicals have contributed a distinctive approach to international public life—one that gives primacy to moral development as the basis for creating and sustaining humane, prosperous societies. Since evangelicals believe that spiritual redemption through Christ is the basis for a meaningful life, their prevailing political doctrine is "moral people make just, humane nations." And although evangelicals have failed to develop a sophisticated political theory to structure thought and action, they have nevertheless contributed to the development of decent, prosperous regimes.

A second claim is that the international work of evangelicals is not a recent phenomenon, but one that dates to the early nineteenth century and the emergence of the missionary movement. While evangelicals were inspired and guided chiefly by spiritual concerns, they nevertheless contributed importantly toward the United States' role in the world and more specifically to the creation of more humane societies. As major agents of cross-cultural engagement, missionaries strengthened understanding of foreign cultures and fostered an appreciation for global concerns.

A third, related claim is that American evangelicals have made a distinctive contribution to the international community through their humanitarianism. Building on the pioneering work of missionaries, evangelicals have established organizations and mobilized public support to care for human needs worldwide, offering aid to orphans and war refugees, food and shelter to people suffering from natural disasters and war, and development assistance to decrease poverty. They have created some of the largest and most effective faith-based NGOs and established a sophisticated organizational network that has structured collaboration among domestic and international organizations in meeting global humanitarian needs.

Finally, evangelicals have contributed to a more principled U.S. foreign policy by highlighting specific moral issues, such as peace, religious freedom, and human dignity. While evangelicals have rarely initiated foreign policy initiatives, they have proved adept at mobilizing believers through grassroots networks.

THE NATURE OF EVANGELICALISM

Evangelicalism is not easily defined. For our purposes, it is conceived as a movement within Protestantism that emphasizes three beliefs: the primacy of the scriptures as the final authority for religious faith, the need for conversion through the personal acceptance of Jesus' atonement on the Cross, and the imperative of sharing the Gospel through evangelism. As Timothy Shah has noted, orthodox Christianity "demands a belief that the Bible enjoys an authority that trumps other sources of authority, such as reason or church tradition; personal and inward acceptance of the gospel message that Christ has atoned for humanity's sins on the Cross and has thereby won eternal salvation for believers; and active and outward mission on the part of all believers, lay and clerical alike, to share the good news of salvation with others" (Shah 2009, 115).

One of the defining social and cultural trends of our times is the growth of evangelicalism in the United States. The leading evangelical denomination is the Southern Baptist Convention, with a membership of more than 16.3 million. Other major evangelical groups include the Church of God in Christ, a predominantly African American denomination with 5.5 million members, and the Lutheran church Missouri Synod, with 2.5 million members. It is estimated that roughly 80 million Americans—roughly 26 percent of the electorate—are considered evangelicals.

Although numerical expansion helps to explain the rise in evangelical influence in both domestic and global affairs, several other factors have contributed to its expanding impact. To begin with, rising evangelical influence in the United States is due to the growing professional success, wealth, and cultural sophistication of evangelical leaders. As Michael Lindsay has recently shown in *Faith in the Halls of Power*, evangelicals have greater influence in politics because a growing number of political leaders and government officials are publicly identified as orthodox believers. The same is true for the leading cultural, business, social, and educational institutions (Lindsay 2008). Second, the media has increased its coverage of religion in public life, and its coverage of evangelical political engagement is fairer and more complete. While the U.S. media remains a largely secular and politically liberal organization, the rising evangelical influence has received much greater and more sympathetic coverage by news reporters and columnists. Third, the dramatic decline in membership of mainline Protestant churches has created a moral vacuum in American public life that evangelicals have attempted to fill. Finally, the influence of evangelicals has increased as their leaders have learned to collaborate with other political groups with similar political goals and legislative goals. At the same time evangelicals, building on their flexibility and grassroots organizations, have learned the importance of mobilizing public opinion. The importance of collaboration and mobilization were evident in the successful passage of the International Religious Freedom Act of 1998 and the Sudan Peace Act of 2002.

Evangelicalism is a conservative tradition, both theologically and politically. Evangelicals emphasize orthodox beliefs and practices that give precedence to an individual's relationship to God and to other human beings. Although sin can manifest itself in collective life, sin, grace, and salvation apply chiefly to individuals in their personal and interpersonal relationships. Moreover, since each person is ultimately responsible for responding to God's gift of salvation and for personally sharing the gospel with others, evangelical ethics give priority to individual belief and action. Unlike Catholic social thought, which emphasizes the common good and communal responsibilities, evangelicalism is an individualistic tradition that places primary responsibility on persons for their own spiritual and temporal well-being. Thus, its conservatism derives not simply from its biblicism and orthodox beliefs but also from its methodology—one that gives primacy to the spiritual over the temporal, the personal over the institutional.

Evangelical political ethics is also associated with conservatism because of the priority given to order, morality, and individual responsibility. For evangelicals, justice is the by-product of a humane order where persons use freedom responsibly. Whereas progressives emphasize the use of public policies and structural reforms to advance social and political justice, evangelicals have historically emphasized reformation and transformation of persons as the best strategy to advance justice. Since good societies are the result of good people, the challenge of orthodox believers is to ensure that human beings are rightly related to their Creator. Once this is achieved, structural reforms can be initiated. Additionally, since human sin is pervasive in personal and social life, especially when power and wealth are involved, evangelicalism has historically given precedence to private initiatives over governmental action. Because of the skepticism about government-initiated reforms, evangelical political ethics are characterized by support for limited government and decentralization (subsidiarity).

Although evangelicalism remains a predominantly conservative religious movement, some observers have suggested that a moderate political center is gaining strength. For example, ethicist David Gushee argues that an evangelical center is emerging, one that that lies between the dominant religious right and the minority evangelical left represented by Ron Sider, Jim Wallis, and others (Gushee 2008). He supports his contention of an emerging center by claiming that a growing number of influential evangelicals have adopted a more moderate and comprehensive approach to national and global public life, taking up issues such as the environment and global poverty from a structural perspective.

THE STRATEGY OF EVANGELICALS

Although evangelicals are informally associated around a core set of religious beliefs, they are not a cohesive, coherent movement. Rather evangelicalism is a religious tendency, allowing for a broad plurality of religious practices and social and political preferences. Unlike the Roman Catholic Church, which has a well-developed body of social and political teachings to guide political and social analysis and action, evangelicals have no similar political doctrine. As a result, they have tended to emphasize personal over political concerns, individual morality over structural and policy issues. Moreover, they have tended to focus on a narrow agenda, believing that individual action is more important than centralized, government-initiated public policies. This pattern was especially evident with the rise of the Moral Majority in the late 1970s and the development of the Christian Coalition in the 1980s. To a significant degree, these movements were inspired by the conviction that government had become excessively intrusive and that public policies were undermining traditional values.

Some scholars attribute the limited scope and ineffectiveness of Christian political engagement to the lack of an established moral doctrine to structure and guide action (Budziszewski 2006). Although there is truth in this claim, the impact of individual moral transformation on social and political life should not be underestimated. Indeed, authentic faith can indirectly contribute to the development of more prosperous and humane political communities by reinforcing the dignity of all persons and by nurturing personal virtues, including integrity, truth-telling, diligence, and honesty. In her case study on development in Guatemala, Amy Sherman has corroborated this claim. She shows that individual conversion, by fostering desirable personal habits and values, can contribute to greater economic enterprise and social stability (Sherman 1997). In a related study of Latin American Pentecostals, Douglas Petersen has shown that, while Pentecostals have rarely developed a sophisticated social ethic, they nonetheless have implemented effective humanitarian practices in meeting human needs (Petersen 1996). Thus, even though evangelicals have not developed political and social doctrines to guide action, they have nevertheless carried out individual and collective actions that have contributed, at least indirectly, to more humane and prosperous political communities.

The distinctive feature of evangelical political ethics is the primacy given to spiritual formation. According to Shah, this approach is a repudiation of the tendency within Western thought of giving primacy to the state in the moral formation of persons. According to classic Western thought, the core task of the state was to make men good—to assist persons in acquiring virtues that were conducive to the good life. Thus, rather than advancing "statecraft as soulcraft," to use George Will's felicitous formula, evangelicals have propounded the opposite doctrine—namely, "soulcraft as statecraft" (Shah 2009, 137). According to this perspective, moral human beings make justice possible. And what nurtures personal morality is individual conversion—the personal, inward acceptance of Christ's atonement for sin. Although state structures and sound public policies are important in fostering a just society, the evangelical perspective gives precedence to spiritual redemption as the basis for developing humane and just political societies. Since salvation demands personal acceptance of the Gospel, evangelical ethics assume that reform emerges from the transformation of persons. Development does not arise from top-down, state-centered initiatives, but from decentralized, bottom-up changes in individual people.

From time to time, evangelicals have tried to broaden the social and political agenda and develop a more comprehensive political ethic. Beginning in the late 1940s, theologian Carl F. H. Henry called attention to the importance of social and political action as part of the Christian faith. As editor of *Christianity Today*, he used his position to advance greater involvement in both domestic and international affairs. Although the National Association of Evangelicals (NAE), the organization representing some forty-five thousand member congregations, issued periodic declarations on global concerns, its priority remained on religious issues and in particular evangelism. One important educational initiative was the Peace, Freedom and Security

Studies Program. Established in 1987 with the aid of external advisors, the program aimed to encourage more informed analysis about the inter-relationship of national security, human rights, and peace (NAE 1986). Perhaps the most significant initiative to date to foster an informed political engagement has been the development of a framework document titled "For the Health of the Nation: An Evangelical Call to Civic Responsibility" (NAE 2004). The study, commissioned in 2001 and prepared by some two dozen evangelical scholars, was formally adopted by the NAE in 2004. The statement, which seeks to encourage a more biblical and comprehensive approach to public affairs, sets forth a biblical and theological rationale for action and identifies principles that should guide moral analysis and political action.

Despite the efforts to develop a broader, more robust political ethic, evangelical political theory remains underdeveloped and its sociopolitical agenda limited. Although evangelicals have been strongly associated with the Republican Party in recent elections, the reason for this is less an inherent religious affinity for Republican ideology than it is the greater sensitivity of that party and its leaders to core values and moral priorities of evangelicals. A close affinity between believers and government, church and state, can be a problem, however, as the moral claims of authentic faith can be undermined. Hence, a number of evangelicals have recently attempted to broaden the political agenda and warn of the dangers of a fusion between believers and political action. This was undoubtedly the justification for "An Evangelical Manifesto," which boldly declares, "The Evangelical soul is not for sale." Since the Christian faith demands "an allegiance higher than party, ideology, economic system or nationality," the manifesto calls on believers to rethink their approach to public life, challenging them to demonstrate a stronger commitment to spiritual values than to temporal concerns. The manifesto states, "We evangelicals see it as our duty to engage with politics, but our equal duty never to be completely equated with any party, partisan ideology, economic system, or nationality" ("An Evangelical Manifesto" 2008, 15).

The irony of evangelical politics is that, even though it has failed to develop a sophisticated political doctrine, the subordination of temporal public affairs to spiritual life in general, and to evangelism in particular, has nevertheless contributed to a distinctive political and social perspective—one that focuses on individual morality as the foundation of social and political ethics. Because evangelical politics entails a preference for decentralization, limited government, and the priority of individual action over public initiatives, it is unlikely that evangelicals will shift their allegiance toward a more government-centered approach to public life. Indeed, to the extent that concerns like global poverty, climate change, religious persecution, and human rights abuses continue at the forefront of American public policy debates, evangelicals are likely to favor small-scale, personal initiatives in addressing such issues.

THE NATURE AND IMPACT OF MISSIONARY SERVICE

The Protestant foreign missions movement began in the early nineteenth century as Congregational, Methodist, Episcopalian, and Presbyterian churches began sending missionaries overseas—first to Hawaii and then to the Middle East and the Far East. Rather than establishing their individual denominational missions organizations, Protestants created a centralized organization—the American Board of Commissioners for Foreign Missions—to manage and direct the missionary enterprise. For more than a century, the American Board shaped the nature and character of American missionary activity. By the end of the nineteenth century nearly five thousand Protestant missionaries were serving abroad. This number increased to roughly ten thousand in 1915 as young adults responded to appeals to support global evangelization and the advance of Christian societies (Reed 1983, 13).

Scholars have widely differing interpretations about the impact of nineteenth century missionary activity. For some, it was chiefly a spiritual activity designed to share the Gospel with peoples unfamiliar with Christianity. According to this perspective, missionaries did not come to impose their own social and cultural values but to educate and uplift underdeveloped peoples and to share with them the good news of salvation in Christ. Although scholars such as Stephen Neill have viewed missionary activity as an expression of cultural imperialism (Neill 1966, 11–12), others, like Arthur Schlesinger Jr., have regarded missionaries as agents of human development—as "a means to advance social progress" (Schlesinger 1974, 336–73).

After World War I, Protestant missionary activity changed, as mainline churches became less concerned with evangelism and more concerned with social justice. As a result, while the number of mainline Protestant missionaries remained largely stable for decades, the number of nondenominational and interdenominational evangelical groups expanded rapidly, eclipsing the number of mainline missionaries by the 1940s. By 1958, evangelical mission groups had over five thousand more missionaries than mainline churches. The gap became even more pronounced when the number of mainline missionaries began to decline in the 1960s while the number of missionaries from nondenominational mission organizations expanded rapidly. By 2001, the total number of full-time U.S. missionaries was more than forty-four thousand, with the vast majority of these serving with evangelical organizations (Moreau 2004, 13 and 35).

Although foreign missionary activity has rarely been involved directly in the conduct of American foreign policy, missionaries have nevertheless contributed to the global engagement of the United States. They have done so in a variety of ways.

To begin with, missionaries have played a critical role in acquiring and disseminating knowledge about foreign societies. Since evangelism required that missionaries learn the language and indigenous customs and cultural traditions, they often were the first Westerners to acquire significant appreciation and understanding of foreign cultures. Because they were often the most knowledgeable persons about foreign societies, they provided much-needed expertise to U.S. diplomats. For example, General Douglas MacArthur relied heavily on the cultural and historical expertise of missionaries who had served in the Far East, especially Burma, China, and Japan. Walter Russell Mead writes that MacArthur's reconstruction of Japan was "essentially an implementation of the missionary program at the point of bayonets." He goes on: "Without the long missionary experience America would have had neither the chutzpah or the know-how that characterized the occupation of Japan, a foreign policy venture that despite all the attendant controversy is generally considered one of the most important successful initiatives in American history" (Mead 2002, 150). To a significant degree, the United States was prepared for global leadership following World War II because of the significant international experience that missionaries had given American society in general and the government in particular. Although many missionary children followed their parents into full-time Christian service, a significant number pursued international careers in business, diplomacy, or related foreign vocations. As the United States assumed a more global perspective, the need for foreign experts increased significantly. Not surprisingly, a growing number of diplomats had missionary backgrounds, especially in the non-Western region of the Near East, Far East, and Asia. According to one estimate, about one half of "foreign-culture experts" at the time of World War II were missionary children (Hutchison 1987, 2).

Missionaries also contributed to America's global role by fostering the development of strong cross-cultural ties. Even more significantly, missionaries contributed to the notion of the world as a global society. Although missionaries tended to identify strongly with the United States and its ideals and interests, the overseas experience also contributed to the emergence of strong transnational ties—to the notion of all persons as part of a human community. This was especially the case for believers, who shared a common bond as members of Christ's universal church. Although the notion of the world as a community was espoused by the ancient Stoics and by medieval Christian thinkers like Dante, the notion of a global society of mediating institutions sharing common ideals—the notion currently expressed as global civil society—is of recent vintage. According to Mead, this idea is best attributed to the missionary movement.

> Apart from a handful of isolated intellectuals, no one before the missionaries ever thought that the world's cultures and societies had or could have enough in common to make a common global society feasible or desirable. Certainly before the missionaries no large group of people set out to build just such a world. The concept that "backward" countries could and should develop into Western-style industrial democracies grew up among missionaries, and missionary relief and development organizations like World Vision and Catholic Relief Services remain at the forefront of development efforts. The idea that governments in the Western world had a positive duty to support the development of poor countries through financial aid and other forms of assistance similarly come out of the missionary world. Most contemporary international organizations that provide relief from natural disasters, shelter refugees, train medical practitioners for poor countries, or perform other important services on an international basis can trace their origin either to missionary organizations or to the missionary milieu. (Mead 2002, 146)

In short, the missionary enterprise, through its international humanitarian and religious work, not only fostered a global consciousness but also advanced the notion of global society—the idea that all societies were a part of God's creation and therefore were part a worldwide community.

A third way that missionaries have contributed to America's global engagement is by fostering human dignity. Since Christianity teaches the infinite worth of all persons, evangelical missionaries taught and modeled values that affirmed the inherent dignity of people, regardless of gender, social class, or ethnicity. For missionaries, human dignity was not a legal doctrine or a political ideology. Rather, it was the basis of their evangelistic mission, which was to share the good news of salvation in Christ with all persons. From the outset of the missionary movement, missionaries were concerned with human well-being—and this conviction was expressed through the provision of humanitarian services and the condemnation of practices considered inhumane, such as slavery and torture.

One way that missionaries have sought to advance human dignity is through education. From the outset, missionaries played a key role in fostering literacy and establishing schools and colleges that equipped and prepared future indigenous leaders. Because women were considered unequal in traditional cultures, making education available to both girls and boys played a pivotal role in many societies. By one estimate, American and British missionaries had, by the beginning of the twentieth century, built 94 colleges, 29,458 schools, 379 hospitals, and 782 dispensaries (Hutchinson 1987, 100). John Fairbank argues that the social impact of foreign missions was probably most significant in the field of education. By 1935 American missionary activity in China was responsible for 13 Christian colleges that enrolled 5,800 students and 255 middle schools that enrolled nearly 44,000 students (Fairbank 1974, 13). American missionary activity in the Middle East was also responsible for the establishment of many educational institutions that profoundly affected Muslim societies. In particular, the humanitarian efforts on behalf of persecuted minorities in the Ottoman Empire prior to and during World War I left an indelible imprint on indigenous culture.

Missionaries also sought to advance human dignity by condemning gross human rights abuses, such as slavery, torture, and degradation of women and children. The important role of missionaries in challenging inhumane practices is best illustrated by William Carey, a British Baptist who carried out missionary work in India from 1793 until his death in 1834. When Carey became aware of *sati*—the Hindu practice of immolating widows on their husbands' funeral pyres—he publicly condemned this traditional practice (Mangalwadi 1999, 83–90).

Evangelicals have also contributed to human dignity by giving impetus to democracy and religious freedom. Robert Woodberry and Timothy Shah argue that Protestant missionary activity played an important role in fostering democratic practices by encouraging the creation of mediating institutions conducive to civil society. Indeed, they argue that missionaries were responsible for much of the development of organized civil society across much of the non-Western world (Woodberry and Shah 2004, 52). Even more importantly, missionaries helped to spread the notion of religious freedom, the basic pillar of democratic government. Since Protestantism lacked an institutional mechanism for resolving doctrinal disagreements, it tended to nurture freedom of thought that expressed itself in a multiplicity of church groups. This pluralism expressed itself in two freedoms, what Alfred Stepan calls "twin tolerations"—the independence of the state from religion and the independence of religion from government (Stepan 2000, 37–57). To be sure, missionaries have not always fostered democratic practices. But to the extent that they have emphasized liberty as a precondition for authentic faith and the creation of vigorous civic institutions for ensuring legitimacy and accountability, they have contributed to the development of values and practices that are conducive to democratic life.

THE RISE OF EVANGELICAL HUMANITARIANISM

A significant by-product of the modern missionary movement has been the expansion of humanitarian concerns and actions. The medical, educational, and relief and development projects of missionary organizations remained relatively small-scale into the early twentieth century. But humanitarian initiatives greatly expanded following World War II with the establishment of relief and development organizations like World Vision—an organization that was created to care for refugee children. Soon many other faith-based humanitarian organizations were established, both denominational organizations like Adventist Development and Relief Agency, Christian Reformed World Relief Committee, and Lutheran World Relief and nondenominational organizations like Food for the Hungry, Opportunity International, Samaritan's Purse, and World Relief. These faith-based NGOs (FNGOs) have played a critical role in meeting human needs in poor countries by providing medical care, delivering food and shelter, promoting education, improving sanitation and health care, and furnishing other similar services. These organizations have become even more important internationally, as the U.S. foreign aid program has relied increasingly on intermediary institutions like FNGOs to distribute disaster relief, provide humanitarian resources, and serve as a catalyst for development.

Much of the humanitarian work of FNGOs is designed to meet immediate human needs, as was the case in the aftermath of the December 2004 Indian Ocean tsunami that devastated coastal regions of numerous Asian countries, including Sri Lanka, Thailand, and Indonesia, leaving some 230,000 persons dead or missing and hundreds of thousands without shelter. Christian charities responded immediately, providing hundreds of millions of dollars of relief and also assisting victims in resettlement and the construction of new communities. It is estimated that private U.S. emergency relief for the devastated areas was more than $1.6 billion, far exceeding the U.S. government aid appropriated by Congress (Eberle 2008, 151). Of course, evangelical humanitarian aid was a significant portion of this private assistance.

Another area where evangelicals have played an important role in humanitarian service is in caring for refugees by providing food and shelter in wartorn environments and in resettling refugees within the United States itself. Historically, the U.S. government has relied heavily on religious organizations to advance humanitarian goals, including the caring of refugees. To be sure, the United Nations High Commissioner for Refugees plays a crucial role in providing overall management of refugee affairs. Yet, when civil war erupts, as in Sudan in the 1990s, some of the first organizations to respond are evangelical humanitarian organizations. Moreover, when regimes abuse human rights, especially religious freedom, Christian groups are able to mobilize significant political pressure in order to alter unacceptable policies.

Historically, the U.S. government has collaborated with religious organizations to meet humanitarian needs overseas. In his fine study on refugees, for example, J. Bruce Nichols shows that American religious organizations have been playing a crucial humanitarian role since the end of World War II. While church-state constitutional concerns constrained government support for domestic social and economic programs administered by churches and religious groups, Nichols shows that church-state constitutional concerns resulted in few limitations on federal funding of FNGOs. Indeed, FNGOs have not only provided specific humanitarian services but they have also helped to define "America's ties with the rest of the world" (Nichols 1988, 3).

U.S. governmental collaboration with FNGOs has greatly increased in the past two decades, as U.S. development policies shifted toward decentralization. Whereas official development assistance in the Cold War era emphasized government-to-government loans and grants, the U.S. Agency for International Development (USAID) has, since the end of the Cold War, placed a premium on poverty reduction through small-scale, local projects. Moreover, rather than relying on its own personnel to distribute funds and resources, USAID has increasingly relied on FNGOS and local grassroots organizations to advance its humanitarian goals. Since the U.S. government depends on civil society organizations to meet humanitarian needs and promote social and economic development, it is not surprising that a large portion of the budgets of FNGOs comes from the U.S. government.

Finally, it is important to call attention to the contribution of short-term missionary work that often supplements the work of evangelical FNGOs. Every year tens of thousands of church volunteers travel annually at their own expense to provide humanitarian services in poor lands. These groups carry out short-term services ranging from one or two weeks to several months, transferring financial resources to poor communities and meeting human needs in countless ways—providing medical care, protecting children from sexual abuse, supporting orphans, building clinics and sanitation facilities, and constructing shelters, schools, and homes.

THE EMERGENCE OF FOREIGN POLICY ADVOCACY

The most visible manifestation of contemporary global engagement by American evangelicals is their increased advocacy for foreign policy initiatives. To a significant degree, political advocacy has been shaped by a commitment to core moral values—the sacredness of human life, the well-being of families and children, religious liberty, and the priority of peace. During the Cold War, evangelicals remained adamantly opposed to Communism because they believed that that ideology was based on atheism and hostile to the Christian faith. Despite their vigorous opposition to Communism, evangelicals rarely mobilized resources to advance specific foreign policy objectives. This began to change in the late 1970s, as evangelicals and fundamentalists became increasingly engaged on domestic social and political issues.

One of the earliest manifestations of evangelicals' quest for increased involvement in foreign policy issues was NAE's program on "Peace, Freedom and Security Studies" (PFSS). The PFSS initiative represented a belated effort by evangelical leaders to respond to the challenge of nuclear arms control that had engaged mainline Protestant denominations and in particular the Roman Catholic Church. In 1983, the U.S. Conference of Catholic Bishops, the decision-making body of the American Catholic church, had issued a landmark pastoral letter on nuclear deterrence titled "The Challenge of Peace." Because the letter reflected a competent command of the issues and involved careful moral analysis rooted in biblical reflection, the letter was regarded as a sound ethical guide on one of the most morally challenging foreign policy issues of the time. Thus, when the NAE leadership launched the PFSS initiative, it did so to assist parishioners in confronting the challenges of promoting peace in the nuclear age. According to the program's forty-seven-page "guidelines," the aim of the PFSS was to encourage evangelicals to "make a distinctive and needed contribution to the debate on security issues in our country and to progress toward a world, safe for free societies, that resolves international conflict without war" (NAE 1986).

The issue that first began to capture evangelical interest in the late 1980s was that of religious persecution in the Soviet Union. As evangelicals became increasingly aware of the persecution of Pentecostals and other believers in the USSR, they demanded greater action by the U.S. government—in particular, calling on the Soviet government to permit greater emigration of such refugees. Partly in response to this initiative, the Soviets began to allow a growing number of Christians to emigrate. Since many of these religious refugees came to the United States, evangelical churches and organizations played an important role in facilitating their resettlement in local communities.

From the mid-1990s to 2005, evangelicals addressed a variety of global concerns, leading to major foreign policy change in several areas of concern. These included religious freedom, human trafficking, the Sudan peace accord, debt relief for low-income countries, and health care, especially the HIV/AIDS pandemic in Africa. Although each of these initiatives entailed cooperation with other political groups, policy reform would have been unlikely without the widespread grassroots support of evangelicals. Moreover, given their skepticism toward ecumenism, what is most surprising about their foreign policy engagement is evangelicals' willingness to cooperate in what Allen Hertzke has called an "unlikely alliance" with Jews, secular public policy advocates, religious minorities, and others to advance human rights (Hertzke 2004).

Evangelicalism remains a decentralized, grassroots movement. As a result, evangelicals find it difficult to assess global problems from an informed, moral perspective and nearly impossible to devise a comprehensive, coherent public policy strategy. Unlike the Roman Catholic Church, which can speak authoritatively from its traditions and through its hierarchical organization, evangelicals have no deep moral traditions or organizational structure to guide reflection and action. They do, however, have one resource that mainline Protestants and Catholics lack—the entrepreneurial activism that comes from a decentralized, grassroots movement. Although developing public policy advocacy is challenging, evangelicals, once mobilized, can exert significant influence. When the World Evangelical Fellowship, a leading international alliance of evangelical denominations, took up the cause of religious persecution in the early 1990s, it spearheaded the cause of religious liberty. It did so by designating a day of prayer to raise awareness about religious persecution. At the height of its influence in the late 1990s, tens of thousands of congregations were participating in the International Day of Prayer for the Persecuted Church. Similarly, when evangelical entrepreneurs like James Dobson, Pat Robertson, Charles Colson, Franklin Graham, and others have taken up issues like religious persecution, global hunger, or the mass killings in southern Sudan through their extensive constituent mailings, television programs, and radio broadcasts, they have mobilized millions of followers. To the extent that evangelicals have influenced U.S. global engagement, they have done so by mobilizing their members to action—providing the "foot soldiers" for moral reform (Marshall 2008). Indeed, what has been so remarkable about evangelical global engagement on human rights issues is that evangelicals had the most extensive ties with believers in the Global South. As Allan Hertzke has observed, "the community most likely to identify with the New Christendom of the global south, with the suffering church, is the very one with social networks and motivation capable of mobilizing pressure on the political system" (Hertzke 2004, 35).

To illustrate the growing efficacy of evangelical public policy efforts, I briefly sketch the important role of evangelicals on two recent issues—*religious freedom* and the *Sudan peace process*. The first issue that led to significant evangelical political advocacy was religious freedom. In the 1980s, evangelical groups, led by the NAE, had lobbied the U.S. government to grant asylum to Pentecostals and other believers facing persecution and discrimination in the Soviet Union. With American prodding, the Soviet government allowed a growing number of Christians to emigrate. Once the refugees arrived in the United States, evangelical churches played an indispensable role in assisting in their resettlement. But with this exception, evangelicals remained unaware of and unconcerned about the plight of persecuted Christians. Mainline Protestant denominations were similarly oblivious to religious persecution, focusing instead on structural issues like global inequality, war and arms control, and racial justice. Secular human rights organizations like Amnesty International and Human Rights Watch did not even monitor religious persecution. Thus, even though two hundred million Christians lived in countries where they faced significant religious persecution and another four hundred million believers faced nontrivial restrictions on their religious freedom, religious liberty remained a neglected problem.

That changed in the mid-1990s, when Michael Horowitz, a Jewish human rights lawyer, began prodding evangelical leaders to address the suffering of fellow believers (Hertzke 2004, 59). A number of developments occurred in

1996 that began to mobilize evangelicals. First, Horowitz and Nina Shea, director of religious freedom at Freedom House, hosted a conference with evangelical leaders to highlight the widespread persecution of Christians. Second, the NAE adopted a declaration that highlighted the problem of religious persecution and called on U.S. government officials to make this religious persecution a priority by increasing monitoring and accountability (NAE 1996). Additionally, Paul Marshall, a leading scholar of religious freedom, published *Their Blood Cries Out*, a book that helped galvanize evangelical support for religious freedom. Ironically, most Protestant Churches, along with the National Council of Churches, remained on the sideline of this debate. Only the governmental affairs office of the Episcopal Church was fully engaged on the issue.

In 1997, a bill sponsored by Rep. Frank Wolf and Sen. Arlen Specter on religious persecution was introduced and overwhelmingly passed by the House of Representatives. But because it called for economic sanctions against regimes abusing the right of religious freedom, it was strongly opposed by the business community. A less demanding, more flexible bill (sponsored by Sens. Don Nickles and Joseph Lieberman) was then introduced into the Senate. On October 9, 1998, the Senate overwhelmingly approved this measure. Since there was no time left to resolve differences in the two bills, Rep. Wolf signaled his support for the more moderate Nickles-Lieberman bill, and the following day the House approved it by acclamation. Although the Clinton administration officials had opposed both measures, President Clinton signed the International Religious Freedom Act (IRFA) into law later in the month.

Even with the passage of IRFA, religious networks and FNGOs continue to play an important role in promoting religious freedom. They do so domestically by disseminating information about religious persecution and by lobbying decision-makers. Internationally, religious actors help advance the cause of religious freedom by serving as a source of information on religious persecution. Since missionaries and faith-based NGOs generally maintain close contact with indigenous people, they are often the best informed about human rights abuses and the best data sources for U.S. embassy reporting on religious persecution.

Sudan Peace Process

Although tribal conflict had long existed in Sudan, a bitter civil war between the Muslim north and the Christian/animist south began in 1983. The war started when the Khartoum government began imposing Islamic law (*sharia*) on non-Muslims in the southern, oil-rich region of the country. When those in the south resisted this development, bitter fighting ensued. To pacify the south, the Muslim regime resorted to scorched earth practices involving rampant killing of civilians, mass deportation, burning of villages, destruction of crops, and the killing of livestock. When relief organizations sought to provide humanitarian aid to the refugees, government forces would confiscate food and medical aid or impede their delivery. The genocidal campaign even involved slavery—a practice that Christian Solidarity International, a Swiss-based Christian NGO, confronted with a "slavery redemption" campaign.

Despite the growing condemnation of human rights abuses by religious and human rights groups, the Muslim regime continued its war of attrition against the Sudan People's Liberation Movement (SPLM). Although some two million Africans were killed in this genocidal war, what mobilized evangelicals was not so much the mass killing as the realization that the war was being waged to persecute and kill persons who did not accept Islam. Thus, when leaders like Charles Colson of Prison Fellowship, Franklin Graham of Samaritan's Purse, and Jim Dobson of Focus on the Family began highlighting Sudan's religiously based genocidal campaign, a broad grassroots movement emerged and began calling on the U.S. government to address the humanitarian crisis in Sudan. One small, informal association—the Midland Ministerial Alliance, a group of some two hundred churches from President Bush's hometown of Midland, Texas—was especially successful in publicizing the suffering of southern Sudanese.

As a result of the growing awareness of the mass suffering in Sudan, a loose coalition of evangelicals, human rights groups, and religious NGOs began lobbying Congress and the president to take action. President Bush responded by appointing former Sen. John Danforth as Special Envoy to Sudan, while the House and the Senate took up the issue in their respective chambers. After intense lobbying, in October 2002, Congress passed the Sudan Peace Act—calling for increased pressure on the Khartoum regime to end the fighting. Fundamentally, the Act provided the president with tools to pressure the Khartoum regime to end the fighting. In particular, it provided for financial aid to the southern area of Sudan not controlled by the government, required that the government and rebels negotiate in good faith, established a timetable by which to achieve a settlement, and authorized the president to curtail oil revenues if the government failed to negotiate in good faith.

As a result of this external pressure, a Comprehensive Peace Agreement (CPA) was signed at the end of 2004. The CPA called for a cease-fire between the ruling Muslims and the southern rebels (SPLM), the sharing of oil revenues, and the creation of a power-sharing government. The parties also agreed that a census would be taken in 2007, and new elections would be held in 2009 followed by a referendum in the south in 2011 to determine whether southern Sudan would remain within the country or become a separate state. To assist in keeping peace in Sudan, the United Nations established a ten-thousand-person peacekeeping force known as UNMIS—UN Mission in Sudan.

Implementation of the CPA has been difficult (I.C.G. 2008). One contributing factor was the death in mid-2005 of John Garang, the head of the SPLM. A second impediment has been the bitter conflict in Darfur, a large, barren region in western Sudan. Although the north-south and Darfur conflicts have not been resolved, a fragile peace exists in southern Sudan, while the killing in Darfur has been reduced with the introduction of an African peacekeeping force. Still, deep distrust remains between the north and the south, and many major challenges remain if a permanent peace is to be achieved. Whether the terms of the CPA can be fulfilled in the future is unclear. Since the Khartoum government failed to complete a census in 2007 as called for by the CPA, the national elections were not held in 2009 but pushed to 2010. More importantly, the inability to settle border issues, especially in the oil-rich Abyei region, is likely to imperil the scheduled 2011 referendum (Winter).

Since the Darfur crisis led some religious and human rights groups to shift their attention to the immediate humanitarian needs in that region, keeping pressure on the Khartoum regime to fulfill the terms of the CPA has become more difficult. For example, while evangelical groups continue to focus primarily on the peace process in southern Sudan, mainline Protestant and African American churches have been much more involved in halting the killing in Darfur.

EVANGELICAL GLOBAL INFLUENCE: LONG TERM AND GROWING

Contrary to conventional wisdom, American evangelicals have played an important role in the world for nearly two centuries. Beginning with the global engagement of missionaries, evangelicals have fostered cross-cultural understanding and highlighted the importance of global concerns. More specifically, they have helped to propagate values and practices conducive to human dignity and democratic governance. Additionally, by modeling modern practices and building transnational institutions in foreign societies, evangelical missions have helped to create civic institutions in foreign lands, providing a foundation for the expanding network of international governmental and nongovernmental organizations. To a significant degree, evangelical global engagement has contributed to an emerging global civil society.

Unlike Roman Catholics, evangelicals do not have a developed social and political doctrine to guide thought and action in international affairs. Nevertheless, the evangelical tradition has produced a distinctive approach to public affairs—one that emphasizes the spiritual over the temporal, the personal over the institutional. The absence of a developed political theory has not prevented evangelicals from carrying out public policy initiatives. Rather, the evangelical tradition has advanced human dignity through a nongovernmental strategy that highlights the spiritual and moral transformation of persons as the basis of justice. Indeed, a major contribution of evangelicals to the less developed regions of the world is the promotion of human dignity. But in advancing humanitarian concerns, evangelicals continue to affirm the priority of the spiritual over the temporal. The priority of the spiritual was recently highlighted by Franklin Graham, the head of the Billy Graham Evangelistic Association and president of Samaritan's Purse, a leading evangelical relief and development organization, who said, "Samaritan's Purse is not primarily a relief and development organization; rather, it is an evangelistic organization that carries out relief and development" (Graham 2008).

In recent years, evangelicals have become more concerned with specific U.S. foreign policies. They have expressed their concerns through grassroots advocacy centering on a limited number of basic moral issues, such as human rights, religious freedom, and global peace. Although evangelicals remain skeptical of governmental action as a way to improve the human condition, they have collaborated in several major public policy initiatives. Even though their contributions to international affairs and U.S. foreign policy remain modest, evangelicals can continue to make an important contribution to a just global order if they remain faithful to the core principles of their tradition.

Chapter Seven

Evangelicals and Foreign Policy in an Era of Conflict

Eric Patterson and Jacob Lenerville

During the 2004 election season, one of us visited Saddleback Church, one of the most influential evangelical churches in the world due to its founder's books on "the purpose-driven life." Pastor Rick Warren had long eschewed explicit political involvement, and with national elections just days away, his only pronouncement was that it was his personal opinion that we should support candidates who value human life. This was tame when compared to many religious leaders, but was also much less energetic than the Rick Warren of 2008, most notably his crusade over the past three years on behalf of "life" in the developing world and his hosting a civil forum for the two presidential candidates at Saddleback Church. Pastor Warren has hardly become a political revolutionary, but he seems to be taking a path well trod by evangelicals that begins with disdain or indifference toward politics and evolves over time into a more complicated and nuanced engagement with political issues. Billy Graham, Pat Robertson, Jerry Falwell, and others have followed a similar trajectory.

American evangelical Christianity is coming of age regarding U.S. foreign policy in at least two ways. One is that each generation of evangelicals proceeds through a period of its own maturation, from political skepticism to political engagement in some form. This is an ongoing feature of evangelicalism. The second is the arrival on the international scene of American evangelicals interested in more than foreign missionary work, whether elected officials in the aftermath of the Republican revolution of 1994, compassionate conservatives in the Bush administration, or thought leaders like Rick Warren. Indeed, in the year prior to this writing, self-appointed evangelical spokespeople have published an "Evangelical Manifesto" and a letter to Muslim clerics worldwide (the Yale Letter).

This chapter examines evangelical Christianity in the United States as it relates to foreign policy and international relations. We briefly consider the theological rationale for evangelicalism and politics, identify trends in evangelical political engagement over the past several decades, and then examine how evangelicals think about foreign policy and conflict in the twenty-first century. While biblical doctrine provides only a modest foundation upon which evangelicals have built their foreign policy views, the combination of religious understanding with evolution in world affairs (e.g., Communism, the birth of Israel, September 11) has indeed informed the foreign policy views of today's American evangelicals.

THE THEOLOGICAL ORIGINS OF AN EVANGELICAL FOREIGN POLICY

Although everyone seems to know who evangelicals are, there is no single, standardized definition. The Institute for the Study of American Evangelicalism (ISAE) at Wheaton College provides three ways of defining evangelicalism. One is to focus, as British historian David Bebbington has, on key doctrinal emphases shared across evangelical denominations: that (1) Christianity can definitively change an individual human being due to (2) Christ's death and resurrection, (3) that the Bible itself is God's expressed message for today, and (4) that Christians should actively spread (evangelize) the faith. A second approach is to define evangelicals as those churches who have a "style" or practice of evangelization. Finally, evangelicalism can be defined as the postwar Protestant movement that rejected both anti-intellectual fundamentalism and liberal mainline denominations. It is characterized by individuals like Billy Graham and cooperative ventures like the National Association of Evangelicals (NAE), which represents fifty member denominations and over thirty million American Protestants.[1] For our purposes, we assume that North American evangelicals are those who would express a commitment to Bebbington's four doctrinal characteristics. Practically speaking, they also are likely to routinely participate in a congregation that is a member of the NAE or embraces its values.

STARTING WITH A FOREIGN POLICY "BLANK SLATE"

At this point, take a step back from your knowledge of American evangelicals and politics in the past quarter century and ask the question, "Starting with a *tabula rasa,* what foreign policy commitments logically flow from the four theological commitments noted above?" In other words, before we look at the evidence of history, surveys, and position papers, it is useful to engage in a theoretical exercise to examine what core foreign policy values might logically arise from the essential doctrinal statements of evangelical Christians.

Starting with that blank slate, we propose that the basic political ramifications of evangelical religious commitments might include these: (1) evangelicals hold strong faith commitments and oppose most restrictions on private conscience, and (2) evangelicals hold strong faith commitments and oppose most public restrictions on faith practice and evangelism. These two bedrock commitments have narrow, but significant, political ramifications.

First, as we note in the historical section that follows, evangelical forms of Christianity routinely emerge in church history as individuals seek a return to the simple doctrines and practices of early Christianity. Although it was not called such in colonial America, the impulse to evangelize Indians and the First Great Awakening were clearly evangelical. Early America witnessed robust religious competition between established and what we would call evangelical denominations. For example, in George Washington's hometown of Alexandria, Baptist preacher Jeremiah Moore was jailed for violating the religious monopoly of Virginia's state church (the Anglican or Episcopal Church). Moore was defended by Patrick Henry, who trumpeted, "Great God gentlemen, a man in prison for preaching the Gospel of the Son of God?" Moore was released and ultimately founded several famous Baptist churches that still operate in northern Virginia and Washington, D.C. [2]

Early America's religious competition was in large part a return to the doctrines and practices of the early Church, which generally meant bucking established institutional religious bodies in favor of individual or small group conscience. Hence, it is unsurprising that it is from the Virginia of that time that we get the Virginia Statute of Religious Freedoms and the U.S. Bill of Rights, the most notable of which is the First Amendment's promise of rights to religion, assembly, speech, and press. Evangelicals strongly support such rights as necessary for the practice of their faith as individuals and collectives. Hence, policies that circumscribe such liberties, either at home or abroad, would be viewed negatively.

So too, evangelicals believe that they have a mission to share their faith with others; indeed, Christ's final command was to take his message around the globe. Evangelicals do not have a history of imposed proselytization like the Counter-Reformation and Catholic conquest of the New World. But they are optimistic that within a marketplace of competing ideas about spirituality and faith, their appeals about Jesus Christ will result in conversions. Consequently, policies that circumscribe the liberty to share one's faith or to do missionary work, either at home or abroad, would be seen as negative.

Thus far, we have suggested that, beginning with a blank slate, evangelicals' essential faith commitments would yield policy goals that protect individual religious and related freedoms as well as the opportunity to share one's faith. Consequently, it should not be surprising that evangelicals surveying the world scene would consider the framework of American liberties a model for all. The tools and characteristics of globalization—easy travel, global access, advanced communications technologies, the opening of closed societies, a competition of values, and the like—are conducive to worldwide evangelism. In turn, policies that circumscribe such liberties would be viewed negatively, be they the overtly anti-Christian persecution in Afghanistan, denials of entry visas by Russia, or Chinese Internet censorship.

In terms of actual policies, evangelicals would likely support at a minimum the rule of law that privileges individual expressions as found in the U.S. Bill of Rights, that such "inalienable" liberties are universal (essential human rights and civil liberties), and that governments should be limited in their powers so as to prevent them from restricting the rights of citizens and religious groups. Indeed, this theoretical constellation of beliefs is largely consonant with mainstream American values, which have always been informed to some degree by religion (and vice versa). Thus the ideal evangelical political platform would likely find tens of millions of sympathizers in U.S. politics who are not necessarily conservative in their Christian faith, from the ACLU to the Libertarian Party.

A HISTORICAL OVERVIEW OF EVANGELICALS AND AMERICAN POLITICS

Were we to anticipate those foreign policy preferences derived from the core religious values shared by evangelicals, we would expect them to advocate for policies that champion private conscience and public expressions of faith. But what does the historical record indicate? From the seventeenth century until well into the nineteenth century—that is, from the First Great Awakening until World War II—the direct impact of evangelical forms of Christianity is difficult to discern. Certainly there was not the interest group-style advocacy on most international issues that we have come to expect today from organizations like the Christian Coalition. But this is unsurprising considering the isolationist thrust of mainstream U.S. foreign policy for the majority of this time, and the tendency to leave international affairs to govern themselves (apart from Western hemisphere sphere of influence issues). Yet it would be unwise to dismiss this period of development. In fact, the ideals of the American Revolution (e.g., liberties of religion, speech, and assembly) and future mass political movements (e.g., abolition, temperance) owe much to religious impulses that were the precursors to contemporary evangelical Christianity. Indeed, the Great Awakenings' emphases on the human condition, as well as the "calling" of America as a bastion of Christian morals and freedom provide a primordial and lasting basis for Christianity-influenced U.S. foreign policy (Kurth 1999).

The early twentieth century proceeded in much the same vein. Pastors and other religious leaders of these times focused on the saving of a nation by the reaching out to millions of individual lost souls. Foreign missionary activity expanded for the same purpose. Most importantly, evangelicals began to define themselves domestically as distinct from "worldly" mainline churches and "otherworldly" fundamentalist churches.

World War II coincided with, and propelled forward, the formal organization of evangelicals. In fact, the NAE was formed in 1942. The rise of the Soviet Union and the fall of the Iron Curtain during the Cold War led to the first, "hard" foreign policy of contemporary evangelicalism—anti-Communism. In his famous 1949 Los Angeles revival message, Billy Graham said, "Communism is not only an economic interpretation of life—communism is a religion that is inspired, directed, and motivated by the Devil himself who has declared war against Almighty God" (Marty 1999, 152). These feelings of anti-Communism were held by Christians on both sides of the political spectrum; Reinhold Niebuhr (1953) titled a chapter in his book *Christian Realism and Political Problems*, "Why Is Communism So Evil?" and wrote that atheistic ideology leads Communism to be "consistently totalitarian in every political and historical environment" (41). Interestingly, evangelicals ultimately were more supportive of anti-Communism than Niebuhr's natural political and religious allies on the left. The policy implications of anti-Communism included support for a foreign policy of containment and a tough, pragmatic approach to dealing with threats continues to mark contemporary evangelical perspectives on foreign policy.

The second specific area of widespread foreign policy agreement among evangelicals following World War II was support for the nation of Israel, which asserted its sovereignty in 1948. This derived from a premillennial dispensationalist eschatology that believes history moves in stages toward an ultimate showdown between good and evil where Christ will return to earth, triumph over evil, and reign supreme. Many evangelicals (and fundamentalists) believe that the birth of a modern Jewish state is a harbinger of the end times and that America will be blessed for supporting the chosen people of the Bible (McMahon 2006; Sifton 2005).

So the first decades of the contemporary evangelical era were marked by support in practice for Israel and anti-Communism. Support for Israel derived directly from evangelicals' understanding of the Bible as "God's message for today" and the anti-Communist/anti-atheist stance aligned with our *tabula rasa* principle of religious freedom.

The cultural revolution of the 1960s and 1970s and Communism's successes abroad presented an increasingly threatening world to evangelicals. Evangelicalism emphasizes the need to challenge popular culture instead of simply withdrawing from it (as in fundamentalism) or capitulating to it (as in the liberal, social justice traditions). In the foreign policy context, this meant moving beyond just preaching against Communism and society's woes to taking overt action to influence society and politics.

This phase of evangelicalism was most evident in the actions of organizations and interest groups such as Concerned Women for America, the Family Research Council, Focus on the Family, the National Federation for Decency, and the premier conservative group of the 1980s, the Moral Majority (Wilcox 2000, 164). Using pamphlets and direct-mail organization, the Moral Majority attempted to influence the government through political mobilization of conservative evangelicals. In the 1980s, domestic concerns trumped foreign policy in evangelical circles, particularly as they pertained to abortion and other family issues. Anti-Communist sentiment continued to run strong, though, like the Soviet Union itself, the issue abated some in importance. For instance, Pat Robertson scarcely mentioned Communism in his 1988 presidential campaign (Martin 1996, 39). Nonetheless, evangelicals remained staunch supporters of Israel. A Moral Majority pamphlet mandated that "one cannot belong to Moral Majority, Inc. without making the commitment to support the state of Israel in its battle for survival" (from Zwier 1982, 48).

Scholars disagree over the level of disappointment with the Carter and Reagan presidencies for their failure to advance the evangelicals' domestic agenda (Martin 1996, 200, 226; Wilcox 2000, 4–5). However, during the next two decades, evangelicals saw the success of the Christian Coalition, the Republican Revolution of 1994, and the election and reelection of George W. Bush, someone whom evangelicals definitely viewed as one of their own. Additionally, the explosive growth of the NAE, the widening and broadening of its constituencies across the political aisle, and recent overt political documents such as the "Evangelical Manifesto" (discussed below) demonstrate a confident sense of identity and a desire to influence both domestic and foreign policy in the United States.

EVANGELICAL OPINION, FOREIGN POLICY, AND CONFLICT
SINCE 9/11

Not long ago, we attended a seminar in Washington, D.C., given by an academic specialist on trends in Africa. The lecture was directed to mid-level government officials, and surprisingly, it made no mention of religion whatsoever. When queried about religion during the question period, the speaker asserted that "fundamentalist forms of Islam and evangelical Christianity" were headed toward a bloody showdown across the continent. This charge—that evangelicals are militaristic and antagonistic—has been leveled at American evangelicals, especially after the election of George W. Bush and the launching of the war on terrorism.

But is this portrait accurate? Is aggressive militancy an identifying characteristic of post-9/11 evangelicals? Are they mostly ideologues willing to export democracy and Christianity at the point of a gun? Are they somehow different than mainstream America on issues of international affairs and conflict? At the broadest level, what foreign policy issues are most important to evangelicals?

While contemporary foreign policy opinion coalesced following World War II, we have suggested that evangelical Christian impulses are at the very root of American history since the founding. Moreover, it is likely that the theological predispositions of evangelicals should make them champions of policies that protect and promote both private and public (and both local and global) expressions of faith in the form of human rights and religious liberty. Likewise, we have demonstrated that evangelicals tended to be anti-Communist and pro-Israel during the Cold War, and unsurprisingly, generally were aligned with the Republican Party during the 1980s–2000.

In this section, we analyze two sources of evidence for the attitudes of evangelicals on foreign policy, international relations, and conflict. The first is survey data, the second content analysis of three widely distributed pan-evangelical documents: "For the Health of the Nation" (2004), the Yale Letter (Yale Center for Faith and Culture 2007), and "An Evangelical Manifesto" (2008).

Evangelical Opinion on Foreign Policy and Global Conflict

Survey research provides a window into the attitudes of evangelicals regarding specific contemporary foreign policy issues. Until recently, the conventional wisdom was that evangelical Christians had their heads buried in the sand when it came to foreign policy. The evidence suggests otherwise. Following the 2004 national election, the Pew Forum found foreign policy to be "very important" to 75 percent of evangelicals surveyed. Indeed, 29 percent of evangelicals felt foreign policy to be "the most important" issue of national politics, putting it just behind social issues (gay marriage, abortion) and far ahead of economic issues (Green et al. 2004). The National Survey of Religion and Politics (2005) found a 7 percent increase in "support for internationalism" among the general population, but a 12 percent increase among evangelical Protestants overall.[3] Exit polls taken by the Pew Forum confirmed the continuation of this trend into the 2006 midterm elections. While "values issues" were still the most important to a plurality (49 percent) of Christians, among white evangelicals the war in Iraq was second at 47 percent.[4] In short, the concerns of evangelicals largely corresponded to those of Americans in general. (In the same survey the Iraq war was the top priority for 53 percent of the general sample.)

However, not all scholars find evangelicals to be uniquely supportive of a broad international agenda. Wuthnow and Lewis (2008, 204) find that Americans with *any* decidedly religious point of view are more likely to support "altruistic" foreign policies; in other words, support for philanthropic and humanitarian concerns is not significant to evangelicals. According to Wuthnow and Lewis, when evangelicals are asked about political trade-offs, they are somewhat more likely to support military strength over altruism.

Greenberg and Berktold (2004, 18) similarly concluded that support for "strength" in foreign policy (strong military, supporting the war on terrorism, etc.) surpassed support for altruistic policies among white evangelicals. However, the survey also noted that white evangelicals gave money and time toward evangelism-focused religious organizations at a much higher rate (74 percent) than did nonevangelical Christians (42 percent) or non-Christians (27 percent). Furthermore, they donated money to the poor and other causes at a higher rate than did non-Christians (84 percent to 75 percent). This reflects the nuanced preferences of evangelicals: they are concerned about world affairs, but are also more socially and politically conservative. Thus they prefer an international agenda that is accomplished primarily through faith-based NGOs (as noted in table 2 of the survey appendix).

What about evangelical opinion in the wake of September 11? Before we look at specific survey data, there were at least two broad impacts. First, 9/11 likely strengthened the sentiments of many evangelicals on certain points— in particular, the spread of democratization, support for Israel, and the dangers of fundamentalism. Second, in those areas that demanded international cooperation, such as opposition to abortion policies in the Third World, such relationships were strained (Kristof 2004).

Evangelicals were consistently the most supportive group of Americans of the foreign actions undertaken by the Bush administration (including the war on terrorism, Iraq, and other international affairs) and of the policy of preemptive war; this support remained positive for evangelicals even when controlled for party, ideology, and other basic demographics (Guth 2004).

Furthermore, many evangelicals, like many other Americans, saw and continue to see the war on terrorism as a battle between good and evil, and thus strongly supported defense spending toward that end. In the late 1990s, evangelical support for defense spending was no different than that of most conservatives and religious voters (Wilcox 2000, 49). But by 2002, evangelicals' support for defense spending had outpaced most other groups (Guth 2004).

Part of the support for the war on terrorism reflects continued support for Israel and a distrust of Islam. Guth (2004) found that evangelicals held the least favorable view of Islam; indeed evangelicalism was the only tradition to be statistically significant both when controlled for political variables and demographics. Nonetheless, some evangelicals have attempted to reach out to Muslims—for example, through the Yale Letter discussed below.

What about using torture on suspected terrorists? A 2006 Pew Research Center survey showed that only 13 percent of white evangelicals believed the use of torture in interrogation can "often be justified."[5] A full 36 percent, however, did believe it can "sometimes" be used. This differed only marginally from the general sample interviewed (at 15 percent and 31 percent).

Finally, what of Israel? Survey data indicates that evangelicals continue to staunchly support Israel, often rejecting attempts to cede land from Israel or to form a Palestinian state (whether led by radicals in Hamas or the more moderate Palestinian Authority). They partially advocate from within the discourse of the war on terrorism, but much of the argument continues to stem from eschatology. Indeed, 69 percent of white evangelicals in the 2006 Pew Forum survey believe God gave Israel to the Jews; that same survey also shows that 59 percent believe in the Israeli state for the fulfillment of eschatological prophesies.[6] When the Bush administration called for Israel to cease military offensives in the West Bank, the White House received more than one hundred thousand critical emails. Nearly 50,000 postcards were sent in opposition to the "Road Map for Peace" (Zunes 2005). Accordingly, in a 2004 survey, 64 percent of evangelicals agreed or strongly agreed with the statement "The U.S. should support Israel over Palestinians in the Middle East" (see table 1 of the survey). This is nearly twice the percentage of the consolidated sample population (35 percent) and more than three times that of those who are religiously unaffiliated (20 percent).

EVANGELICALS ON RELIGIOUS FREEDOM, POVERTY, TRAFFICKING, AND OTHER ISSUES

When it comes to the "high politics" issues of war, particularly in the context of post–September 11, we found that evangelicals are not oblivious to foreign policy. Indeed, evangelicals tended to be among the most supportive of the Bush administration's policies regarding the war on terrorism, and on many issues—for example, the use of harsh interrogation techniques—evangelicals are in the mainstream of America.

Evangelicals also are concerned about other issues in international life. For example, they support international action (both in terms of influence and possible intervention) to support human and religious rights. While the origins of this lie in the 1970s with the persecution of Christians and Jews behind the Iron Curtain, evangelicals have placed greater stress on this issue in the post–Cold War years. William Martin (1999, 75–76) noted that in 1996, members of the State Department started speaking of the "10/40 Window"—the geographical segment of the world with the highest persecution of Christians.[7] Yet the term had been used by missionaries for a decade before it was picked up by the foreign service.

Three states tend to get the most negative attention from evangelicals: China, North Korea, and Sudan. Evangelicals opposed granting "most favored nation" trading status to China and have vocally condemned religious persecution there. Due to its nuclear threat and atrocious human rights record (against religion in particular), North Korea is considered a major political issue by the NAE, which pushed for the North Korea Human Rights Act. In the case of Sudan, much of the Darfur conflict is directed by Arab Muslims against black Muslims and Christians. Consequently, as the *New York Times* noted, President Bush's "core constituency . . . [evangelicals have] been pushing him to be more active on Sudan," with the United States the sole major power to define the conflict as "genocide" (see Kristof 2004). Interestingly, both North Korea and Sudan were isolated in 2000 by the NAE, which cohosted the "Second Summit of Christian Leaders on World-Wide Religious Persecution: An Examination of Sudan and North Korea."[8]

The Fourth National Survey of Religion and Politics questioned its participants on international issues (outside of national security) and asked whether such issues should be given "high priority," "some priority," or "low priority." While no majority in any group believed religious persecution should be a high priority for foreign policy, a plurality (43 percent) of traditional evangelicals held this belief. This is significant, since it is double the number among the general population. For sake of comparison, for evangelicals this figure was 10 percent lower than fighting AIDS and 3 percent lower than famine relief (table 2 of the survey).

Evangelicals' interest in religious freedom is interwoven with related issues, from "good Samaritan" concerns about poverty and disease to strong sentiments in favor of democracy. Evangelicals largely supported AIDS relief under the Bush administration (President's Emergency Program for AIDS Relief-PEPFAR), in part because he advocated congruent positions on sex education and abstinence. Similarly, evangelicals are likely to support democracy promotion in some form. Rooted in the Great Awakenings, these sentiments have lent a religious tone to the American democratic experiment that persists to this day. Moreover, many evangelicals hold to a version of Max Weber's Protestant ethic thesis, that the Protestant Reformation laid the foundation for the development of capitalism and democracy in the West (Anderson, 2004; Patterson, 2005). Huntington (1991, 75) argued that Protestant doctrines of individualism underlay both the "first wave" and later waves of democracy. He also asserted that Protestant churches (as civic institutions) are more democratic, a point supported by the broader resource mobilization and civil rights literatures. Many evangelicals tend to support international democratization, at least in theory, because it facilitates for individual religious freedom and is more likely to set conditions for peace with the United States.

Another foreign policy topic is the relationship of the United States to international organizations. Evangelicals traditionally have distrusted multilateral organizations such as the United Nations, largely due to an eschatological concern that the consolidation of power in the UN will result in a loss of, or adversely affect, personal freedoms, and ultimately may result in an ungodly, one-world government. Such institutions are often seen as tainted by European atheism (leading to views such as population control) and lack of democratic accountability. The survey data reflects this concern: significant negative feelings exist among evangelicals concerning U.S. cooperation with the UN or with having our troops operate under UN control (Guth 2004). When controlled for demographics and political party, these negative feelings remained statistically significant, a finding unique to evangelicals. Political conservatives, evangelicals included, tend to deride the UN and other international agencies as wasteful, bureaucratic, meddling, and unaccountable, and prefer the actions of missionaries and charitable organizations (e.g., World Vision, Samaritan's Purse) over UN diplomats and ICC judges.

In the past decade, evangelicals have networked with other faith groups and the wider human rights community on a variety of issues, resulting in significant legislative victories—primarily on behalf of religious freedom. The first such victory, sparked interestingly by a non-Christian whose activism was critical to long-term success, was the passage of the landmark International Religious Freedom Act (1998). The act made the promotion of religious and related freedoms abroad and the denunciation of persecution key elements of U.S. foreign policy. It included the creation of an indepen-

dent U.S. Commission on International Religious Freedom and a State Department Office of International Religious Freedom headed by an ambassador-at-large. Other legislative victories followed—the Trafficking Victims
Protection Act (2000), the Sudan Peace Act (2002), and the North Korea
Human Rights Act (2004).[9] In recent years, evangelicals have emphasized
global "creation care"—that is, foreign policy that addresses climate change
and other environmental policies (McMahon 2006).

RECENT EVANGELICAL WRITING ON INTERNATIONAL AFFAIRS

In recent years evangelical spokespeople have taken public stands on political issues ranging far beyond the narrow domestic "values" issues of the
Moral Majority in the 1980s or the Christian Coalition in the 1990s. More
importantly, the notion that evangelicals only reside in the Republican Party
has come under assault, led most notably by former president Jimmy Carter
and the prolific author Jim Wallis. Indeed, polls indicate that, at least among
younger voters, many defected from the GOP to vote for Barack Obama in
the 2008 election. At the same time, gubernatorial victories for Republicans
in Virginia and New Jersey in 2009 suggest that it is too soon to render long-
term judgments on changes in the partisan attachments of evangelicals.
Nonetheless, we may be in the midst of a demographic effect of the coming
of age of a millennial generation which prioritizes issues such as the environment differently than their parents. Such potentialities notwithstanding, the
vast majority of American evangelicals, according to the data, remain political conservatives in tune with the trends noted above.

To provide a flavor of the broadening interest of evangelicals in international affairs, we close this essay with a few observations regarding three
recent public documents that touch on foreign policy: "For the Health of the
Nation: An Evangelical Call to Civic Responsibility" (2004), the Yale Letter
(2007), and "An Evangelical Manifesto" (2008).

The process of drafting "For the Health of the Nation," often referred to
as "the Call," began in March 2001 at the annual convention of the NAE, and
finally was adopted in October 2004.[10] In light of prior evangelical "ambival-
en[ce] about civic engagement," the document argues for the public engagement of evangelicals on a broad array of sociopolitical issues (4). After
asserting a biblical worldview for a Christian's responsibility to be civically
engaged, the document adumbrates seven principles of Christian political
engagement:

• We work to protect religious freedom and liberty of conscience.

- We work to nurture family life and protect children.
- We work to protect the sanctity of human life and safeguard its nature.
- We seek justice and compassion for the poor and vulnerable.
- We work to protect human rights.
- We seek peace and work to restrain violence.
- We labor to protect God's creation.

Although the document projects a broad, general vision, it nonetheless incorporates many of the key themes noted in the survey data, particularly that evangelicals tend to agree on just war, religious freedom, human rights, and poverty alleviation. For example, the Call states, "Military force must be guided by classical just war principles, which are designed to restrain violence by establishing the right conditions for and right conduct in fighting a war." Not surprisingly, the Call also emphasizes the importance of "practical peacemaking" and nonviolent conflict resolution (23).

The Call uses much stronger language on humanitarian and civil/human rights issues. It calls on governments everywhere to support religious liberty, freedom of expression, and the right to assemble, and argues that

> extreme poverty, lack of health care, the spread of HIV/AIDS, inadequate nutrition, unjust and unstable economies, slavery and sexual trafficking, the use of rape as a tool of terror and oppression, civil war, and government cronyism and graft create the conditions in which large populations become vulnerable. *We support Christian agencies and American foreign policy that effectively correct these political problems and promote just, democratic structures.* (20; italics added)

If an unwieldy organization like the NAE, made up of constituent denominations and parachurch groups, can agree to this language, then it likely reflects the rooting of such sentiments among individual parishioners. A second document is the Yale Letter (2007), a public letter signed by over 130 Christian leaders from across the religious spectrum. Titled "Loving God and Neighbor Together: A Christian Response to 'A Common Word between Us and You,'" the letter responded to "A Common Word between Us and You" (an open letter from Muslim clerics following the pope's Regensburg speech). In the Yale letter, the writers expressed happiness at the outstretched Muslim hand and anticipated finding common ground between Muslims and Christians upon which to peacefully coexist. The Yale Letter was criticized in some conservative evangelical circles for apologizing for historic grievances (e.g., the Crusades) without noting recent atrocities in the Muslim world, such as suicide bombings, terrorism, or Darfur. Yet the letter is a terse call to engagement by religious peoples from East and West to promote peace and reconciliation. Bolstering its widespread credibility as a "starting place for dialogue" was its unusual constellation of signatories, including the NAE's vice president for governmental affairs, the editor of *Christianity Today*, the pastors of the world's largest church and of two of America's most influential contemporary churches (Saddleback and Willow Creek), and representatives of conservative places of Christian higher education like Fuller Seminary, Biola University, and Wheaton College.

Finally, "An Evangelical Manifesto" was released in May 2008.[11] The manifesto offers a strict, theological definition of evangelicalism that eschews political language (8).[12] As to politics, the writers exhort evangelicals to commit to being involved in changing society, instead of running away from (fundamentalism) or succumbing to its evils (liberalism). They acknowledge the historical period in which it is written—the "global era" in which conflict of ideologies (read broadly to include religion) seems "inevitable" (18). While not restricting evangelicalism to any ideology, including pacifism or just war theory, they argue that evangelicals are committed to a biblical, moral worldview which comes with certain value commitments that simply are non-negotiable. The authors take direct issue with the notion that a certain relativism might govern morality in international life. Hence, issues of genocide and oppression have ethical and spiritual significance:

> More tolerant sounding at first, this position [of avoiding inter-cultural judgments of morality] leads directly to the evils of *complacency*; for in a world of such evils as genocide, slavery, female oppression, and assaults on the unborn, there are rights that require defending, evils that must be resisted, and interventions into the affairs of others that are morally justifiable. (18)

From this paragraph, it is clear—"An Evangelical Manifesto" justifies and possibly mandates intervention to ensure the rights of others and to restrain evil.[13] It parallels in many ways the "Responsibility to Protect" concept that arose in the wake of the genocides of the 1990s and was documented in a 2005 UN General Assembly document with the same name. In sum, just as the survey data indicates the strong interest of rank-and-file evangelicals in international issues, the statements of evangelical elites are similarly engaged across a wide variety of global policy areas.

EVANGELICALS: ISOLATIONISTS NO LONGER

Notwithstanding the above data, there remain those who predict that evangelicals will be the first to return to the days and ways of isolationism. Considering the number of years—indeed, decades—over which evangelical foreign policy matured and evolved into its current form, a rapid regression to isolationism is unlikely, for evangelicals and for Americans in general. For evangelicals, no single government doctrine, be it Monroe or Bush, forms the basis of foreign policy. Their policy views cannot be separated from the Great Commission to share the Gospel, the Great Commandment to love one's neighbors, and the belief in the unity of all believers. For evangelicals, foreign policy actors include not only states and interstate institutions, but also missionaries and global faith-based organizations. Evangelicals were engaged in foreign affairs long before their leadership started to offer coherent official foreign policy recommendations, and evangelicals will continue to be interested in a host of international issues. Moreover, it seems likely that, for the foreseeable future, evangelicals will continue to be interested in the fate of Israel, press for action (be it through economic policies or intervention) against states that threaten religious freedom and human rights, and closely follow the war on terrorism and religious conflict in the Muslim world. And since evangelicals make up a quarter or more of the American electorate, their views will continue to influence American foreign policy.

NOTES

1. This information is taken from the ISAE website and can be found at www.wheaton.edu/isae/defining_evangelicalism.html (accessed March 15, 2008). For a historical perspective, see David Bebbington, *The Dominance of Evangelicalism: The Age of Spurgeon and Moody* (Colorado Springs, Colo.: InterVarsity Press, 2005).

2. This anecdote is characteristic of a hundred others from colonial times and the early years of the republic. For more on Moore, see the website of a church he helped found at fbcalexandria.org/page.asp?page_id=271.

3. From the Fourth National Survey of Religion and Politics, Bliss Institute—University of Akron, March-May 2004 (N-4000). Available at http://pewforum.org/docs/index.php?DocID=55.

4. From the Pew Forum on Religion and Public Life, "Religion and the 2006 Elections," http://pewforum.org/docs/?DocID=174.

5. Survey data available at http://ncronline.org/NCR_Online/archives2/2006a/032406/032406h.htm.

6. Available at http://pewforum.org/docs/?DocID=153.

7. More information comes from the website 1040window.org.

8. See www.nae.net/index.cfm?FUSEACTION=editor.page&pageID=91&IDCategory=8.

9. These accomplishments are covered in Alan Hertzke's *Freeing God's Children: The Unlikely Alliance for Global Human Rights* (Lanham, Md.: Roman and Littlefield, 2004). Jewish activist Michael Horowitz was an important catalyst for international freedom.

10. The Call can be found at www.nae.net/images/civic_responsibility2.pdf.

11. The manifesto can be found at www.anevangelicalmanifesto.com/docs/Evangelical_Manifesto_Summary.pdf.

12. While never strictly stated, the response is against those who equate evangelicals with the Christian Right.

13. An additional document was released under the title "evangelical," but as it only had seventeen original signatories, we feel that its scope is much smaller than this work. In March 2007, seventeen American evangelicals under the guise "Evangelicals for Human Rights" drafted "An Evangelical Declaration against Torture: Protecting Human Rights in an Age of Terror." The document calls for a ban against torture and the extension of rights to all held combatants based on "the sanctity of human life" endowed by their creator and the need to be "faithful to Christ and his teachings." Significantly, the NAE has endorsed the declaration.

Chapter Eight

"The New Internationals": Human Rights and American Evangelicalism

Zachary R. Calo

In the fall of 2004, the Government Affairs Office of the National Association of Evangelicals (NAE) issued "For the Health of the Nation: An Evangelical Call to Civic Responsibility." The NAE has produced statements on political issues for over fifty years, during which time it has voiced opinions on matters ranging from civil rights, Communism, and the death penalty to budget deficits and serving alcohol on airplanes. These policy statements are not authoritative for evangelicals in the way that those issued by the U.S. Conference of Catholic Bishops are for Roman Catholics. Evangelicals have no obligation to seriously entertain, much less embrace, views of the NAE. Evangelicalism, which locates authority in the local church and ultimately Scripture, possesses no central teaching authority. It is problematic to speak of an evangelical position on political questions, for such a position does not exist in any formal sense. Nevertheless, NAE statements have often served as an accurate barometer of the leading views and priorities within evangelicalism at a given moment. It is for this reason that "For the Health of the Nation" is so significant for the document does nothing less than calls for a reordering of evangelical politics. If it reflects the deeper impulses now shaping American evangelicalism, it may augur the political transformation of this religious community.

The most striking feature of "For the Health of the Nation" is its commitment to expanding the scope of issues on which evangelicals stake their public witness. "For the Health of the Nation" continues to emphasize the importance of abortion, gay marriage, family life, and other cultural concerns. Yet it also urges evangelicals to move beyond these core issues in order to promote economic justice, peacemaking, environmental stewardship, and international human rights. Mark Totten correctly notes that the political profile of white American evangelicals has traditionally been "fairly predictable: strong allegiance to Republicans and focus on a few social concerns" (Totten 2006). But this profile is changing, particularly among young evangelicals. Michael Gerson, former speechwriter and advisor to President George W. Bush, alluded to this in observing that "I think there are lots and lots of young people, in their 20s to 40s, who are very impatient with older models of social engagement like those used by the Religious Right." Gerson, named one of America's twenty-five most influential evangelicals by *Time*, added that many young evangelicals "understand the importance of the life issues and the family issues, but they know the concern for justice has to be broader and global" (Hansen 2006). Recent polls support Gerson's assessment. A Pew Research Center poll, for instance, found a 15 percent drop in the number of white evangelicals who identify as Republican. Evangelicals have not, by and large, forsaken the social and cultural issues which have long defined their political profile. But such issues no longer have a stranglehold on the evangelical political imagination. "The old religious right led by Jerry Falwell and Pat Robertson, trying to battle Satan with school prayers and right-to-life amendments, is on the ropes," writes one commentator (Kristof 2002).

Among the most important characteristics of this new evangelical politics is its global scope, particularly as to international human rights. From pressing the Bush administration for increased funding to combat AIDS in Africa to criticizing China's human rights abuses, a new evangelical assertiveness in international issues is taking form. This marks a sharp break from the dominant political practices of the past. Allen Hertzke, the leading chronicler of evangelical human rights activities, notes that American evangelicals "burst unexpectedly onto the international stage with the dawning of the twenty-first century" (Hertzke 2004, 13). Foreign policy, human rights, and media elites, dominated—in the words of a former high-ranking State Department official—by a "secular myopia" and "aversion to religion," failed initially to appreciate the growing interest of evangelicals in these issues (Farr 2006). But this is changing. Nicholas Kristof has observed in the *New York Times* that the movement of American evangelicals into international politics represents a "broad new trend that is beginning to reshape American foreign policy" (Kristof 2002). Kristof has praised evangelicals for their "superb work on poverty, AIDS, sex trafficking, climate change, prison abuses, malaria and genocide in Darfur" (Kristof 2008). Another *New York Times* writer has noted interest among evangelicals "in moving beyond the divisive domestic issues that consumed them a generation ago . . . into an international arena" (Bumiller 2003). Walter Russell Mead, writing in *Foreign Affairs*, similarly observed evangelicals' "growing influence" in humanitarian and human rights efforts (Mead 2006). In line with "For the Health of the Nation," evangelicals are adopting a broader conception of social justice, of which international human rights is a foundational component. American evangelicals, in Kristof's bold words, are becoming "the new internationalists" (Kristof 2002).

This international turn in evangelical politics, should it sustain itself, has the potential to transform the political life of evangelicalism and the landscape of American foreign policy. Most obviously, evangelicals bring to politics a moral passion rooted in the certainties of faith. If patterns which have defined evangelical involvement in domestic politics over the past three decades carry over into international politics, this community of religious believers will have the ability to generate profoundly intense grassroots support for human rights issues. This possibility alone could bring broad-based, even populist, interest to issues which often fail to garner such attention. Indeed, evangelicals did just this during the human rights crisis in southern Sudan, and they continue to do so with such issues as religious persecution and sex slavery. Yet perhaps the most intriguing question concerns how evangelicals might influence the broader human rights movement. The institutions and networks which dominate the human rights movement have long been the province of a secular elite. While evangelicals certainly share many of the same priorities and concerns, they also bring to their efforts a distinctive worldview rooted in the particularities of Christian theology. The extent to which evangelicals will merge into this broader human rights movement instead of creating their own parallel movement remains unclear. But a human rights movement based not only in New York and Geneva but also in churches in Kigali and Jakarta will certainly look very different.

THE INTERNATIONAL TURN IN EVANGELICAL POLITICS

Evangelicals are not simply "new internationalists"—they were among the first internationalists. While the foray into human rights politics is of recent origin, evangelical Protestantism has long been international in ambition and outlook. Driven by the universalistic impulses of the Gospel, evangelicals have taken Christianity throughout the world. As announced in the Lausanne Covenant, a 1974 statement on Christian conviction and global mission developed by leading evangelicals, "We believe the Gospel is God's good news for the whole world, and we are determined by his grace to obey Christ's commission to proclaim it to all mankind and to make disciples of every nation." Evangelicals have a long history of international relief work that took place largely outside the bounds of politics. World Vision was founded in 1951 and is now one of the largest Christian relief organizations, assisting seventy million people each year. Samaritan's Purse, another Christian relief organization founded in 1970, similarly has a long record of aiding victims of poverty, war, natural disaster, and famine. Yet in recent years the international impulse long present within evangelicalism has turned more toward social and political action. Moving beyond missionary work and private relief efforts, American evangelicals have joined debates about the just ordering of the institutions, policies, and laws which shape the global order. The following section considers three of the most important events which triggered this recent shift in focus: the globalization of Christianity, the crisis in southern Sudan, and the Religious Freedom Restoration Act.

THE GLOBALIZATION OF CHRISTIANITY

The shifting axis of Christianity from the West to the global south was one of the seminal sociological developments of the past century. In a relatively short period of time, Christianity has been transformed from a predominantly European and North American religion to one centered in Africa, Asia, and Latin America. By 2000, 60 percent of the world's Christian population was in the global south (Hertzke 2004). The demographic shift to the developing world continues to grow apace.

This shifting axis has transformed the life and practice of global Christianity, with implications which are both demographic and theological. The growth of Christianity in Africa, Asia, and South America has largely involved conservative traditions, specifically Roman Catholicism and evangelicalism (broadly interpreted as including Pentecostals as well as Anglicans, Presbyterians, and Methodists). Christian communities outside the West, as they mature and grow more assertive, have increasingly challenged liberal elements within the Western churches. This is particularly visible within Anglicanism and Methodism, which have endured divisive internecine feuds between liberals and conservatives over such issues as homosexuality. Speaking at the 2008 Global Anglican Future Conference (GAFCON), a gathering of conservative Anglicans, the Anglican Primate of the Church of Nigeria, denounced the theological liberalism of Western Anglicanism, particularly the Episcopal Church USA, as a form of a spiritual imperialism analogous to earlier forms of political and economic imperialism:

> We are here because we know that in God's providence GAFCON will liberate and set participants [particularly Africans] free from spiritual bondage which the Episcopal Church of the United States and its Allies champion. Having survived the inhuman physical slavery of the 19th century, the political slavery called colonialism of the 20th century, the developing world economic enslavement, we cannot, we dare not allow ourselves and the millions we represent to be kept in religious and spiritual dungeon. (Akinola 2008)

For American evangelicals, who are by and large theologically conservative, Akinola and other global South leaders have become important allies. As Philip Jenkins notes, the conservatism of "Southern believers is music to the ears of North Americans or Europeans who find themselves at odds with the progressive leadership of their own churches" (Jenkins 2002, 202). The globalization of Christianity has thus brought about an ecclesiastical realignment in which American evangelicals have joined with African, Latin American, and Asian evangelicals in challenging theological liberalism in the Western churches.

The political implications of Christianity's southward shift have been no less significant. For one thing, this development has internationalized the domestic culture wars and given American evangelicals new allies in their political battles at home. This might well augur a broader global transformation in battles over the meaning and the limits of freedom, personhood, gender, and family which will pit orthodox religious believers against secular modernists. More subtly, these new connections between evangelicals in America and the developing world have challenged the parochial political worldview that has defined American evangelicalism since the rise of the religious right in the 1970s. In particular, the rise of a more globally interconnected evangelicalism has drawn American evangelicals into contact with the sufferings and persecution faced by Christians around the world. For instance, American evangelical Anglicans who have partnered with Rwandan, Nigerian, and Sudanese Anglican churches have been introduced to intimate accounts of genocide, poverty, and religious persecution. Moreover, evangelical growth throughout the global south, particularly in Latin America, has occurred among the poorest segments of society. A Baptist pastor in Brazil noted, "The Catholic Church opted for the poor, but the poor opted for the Evangelicals" (Ostling 2001). The flattening of the world has flattened the church, and American evangelicals now find themselves embedded within a global church community, much of which suffers from poverty and oppression.

The experience of Rick Warren, pastor at Saddleback Church and author of *The Purpose-Driven Life*, offers one example of how the global interconnectedness of evangelical Christianity is transforming the attitudes and practices of the American church. With little previous interest in such international issues as poverty, economic development, and disease, Warren took a 2003 trip to South Africa. There he "came across a tiny church operating from a dilapidated tent—yet sheltering 25 children orphaned by AIDS." The encounter awakened Warren to the needs of the global church and led him to exert his considerable influence to shape evangelical opinion. Thousands of Saddleback Church congregants have subsequently traveled to Africa to volunteer in relief efforts (Kristof 2008). Similarly transformative events have happened throughout the evangelical community, generating a network of institutions committed to advancing evangelical work globally. The International Day of Prayer for the Persecuted Church was established in 1996. International Justice Mission, a Christian human rights organization, was founded in 1997 to aid victims of oppression throughout the world. The Institute for Global Engagement was established to promote religious freedom in academic and public policy debates. More recently, Evangelicals for Human Rights was formed in response to the United States' use of torture. In these and many other ways, evangelicals have become international actors working for the rights of persecuted Christians and the cause of human rights more generally.

SOUTHERN SUDAN AND THE BIRTH OF AN EVANGELICAL HUMAN RIGHTS MOVEMENT

The globalization of Christianity fueled evangelical interest in human rights, but debates about Sudan and international religious freedom birthed the evangelical human rights movement. For twenty years, the Arab Muslim government in the north of Sudan moved to impose sharia law on the largely Christian south. Government-armed militias raped and killed over two million people in the course of the conflict. The 2002 report of the U.S. Commission on International Religious Freedom identified Sudan as the world's most violent human rights abuser. In spite of its genocidal characteristics, the Sudan conflict failed to gain currency among Western political leaders. Secretary of State Madeline Albright notoriously stated in 1999 that "the human rights situation in Sudan is not marketable to the American people." What Albright did not count on, however, was the growing concern with the Sudan crisis within religious communities and particularly among evangelical Christians. Allen Hertzke writes, "The plight of the southern Sudanese people would have remained in the backwater of American concern had not the Christian solidarity movement picked up the case" (Hertzke 2004, 246). Evangelical influence proved essential to gaining congressional passage of the 2002 Sudan Peace Act, which condemned human rights violations in Sudan and established mechanisms for advancing a peace process. This act led, in turn, to a 2005 peace agreement between the north and south.

The crisis in southern Sudan galvanized evangelical interest in international human rights. It also revealed the character this evangelical movement would take in its formative stage. Because evangelicalism is decentralized, political action relies more on bottom-up populism than top-down directives. A few leading organizations and evangelical leaders lit the spark on Sudan, but it was moral passion and grassroots organization that produced a mass movement. Local churches played a seminal role in this process by providing information about Sudan, hosting films and speakers, organizing political action, collecting donations, and even sending members to the country. The British weekly *New Statesman* went so far as to describe evangelical activism on behalf of Sudan as a "crusade" (Higham 2004).

This crusade approach to human rights, of course, has limitations. It encourages treating complex international issues as populist religious campaigns. It focuses on short-term solutions to problems which may require a long-term response. It tends to limit evangelical interest to those issues which directly impact Christians. The crusade mentality also relies heavily on an emotional energy instead of developing permanent institutions to direct evangelical human rights work. At the same time, evangelical populism brought attention to the long-neglected humanitarian crisis in Sudan. Evangelical relief workers entered Sudan when others deemed it too dangerous. The evangelical community labored tirelessly for Sudan when the situation was being ignored "by secular groups, the mainstream press, and the foreign-policy establishment" (Hertzke 2005). In short, evangelicals succeeded where other human rights advocates did not because their faith-driven idealism refused to be stifled by the norms of realpolitik.

The approach evangelicals employed in the Sudan is not a long-term model. A moral crusade might achieve important short-term goals, but it cannot sustain a mature and influential movement over the long term. The evangelical human rights movement which first formed during the Sudan crisis must ultimately take a different shape. And it has. Evangelicals have increasingly sought common cause with the broader human rights movement, developing leaders and institutions to guide future political action. Only a decade later, the evangelical human rights movement has become a more settled, mature, and lasting presence in American public life. Yet the response to Sudan revealed qualities of the evangelical human rights movement which distinguish it from the mainstream movement. Properly harnessed, these qualities will allow evangelicals to advance human rights in ways, and perhaps in places, which others cannot.

THE INTERNATIONAL RELIGIOUS FREEDOM ACT AND THE POLITICS OF HUMAN RIGHTS

The final galvanizing issue we consider is evangelical participation in the debate over the International Religious Freedom Act (IRFA) of 1998, legislation which authorized the use of American foreign policy to advance religious freedom. The text of the IRFA established the importance of religious freedom to American democracy: "the right to freedom of religion undergirds the very origin and existence of the United States. . . . From its birth to this day, the United States has prized this legacy of religious freedom and honored this heritage by standing for religious freedom and offering refuge for those suffering religious persecution." In light of the foundational significance of religious freedom to democracy and human rights, the IRFA announced that the "policy of the United States" is now "to promote the right to freedom of religion" and "to oppose violations of religious freedom that are or have been engaged in or tolerated by the governments of foreign countries."

The IRFA employed a number of mechanisms for achieving these goals. First, it established the Office of International Religious Freedom within the Department of State and provided that the president shall appoint an ambassador-at-large whose primary responsibility is "to advance the right of freedom of religion abroad, to denounce the violation of that right, and to recommend appropriate responses by the United States Government when this right is violated." Second, the legislation required that the secretary of state, with the assistance of the ambassador, provide Congress with an annual report describing the status of religious freedom in each foreign country, assessing the nature and extent of violations of religious freedom in each country, and describing the policies of the United States toward each foreign country engaging in or tolerating violations of religious freedom. Third, the IRFA established a Commission on International Religious Freedom responsible for reviewing the facts and circumstances of violations of religious freedom and making policy recommendations to the president, secretary of state, and Congress on matters involving international religious freedom. Finally, the IRFA set forth a number of actions the president may take in response to violations of religious freedom, including a private or official public demarche, a public condemnation, delay or cancellation of scientific or cultural exchanges, denial or cancellation of state visits, withdrawal or suspension of development or security assistance, requiring U.S. directors of international financial institutions to oppose or vote against loans primarily benefiting the foreign government, and prohibiting the U.S. government from procuring goods or services from the foreign government found to be in violation.

Although some liberal religious organizations such as the National Council of Churches opposed the IRFA, religious groups were among the legislation's strongest supporters (Danchin 2002). In Allan Hertzke's phrase, an "unlikely alliance" took shape in which evangelicals, Catholics, and mainline Protestants found common cause with Buddhists, Muslims, and Bahai. Evangelicals played a central role in this new alliance. One commentator, writing in the *New York Times*, described the political coalition bringing new attention to the issue of religious persecution as including "Reaganite conservatives, labor activists, veterans of the Soviet Jewry movement and, most important, evangelical Christians" (Goldberg 1997, 46). Hertzke has similarly written in detail about the indispensable role of evangelical church-based networks in advancing the legislation.

Evangelical action on behalf of the IRFA was primarily driven by grass-roots efforts, meaning it often failed to capture widespread attention among media and policy elites. Elliot Abrams, writing just months before passage of the IRFA, stated that "there is little evidence of a wave of grass-roots Christian activism" on behalf of international religious freedom (Abrams 1997). Yet the same powerful evangelical network which had effectively promoted conservative positions on domestic cultural matters had been quietly marshalling its strength on behalf of international religious freedom. As with the evangelical response to Sudan, the movement which drew attention to religious persecution relied on an ad hoc network of local churches, umbrella organizations, and unheralded leaders. This approach has limitations as a long-term model for developing a broad-based human rights movement with evangelicalism. It also led critics to attack evangelicals for their narrow concern with the rights of persecuted Christians. Both of these issues will need to be addressed as the evangelical human rights movement matures. Nevertheless, the importance of the IRFA in creating a nascent evangelical human rights movement cannot be overstated. It also served notice to political elites that evangelicals were entering the human rights arena and had tremendous potential to influence policy. The evangelical human rights movement in American continues to exist in the shadow of the successes enjoyed during the debates over Sudan and the IRFA.

AN EVANGELICAL POLITICAL THEOLOGY OF HUMAN RIGHTS?

The recent explosion of evangelical activity on behalf of human rights issues has largely focused on political organization, activism, and institution building. Evangelicals have given far less attention to intellectual and theological reflection on the issue of human rights and the role of the church in global politics more generally. A significant challenge confronting the evangelical church as it moves forward will be to develop an account of human rights informed both by the Christian theological tradition and broader intellectual currents in politics, law, and philosophy. Theory and praxis must unite if the evangelical human rights movement is to emerge as a culture-forming movement.

One cause for evangelicalism's failure to inaugurate a robust philosophical and theological conversation about human rights is a lingering anti-intellectualism. Much has changed since Mark Noll penned his much-commented-upon book *The Scandal of the Evangelical Mind* in 1994. Yet many of Noll's criticisms still apply, particularly in the area of politics. Evangelical politics continues to be an affair of the heart more than the mind, as illustrated in the evangelical responses to Sudan and the IRFA. Along these lines, Ronald Sider recently scolded evangelicals for failing to cultivate an adequate political philosophy, a matter of particular relevance to human rights efforts (Sider 2005).

Another challenge is the lack of intellectual resources upon which to draw in cultivating a political philosophy. Catholic scholar Robert Delahunty makes this point in writing that American evangelicals "lack the comprehensive intellectual framework that is necessary to guide and inform policy" (Delahunty 2008, 281). This lack of a "comprehensive intellectual framework" reflects, at least in part, the dominant role of scripture in evangelical theology. Because evangelical theology is biblical theology, evangelicals have struggled to find a language and methodology for mediating between scripture and the political discourses of a pluralistic democracy.

In contrast to the evangelical tradition, Roman Catholic social thought has long sustained critical reflection on law, politics, social justice, and human rights. Beginning with Pope Leo XIII's 1891 encyclical letter *Rerum Novarum*, and subsequently developed in such seminal documents as *Quadragesimo Anno* (1931), *Dignitatis Humanae* (1965), and *Centesimus Anno* (1991), the Catholic Church has used its teaching authority to advance a conversation between Christianity and the political and economic ideas which inform the modern world. This conversation has been particularly fruitful in the area of human rights, where Catholic social thought has developed rich accounts of human personhood, religious freedom, the family, and the state.

The success of the Catholic Church in developing a tradition of thought about human rights reflects its ability to mediate between the theological and the political. Whether by means of the neo-Thomistic natural law tradition, which dominated Catholic social thought before Vatican II, or by means of recent developments in theological anthropology, Catholic thinkers have at their disposal a set of concepts and categories which facilitate speaking ethically about the foundations and ends of human rights. Catholics have been particularly effective at incorporating the liberal language of rights into their social thought, while at the same time refusing to subordinate Catholic thought to the dictates of secular liberalism. As such, the Catholic social thought tradition has allowed Catholics to fluently participate in debates employing the language of rights, the dominant moral vocabulary of modern politics, while also offering a distinctive perspective on the content and meaning of these rights.

Evangelicals have yet to find a way to critically engage the liberal rights tradition. The primary reason for this difficulty is that evangelicalism's *sola scriptura* approach to theology leaves little space for reason, natural law, and other mediating categories which facilitate a discussion about political goods within the context of a liberal pluralistic society. One scholar explains the origins of the difficulty as follows:

> Reformation theorists, drawing on nominalist strands in Catholic thought, blasted through the whole elegantly conceived organic/epistemological/juristic medieval unity by emphasizing the free will of God, not his reason. . . . This emphasis on God's unfettered will meant that God related to humans not because of any ontological unity linking his reason to ours but rather by the words he has chosen to utter (*sola scriptura*). (Mensch 2001, 63)

Put in less abstruse terms, the evangelical tradition provides few resources for thinking and speaking about politics without recourse to explicitly theological categories.

At the same time, evangelicals have become ever more willing to invoke the language of human rights to make political claims. Paul Marshall, a leading figure within the evangelical human rights movement, writes, "Paralleling developments within the Roman Catholic Church, most evangelicals now believe that human rights are an essential expression of the gospel, that the language of rights is a good way to express Christian concerns, and that any responsible faith-directed politics must be committed to defending and promoting human rights" (Marshall 2005, 307). In fact, evangelicals employed the language of rights well before they became involved in international human rights. In debates over abortion, homosexuality, and religious freedom, for instance, evangelicals have long made claims about the meaning of certain legal rights within the context of American democracy. The human rights movement within American evangelicalism, as it has taken shape within recent years, has appropriated this facility with rights talk and transferred it to a new set of international political issues. Yet this appropriation of rights language does not negate the fact that evangelicals still lack "ready access to a public philosophy that would enable them both to articulate a secular vision of the common good and to convince a substantial number of non-evangelical elites to join with them in pursuit of that good" (Wilcox 2007). A disconnect remains between the facility with which evangelicals have embraced rights talk and the difficulties they have in articulating a critical account of rights from within evangelical tradition.

The ease with which American evangelicals make rights claims reflects, in large measure, the fact that Protestantism, and in particular American Protestantism, emerged hand in hand with the forces of modern politics. American evangelicalism was naturally wired to find itself at home with modern democratic politics. It is the quintessential democratic faith. This stands in stark contrast to the Roman Catholic experience. The Roman Catholic human rights tradition took shape only after a long and contested battle with liberalism and democracy. For much of the eighteenth, nineteenth, and early twentieth centuries, Catholic social teaching defined itself against the foundational claims of political liberalism. As Pope Pius IX famously stated in the 1864 *Syllabus of Errors*, it is false to assert that "the Roman Pontiff can, and ought to, reconcile himself, and come to terms with progress, liberalism, and modern civilization" (§80). It was not until Catholicism found, in Charles Taylor's words, a "voice from within the achievements of modernity," that it became one of the leading advocates of social and political justice, democratic governance, and human rights (Taylor 1999). Finding this voice within modernity required, above all else, that Catholicism reconcile itself with liberalism. This rapprochement did not mean Catholicism uncritically embraced liberalism. Rather, through the course of a long and often tortured process, Catholic social thought produced an account of rights which was conversant with the liberal tradition but nevertheless distinctively rooted in the Catholic worldview.

Evangelicalism has never gone through a similar intellectual process. There has never been an evangelical modernity akin to the Catholic modernity Taylor describes. Evangelicalism is a creation and expression of modernity. Its easy compatibility with modern politics has, on one hand, facilitated evangelicalism's movement into human rights. Yet it also has allowed evangelicalism to reflexively endorse the idea of human rights without doing the hard work of developing a public philosophy which sets the terms of evangelical participation. This has left evangelism ill positioned to influence the direction of the human rights movement, politically as well as intellectually. Without access to a public philosophy both liberal and evangelical in its composition, evangelicals have little to offer the current human rights conversation which reflects their unique perspective. Until evangelicals develop such a political philosophy, they will remain a class apart from the broader international human rights movement.

Going forward, evangelicals will need to bridge the gap between their biblical and political commitments. One approach will involve following Catholic social thought in developing an account of human rights which rests on such concepts as human dignity, the common good, the universal destination of goods, reason, and nature. Catholic social thought has had a pronounced influence on Protestant thinkers in recent years, and intellectual cross-fertilization undoubtedly will continue as evangelicals develop a vocabulary for speaking about human rights. Yet this process is likely to follow a path different from that traveled by Catholics over the past century. In particular, the evangelical voice within the human rights movement will adopt the characteristics which define evangelical thought, notably the centrality of Scripture. Paul Marshall offers one example of how a rich account of human rights can emerge from the biblical narrative rather than the liberal rights tradition. "We should base our view of rights on who we are," Marshall writes, "created by God . . . [and] made in the image of God" (Marshall

2005, 311). Much remains to be done in developing such a project, but there are certainly resources available within the evangelical tradition for constructing a social ethic that establishes points of contact between the language of rights and the scriptural account of justice. This tradition will differ from the main of the human rights movement in that it does not take the Enlightenment as its starting point. But as Marshall notes, "Human rights properly understood are compatible with and, indeed, flow from a Christian [worldview]. . . . The basis of human rights need not be human will or autonomy but can be understood as an expression of the grace of God extended to all" (Marshall 2005, 322).

A DISTINCTIVE WITNESS: THE FUTURE OF THE EVANGELICAL HUMAN RIGHTS MOVEMENT

Evangelical human rights work has blossomed in recent years, but questions remain as to whether evangelicals are prepared to establish a distinctive, permanent, and influential voice within the broader human rights movement. One reason for this questioning is that evangelicals have not yet committed themselves to working en masse with the full range of international issues such as poverty and economic development, genocide, torture, sex trafficking, and the environment. There are significant exceptions, to be sure, but as David Gushee, president of Evangelicals for Human Rights, correctly notes, "Conservative evangelicals generally offer an unbiblically narrow policy agenda focused on just a few moral issues such as abortion and gay marriage instead of tackling the full range of biblical concerns, which include poverty, oppression and war" (Gushee 2008). The same narrowness of concern that has defined evangelical work on domestic politics has carried over into the international arena, where the most passionate evangelical work has involved issues directly impacting the rights of Christians. While evangelicals rallied in response to the crisis in southern Sudan, for instance, they have not exhibited nearly as strong an interest in Darfur.

The narrowness of evangelical concern became an issue during debate over the International Religious Freedom Act. Numerous commentators critically noted the disproportionate influence of conservative Christians in pushing the legislation and their seemingly narrow concern with protecting the rights of Christians. William Martin of Rice University, for one, dismissed the IRFA as a by-product of the Christian Right's opposition to such international organizations as the United Nations, the European Union, and the Council on Foreign Relations (Martin 1999). Similar criticisms were advanced by leaders within the mainstream human rights community. The executive director of Human Rights Watch criticized the IRFA as a form of "special pleading" on behalf of persecuted Christians (Philpott 2004). John Shattuck, the former assistant secretary for Democracy, Human Rights, and Labor at the U.S. State Department, described the IRFA as an effort "by the American Religious Right to advance a political agenda within the United States government that seeks to promote special religious interests overseas" (Shattuck 2003). In short, many commentators viewed the IRFA, regardless of its merits, as pandering to the particular concerns of evangelicals and other religious believers at the expense of a more holistic approach to human rights.

These critics are right to attribute evangelical involvement in the religious freedom debate to a concern for persecuted Christians around the world. Evangelical commentators concede as much. Alan Hertzke, for instance, has written that religiously based human rights work was "initially animated by concern for the persecution of Christians around the word" (Hertzke 2005). Paul Marshall, albeit more skeptically, acknowledged the oft-cited claim that evangelical enthusiasm for the IRFA and the crisis in Sudan were "at bottom, only efforts to help Christians overseas and thus not a genuine universal concern for rights" (Marshall 2005, 307). At the same time, Marshall, Hertzke, and other sympathetic observers see vast potential for the development of a comprehensive evangelical human rights movement. Reaching this point, however, will require moving beyond the bounded concerns which have defined the movement in its infancy. There are certainly indications that this is happening. The establishment of such organizations as the Institute for Global Engagement, Evangelicals for Human Rights, and International Justice Mission indicates that evangelicals are committed to establishing a permanent foothold in international affairs. The legal and political focus of these efforts contrasts with the mission and relief focus of established organizations such as World Vision. Even more significantly, the political priorities of younger evangelicals, particularly the emergent cosmopolitan elite, augurs well for a future in which human rights issues are a central part of evangelicalism's public witness. While the old guard of evangelical leadership maintains significant influence, a tipping point might have been reached. Questions certainly remain about how broadly based the evangelical human rights movement will be, what it will adopt as its political priorities, and what will be its relationship with the broader human rights movement. Yet evangelicals have unquestionably begun to find a voice within human rights debates.

The broad participation of evangelicals could transform the human rights movement, both in the United States and throughout the world. The mainstream human rights movement, as it took shape in the years after World War II, has been dominated by a westernized and largely secular outlook. As sociologist Peter Berger notes, the conventions and declarations which inform the modern human rights movement "were not adopted by nations but by a small clique of lawyers, bureaucrats, and intellectuals who are highly westernized and most of who have absolutely nothing to do with the cultures in which most of their fellow nationals live" (Smolin 1995–1996, 15). Many intellectuals and policy elites within the human rights movement continue to operate as if religion can be ignored. Yet religion endures as a powerful force. Recent events have certainly demonstrated that the secularization thesis, which proposed that modernization would bring about a decline of religion, is profoundly inadequate, if not fundamentally wrong. As Alan Hertzke writes, "One cannot understand international relations today without comprehending the new faith-based movement" (Hertzke 2004).

The once monochrome tapestry that constituted the human rights movement is fragmenting into a more colorful ensemble in which diverse groups, many of them religious, speak about rights in terms informed by their particular traditions. Evangelical movement into the human rights area provides a particularly vivid example of this fragmentation. As Walter Russell Mead observes, "Evangelicals have not . . . simply followed the human rights and humanitarian agendas crafted by liberal and secular leaders" (Mead 2006, 6). They rather have brought to human rights work an agenda and worldview rooted in their particular concerns and commitments. The major mainline Christian denominations—Episcopalian, Lutheran, Methodist, Presbyterian—vocally support international human rights, particularly through policy offices within the national hierarchy. But their support typically parrots the already dominant views of the human rights establishment. Mead notes, "Liberal Christianity has a much lower estimate of the difference between Christians and non-Christians" and is therefore willing to endorse human rights activities which take place in the secular world on secular terms (Mead 2006). Unlike their liberal Protestant counterparts, evangelicals have resisted defining their human rights work to secular norms, cultivating instead a more distinctively Christian human rights witness. As discussed above, this sectarian approach to human rights has complicated the ability of evangelicals to establish a prominent voice within the broader human rights movement. The challenge of cultivating a public philosophy remains. At the same time, the willingness of evangelicals to engage human rights issues on unashamedly Christian terms represents an important challenge to the secular stranglehold over human rights discourses.

The movement for universal human rights will find its future in particularity, as the unitary secular account of rights is increasingly challenged by the claims of religious communities. The evangelical human rights revolution is part of a broader trend that is reshaping international human rights. Going forward, the critical issue will be how the human rights movement adapts to the particularity of religious communities and how religious communities adapt to the universality of human rights claims. The increased presence of religious communities, however, need not undermine the goals of the human rights movement. If anything, it has the potential to vivify the human rights movement and draw in participants otherwise left at the margins.

As evangelicals develop a more prominent role within the human rights movement, points of tension will certainly emerge. An account of human rights rooted in the Christian worldview will differ from that emerging out of a secular Enlightenment worldview. On matters such as abortion, sexual rights, children's rights, and the role of the family, evangelicals almost certainly will clash with the human rights elite as the Catholic Church long has (Glendon 1996). Yet it might be hoped that the evangelical human rights movement will bring about more than an internationalization of the culture wars. Evangelicals also have the capacity to establish common cause with the broader human rights movement on such matters as economic justice, environmental protection, and religious freedom. Evangelicals will operate from distinctive first principles, to be sure, but this distinctiveness need not overshadow the shared goal of advancing the common good of global society. In the end, the evangelical entrée into human rights does not pose a challenge to the broader human rights movement. Far from undermining the human rights movement, evangelicals are involved in restoring a religiously informed perspective to the debate. John Witte writes that Christian communities "participated actively as midwives in the birth" of the modern human rights revolution, but were soon exiled to the margins of the movement (Witte 1996, 5–6). The re-emergence of religiously based human rights movements marks a return to an earlier moment when theology and enlightenment liberalism engaged in a creative partnership that changed the world. The restoration of this partnership will be fruitful both for religious communities and for the cause of human rights.

Chapter Nine

Evangelicals, Pakistan, and the War in Afghanistan: Scriptural Resources for National Security Issues

Ron Kirkemo

The United States is at war in the far-off lands of Iraq and Afghanistan, fighting vicious wars on the ground against enemies who blend into the civilian population and attack with snipers, suicide bombers, and improvised explosive devices. "I had faith until I got to Iraq," said Army Specialist Joe Schaffel, "I haven't gotten it back since. Once you get there, you wonder how God could let anyone go through that" (Conant 2007, 28).

National Guard Specialist Charles Graner was involved in prisoner abuse at Abu Ghraib. "The Christian in me says it's wrong," he told a friend, but he enjoyed abusing the enemy. He showed pictures of the widespread abuse to his friend Specialist Joseph Darby, who was not an evangelical Christian, yet knew it was morally wrong and knew he had to do something about it (Higham and Stephen 2004, A01). So broke the scandal of Abu Ghraib prison and the attendant moral failings and courage at the individual level.

During the 1962 Cuban missile crisis, President Kennedy's advisors were nearing a decision to launch a surprise attack on Cuba that would kill Soviet soldiers there, likely sparking a Soviet retaliatory strike and a possible nuclear exchange. Robert Kennedy argued that such a sneak attack would violate American values and morality. He convinced one, and then another, of the advisors, and an effective but much less dangerous policy was adopted that constrained the momentum of events. One of the participants later said, "Bobby Kennedy's good sense and moral character were perhaps decisive" (Schlesinger 1979, 549).

These stories demonstrate that American national security involves not just questions about numbers and types of guns and bombs, but also important theological issues, the level of God's involvement in history, and personal morality. This chapter provides an evangelical Christian perspective on those broader questions. It explores them through the lens of the war in Afghanistan and ties together three elements: (1) the broad political and strategic aspects of the war from the view of Winston Churchill's perspective on the outbreak of World War I, (2) the scriptural and theological perspectives of a range of Christian groups, and (3) a Wesleyan view of scriptural principles, narratives, and biographies. Together they inform evangelical struggles to reconcile God's role in history with national security policy in the early twenty-first century.

FROM 1914 TO 2014?

The war in Afghanistan is a focal point for U.S. defense in the first half of the twenty-first century. At the time of this writing, the war is proceeding poorly for the United States. General McChrystal has been unceremoniously sacked by President Obama, and General David Petraeus, architect of the turnaround in Iraq, has been elevated to the top command spot in Afghanistan in hopes of achieving a similar result. The war represents a new era of strategy but with a 1914 tinderbox potential for the future of American foreign affairs. In short, American military strategy in Afghanistan is very important.

World War II was a symmetrical war fought between highly industrialized nations with comparable weapons, strategies, and firepower. As a war between nations, no distinctions were observed between warriors and civilians as cities were bombed into oblivion. That kind of war remains a possibility as nations rise in power and ambition. In Afghanistan, however, the United States faces not an antagonistic nation, but a quasi-state and partial government which has given harbor to networks of religious radicals using snipers, suicide bombers, and inexpensive and easy-to-build weapons like improvised explosive devices. The enemy spins their view of themselves and the Americans through radio, websites, sympathetic news stories, and threatening hand-delivered "night letters" to Afghan villages. Against those threats, the technological marvels of U.S. air and sea power are irrelevant. In this asymmetrical war, the number of insurgents killed or captured is less important than the attitudes and perceptions of civilians. The war is fought by protecting civilians engaging local civilian leaders (Ricks 2009, 24–73).

Afghanistan lies between nuclear Pakistan and soon-to-be-nuclear Iran. India has nuclear weapons and supports Afghanistan, thus creating security issues for its hostile neighbor, Pakistan. Nuclear China supports nuclear Pakistan, creating multiple nuclear security issues for India. These interconnections exist in proximity to Saudi Arabia and Yemen, both of which are home to al Qaeda operatives and whose security will be complicated when Iran achieves its goal of developing nuclear weapons. Further complicating the politics of the region is the diversity in governments and social values: communist China, democratic India, theocratic Iran, autocratic Saudi Arabia, unstable Pakistan and Iraq, and the propped-up quasi-state of Afghanistan.

A takeover of Afghanistan by the Taliban and al Qaeda would increase the chances of a coup in neighboring nuclear Pakistan, thus giving radical Islamists control of nuclear weapons. Pakistan has suffered four military coups and twenty-two years of military dictatorship in its sixty years of existence. General Zia strove to "Islamify" the country and currently Pakistan supports Islamist militia groups that carry out attacks on India. If Pakistan were to fall to militants, odds of a Pakistani-Indian war would increase, and with it the threat of nuclear escalation. There have been forty-three militarized disputes between the countries since 1947. The most recent—the 2002 conflict—took the nations to "the brink," and left them "One Misstep Away from Nuclear War" (Geller 2005, 11; Richter and Maugh 2002, 1). The nuclear deterrence policy that effectively stabilized the Cold War does not work in South Asia, and there are few "red lines" to prevent a rapid escalation to nuclear war. Faced with the prospect of a nuclear Iran and nuclear Pakistan, Saudi Arabia would certainly obtain nuclear forces. Israel's paranoia would be amplified.

While the setting does not mirror 1914 Europe, there are disturbing similarities. Churchill saw Europe's fateful descent into World War I as a result of the "limited minds of even the ablest men," the pressure of public opinion, the machinations of governmental "wheels within wheels," and forces moving in the shadows. Those who tried to manage the opportunities and risks of this vast and detailed historical problem were overwhelmed by a "momentum that could not be derailed, creating a convulsion of unfathomable catastrophe" (Churchill 1931, 6, 14).

The current nuclear states between Israel and China have divergent interests and intentions, and already are home to war and forces moving in the shadows. For a decade, security experts have called it "the likeliest place for the world's first nuclear war" (Schulz 2002, 1). If Pakistan falls to militants—a real possibility—the odds of provocations followed by a serious war between India and Pakistan are highly likely. If Pakistan strikes valued targets in India or if India's much larger ground forces invade Pakistan, the chances of war with nuclear strikes could be as high as 75 percent, as national fears and religious hopes overwhelm national security calculations. The road to such convulsions runs through our asymmetrical war in Afghanistan.

U.S. security is bound up in reducing the dangers of al Qaeda and in containing the potential for a wider war. Complicating these two goals are the perceptions of the U.S. forces as secular outsiders in a conflict among corrupt allies and ruthless religion-fired enemies. The stakes are high for the United States and its future trajectory of renewal or decline. Do its leaders have any freedom of choice and policy in this setting, or is everything determined? For evangelicals with a high view of scripture, are there biblical resources to understand and guide their understanding on this era of national security issues?

FAITH PERSPECTIVES

Key elements that define evangelicals are the sovereignty of God, the authority of scriptures, the reality of a personal relationship with God, and faith in the world to come. Those involve mystery and second-order commitments over which there is disagreement. If God is sovereign, what role is played by human freedom, the machinations of governments, and historical forces? How fixed or contingent is history? Various Judeo-Christian traditions bring differing theological frameworks to the mysteries of sovereignty, freedom, and fate.

Jewish writers of the Old Testament saw history dominated by God's promises to the people of Israel and his interventions to protect them. Morality was embedded in national security, for history was fully contingent on the will and action of a warrior God who had no reticence about demanding genocide against enemies. Many evangelicals continue to give a prominent place to God's purposes for Israel, while others believe that the Christian church has replaced Israel at the center of God's purposes. In the New Testament, the writers of the gospels and letters focused on the individual Christian life within the early church and the Roman Empire, in expectation of the not-too-distant return of the Lord.

Christian fundamentalists also merge God and history. They insist on the literal inerrancy of scripture in all things to protect belief from critiques by modern science and biblical scholarship. Israel remains central to history, and there is little human control in light of God's hand on human events. War and nuclear danger are not a failure of humanity, but rather implicit in God's movement of history. The wars in Iraq and Afghanistan are part of the "wars and rumors of war" that signal the coming of the end times. Rational strategic analysis apart from the prophecies of Daniel is useless.

An opposite perspective is dualism—the existence of two moralities, one personal and one for government and politics. Lutherans understand government as a nonreligious institution that is needed to limit the social consequences of sin, so Christians should acquiesce in the policies of the state. Political necessity equals political morality. Not so for Christian liberals. Morality is personal and must be applied at the macro level of national policy. War is a failure to live up to God's pronounced will in New Testament scriptures for love, peace, and justice among people. Christians should lament the personal and national distortions of the war establishment and the global war system. Peacemaking and humanitarian programs constitute a better foundation for the security of the United States and a better hope of leashing the dogs of war.

Evangelicals take seriously the responsibility to live holy lives that witness to a world torn by conflict and war. At the heart of their orthodoxy are the words of Jesus when he told Nicodemus "You must be born again," and invited his disciples to "abide in me." These constitute the heart of life in the kingdom of God, further expressed in Christ's Sermon on the Mount and his farewell discourse. To live as an evangelical is to live in an ecclesiastical community of orthodoxy and pastoral care, and in a position of personal piety and judgment.

On U.S. policy in Iraq and Afghanistan, evangelicals do not hold to a single view. Sixty percent of evangelical voters in 2004 favored decreasing or withdrawing troops from Iraq, but they were split nearly evenly on the need for a new approach to foreign policy and on whether the United States should emphasize military or diplomatic means (World Public Opinion 2006). Another poll revealed disagreement among evangelical leaders over the war in Iraq. While most still supported the war, opinions varied. Some thought the war a mistake. Others thought it a proper application of just war theory. Still others believed nonmilitary measures ought to have been used. Some evangelicals sought an alternative "humanitarian surge" (Wallis 2009), while others believed U.S. policy to be "on the right track" (Miller and Miller 2009). Mercer University ethics professor David Gushee captured the ambivalence of many toward a costly war that seemed increasingly stalemated when he said, "We must become more discerning when our nation's leaders advocate a military solution" (Gushee 2007).

Evangelicals wish to avoid both dualism and not applying personal morality to nations. There are two rationales for doing so, an intellectual commitment to the Christian faith and a personal commitment to a living Christ, basically represented in the Calvinist or Reformed tradition and the Wesleyan tradition.

In the Reformed tradition, God is creator of all things, and in his sovereignty chooses the redeemed who are given the "cultural mandate" to form a culture in which all facets of creation can come into being. Authority is vested in scripture alone (*sola scriptura*). Scriptures are God's revelation, the foundation for a coherent Christian worldview. God is sovereign; there is nothing outside his will. His creation and all its spheres are orderly and drawn to his ends. In the reformed tradition, history and particular international orders are not a product of chance or social compact; they are rather purposeful, with their ultimate origins in God and embedded in God's continuing creation. Nations and international organizations within that order have a "natural obligation to God" to fulfill the good for which the realm exists. That good includes preserving order, promoting justice, and moving within the process of redemption toward God's ultimate consummation and fulfillment (Adams 1997, 37, 40–41).

Dean Curry's *A World without Tyranny* reflects that tradition. The authoritative principles of the Bible are absolute. God is in control of history, so that nothing happens apart from God's will. The main principle to be applied in politics is prudence, which is the wise use of biblical principles (Curry 1990, 74, 83). Mark Amstutz is less absolutist about scripture, but also seeks those principles of biblical justice that can be promoted in the world. Amstutz identifies those principles as God's sovereignty and love, the reality of sin, and justice defined as shalom. However, he recognizes that, while there may be agreement on such general principles, their application may well differ (Amstutz 1987, 41–47, 60).

The other strand in evangelicalism is Wesleyan thought, which begins with the resurrection rather than creation. Wesleyan theology emphasizes the personal orientation of the sermons of Jesus and the power of his grace to transform lives and enable Christians to bend and shape history toward shalom. Wesleyan evangelicals find their call in the Great Commission rather than the cultural mandate. Arising during and after the Enlightenment, Wesleyan thought and exegesis take seriously individual engagement of the world, embracing reason as a source of authority and accepting the use of such varied methodologies as historical and literary approaches to scripture. Scripture is not static, but is always considered in light of ongoing world events and with the inspiration of the Holy Spirit.

God is present in the structure of this world through general sovereignty, and he moves to accomplish his redeeming will through grace, which is his kindness and loyalty to humanity, his call to all who will recognize and accept him, and his presence that guides, sustains, judges, and gives us hope. Saving, sanctifying, and guiding grace is available to all people, and no person or element of creation is beyond his grace. People can reject God's grace and act in ways that pervert God's good creation, and they can become widely destructive as they shape and lead nations. In the interplay between leaders and nations, the forces of good and idolatry struggle against each other. Since they are rarely absolute, there are margins of freedom in the midst of peril. Though the war system is far removed from the Gospel, Wesleyans can find their calling in national security issues as agents of grace in situations of peril.

A Wesleyan framework that links theology and history is Jurgen Molt-mann's theology of hope. The resurrection validates God's claim as the final victor in history. We have a responsibility within history to promote a better world because we know the end of history is God's triumph (Moltmann 1967, 334–38). Faith must be more than personal piety, for Auschwitz showed faith is not a private matter and Hiroshima showed that time is finite. Love of enemies means reducing hostilities and acting toward the just peace of shalom (Moltmann 1990, 32, 34, 36, 40). Alternatively, Wesleyan scholar Stanley Hauerwas argues that the Christian life is group centered, defined by being part of an authoritarian community of faith, habits, language, and virtues. Christian rationality is not individualistic or utilitarian, but is com-munity-based and tradition-constituted. Christians are resident aliens, stand-ing against the nations. Without that separation, Christians will continue to live within the liberal ethos of democratic government and the "progressive dechristianization" of the country (Hauerwas 1985, 7, 9, 11–12, 153).

Other Wesleyans recognize the importance of history and life experience as supplements to scripture and reason. They are unsure that biblical princi-ples exist in sufficient specificity to guide history or to move actual events toward biblical justice. They are unable to see the will or hand of God in global tragedies like World War I. They take the risks and uncertainties of international politics seriously. They place more emphasis on personal free-dom than on absolutist principles or historical fate, more emphasis on reason than authoritarian communities.

Life in Christ is dialogical with this world, rather than dualistic or propo-sitional. Evangelicals belong to communities of faith, but each person must struggle to understand God's goodness and will in the face of the realities of our world. Structures of reality are too diverse and dynamic, and the rate of new scientific and social discoveries too rapid, to claim much finality or to defer to the authoritarian answers of a faith community. Faith and politics are held in a conjunctive relationship, with the individual finding a satisfactory relationship under the guidance of the Counselor while journeying with the scripture and building intellectual constructs of theology and politics.

Wesleyans see ambiguity and tension in efforts to understand the two realms, and are comfortable with differing viewpoints and efforts at reconcil-iation. At the same time, the pressure of immediate and dangerous events must not overwhelm one's faith or moral principles. Thank God for his grace in all situations. People are called to remember that, unlike those in the hallowed halls of the ivory tower or other detached communities, the actual decision-maker must act, and then accept the consequences of those policy choices and actions.

JOURNEY WITH THE SCRIPTURES

While scriptures are viewed as divine revelation, they did not fall from Heaven intact as God's first-person statements. They were written by humans in their times or later (much of the Old Testament was written during and after the Babylon exile), a compilation of writings comprised of history, law, poetry, war oracles, prophecy, and letters. Evangelicals consider scripture to be inspired by God and inerrant in all things necessary to salvation. But the Bible is not a book of divine propositions on politics or a treatise on war and peace. The scriptures reflect the time, place, knowledge, and literary forms of the writers. Like Jesus, scripture is both divine and human.

Nothing in scripture should be taken in isolation. Evangelicals are to live in the scriptures as the inspired self-disclosure of God and also in in-depth conversation with each other, with the writers' historical context and ours, and with the firm belief that all scripture should point the way to Christ. Christians are to journey with the scriptures in the living company of Christ, with the inspirations, insights, and guidance of the Holy Spirit as they confront the realities of the present world. The scriptures can provide three kinds of instruction: (1) general principles, (2) specific biographies that demonstrate moral struggles and moral courage, and (3) narratives that bring insight into current affairs and the intersections of providential and political history.

BIBLICALLY DERIVED PRINCIPLES

There are clear biblical principles that are distinguishable from nonbiblical principles—God's purposeful creation, human alienation from the creator and one's fellowman, redemption through Christ, and a life motivated by love of others. These core beliefs establish boundaries for the nation and the individual, though the specifics of those boundaries are contested. The nation itself can never be allowed to become an idol, but that ought not to denigrate patriotism or the men and women willing to serve to protect and advance the interests and values of their nation, even to the point of self-sacrifice in war. The principle of creation says our world is orderly, rational, and good—violence came from freedom and was not of God's purpose (Gen 4:10, 6:11–12). All humanity carries the image of God as we live as individuals within both God's creation purpose and human reality. Thus compromised, the resurrection and the coming of the Holy Spirit mean the power of God is in play to help individuals see beyond their own private interests, to have hope for a better world, and to become aware of the only true God.

Principles such as purposeful creation are *normative*; they establish moral values and perspectives. The theology of creation is not simple. God created an orderly, rational, and good creation. From that come contestable second-order principles. So does purposeful creation mean social life should be oriented toward preservation of the status quo in the name of orderliness? Or should there be active seeking after change toward the end of increasing justice for the common good (Middleton 1994, 262, 266–67, 275–76)? From those second-order principles, different theologies and philosophies can be constructed. So change in the interests of justice shaped an expanded view of morality and moral intuition on the issue of Southern slavery, in contrast to the culture-bound absolutes of southern biblicism. It was through a process of change that northern Christians found a biblical basis for abolition of slavery (Harrill 2000, 149). That process ultimately produced the 1964 Civil Rights Act, which was made possible because of an expanded moral imagination that led a government to make and enforce a policy that moved the country into a new social sphere. The morality that flowed from evolving principles led people to push against boundaries that constrained a just world.

Principles have to be *operationalized*—that is, they must move from high levels of abstraction to fit into unique factual situations, to analyze risks, and to define second-order consequences. Doing so inevitably compromises those principles. For example, the Golden Rule was applied to nuclear strategy through the "no cities" doctrine. Nuclear strategy rests on a "usability paradox"; to make deterrence work and to avoid a nuclear war which would devastate this country, the United States had to actually intend to use nuclear weapons in a devastating attack. If our leaders would never use them in a crisis, there would be no fear among Soviet leaders and no deterrence. In the 1950s, military leaders saw nuclear weapons as just bigger and better weapons to be used in traditional Napoleonic style.

A group of defense intellectuals devised a strategy of rational control to prevent easy use, preemptive strikes, unauthorized use, or unintended escalation. A part of that deterrence strategy was the no cities doctrine, meaning we would not strike Soviet cities if they did not strike ours. When that proved impossible because of the size of weapons and their locations near urban centers, Freeman Dyson advocated a debased operational form of the principle he called the "Brass Rule," which held that we should be able to do at least as much damage as the Soviet could do to us (Dyson 1984, 273). That was a "minimum deterrence" approach which could minimize the size of nuclear forces and their consequences. That strategy was not adopted, so Christian strategists like Jack Swearengen adopted the biblical principle of reconciliation between enemies, another form of the Golden Rule, from which arms control could be adopted as an approach to nuclear weapons (Swearengen 1992, 25–35). In Afghanistan, there is no central enemy with whom to seek mutual understandings on strategy. The Golden Rule cannot be operationalized, and the U.S. is relegated to being guided by its own principled self-control.

As recorded in the New Testament, God made a decisive intervention into human history with the coming of Jesus. At the heart of Christ's sermons is life in the kingdom of God. Embedded in the Sermon on the Mount and the farewell discourse are the principles of love your enemies, accept physical assault rather than use violence, and forgive those who wrong you. Those principles are normative, but not absolute, for individuals and nations. In his life, Jesus castigated the Pharisees as snakes, escaped from the danger of those who would hurt him, and violently drove the money changers from the temple (Matt 12:34, John 8:59, John 2:13–16). He healed the child of a centurion without requiring him to end his military career (Matt 8:5–13).

To avoid dualism, ways must be found to relate the principle of love to the reality of national security. Love is an attachment to, and preference for, another. Though the principle of loving one another relates to personal relations, it can be operationalized in domestic politics as justice for legislatures who define it, administrators who program it, and courts who adjudicate it. What would the spirit of that principle resemble in national security policy in a world without those governmental structures? Among allies, love would be defined as cooperation for mutual benefit. Among poor and failed states, love would take the character of support and help. Among enemies, it would be operationalized as avoiding conflict and seeking reconciliation. Love could be defined as patience and perseverance in peace-making diplomacy. The possible failure of those efforts moves the dispute to a militarized dispute, and the United States must be prepared to defend itself and its interests through sanctions if possible, through threat of violence if necessary, or through war. In war, love would be marginalized, but it might still be important as an ethic of proportionality. After the war, love could become a dominant feature of policy through reconciliation, reconstruction, and ultimately forgiveness of the defeated enemies, as with U.S. policy toward its former World War II enemies, Germany and Japan.

Principles must be made into doctrines of *action*. Pacifism is one, just war theory another. The first may attempt too much and the latter is a poor fit for current military conflicts with quasi-nations, failed states, and subnational terrorist organizations. Jesus blessed the peacemaker, but he did not condemn the centurion, and was not above using force himself. He was a preacher, not a national leader with responsibility for the physical welfare of the nation and its peoples. With miraculous power, he calmed the sea and fed five thousand, but he did not use that power to abolish war. He blessed the peacemaker, not the pacifist. But while he relied on the centurions to maintain the peace that allowed him to travel and preach, he also was prosecuted and executed by those same centurions.

How should love and peace be actualized among nervous and hostile nations with nuclear weapons? Humanity was saved from a nuclear World War III due in large part to the doctrine of nuclear deterrence developed in the 1950s by RAND Corporation and summarized in Herman Kahn's *On Thermonuclear War*. Kahn had many moral critics. How could a nuclear war be anything but evil? Or nuclear deterrent strategy, with the severe risks it ran and the consequences it might cause? Yet abandoning nuclear weapons in favor of the principle of peace runs the risk of national dismemberment and subservience. Which risk was more likely and which had the better chance of deterring war, death, and violence? Nuclear deterrence was not a lesser evil; it was a risky, prudential evil that helped to effectively avoid a catastrophic evil. Principles should be moral, but they also must reflect reasonable calculations in a world of danger and uncertainty.

Yet critics of Kahn and his work also charged that he represented a reasoning that was speculative rather than historical and offered a closed mathematical rationality divorced from ethical considerations. Moral choices can be purely rational and secular—more or less troops and causalities for this or that goal. In Vietnam, rationality was personified by Robert McNamara and his advisors. Leaders can fail by avoiding choices, events can overwhelm intentions, and in the face of miscalculations, leaders may stay with a policy for political reasons or emotional commitment (Shapley 1993, 305, 359). Game theory and matrixes of options are reasonable modes of analysis for understanding conflict and weighing potential decisions, but analyses based upon pure rationalism will not adequately grasp the nature of the enemy or the war in Afghanistan. The Israel of scripture is a reminder of the power and danger of identity politics and particularism. It demonstrates the religious fervency that renders rationality inadequate, diplomacy impotent, and military operations outside the bounds of international laws of war. Rationality must be augmented with an appreciation of the impact of a religiosity that promotes jihad and suicide bombers. Rationality in choices is crucial, but it also is constrained by personal and historical factors, and it must include ethical reasoning that encompasses moral factors.

The suffering and dislocation caused by war are a tragedy recognized in Genesis, yet life on earth is organized under the verdict of Babel—division, misunderstanding, ambition, and failure of universalizing projects. Rather than re-creating Eden, God has left us to the processes of history that combine hope and fear, risk and the unknown. A popular derivative principle is that war should be the last resort. Yet Afghanistan demonstrates the possible dangers of waiting too long and forfeiting successful defenses. Trying to avoid miscalculations by going to war too early risks a fearsome response from a wide spectrum, from nuclear to terrorist, and may well provoke formerly reluctant neighboring adversaries to get involved. "It's kind of like World War I," said retired U.S. Marine General Anthony Zinni, "with both sides mobilizing on automatic . . . which makes it extremely dangerous right now. What I worry about here is a miscalculation" (Graham and Ricks 2002, A10).

The present is not like 1939, where one or two madmen drove the conflict. This is far more complex, with multiple nations existing in ambition and fear, where miscalculations could spark a series of military actions that might quickly spread and escalate. Working for peace in the near future means defining that term short of shalom. Rejecting dualism and fundamentalism, evangelicals recognize that the United States must be deeply involved in the region, utilizing the best modes of rationality possible, combining the normative concern for peace with the cold rationality of Kahn. A U.S. security policy for the region will use multiple means of calculation—defining the stakes involved, empirical studies of war, war gaming, negotiating decisions on arms sales to the region, profiling leaders in the region, and preparations for postwar planning.

Devising policy that operationalizes principles like love and peace is serious, for God refrains from directing the processes of international politics and affairs of nations. In the midst of those processes, however, one scriptural principle is normative, operationalized, and active—God is present with us through the Holy Spirit who is the manifestation of God's grace. We, then, are responsible for conducting a grace-infused dialogue that balances a commitment to moral norms of scripture with the political realities and military necessities. This is a dialogue between experience, reason, and speculation, between ethical and empirical modes of reasoning.

Evangelicals who reject fundamentalism, dual morality, and group think recognize the imperative of a national security policy that is relevant to actual dangers from nations, quasi-nations, and terrorist groups. It must be relevant enough to prevent 2014 from becoming a repeat of 1914, moral and courageous enough to minimize the depravity and despair of wars without bounds, and prophetic and politically farsighted enough to avoid laying the foundation for future war. This kind of evangelical recognizes the necessity of living with operational principles that seek rational control of the means of violence while trusting God to lead believers in times of paradoxes and through dilemmas without clear answers. They accept the responsibility to devise and pursue national security policy that seemingly compromises principles and stabs the conscience. They must hold steadfastly to their First Love in the midst of the complexities around them. Responsibility and piety must be bound together with the principles of this world.

BIBLICAL BIOGRAPHIES

Four biographies from scripture reflect the application of morality to politics. Joseph was sold by his brothers into captivity, then jailed after false accusations of sexual misconduct. But when he got a chance to impress the Pharaoh, he correctly interpreted the monarch's dream as a risk analysis. He then took the further step of proposing a plan that enriched the Pharaoh and destroyed the wealth of the people. Perhaps because of his background, Joseph was determined not to be cast down again. So his proposal was self-serving for both him and the Pharaoh. He turned out to be an efficient administrator in implementing the plan, but lacked moral perspective on the common good, choosing instead to ingratiate himself with the Pharaoh.

Daniel was an exile in Babylon, living without choice at the time of empire, just as we have no choice about living in the time of war in Afghanistan. Daniel actively engaged his times and served as a regional administrator. He rejected part of his inculcation into their culture (rich food), and continued his practice of prayer despite a public edict outlawing such prayers, a law aimed at him. He was convicted and sentenced to death, but survived. When he later interpreted a dream for Nebuchadnezzar, he (unlike Joseph) attributed his insight to the guidance of his God. He fit himself into the empire, but without sacrificing his faith in God's sovereignty.

Esther was a Jewish exile living as queen to the Persian monarch. She uncovered a plan to kill all the Jews in the empire and faced a choice—stay quiet and safe, or risk her position and perhaps even her life by lobbying the king. She chose the latter, skillfully working the wheels of court politics and ultimately prevailing. Unlike Esther, Sergeant Graner lacked moral courage despite his Christianity. In contrast, Sergeant Darby acted with courage and paid a high price professionally and socially.

Joab was King David's military chief who sabotaged David's summit with Abner to reunite the two factions of Israel after Saul's death by assassinating Abner. There was miscalculation. Personally hating Abner and lacking the intelligence (spies) to discern Abner's real motives, Joab assumed the worst-case scenario that the summit was a pretext to prepare an attack on David. Later he protected David's flight from Jerusalem when Absalom overthrew his father, killing Absalom against David's specific orders because he knew Absalom would always be a threat to David's rule. With political insight, he spoke truth to power, bluntly telling David that his mourning for his son was not good for the nation or for maintaining the loyalty of the people. Yet he arranged the death of Uriah at David's instruction and complied with David's demand for a census. His opportunism led him to ally himself with Adonijah, the presumed successor to David, and as a result he missed the conspiratorial alliance of Nathan the prophet and the adulteress Bathsheba. They made Solomon king and had Joab killed for treason. Joab exemplified, in Churchill's terms, the limited minds of even the ablest men, who may have a good political compass but who look out for themselves without a personal moral compass.

BIBLICAL NARRATIVES

Four narratives likewise offer important insights into the challenges faced by Christians participating in the defense establishment. Consider Samuel and Saul. Samuel had been the reigning prophet judge and expected his sons to follow him as leaders of Israel. But they were corrupt, and the people wanted no part of them, instead demanding a king. Without his own military forces to maintain his position Samuel relented, and anointed Saul as king. The Spirit came upon Saul, and the Lord changed Saul's heart (I Sam 10:6, 9). But would the prophet still prevail in the new realm of politics?

Samuel went to Saul to inform him of God's command to attack the Amalekites. They had lived in the area since Abraham and had attacked the invading Israelites, for which Moses had pronounced historical enmity and judgment against them (Exodus 17:14–15). Do not merely defeat them, Samuel said; the God of revenge and genocide demands that you utterly destroy the men and women, the infants learning to talk, and the teens about to marry—even destroy all their livestock and possessions (I Sam 15). Saul led the battle and destroyed the people, but yielded to the demands of his soldiers that they keep some of the possessions as plunder.

Samuel told Saul that, because he had disobeyed, the Lord had abandoned him and rejected Saul's repentance. Saul faced a dilemma, caught between a religious leader demanding a moral absolute and his people presenting their selfish demands. Samuel recognized his powerlessness to dethrone the king, so he withdrew, content to criticize from the sidelines like a resident alien. Nor did God dethrone the king. Saul ruled for four decades, fighting enemies and growing increasingly despondent and paranoid. In the war between the houses of Saul and David, similar stories delegitimized Saul and legitimized David's claim to the throne and to establish an alternate family dynasty. They also reflect the dilemma of Christians in Congress caught between the multiple political values of the needs of the Pentagon, the power competition between parties, and the demands of their electoral districts for jobs in defense industries. Each member must prioritize these competing demands, with the risks that accompany them.

The story of David and Goliath has a dual reading. The giant was clothed with the latest in military technology, a thick coat of mail, bronze helmet, armor on his legs, and massive spear and iron spearhead. He challenged the

Israelites to send out a champion to fight, and Saul declined. The Israelites had the same Bronze Age military assets, but calculating power is not simple. It can be calculated empirically by totaling the various armaments. That calculation means little if the power cannot be used. Power can be great, must be usable, but can also be irrelevant. David rejected the latest military technology in favor of a primitive weapon, against which Goliath's armor was of little use. All the measurements of power identified with Goliath were irrelevant to the battle with the small and nimble David; David avoided the giant's spear and used a slingshot and a rock to attack his point of vulnerability. With the right weapons, the weak can render the military forces of the powerful irrelevant.

The United States is Goliath and the insurgents in Afghanistan are Davids. The United States has technologically sophisticated military means, which are largely irrelevant to the insurgent battles waged in the city streets. And the insurgents' improvised explosive devices are just as deadly as David's stone and slingshot. This is asymmetrical warfare.

As a modern-day Goliath, the United States must take care to avoid the assumptions and trappings of imperialism and the "Egyptianization" of its people in public service as happened to Joseph (Brueggemann 2007, 28). The Pentagon and the defense firms are massive bureaucracies, susceptible to arrogance, blind policy, and loss of moral imagination. Isaiah criticized the leaders of Babylon for letting their knowledge warp their thinking (Isaiah 47:10). As President Kennedy put it, we must be sure to "determine whether we use power or power uses us" (Kennedy 1963, 816). Evangelicals must relate to Daniel rather than Joseph, who accommodated himself to the Pharaoh, his empire, and its increasingly inhumane modes of thinking.

National security policy is further complicated by the rise in new kinds of threats and the need for highly technological forces. Cyber-attacks against the Pentagon are now commonplace. Space is becoming a new area of conflict, with China joining Russia as a nation capable of placing satellites and weapons in orbit and of destroying U.S. satellites, upon which so much commercial business and military operations depend. The United States must emulate David, aiming for nimble and technologically agile forces that can be employed in relevant ways to the modern era. This is already occurring, as the CIA is evolving in the midst of the asymmetrical war in Afghanistan and elsewhere into a paramilitary organization of great value.

Perhaps God is in control of history, but if so, one hopes that his plan for 2014 is not the same as 1914. Richard Bauckham argues that nuclear weapons give humanity the power to do what we once thought only God could do—blow up the world. Consequently, we must rethink the theological meaning of history and take human freedom more seriously (Bauckham 1985, 590, 595–96). God's good grace has transformed individual lives, but it has never transformed international politics. History is neither contingent nor determined. We must use the margins of freedom allowed by God and circumstances, and we must prove more able than those in 1914. Forces and doctrines must be designed to control fate, make peace, and give time for diplomats and humanitarians to build a more prophetic future of peace. This is the work for analytical evangelicals more than fatalistic fundamentalists who would welcome Armageddon.

The narrative of Samson and Delilah provides perspective as we move from war issues to intelligence in the context of Afghanistan. The United States faces al Qaeda religious terrorists secretly planning attacks in Afghanistan and within the United States. The United States must obtain clandestine information about threats abroad while protecting itself against attacks on its own soil. The strong are defeated only by weapons or strategy; they can be defeated by their own inattention, duplicity, or naivety in the face of enemy activity. Jeremiah lamented the foolishness of his people in dismissing the sounds of war and the approaching disaster (Jeremiah 4:19–22).

The fourth narrative involves the invaders who overthrew Belshazzar and the Babylonian Empire by using its infrastructure and water works to secretly enter the capital city. Much of the U.S. infrastructure is vulnerable to physical and cyber-attack. The loss of a few communications satellites would cripple the banking industry and the "net-centric" military forces; likewise, the loss of power generation or transportation centers would cause havoc with our ability to respond.

BIBLICALLY INFUSED WISDOM

In the name of national security, we send our troops to fight in far-off lands. They are volunteers who, like Army Specialist Schaffel, may end up feeling betrayed by a government stumbling into war or just lose their way in the midst of war's depravity. There is too much blood on the pages of history to believe that a good God specifically controls history. There is too little evidence for an expansive view of creation that asserts the international order is part of God's creative plan and purpose. If evangelicals in the twenty-first century are not awaiting Armageddon or the fuller revelation of Christ's Kingdom, is history just sound and fury signifying nothing?

A relevant set of scriptures for these questions is the wisdom literature of Ecclesiastes and Proverbs. That literature is philosophical, practical, and personal. It is not about military strategy per se, but it does offer an important view of the world. It moves away from national particularity and sacred space to a more personal glimpse of time and of earth and God's presence in it. It connects individuals directly to God and humanizes history as a series of personal opportunities (a time to . . . a time to . . . a time to . . .). This is different than the wisdom of James, which is interpersonal and which portrays our lives as only a mist with little value except in being good to others (James 3:17, 4:14). Though Ecclesiastes exudes pervasive meaninglessness, when taken together with Proverbs, it provides a global perspective on individuals and nations and for bringing our faith to a troubled world. Wisdom is gained through effort, gleaned from studying the reality of international politics in the light of the "fear of the Lord" (Prov 1:2–7, 2:1–6). It melds intellect and piety to better understand the providence and moral order of God (Clements 1992, 157, 153–56). It offers a path between moral dualism, group think, and the nationalizing of personal morality.

It is a crucial path because the power which leaders wield through nuclear weapons means that we are more at the mercy of miscalculation. The good news is that, though God may refrain from directing the affairs of nations, he is not necessarily absent. Evangelicals know that decision making is not merely good judgment—that is, a correct assessment of the situation and the prescribing of effective policy to be achieved at the lowest cost (Haas 2003, 252). Our wisdom perspective affirms a positive, global, moral order beyond mere rational choice or national self-interest. An example is the international law of war. Even as the value of that law in the context of asymmetrical war is up for debate, it still offers a global perspective beyond cold calculation and sound judgment. It allows evangelicals to partner with secularists to affirm a morality beyond national particularism. God moves within individuals to plant a moral intuition, empowering them to articulate that moral view and to advance it with prudence and courage. Thus can men support, defend, and advance a moral world, as Robert Kennedy did when he spoke morality to power and successfully persuaded his colleagues.

Yet that movement is not always smooth or successful. We know from the example of July 1914 of the potential for disastrous miscalculations and the overriding of moral issues by military strategy and human stubbornness. That dynamic is still possible, especially between India and Pakistan, where military disparity and differing assumptions about transcendence make for grave uncertainty. These national security issues carry the highest of earthly stakes. Nevertheless, pessimism should never overcome hope, even in the darkest of times, as the defeat of Hitler and other achievements demonstrate.

Wisdom means finding moral coherence in the rise and fall of nations. It means subordinating oneself to the overarching sweep of history, accepting the mystery of God's involvement in time, and acting when opportunities present themselves in the midst of God's larger providence (Brown 1996, 44). It avoids conditioning faith on nationalism, dismissing the here and now while awaiting Armageddon, or indulging utopian self-deceptions. It comes from a combination of moral character, grace, political and military skill, and common sense.

The war in Afghanistan cannot be considered in isolation, for it is a piece of the broader sweep of history involving neighbors, the rise of militant religion, regional nuclear power, and the security and future leadership of the United States. Evangelical wisdom can offer counsel that this is an opportunity to act wisely and aim for control of events. For war planners, this wisdom means that the principle of love can be operationalized before, during, and after war. It reminds our leaders that the continuing struggle for a moral order requires avoiding Joseph's Egyptianization and Joab's lack of moral principles. It expresses the need to exhibit Daniel's faith and Esther's courage, to be alert enough not to be deceived, and to be transcendent enough not to let service rivalries and the allure of new weaponry warp the understanding of the nature of relevant power.

This chapter ends where Bauckham does, with a trust and hope in God that does not deny human freedom and the potential for miscalculation, nor does it detract from human responsibility. Instead, it sustains us against despair in our efforts to manage events and realize continuing proximate peace (Bauckham 1985, 600).

Part III

Engaging Culture: Counterforce or Capitulation?

Chapter Ten

Love Rightly Understood: Reflections on the Substance, Style, and Spirit of Evangelical Activism and (Same-Sex) Marriage Policy

David K. Ryden and Jeffrey J. Polet[1]

It has been suggested by no less an authority than President Obama that America's culture wars are behind us. In support of this, some cite the declining importance of same-sex marriage as a priority to much of the public. Yet the following items indicate that the same-sex marriage as a public policy debate is unlikely to subside any time soon.

- On May 15, 2008, the California state Supreme Court overturned a state law and required that the state recognize marriage between couples of the same sex. In October, Connecticut's high court followed suit, holding that gays have the legal and constitutional right to marry. Previously, Massachusetts had similarly relied upon judicial action to validate same-sex marriage.
- On November 4, 2008, California adopted a ballot initiative that amended its state constitution to ban same-sex marriage. Ballot measures prohibiting same-sex marriage also passed in Arizona and Florida, bringing to thirty those states that have legally defined marriage as exclusively limited to a man and woman.

These events suggest an increasing tension around the controversy over the legal status of gay marriage. A growing body of law at the state level prohibits same-sex marriage, even while popular resistance to the idea gradually softens, suggesting, perhaps, a last-ditch effort by traditionalists to hold on to their position.

One is hard pressed to think of an issue of similar import that has undergone such a transformation with respect to public sentiments. Two decades ago attitudes on gay marriage were not even polled. While majorities today still disapprove of gay marriage, the size of that majority is shrinking. Younger Americans fancy themselves more open-minded about same-sex marriage, enough so that changing generational demographics may inevitably lead to legal recognition of gay marriage.[2]

Consequently, the ballot victories for opponents of same-sex marriage may prove short-lived. Evolving public attitudes combined with a judicial willingness to review and possibly overturn ballot initiatives—as seen in the Court's rulings in *Lawrence v. Texas* and the recent Massachusetts rulings striking down provisions of the Defense of Marriage Act—almost assures a looming constitutional battle on this central front in the culture wars. This has important implications for evangelicals who oppose same-sex marriage in far greater numbers than the rest of the country. Almost two-thirds of white evangelicals think homosexuality should be discouraged, while 81 percent oppose same-sex marriage (2008 U.S. Religious Landscape survey).

These data may suggest that evangelical Christians are on the wrong side of history, or are agents of homophobia and bigotry. Such negative perceptions of some Christians threaten to undermine the ability of evangelicals to be taken seriously as reasonable participants in public debates over gay marriage. For this reason, evangelical Christians need to develop a thoughtful, publicly accessible set of arguments on gay marriage, and be especially attentive to avoiding behavior that makes them easy targets of such charges.

This chapter seeks to articulate a constructive approach by which evangelical Christians might engage others on the issue of same-sex marriage. To accomplish this, we focus on two sets of arguments: first, to address the issue within the Christian community; second, to help the Christian community make arguments that might be publicly acceptable in a pluralistic social sphere. The first set of arguments might be thought of as *theological* while the second set is *political*. We are skeptical of the claim that any opposition to gay marriage is necessarily a religious one and thus a violation of the religion clauses of the First Amendment. This is the argument offered by Geoffrey Stone, a faculty member at the University of Chicago Law School. Stone argues the following: Prop 8 passed by a margin of 52–48. Those who identified themselves as evangelicals voted for it by a margin of 81–19 while non-Christians voted against it 85–15. For this reason, Stone believes, Prop 8 is an establishment into law of a particular religious belief. But consider that black voters voted 70–30 in favor of Prop 8. One can't imagine Stone making the claim that the law is an instantiation of racial preferences, or because elderly people were more likely to favor Prop 8, that it entrenched age preferences. Why single out religion? We raise this point in this context to entertain the possibility that charges of bigotry against evangelical Christians may themselves be informed by bigotry against evangelical Christians, and further obscure the relationship between theological and political arguments.

THE THEOLOGICAL ARGUMENT CONCERNING MARRIAGE

Our examination of the theological argument against same-sex marriage derives from two sources: the Christian Bible and tradition. As to the latter, we suggest that Christian practice through the ages carries with it a certain weight, and those who seek to change the practice or, in this instance, fundamentally alter a bedrock social institution, have the onus placed upon them to provide compelling reasons to do so.

The framework for assessing gay marriage both from the biblical and secular perspectives is found in the broad context of marriage itself. The scriptural stance on same-sex marriage must be linked to marriage as a central dimension of God's creative design for humanity. Note the emphasis here on God's design for marriage, which is independent of how particular cultures, even those who occupy a central place within the scriptural narrative, may have arranged the institution of marriage. A criticism of the "biblical case for marriage" has centered on the fact that marriage and commentary on marriage takes many forms in the Bible, ranging from Pauline devaluing of marriage to Old Testament polygamy and concubinage.[3] Independent of particular cultural forms of marriage, however, there remain biblical injunctions for marriage as well as the delineating of the design and purpose of marriage, which transcend those particulars.

A defining attribute of evangelicalism is the confidence in the Bible as the revealed word of God. Evangelicals are more inclined to adopt a literal reading of scripture than are other theological traditions. They also are more likely to look to scriptural authority for explicit answers to policy questions.[4] Evangelicals examine the "length and breadth of scripture" for guidance and direction in what is moral and right (Gushee and Hollinger 2005, 137).

The evangelical position on same-sex marriage begins with those specific biblical references to homosexuality, what evangelical theologian John Stott calls *the negative proscriptions* (Stott 1998, 122). Several explicit scriptural passages (NIV) speak directly to homosexual behavior:

- Leviticus 18:22: "Do not lie with a man as one lies with a woman; that is detestable."
- Leviticus 20:13: "If a man lies with a man as one lies with a woman, both of them have done what is detestable."
- Romans 1:26–27: "God gave them over to shameful lusts. Even their women exchanged natural relations for unnatural ones. In the same way the men also abandoned natural relations with women and were inflamed with lust for one another. Men committed indecent acts with other men."
- I Corinthians 6:9–10: "Neither the sexually immoral . . . nor homosexual offenders . . . will inherit the kingdom of God."

Evangelicals find little ambiguity in these provisions. Homosexual relations are sinful, and to be discouraged. By extension, they cannot be the foundation for the marriage relationship.[5]

It has been argued against a straightforward reading of these texts by, for example, Lisa Miller in *Newsweek*, that neither the Bible nor Jesus defines marriage as the relation between one man and one woman. "No sensible modern person," she writes, "wants marriage—theirs or anyone else's—to look in its particulars anything like what the Bible describes." More pejoratively, she notes that "Ozzie and Harriet are nowhere in the New Testament." The above passages are regarded by her as "throwaway lines" with no more normative weight for us than Levitical dicta on haircuts or blood sacrifices (Miller 2008). Her claim, however, confuses context with significance. In the passages from Leviticus, only the offense of homosexuality is taken as an "abomination," a word used infrequently enough that we generally take the prohibitions seriously even today. The condemnation of homosexual practice is grouped with other impure sexual offenses that don't admit of simple cleansing rituals. Additionally, the proscription carries within itself its reasoning as grounded in the ordered nature of things. Homosexual practice is thus against the nature of things, for it treats another male as if he were a woman.

Miller, noting that the Bible as a "living document" gives us no reason to oppose same-sex marriage but many reasons to support it, also claims that it's male-on-male sex that is condemned, not lesbianism; that in Romans Paul is condemning in particular the craven violence of the Roman emperors; and that Paul condemns divorce more than he does homosexuality. As to the first point, the infrequency of condemnation doesn't decide the issue. Paul condemns divorce more than he does bestiality or incest, but one would be hard pressed to suggest that he therefore approved of the latter. Rather, more likely he rarely condemned such things because they were self-evidently wrong and required no condemnation, while divorce was still an unsettled area of Jewish law and required more reflection. This makes more sense of his infrequent references to male-on-male sex, and singular reference to lesbianism (Miller wrongly asserts that lesbianism is never mentioned; see Romans 1:26). Lesbianism was, in the ancient world, a self-evidently wrong sexual practice, and therefore Miller mistakenly states that "sex between women . . . never raised as much ire," for it did not need condemning.

As to her second point, that it was not male-on-male sex to which Paul was voicing opposition, but violence, that can only be the case if we accept the claim that all discussions concerning sexuality address themselves only to the conventions of sex, but not to the nature of sex itself. This is a distinction Miller never bothers to make, but the Bible and Jesus do (see Christ's narrative in Mark 10 and Matthew 19, for example, where he explicitly invokes the creational distinction between male and female). For this reason, Miller claims that objections to gay marriage among Christians can only come from "custom and tradition." But if that were true, the same could be said of the advocacy for gay marriage and doesn't address the issue of whether something could be wrong in itself. In this regard Miller's reference to the Bible's apparent "endorsement" of slavery is misplaced. The Bible doesn't present slavery as part of God's created design for humanity, the way it does male/female relationships. The Bible tolerates slavery, but doesn't display any interest in preserving the institution the way it does marriage as a male/female union. Furthermore, the push of the scripture is toward slavery's curtailment and eradication; no such claim can be made about heterosexual marriage.[6]

The evangelical perspective, however, contains not only specific negative prohibitions, but locates them within a positive view of marriage.[7] Beyond the particularity of explicit proscription is the *positive message of creation*, the emphasis on the Bible as God's revealed and life-affirming truth writ large. Beyond word-for-word biblical literalism is a view of scripture as the source of God's creative design for the world. It sets forth the "essential positives of divine revelation on sexuality and marriage" (Stott 1998, 43). According to this view, the Bible is more than a list of dos and don'ts. It reveals the essence of God's creative order, offering a holistic understanding of the goodness of God's creation, including His provision for human sexuality.

At the center is the creation story, man and woman made for each other and for sexual intimacy in the context of lifelong marriage and procreative actions (it is in the genetic creation of new life that two beings in love literally become one new creature). The biblical creation narrative makes clear the differentiation and complementary nature of the two sexes. God not only created man in His image, but "male and female he created them" (Genesis 1:27). Genesis expresses the human need for companionship ("It is not good for the man to be alone") and God's meeting of that need via the special creation of male and female. God's design culminates in sexual differentiation, the institution of marriage, and human sexual ordering and fulfillment within that marriage. Man and woman are joined together before God, becoming one in a relationship of love, intimacy, creativity and procreation, exclusiveness, and permanence (Minnery and Stanton 2005, 250–51).[8] Moreover, in the becoming of one flesh in the act of procreation, man and woman reflect God's creative work and love.

Christ himself confirmed the Genesis account of sexuality and marriage as normative and prescriptive. His explicit references to Genesis reinforced the centrality of exclusive heterosexual intimacy within the framework of marriage. He left no doubt that the differentiation of the sexes is a divine creation, heterosexual marriage a divine institution, and heterosexual fidelity the divine intention (Stott 1998, 36).

Sexuality, then, is grounded in the scriptural revelation of marriage as a central piece of the created order wherein the complementary differences of men and women find their expression and fulfillment. It is a covenantal relationship between human beings that mirrors God's promises to us. As one pair of scholars put it, marriage is "not an incidental human construction but a creational reality. Any sexual ethic constructed without a clear connection to a theology of marriage is destined to be deficient" (Jones and Yarhouse 2000, 164).

Human sexuality is part of God's gift to and design for human beings. Miller claims that Paul's seemingly cool attitude toward marriage results from a "lack of interest in things of the flesh," and therefore has no normative weight. But conversely, Paul might have thought so highly of marriage that he uses it as the predominant metaphor for the relationship between (the male) Christ and his (female) church. Paul's point may be summed up with two considerations: first, he accepts a distinction between holiness and righteousness, and that while married life is an unmitigated good, the life of holiness and celibacy can be better still; second, that there is no moral imperative for sexual activity (that is, we are not morally required to engage in sex in the same way we are required to engage in acts of charity). Certainly there is a biological imperative for sexual activity, but it is not a biological function in which all persons need to engage.

If homosexual behavior stands outside the bounds of God's creative plan for humanity, then those who experience persistent same-sex attraction obey through celibacy. In general, we are agnostic on the question of the etiology of same-sex attractedness. Let's assume, however, certain persons have a natural disposition toward same-sex activity. This disposition can no more become a justification for action than a disposition toward pedophilia could become a justification for pedophilic action or toward animals could for bestiality. Scientists have identified genes related to a proclivity for alcoholism, but we don't conclude from this that persons with the gene ought to be allowed to drink freely. Quite the contrary—those are the persons we would most likely attempt to dissuade from drinking at all. It may be argued that pedophilia and bestiality do not involve consensual sex, but we'll argue below that consent isn't a strong enough concept to ground human sexual activity. It will also be argued that, unlike pedophilia or alcoholism, homosexuality is not a pathology. But that isn't a scientific judgment, it is a moral or political judgment, and at the heart of the debate.

The point is not whether same-sex orientation means a person can or cannot be a Christian; rather, the question is simply whether homosexual behavior is acceptable Christian practice, and on this score Christian theological thinking indicates the negative. Biblically grounded sexual ethics requires refraining from behavior in conflict with God's created order—whether it be homosexual intimacy, adultery, fornication, or other sexual sin. This implies several things. First, disputes over sexual orientation (a problematic term in itself) as nature versus choice are largely irrelevant to the underlying morality of homosexual behavior. Whatever one's sexual inclinations in the first place, Christians are not helpless victims of their own fleshly desires. One cannot be faulted for one's orientation, but one is responsible for what he or she does with that orientation (Gagnon 2005, 298). As John Stott states:

> In every discussion about homosexuality we must be rigorous in differentiating between this "being" and "doing," that is, between a person's identity and activity, sexual preference and sexual practice, constitution and conduct. (Stott 1998, 14)

This standard of obedience is not imposed solely on homosexuals. While gay persons are called to a life of celibacy, all Christians are called to the proper ordering and disciplining of their sexual desires. The homosexual's burden—desires and passions that he or she did not choose—is the common plight of all humanity: "[H]ow are we to live when what we want is out of accord with what God tells us we should want in this life?" (Jones and Yarhouse 2000, 181).

It also means Christians must guard against selective denunciation of gays. While demanding celibacy from the homosexual, conservative Christians often fail to apply the same standard of sexual purity to all Christians. Yet they are as apt to live in disobedience of biblical imperatives on sexual immorality as nonbelievers. They divorce, engage in premarital sex and adultery, and suffer from marital abuse at rates that equal those of non-evangelicals (Sider 2005b, 17). Evangelical Christians are so habituated to pervasive cultural habits as to deserve the charges of hypocrisy for railing against homosexuality without reflecting on their own behavior and that of their fellow Christians. Their hypocrisy, however, doesn't discount the principle itself.

Christians also must acknowledge the magnitude of what is being asked of the gay Christian. It is difficult to forego the unique human connection expressed in sexual intimacy; it is a self-sacrifice to which most heterosexuals will never have to relate. Hopefully gay Christians are able to bear witness to Christ's work in them, and testify to a new sense of personal fulfillment as children of God. But even this does not necessarily mean delivery from one's sexual inclinations; hence there is likely to be no small amount of pain and struggle over matters of sexual temptation (Stott 1998, 76). Part of the failure of the church has been its inability or unwillingness to provide an alternative self-concept from the cultural construction of a gay identity to those who experience persistent same-sex attraction (Yarhouse 2007). The Christian church must help persons with those attractions to think of themselves not in terms of a gay "identity," but as Christian brothers and sisters who, like all of us, struggle with concupiscence.[9] Gay or straight, we are invited to become new creations in Christ, free from the sinful nature that enslaves us. That holds true for all sexual activity that contradicts God's ordering of our lives as morally good. All Christians will be alien in a culture that eschews self-denial, sacrifice, and a willingness to admit our guilt before God, to seek forgiveness, and to follow Christ in obedience to his revealed will.

BIBLICAL LOVE AND COMPASSION RIGHTLY UNDERSTOOD

Probably the most significant theological challenge to the above understanding of same-sex behavior is the idea that Christianity is an inclusive religion which accepts all sinners. This is not simply an argument for toleration, however—that is, learning to live with something you think is wrong. Rather, it is an argument for acceptance and compassion: to embrace the other in the fullness of his or her identity. As one gay Christian theologian puts it, "A gay person is not simply a homosexual, but one who recognizes his or her loving impulses towards members of the same-sex as so deeply definitive of his or her personhood that disowning them would be an act of self-betrayal" (Long 2005, 53). The conjoining of two persons who have a mutual desire for one another is thus understood as a basic human right and good. Furthermore, writers who defend this argument point out that Jesus' ministry was to everyone, but particularly to those "on the margins," those scorned and rejected according to social customs.

This biblical case involves a selective reading of the texts. Jesus tells the adulteress in John 8 that he doesn't condemn her, but she should "go now, and leave her life of sin." Clearly Jesus is distinguishing between the sinner and the sin, condemning the latter but not the former. The plain meaning of the gospel is that Jesus came to sinners, and that we are all sinners in need of his mercy. At the same time, such mercy requires repentance and a transformation of the self so that we no longer engage in sin and that we "pluck out" the offending organ that causes us to transgress. Indeed, the gospel demands sacrifice, a difficult and arduous task of obedience which may require of us that we abstain from deep desires and follow the way of the cross.

For this reason "compassion" is an inadequate basis for managing human relations, for it requires us to accept the other as they are. It loves people not enough, for it doesn't require of them the disciplining of the sexual desires that is expected of all of us. It holds gay persons to be less responsible for the use of their sexuality than other Christians according to the design for human sexuality as laid down in scripture. A theologically informed understanding of love undermines those justifications offered in favor of gay marriage. The evangelical tradition rejects these views as elevating a shallow understanding of happiness over the promise of God's redemptive grace and the happiness that comes from living in His will. God "welcomes us in order to redeem and transform us, not to leave us alone in our sins" (Stott 1998, 59).

Faith in the revealed truth of God and His creation means accepting that this truth is good and good for us. The preference for exclusive, heterosexual marriage flows from a genuine belief in God's created order as good—indeed, best—for individuals and communities. Leading a sexually active gay lifestyle means satisfaction on a personal level, but undermines the far greater good of living according to and in harmony with God's created order. Christian efforts to normalize homosexual behavior show a "widespread loss of faith in a just but gracious transcendent God" (Satinover 1996, 166). In Stott's words, "[gay relationships] are incompatible with true love because they are incompatible with God's law. Love is concerned for the highest welfare of the beloved. And our highest human welfare is found in obedience to God's law and purpose, not in revolt against them" (Stott 1998, 55). That is love rightly understood.

At the same time Christ's love must infuse both word *and* deed. The celibate homosexual condition is undeniably one of loneliness and unfulfilled desire for mutual love and affection. But the choices are not merely between "the warm physical relationship of homosexual intercourse and the pain of isolation in the cold. There is a third option, namely a Christian environment of love, understanding, acceptance, and support" (Stott 1998, 81). Where ought the celibate gay Christian to find this, but in the church? Christian churches should not reject homosexuals, but ought to accept them as fellow sinners and support them in a life of obedience.

THE PUBLIC CASE FOR TRADITIONAL MARRIAGE

For evangelical Christians, the scriptural response to same-sex marriage is straightforward: it is not only possible for gays to lead a celibate life, but, with God's grace, for that life to be rich and rewarding. However, policy debates are rarely won with such overtly religious arguments. In a liberal polity evangelical Christians must connect *in secular terms* God's rule for creation to societal well-being. This requires translating arguments from an explicitly religious cast into public language based upon considerations of the common good. Our pluralist society challenges Christians to persuade from common principles of social science, policy analysis, common sense, and logic. Perhaps most importantly, Christians must work to hold on to a moral system grounded in nature and not one grounded in convention.

This creates a paradox for Christians, for they must articulate in culturally relevant language ideas that are frequently countercultural. The problem is made more complex because of the vagueness of many of the moral ideas which dominate our public life: tolerance, inclusiveness, compassion, and equality. Most of these terms are philosophically problematic, and are used with little understanding or precision. Too often, however, evangelicals can be criticized for a lack of rigor in their own thinking, and in the terms they use. They fall back on a once widely accepted Judeo-Christian moral framework, even as the moral rightness of their positions is no longer intuitively clear to society.[10]

The dynamic deepens when we realize that the argument against same-sex marriage is in many ways, especially in a liberal polity, much more difficult to make than the argument for it. This is so for two reasons: first, the issue can seem resolved readily with reference to the claim that no one is harmed by allowing same-sex marriages; and second, our understanding of the nature of a person is ensconced in the language of rights, and it is difficult to make any morally persuasive argument outside the language of rights. This also provides an opening, however, for whatever else the understanding of a human being as a rights-bearing agent is—it is not given in the nature of things. It is no less an article of faith to suggest that human beings possess rights than to suggest they are responsive creatures to divine command. Furthermore, as Mary Ann Glendon has demonstrated, recourse to the language of rights undermines public discourse and democratic processes, for it isolates citizens, absolutizes claims, disconnects from discussions concerning responsibility, falsely creates insoluble dilemmas, and generally makes democratic negotiation impossible (Glendon 1993).[11]

The liberal position, therefore, is not a neutral one, for it presupposes ideas of human nature, human community, and human happiness. It generally reduces questions of sexuality to three considerations: the nature of consent, the nature of desire, and whether anyone is harmed. So in making the public argument for the traditional position, we will first proceed *negatively*—that is, as a critique of these ideas—and then *affirmatively*—that is, how the Christian understanding contributes to a public good independent of whether someone is a Christian.

First, is any sex permissible so long as the parties are consenting? This would seem to rule out pedophilia, for children are thought to be short of the age of informed consent. Mind you, it is difficult to determine at what point a person is no longer a child, or whether that point can be fixed on an age continuum. The age of consent is largely arbitrary, and itself a cultural standard that is susceptible to being moved as people desire. That aside, such a standard wouldn't preclude either incest or varieties of polyamorous relations. Someone who says homosexuality is natural would be hard pressed to make the argument that incest isn't natural. Indeed, scripture is as condemnatory of incest as it is of homosexuality, and for similar reasons. An argument that can be made against homosexuality is that it is having sex with a sexual being already like oneself; in other words, it is not the quintessential union of differences, but sex as an extension of one's own sexuality. Sex then doesn't encourage the kinds of selflessness that genuine sexuality requires. All sex done primarily for pleasure has that fundamental quality of selfishness. In incest also, sex is unwarranted intimacy with someone with whom one is already too similar or familiar. There isn't a complementary difference between the parties.

There also are contingent reasons why incest may be considered a bad idea. We know that incestuous relations produce higher levels of birth defects, but we would resist incest even if that were not the case. For more than that, incest strikes at the order of the family itself; it confuses and obscures the proper ordering of the household, and it obfuscates the proper nature of a jealousy which renounces sexual competition. Civilization requires the confining of sexual desire to its proper sphere. If, however, consent becomes the sole ground of sexual propriety, then we see no reason why incestuous relations among adults shouldn't be openly embraced.[12]

Likewise, monogamy could enjoy no privileged status over polyamorous arrangements. Stanley Kurtz has effectively demonstrated that the same-sex marriage argument is a wedge to open the door to a multiplicity of marital arrangements. The advent of shows such as *Big Love* and the sympathetic interviewing of polygamists on *Oprah* should serve as fair warning that this question is not purely hypothetical. Indeed, law reviews are publishing an ever-increasing number of articles openly advocating for legal recognition of polyamorous arrangements.[13] Such arrangements, however, would require a radical redefinition of the term "marriage" itself; the traditional Christian understanding of marriage as a mutual and binding promise between one man and one woman to enter a procreative bond with each other alone, for life, would be transformed into "a bond of affection between consenting parties so long as they desire."

Indeed, this broad redefinition may be precisely the point. Scott James reported in the *New York Times* (January 28, 2010) that a San Francisco area study of long-term gay couples revealed that 50 percent of them have "open" relationships wherein they are allowed and encouraged to have sex with other persons, even though typically (largely arbitrary) restrictions are put in place. The article notes that this is a well-known arrangement in the gay community but that it isn't publicized for fear that it will undermine their claims to same-sex marriage. Gays are lauded for "bringing a fresh perspective" that might save a dying institution, with the resultant claim that "if innovation in marriage is going to occur, it will be spearheaded by homosexual marriages." Such innovation will necessarily destroy older forms, the loss of which might be keenly felt by its adherents, many of whom still believe in marriage as a vivified institution. In this "open" arrangement, we see how consent trumps all other considerations such that it deinstitutionalizes marriage itself. Consent proves to be too weak of a concept to undergird an institution as weighty as marriage, for it is too arbitrary, too ephemeral, and too likely to be a slave to desire.

Innovation introduces instability into marriage commensurate with the instability of our desires. That is not the only problem, however, for once again it makes hash out of a loving jealousy which recognizes in one other person someone with whom we are fitted to live. Without that, how would one deny to someone their polyamorous desires? How could they legitimately experience or express the hurt and pain they feel when preference has been expressed for someone else? Is, in fact, the restricting of any sexual desire unjust? To suggest that someone has been treated unjustly, we would have to discuss the nature of what they have been denied, that what they have been denied is a good, and that one is entitled to that good (Beckwith 2005, 42). None of these are self-evident. If the nature of marriage is evolving, however, it would be difficult to make any of those claims; we can't really know anything about the topic under discussion, since the reality of marriage is too fluid to provide a basis for discussion. This makes the claim of *anyone* to marriage as a good to which they are entitled problematic.

"Desire" as the foundation for marital freedom proves insufficient. Perhaps the problem goes back to Hume's observation that "reason is, and ought to be only the slave of the passions" (Hume 1965). Whether that is an acceptable view of human nature is a large part of the conversation, but those are precisely the questions advocates of same-sex marriage typically avoid. While most would link desire to consent as a means of limiting the former, desire raises the question of ordered and disordered desires, with an extreme form in bestiality. The moral case for bestiality has been made most forcefully by the well-known Princeton ethicist Peter Singer in his notorious essay "Heavy Petting" (Singer 2001). Singer argues that not only do a significant percentage of Americans have sex with animals but that the practice itself also "ceases to be an offence to our status and dignity as human beings." The taboo against sex with animals, Singer believes, arises from the human desire to differentiate themselves from other creatures and retain a higher status. Singer finds such differentiation ethically unwarranted, for we are simply animals. He opines there is no reason to assume bestiality involves cruelty to animals—indeed, they may find it pleasurable as well. This highlights a related point: if desire becomes the sole justificatory basis for sex, pleasure becomes its sole, or at least overarching, purpose.

The final argument, that no one is harmed by same-sex marriage, in part is legitimated by reference to the first two arguments, for the parties in question are not harmed so long as we accept that consent and desire are legitimate bases for sexual activity, and so long as we don't consider the interests of children to be enmeshed in such arrangements. One need not go as extreme as bestiality to make the case, however. Does the desire for someone of the same sex constitute "harm" for either party, or for other members of the polity? In answer to the first question, we might suggest the following: to understand same-sex intercourse as the proper end of sexual action for a gay person is akin to suggesting that risk-taking is the proper end of the adrenal glands for a person. It may be descriptively true, but it suggests that something is disordered. We would understand, then, that the pursuit of a disordered action, while desirable to the person in question, nonetheless constitutes harm for that person. It will be argued that the analogy is not apt, for same-sex desire is not disordered desire. That, however, must be determined. The fact of a desire does not provide its own justification, which can only be achieved with reference to whether the desire is aimed at something genuinely good.

Providing satisfaction, either of a fleeting pleasure or of a heftier variety ("It brings me a feeling of happiness or well-being"), provides no sufficient basis for justifying an action. A version of this argument is used by David Myers and Letha Dawson Scanzoni in *What God Has Joined Together? A Christian Case for Gay Marriage*. They argue that since marriage itself is good for society, and produces good things for those who inhabit it, there is no compelling reason to limit it to heterosexuals. A good deal of the argument hinges, however, on the contention that the good of marriage is found in the self-perceptions of those who are in it, and is predicated on the belief that the definition of marriage is itself fluid. It doesn't help us answer the question of whether consent, desire, and the absence of harm are sufficient warrants for marital alteration. So we come to a central political question: is marriage an institution natural to human beings that prefigures political society, or is it a socially constructed institution whose nature is what we will it to be? If the former, then the state not only has no authority to alter it, but it must also, as one of its fundamental functions, work to preserve and protect it. If there is by definition no such thing as gay marriage, the argument over whether it ought to be legally recognized is largely irrelevant. It only becomes relevant if one accepts that the definition is up for grabs.

Having considered arguments for same-sex marriage, let us now make the affirmative public argument for traditional marriage as the best mechanism yet developed for the birthing and raising of children. Marriage is the structure by which man and woman are brought together to have and care for children. It is how society ensures that parents with "a biological stake in a child cooperate together to raise and provide for that child" (Minnery and Stanton 2005, 262). It is premised upon the simple notion that the best way to have healthy, well-adjusted children is within a family of one mother and one father in a committed, permanent, and ideally loving union. Simply put, children need fathers and mothers, and marriage accomplishes that uniquely (Gallagher 2002, 791).

The social science research overwhelmingly validates a simple fact: healthy children are most likely to come from a family structure consisting of two biological parents. (This, of course, is an argument of contingency, for it's a relevant question to ask whether we would affirm traditional marriage or oppose same-sex marriage if social science were to prove the opposite. While we would be skeptical of any claim that there's a better arrangement for the creation and nurturing of children, our case doesn't stand or fall on the social science data concerning their well-being.) Children who are born to unmarried mothers, who live in an environment of cohabitation, or who live in a stepparent situation face significantly higher risks of suicide and emotional problems, physical illness, criminality, conduct disorder, and a host of other dysfunctions. Children lacking the two-parent structure are more prone to fall into criminal habits, suffer from child abuse at greater levels, and have higher infant mortality rates. Divorce and nonmarriage have a measurable detrimental impact on children's educational achievements and their subsequent socioeconomic well-being. Finally, children of divorce are more likely to become unwed mothers, experience divorce, or be involved in unhappy relationships (Gallagher, 783–88). Thus family scholars have concluded that "[m]arriage is an important social good, associated with an impressively broad array of positive outcomes for children and adults alike. . . .Whether American society succeeds or fails in building a healthy marriage culture is clearly a matter of legitimate public concern" (Gallagher 2003).

Marriage is a public institution and not merely a private one. It does not exist solely to validate feelings of love, affection, or commitment between adults. Rather, it best benefits society when structured around the care and well-being of children, as well as deepening the human capacity for the subordination of self-interest (Gallagher 2002, 781–82). The public has an interest in couples reproducing children and, in the process, regenerating society. Without it, "marriage becomes . . . a mere contract, a vessel with no particular content, one of a menu of sexual lifestyles, of no fundamental importance to anyone outside a given relationship" (Gallagher 2003).

These public benefits of marriage account for the legal distinctions between different kinds of relationships. The positive public aims of marriage—to protect and advance the interests of children (and of society along with them)—do not exist in other family forms. There is no similar public interest in promoting the union of same-sex couples (who operate under no procreative principle) or cohabitating couples. Only marriage reflects our "deep cultural commitment to the equal dignity and social worth of all children. All kids need and deserve a married mom and dad" (Gallagher 2003). Marriage may have other meanings—private, religious, emotional. But its core *public* meaning is a legal recognition that "having children is not only tolerated but welcomed and encouraged, because it gives children mothers and fathers" (Ibid.).

There remains the macro-level question of what gay marriage will do to the institution of marriage, and by extension to subsequent generations of children. The oft-heard refrain from gay marriage proponents is that it has no direct bearing on the health of heterosexual marriages. This is a profoundly misleading point which overlooks the primary objection to the legal recognition of gay marriage—its future impact on marriage as an institution, the public purpose of which is to ensure the perpetuation of a healthy society through the well-being of subsequent generations of children. In other words, might the acceptance of gay marriage negatively affect the delicate social ecology that helps marriage itself survive and flourish? We argue that accepting gay marriage as a viable alternative requires a radical enough rethinking of the way we define things that marriage itself becomes an accoutrement. Marriage traditionally understood is crucial to stable families, which in turn are crucial to a stable society. All of this has hinged on monogamous male-female unions: "Gay marriage will break that connection. . . . What lies beyond gay marriage is no marriage at all" (Kurtz 2003).

In the end, same-sex marriage arguments are in deep conflict with, and cannot be reconciled to, those for marriage itself. The logic of same-sex marriage points to what scholars call *deinstitutionalization*—the "overturning or weakening of all of the customary forms of marriage, and the dramatic shrinking of marriage's public meaning and institutional authority" (Blankenhorn 2007). Thus, a simple recourse to the problematic language of "rights" is not sufficient to change marriage law.[14]

As can be seen, the issue of whether persistent same-sex attraction is natural to certain persons is largely not relevant to our presentation. Given the inability of science to settle this question, there is no compelling reason to go into it. Those who make the argument that gays are born that way often do so for the purpose of suggesting that they find themselves in the same rights position as blacks during segregation. But unlike sexual orientation, race is not a behavioral characteristic, is largely benign, and is completely immutable. The data on whether persistent same-sex attraction can be altered are too mixed to warrant any conclusion one way or the other, but at least one cannot say with certainty that the condition is immutable. Even if it were, however, it would not alter the fact that biological causation is not a sufficient basis for making legal and policy decisions (a variation of what philosophers call "the naturalist fallacy"). The consequences of suggesting that genetic makeup ought to be determinative of moral duty and policy choices are revolutionary. Morality and law are predicated on the belief that human beings operate out of freedom, and can be held accountable for their actions. Couldn't a man say that he is wired for multiple sexual partners? Couldn't persons say that they have no choice but to be pedophiles, and thus are not culpable for behaving accordingly? Furthermore, the inclusion of persons of others races is consistent with the principles of our social institutions and doesn't undermine them. In that sense, such inclusion enhances and doesn't destroy.

If the proper focus for evangelical Christians is on the entirety of marriage, then their opposition to gay marriage must be embedded in a broader pro-marriage policy and a comprehensive accounting of human sexuality. Integrity in the policy realm compels a coherent, inclusive policy agenda aimed at preserving marriage. This means addressing the range of behaviors that undermine marriage as society's primary pro-children institution. It should oppose "with equal clarity and intensity the host of trends pushing our society toward 'postinstitutional marriage'" (Blankenhorn 2007). This might ease the hypocrisy of Christians who target same-sex marriage with nary a word about easy divorce or other heterosexual practices that have been hugely damaging to the institution of marriage. Resistance to same-sex marriage is not an attack on gays, but part of a larger effort to safeguard and strengthen marriage (Ibid.).

An encompassing pro-marriage policy agenda would regulate both the entry into marriage and the exit from it, to make sure children are cared for when marriage fails. It must articulate a set of rules that would increase the likelihood of strong, permanent marriages; these might include legally imposed waiting periods prior to entering marriage, mandatory completion of counseling, and making provision for an alternative covenantal marriage track. A comprehensive marriage policy also would address divorce: reforming no fault, or even eliminating it when children are involved. It would require additional waiting periods and mandatory negotiation when divorce is not mutual, premarital agreements that would specify the explicit grounds for divorce, and more. Finally, a pro-marriage agenda would seek to reinforce the norm of the family unit as two-parent, male-female structure. Adoption and foster care placement would favor homes with a traditional marriage structure over alternative domestic situations such as cohabitation or single parenting by choice. It might also include revisiting welfare laws so as to confront the alarming trends toward unwed motherhood. [15]

THE TONE OF POLITICAL INVOLVEMENT AND POLICY DEBATE

Evangelicals too often have failed, and failed miserably, to ensure their beliefs are delivered with a Christ-like spirit. This has resulted in no small harm to the public reputation of Christians, to the hope of sharing their faith with the world, and especially to their Christian brothers and sisters who struggle with same-sex desire. The Christian policy presence must be placed in the context of biblical demands. First and foremost is the obligation to *love and affirm* every human being as God's creations. The biblical concept of human dignity demands that genuine love of the gay person must always overwhelm the disapproval of gay behavior or the political opposition. A second facet is the necessity of *sensitivity and modulation*. In this issue context, Christians need take care to avoid flippancy and harsh rhetoric. Human sexuality is a complex and important piece of each person's makeup. It goes to the heart of how many people perceive themselves, and cannot be taken lightly. It requires high degrees of empathy to recognize the sorts of sacrifices persons are being asked to make. The entire discussion requires an unusual degree of sensitivity. Any thoughtful individual ought to be able to imagine how they would in love deal with one of their children should that child be gay.

In this light, Christians ought to take seriously the claim that opposition to gay marriage is part of a mode of discrimination that harms individuals to the extent that suicide rates among gay teenagers is "murderously" high. The argument goes like this: the rates of suicide among gay teenagers is alarmingly high and they commit suicide because of discrimination, so eliminating all forms of discrimination will lower the suicide rates. Obviously each suicide is a tragedy, and Christians ought to dissociate themselves from activities that lead to suicide. At the same time, there is reason to be wary of this argument. First, the data on suicide rates among gay teenagers are deeply flawed, and mostly inconclusive. There is much more nuance to the issue than is typically suggested. Second, it is not obviously the case that these individuals commit suicide because of discrimination. There are other possible explanations. Third, neither is it clear that legally allowing gay marriage would necessarily lower these rates. Fourth, there are other variables associated with high teenage suicide rates, but the advocates of gay marriage don't focus their attention on any of these variables with subsequent policy initiatives (what policies, for example, might you put into place for unrequited or spurned heterosexual love?). Finally, any such conversation must take place within the context of accounting for the culpability of the person who commits suicide. While the issue is indeed a serious one that requires great sensitivity, simply noting the problem doesn't settle the issue.

According to the third principle, Christians must be *humble*. All are sinners, and likely guilty of sexual sins of one sort or another. There is no room for arrogance, self-righteousness, or airs of moral superiority. Evangelicals cannot view homosexuality as some special sin, somehow worse than those that plague us all. If anything, the pride and hypocrisy that afflicts much Christian involvement in politics is as bad as any sexual sinfulness (Stott 1998, 12). Even as they speak with boldness and clarity on the issue, evangelicals need to exhibit an equal measure of humility and empathy.

It also means eschewing the language of judgment and division that offends and wounds. Taking positions "for righteousness in the public arena without being seen as self-righteous requires spiritual discipline and enormous effort. . . . But it is an effort that must be made" (Cromartie 2001). Christians will be judged in the public square. Their involvement therefore demands humility, modesty, and charity toward even their strongest of opponents. Evangelicals need to employ a Christ-infused rhetoric and action always (Cromartie 2001).

Opposition to gay marriage need not be equated with close-mindedness or intolerance, if the connection to the larger good of marriage, children, and society can be made. It need not represent hatred or fear toward gays, but rather an affirmative concern for the peculiar benefits of marriage understood as the permanent union of male and female—namely the bearing and rearing of children. This is love rightly understood, the pursuit of that which is best for all concerned—both individually and for our society.

NOTES

1. The authors are, respectively, an evangelical and a Catholic Christian. We mention this for two reasons: first, to suggest that the importance of the issue stretches across intrareligious divisions and is not simply a "Christian Right" issue; and, second, to indicate to evangelicals they would do well to draw on the rich intellectual history of Catholic Christianity in grappling with significant issues of public importance.

2. Not calculating into the mix are the following two factors: evangelicals tend to oppose same-sex marriage at higher rates than the rest of the population, and they tend to reproduce at higher rates than the rest of the population. Assuming that children are likely to replicate the views of their parents, the triumph of gay marriage can't be considered a *fait accompli*.

3. For our purposes, we will take as the religious case for gay marriage the controversial December 15, 2008, *Newsweek* cover story "Our Mutual Joy" written by religion editor Lisa Miller, as well as the editorial introduction by Jon Meacham. Meacham in particular makes the objection that those with religious objections to gay marriage are on the wrong side of history, and likens them to the segregationists of old.

4. A U.S. Religious Landscape Survey found that evangelicals are far more likely than any other religious group to fall back on religious and scriptural views as the primary influence on their thinking about politics.

5. These references certainly do not resolve the question for all Christians. There is spirited debate among biblical scholars from a variety of traditions, whose notions of biblical revelation diverge from the more literal approach. Among these are supporters of same-sex marriage, who have sought to rebut the specific references to homosexuality. Evangelical Christians also are frequently accused of proof-texting, of first settling upon a particular issue stance, and then trolling after the fact for the scriptural reference to support the pre-ordained position. For example, historian Randall Balmer indicts the religious right for their use of a "[s]elective literalism . . . [which] allows them to locate sin outside of the evangelical subculture (or so they think) by designating as especially egregious those dispositions and behaviors, homosexuality and abortion, that they believe characteristic of others, not themselves" (Balmer 2006, 10). Hence they tend to externalize sexual immorality and focus on the sexual sins of others rather than their own.

6. Our reading of the biblical texts here is informed by the work of Robert Gagnon, a New Testament scholar at Pittsburgh Theological Seminary.

7. Stott notes that there is not a single reference in the Bible that gives explicit support to the acceptance of same-sex marriage: "Scripture envisages no other kind of marriage or sexual intercourse [than heterosexual monogamy], for God provided no alternative" (Stott 1998, 39). Its supporters end up arguing for gay marriage from general biblical principles such as love, compassion, and justice.

8. Stott describes this broader biblical context for human sexuality in terms of the "complementarity" of the sexes as the basis for heterosexual marriage. Marriage as defined and designed by God is the union of a man and a woman, "which must be publicly acknowledged (the leaving of parents), permanently sealed (he will 'cleave to his wife'), and physically consummated ('one flesh')" (Stott 1998, 32, 39).

9. *The Kingdom of God and the Homosexual* by Andrew Comiskey (Anaheim: Desert Stream, 2000) is his confession related to his struggle as a Christian who experiences persistent same-sex attraction.

10. Indeed, this challenge has led some thoughtful Christians to give up trying, and to assert that the only convincing basis for opposing same-sex marriage is the core religious and moral traditions grounded in biblical admonitions. David Gushee suggests that "[w]e should honestly acknowledge that the primary reason we oppose [gay marriage] is we believe the Bible, as God's inspired word, teaches that heterosexual relationships are normative and homosexual behavior falls outside God's plan, and this is reinforced by two thousand years of unanimous Christian tradition" (Gushee 2008, 169). He finds that "the various 'publicly accessible' arguments that evangelicals . . . array against gay marriage . . . appear to be unpersuasive to those who are not already pre-persuaded on the basis of their religious beliefs—rooted in the authority of the Bible (or the Christian tradition) and the nature of its teaching on this matter" (170). For Gushee, the logical conclusion of this belief is to leave the matter to individual states to deal with in ways befitting their religious and social views on the matter.

11. See Glendon's *Rights Talk: The Impoverishment of Political Discourse* (New York: Free Press, 1993).

12. This is not a simple debater's point. The argument is being made. Larry Constantine, a professor of psychology at Tufts University, has suggested the incest taboo is an outmoded relic and that "children have the right to express themselves sexually, even with members of their own family." The conclusion is drawn from the premise that "all forms of consensual sexuality are good"—the only things that are bad are guilt and shame. See "Sexes: Attacking the Last Taboo," *Time*, April 14, 1980. See also "I Had Sex with My Brother But I Don't Feel Guilty," *The Sunday Times*, July 15, 2008.

13. See, for example, Ann E. Tweedy, "Polyamory as a Sexual Orientation," and Elizabeth Emens, "Monogamy's Law: Compulsory Monogamy and Polyamorous Existence," in *New York University Review of Law and Social Change* 29(2), 2004. Maura Strassberg, in "The Challenge of Postmodern Polygamy: Considering Polyamory," in *Capital University Law Review* (31:139), argues that arrangements of polyamory and polyfidelity are "flexible and re-

sponsive to the needs of the individual" and not a "rigid institution imposed in cookie cutter fashion on everyone." This sort of enshrining of individual desire with the concomitant need to shape social institutions to fit those desires is precisely the sort of antinomianism to which we object. One wonders who is minding the children while the adults are busy indulging their needs.

14. This is also consistent with the biblical understanding of rights as ultimately grounded in God's ordained creation. Society's refusal to recognize homosexual partnerships as a legal alternative to heterosexual marriages is not a denial of rights, "since human beings may not claim as a 'right' what God has not given them" (Stott 1998, 57). Gays are free to avail themselves of marriage as traditionally understood, but they have no right to marriage in whatever form they prefer or define it.

15. Space constraints prevent any in-depth consideration of other important aspects of the policy debate. One of these is the issue of federalism, and the wisdom of a federal constitutional amendment versus deference to allowing individual states to pursue their own policy. Another is the possibility of civil unions as a legal alternative to gay marriage for committed, long-term gay relationships. Steadfast opposition to gay marriage may not necessarily require that Christians similarly oppose every form of civil union for gay couples. Christians can adhere to the biblical imperatives of marriage as an exclusive male-female arrangement, and accommodate the extension of benefits to same-sex couples in the name of a pluralist commitment to justice (Wallis 2005, 332). This would acknowledge that gay couples have the same economic, financial, and legal concerns as others. Legal recognition of same-sex unions could provide for medical decision-making rights, access to health insurance, inheritance rights, retirement benefits, or some combination (Gushee 2008, 174). Considerations of fairness and Christian charity—apart from biblical truth—may favor legal recognition of gay unions in the name of reinforcing committed relationships without a fundamental shift in our understanding of the nature of marriage.

Chapter Eleven

Evangelicals and the Elusive Goal of Racial Reconciliation: The Role of Culture, Politics, and Public Policy

David K. Ryden

The 1990s were when American evangelical Christianity caught the racial reconciliation fever. Within a few short years, countless books were written exhorting churches on to multiracial ministry. Evangelical denominations and organizations publicly owned up to the historical sin of racism, issuing formal apologies and committing themselves to improving race relations. And individual evangelical Christians likewise sought to build relationships across racial lines.

It did not take long, however, for the fever to cool. Looking back, the fruits of the reconciliation movement of a decade ago seem largely illusory. Evangelical churches remain overwhelmingly segregated. White and black Christians still live mostly apart from each other. While there undoubtedly are exciting models of multiracial ministry, they are few and far between. In sum, genuine far-reaching racial reconciliation remains a frustratingly elusive goal.

This essay explores why evangelicals' well-intentioned reconciliation efforts yielded such meager tangible success. The answer is intriguing—and troubling for the future of black/white race relations. It suggests that the respective cultural identities of blacks and whites lead to much different, even contradictory, views of what constitutes racial reconciliation and how best to address racial problems. This cultural conditioning is interwoven with a complex web of political considerations; black and white evangelical Christians are poles apart in their partisan attachments, ideological predispositions, and policy orientations on matters of race and inequality. With the benefit of hindsight, these culturally ingrained political differences are so stark as to make the earlier efforts at reconciliation appear doomed from the start.

It remains to be seen if stronger, more permanent bonds between black and white evangelical Christians are genuinely possible. It almost certainly would require a softening of the hard partisan loyalties that generate no small amount of distrust between each of the two groups. It also demands an acknowledgement by white evangelicals of the reality of the societal and structural causes of persistent racial inequality. Finally, it may mean that they also be open to a more proactive policy agenda that would demonstrate real commitment to bettering the condition of so much of black America. The open question is whether there exists some common policy ground that would accommodate both the conservative political instincts of white evangelicalism and the more progressive policy inclinations of their black fellow believers.

THE SCRIPTURAL AND THEOLOGICAL BASIS FOR RECONCILIATION

> Now all things are of God, who has reconciled us to Himself through Jesus Christ and has given us the ministry of reconciliation. (2 Corinthians 5:18)

> For He himself is our peace, who has made both one, and has broken down the wall of separation . . . and that He might reconcile them both to God in one body through the cross, thereby putting to death the enmity. (Ephesians 2:14, 16)

The theological foundations for racial unity and reconciliation are straightforward and incontrovertible. A central tenet of evangelical Christianity is its reliance upon scripture as an authoritative guide to ethical and moral behavior. Hence, much work has been done by those in the reconciliation movement to flesh out a biblical mandate for the cause. That mandate is rooted both in explicit provisions of the Bible and in broader, overarching biblical values.

At the heart of the biblical case for reconciliation is the vision of Christ as the ultimate agent of reconciliation, between God and man, and by extension between all men.

> All this is from God, who reconciled us to himself through Christ and has given us the ministry of reconciliation; that is, in Christ God was reconciling the world to himself, not counting their trespasses against them, and entrusting

the message of reconciliation to us. So we are ambassadors for Christ, since God is making his appeal through us; we entreat you on behalf of Christ, be reconciled to God. (2 Corinthians 5:17-20)

The theological concept of reconciliation in Christ reaches in two directions. He reconciles all humankind to their Creator, while also bringing the ministry of reconciliation to those who accept Him. All believers are to be agents of Christ's reconciling power, in extending that power to their fellow man. In short, scripture calls people to be reconciled to God *and* to each other.

The corollary to the explicit message of reconciliation is the broader goal of Christian unity, the desire for harmony and brotherhood among believers. Biblical reconciliation is a concept that combines relationship with God with the transformation of one's human relationships, toward the end of restoring harmony among believers. Reconciliation is reserved in scripture "as the most powerful way of expressing the meaning of the life, death, and resurrection of Jesus Christ" (DeYoung 1997, 45).

The New Testament is replete with references to the central importance of unity among members of Christ's body. In Colossians 3:11, Paul proclaims that all are "one in Christ," whether Jew or Greek, male or female, circumcised or uncircumcised. Ephesians 2:11–22 and Galatians 3:28 describe Jew and Gentile as becoming one in Christ. He "has made the two one and has destroyed the barrier, the dividing wall of hostility . . . to reconcile both of them to God through the cross, by which he put to death their hostility." Christ's explicit prayer is that "all of them may be one, Father, just as you are in me and I am in you" (John 17:21).

This call to Christian unity certainly encompasses race and ethnicity, as inferred from Jesus' great commission in Matthew 28:19 to "make disciples of all nations." God desires an "all-nations church," comprised of all ethnic, racial, and national groups. Just as unity was possible for Jew and Gentile, it is possible for black and white. As the apostle Paul says, "[we] are no longer strangers and sojourners, but [we] are fellow citizens with the saints and members of the household of God" (Pannell 1993, 36). John Perkins, one of the elder statesmen of racial reconciliation efforts, sees reconciliation at the very center of the Gospel, which

> crosses cultural, racial and international barriers. If the Gospel we preach is genuine, it is the power to reconcile alienated men and women to a holy God and to one another across all these barriers. It is the only means and hope for international brotherhood and peace, and the only means and hope for brotherhood and peace between different races and ethnic groups here at home. (Perkins and Tarrants 1994, 177)

Unity under the common lordship of Christ must encompass racial brotherhood and relationships. Christian unity demands that we love each other
across racial barriers.

THE TWO WAVES OF THE RACIAL RECONCILIATION
MOVEMENT

[T]he emphasis on racial reconciliation [by white evangelicals] appears to be
opening a space for emotional expression, dialogue, and even potentially a
kind of cultural healing, and this in a national culture deeply scarred by racism
where very few such forums exist. (Wadsworth 1997)

The scriptural foundation of racial reconciliation notwithstanding, white evangelical Christians' record on race for most of the twentieth century left
much to be desired. It was marked by passivity, if not active opposition,
towards civil rights and social justice for blacks. White evangelical churches
and organizations typically acquiesced to, and often embraced outright, the
segregationist practices that existed in much of the country at mid-century.
At the height of the civil rights battles of the 1950s and 1960s, the differences
in the respective behavior of black and white evangelicals could not have
been greater. Black civil rights activism had a decidedly Christian cast to it; it
was often rhetorically grounded in the Gospel message of justice for all.
Meanwhile, most white evangelicals stood on the sidelines. Southern whites
generally sided *against* black evangelicals on matters of civil rights and
segregation, while northern evangelicals were too distracted to take much
notice. To the extent that religiously motivated whites joined in the civil
rights crusade, they tended to be Jewish or liberal mainline Protestants.

The indifference of white evangelical Christians on matters of race continued, even with the emergence of a first wave of the racial reconciliation
movement in the late 1960s and early 1970s. Tom Skinner, John Perkins,
William Pannell, and other black voices represented the spirit of the times, as
they implored white evangelical America to make the cause of economic and
social justice for blacks their own. Those pleas largely fell upon deaf ears
(Alumkal 2004, 201).

It would take two more decades before white evangelical Christians
would get serious about the business of reconciling with their black believing
brethren. The mid-1990s brought about a remarkable level of activity—intellectual, institutional, individual—the purpose of which was to atone for past
sins and build relationships between black and white evangelical Christians.

On an intellectual level, serious theological effort was devoted to the
subject of racial reconciliation, and making the case for why it warranted the
attention of evangelical Christians. Dozens of books addressed racial healing

within the church—many of them written by black/white teams of authors. *Christianity Today*, the leading periodical voice for white evangelical America, along with other religious journals, began to devote serious space to black/white relations and the need for reconciliation.

There also were dramatic developments on a collective and organizational level, as religious groups and denominations openly confessed to sins of the past and engaged in highly public acts of contrition. In 1994, the overwhelmingly white Pentecostal Fellowship of North America (PFNA) joined with black Pentecostal denominations in what came to be known as the "Memphis Miracle." The PFNA abruptly dissolved itself, merged with black Pentecostal churches to form the Pentecostal Charismatic Churches of North America (PCCNA), electing a black bishop to lead it. In the *Racial Reconciliation Manifesto*, they covenanted to work together to combat racism (*Racial Reconciliation Manifesto* 1994).

A year later, the Southern Baptist Convention publicly denounced racism and issued a formal apology for its segregationist past. The NAE and the National Black Evangelical Association held joint meetings to encourage racial cooperation. Numerous organizations and ministries were formed around a mission of racial harmony and reconciliation: Reconcilers Fellowship, the Twin Cities Urban Reconciliation Network, Chicago's Urban Reconciliation Enterprise, and the John M. Perkins Foundation for Reconciliation and Development, to name just a few (Emerson and Smith 2000, 63–65).

Perhaps the most dramatic of these efforts occurred within the men's worship movement known as PromiseKeepers, which in the late 1990s was organizing huge gatherings of evangelical Christian men across the country. Led by former University of Colorado football coach Bill McCartney, PromiseKeepers adopted as a primary tenet a personal commitment to the pursuit of racial reconciliation. The organization challenged men and pastors attending the rallies to covenant to "confront racism and build cross-cultural friendships" (Gilbreath 2008, 181).

As the PromiseKeepers commitment to building cross-cultural relationships suggests, this "second wave" of racial reconciliation was not confined to the institutional or elite level. Rather, it aimed to plant in individual Christians the seeds of reconciliation. Racial harmony was not just a political tactic or an organizational necessity, but a Christian imperative. Individuals were urged to "overcome their racism through direct contact and association with people of color," to acknowledge the sin of racism and repent. Evangelicals were called to openly engage racial issues, rather than minimizing or evading them.

In short, there was a palpable energy and enthusiasm directed toward the realization of racial reconciliation. White evangelicals took concrete action that demonstrated an acknowledgment of racial division and a commitment to reconcile with fellow black Christians. To one observer, these efforts were "some of the most significant, and potentially radical, moves ever made within American evangelicalism" (Wadsworth 1997, 343). Moreover, there was genuine optimism that reconciliation was in fact attainable. The hope was that repentance and forgiveness might provide the foundation for a lasting racial healing otherwise not possible. The movement appeared to be carving out a space for "a kind of cultural healing . . . in a national culture deeply scarred by racism *where very few such forums exist*" (Wadsworth 1997, 365).

CULTURE, POLITICS, AND THE COMPLEXITIES OF RACIAL RECONCILIATION

Race/ethnicity serve[s] as a prism through which common religious and theological tenets are refracted at sharp angles, yielding divergent values and political allegiances. (McDaniel and Ellison 2008)

The optimism of a decade ago regarding the potential for racial healing among black and white evangelical Christians seems naïve in today's light; despite the efforts chronicled above, a deeper and more encompassing racial reconciliation among evangelical Christians failed to materialize. Despite some success stories, reconciliation efforts on a larger scale stalled out. From a contemporary perspective, the 1990s reconciliation movement seems more a passing fad than a serious reordering of race relations among evangelical Christians. The remainder of this essay examines why, focusing on the influences of culture and politics as obstacles to a lasting and comprehensive reconciliation among white and black evangelical Christians.

A central question running through this book is whether there even exists a coherent political perspective or policy approach that can be categorized as evangelical. To approximate a cohesive or distinctive normative evangelical policy framework suggests a commonly accepted theological mind-set, which in turn generates a consistent policy position.

At first glance, the common theological commitments of white and black Christians seemingly offer a strong foundation for consensus on issues of race. Despite the tendency to equate "evangelical" with white Christians, blacks tend to be *more* theologically evangelical than whites. They are *more* likely to adopt evangelical doctrinal beliefs, attend evangelical or Pentecostal churches, and exhibit higher levels of personal religiosity. One would expect that the substantial overlap in adherence to evangelical tenets among black and white Christians would generate a common framework for thinking about race and black/white relations.

In fact, the similar theological dispositions of white and black evangelicals have not translated into similar political or policy views on race. Indeed, the extent to which they have reached utterly divergent policy positions despite their common faith is striking. Instead, the combination of starkly contrasting historical and cultural backdrops, partisan allegiances, and contrasting ideological orientations, when refracted through the prism of race, have led to profoundly dissimilar answers to how best to address race relations. This complex brew of culture and racial identity has made the goal of genuine racial reconciliation between black and white evangelical Christians far more difficult than it otherwise might appear. Indeed, it leaves blacks and whites unable to agree on what even constitutes racial reconciliation.

In short, huge hurdles to racial reconciliation can be found in the deep political divisions that separate black and white Christians—in their party loyalties, ideological orientations, and policy preferences. Nine out of ten blacks support the Democratic Party in their voting; close to two-thirds of white evangelicals vote Republican. Blacks accept a far more expansive role for the state in seeking economic and social equality. White evangelicals typically prefer smaller government, lower taxes, and less social welfare. Unsurprisingly, these differences in party and ideology lead black and white evangelicals to policy stances that more often than not are at odds. This begs the obvious question: How can two groups, both purporting to treat scriptural authority as literal truth, interpret that scripture so differently in its policy applications to matters of race?[1]

The Cultural Shaping of Racial Reconciliation Theology

A central piece of the answer is the formative influence of culture in shaping textual meaning, including scripture. Cultural lenses belie the easy assumption that one need only locate the apt biblical passage to determine the correct policy on a given issue. Simply put, scriptural interpretation is socially constructed and shaped. The message and meaning of the text for one's life is very much the result of the cultural history, character, and experiences of the community to which one belongs. The vast complexity of the Bible ensures that these cultural influences will play out in how members of different communities elevate some passages while diminishing or dismissing other, favoring some themes at the expense of others (McDaniel and Ellison 2008, 182).

Unsurprisingly, white and black Christians operate from much different premises when reading and applying the Bible (McDaniel and Ellison 2008, 182). Even as black and white evangelicals employ a literal interpretation of scripture, the specific product of that literalism for each is dictated by their respective collective religious identities, and the socioreligious values within each group. Moreover, the differing social cues and cultural influences dramatically effect how each group envisions problems of race and the path to racial reconciliation in a biblical context.

The cultural framework for white evangelicals is characterized by what Emerson and Smith call "accountable free will individualism" (2000, 79). It is a highly individualistic theological orientation emphasizing sin, repentance, salvation, and the redemptive grace of Christ. The focus is on personal responsibility and the sin in one's life (Emerson and Smith 2000, 79). What matters is one's spiritual well-being and the state of one's relationship with Christ.

The black cultural identity manifests itself in a markedly different orientation. It developed as part and parcel of their collective existence and their historical struggle to define themselves within their American experience, an experience shaped by slavery, Jim Crow, and overt discrimination. While one's relationship with Christ is important, the black tradition incorporates prophetic concern for injustice, exploitation, and neglect of the less fortunate. For black Christians, biblical concerns include values of fairness and equality, and stress collective responsibility for treating all people with justice and mercy (Alumkal 2004, 183).

These contrasting sensibilities ensure that whites and blacks will see race and reconciliation differently. White evangelicals place primary emphasis on personal behavior. Racial tensions are caused by individual sin and the failure to love one's neighbor. Racism is at its core a spiritual problem demanding a spiritual solution—namely, repentance, forgiveness, and unity through a common identity in Christ. Reconciliation is effectively distilled down to the actions and efforts of individuals (Alumkal 2004, 202). Whites need to own up to their sin, repent and apologize to their black brethren, and seek forgiveness in return.

These attitudes are of a piece with dominant American values. They fuse the evangelical faith with a faith in the American ideals of individualism, independence, and self-determination (Emerson and Smith 2000, 129). The individual is "an entity independent of macro social structures and institutions" (Emerson, Smith, and Sikkink 1999, 400–401). The result is a white "cultural tool kit" that treats race problems as "profoundly individualistic and interpersonal: become a Christian, love your individual neighbors, establish a cross-race friendship, give individuals the right to pursue jobs and individual justice without discrimination by other individuals, and ask forgiveness of individuals one has wronged" (Emerson and Smith 2000, 130). The answers to racism are relational and interpersonal. And a personal relationship with Christ will infuse one with the love, respect, and dignity needed to build those relationships.

Black evangelicals see the world much differently. While individual behavior matters, there also is an acute awareness of institutional and societal influences that is utterly absent from the white evangelical consciousness. The black religious tradition places considerable importance on social, economic, and political institutions—both as contributing to racial problems and as part of the remedy. There is a strong element of group solidarity in challenging the broader sources of racial inequality (Alumkal 2004, 183). Black religious discourse emphasizes both individual and collective action to overcome poverty and level the economic playing field (Edgell and Tranby 2007, 282). Their theology incorporates an attention to the social disparities in access to quality housing, education, economic opportunities, and more.

These contrasting foci were evident in the respective racial reconciliation movements of the 1970s and 1990s. The black leaders of the first wave of racial reconciliation were unequivocal in highlighting societal sin and challenging systemic injustice and inequality. A distinctive piece of the movement was a call to address the inequities of the existing economic, social, educational, political, and religious structures (Emerson and Smith 2000, 67). Personal relationship building had to be accompanied by collective justice; reconciliation required attacking the institutional barriers to true political, economic, and social equality for blacks.

When the second wave of reconciliation surfaced two decades later—with significant white evangelical involvement—the system-altering facets of the original formulations were gone. They had been lost in translating and popularizing the message for a larger white evangelical audience. The popularized version reflected the crabbed white evangelical vision of reconciliation. It focused mainly on individual-level reconciliation, without seriously addressing racialized social structures, institutions, and culture (Emerson and Smith 2000, 52).

These divergent orientations toward the problems of race help to explain the dissipation of the reconciliation movement of the late 1990s. White evangelicals' cultural blinders left them ill equipped to attend to factors at the center of the black evangelical cultural experience. Systematic injustice and inequality are not part of white evangelicals' consciousness. The individualistic social construct obfuscates racialized patterns that are deeply embedded in society and its institutions. It leaves little room for concerns of collective sin or societal responsibility, or for working against structures of inequality that disproportionately impact black communities and neighborhoods (Gilbreath 2008, 74). For black evangelicals, the exclusive focus on personal relationships is woefully incomplete and sure to be ineffective. Little wonder blacks eventually wearied of the talk of personal reconciliation and relationship building.

Indeed, this individualism is so deeply ingrained in conservative Protestant culture that it goes beyond mere indifference to structural aspects of race problems. It actually morphs into an anti-structuralism that opposes governmental efforts to address racial inequality. A perspective that reduces the race problem to individual prejudice and personal bigotry views structural explanations as actually wrong-headed and counterproductive. Stressing the institutional and social causes of racial tension obscures the root source—the accountable, responsible individual (Emerson and Smith 2000, 79). Thus the dominant white evangelical racial mind-set, while perhaps supportive of formal legal equality for minorities, opposes governmental action to remedy on a broader institutional level the disparities between white and black economic, social, and political success (Alumkal 2004, 201).[2]

Racialized Stereotypes and the Maintenance of the Status Quo

Finally, and perhaps most insidiously, the hyperindividualism that characterizes the white evangelical perspective does more than just mask the structural inequalities involving race. When melded with commonly held negative stereotypes of blacks, it also gives white evangelicals—and whites in general—a mind-set and rhetoric that provide a rationale for justifying and legitimizing the racial status quo in America (Tranby and Hartmann 2008, 342).

Evangelicals, like many white Americans, put great stock in the Calvinist work ethic and its tangible rewards. Social outcomes, rather than being influenced by larger cultural forces, are essentially the product of merit and hard work. The emphasis on individual effort becomes the primary means of accounting for the economic disparities between blacks and whites. Those inequalities are not due to societal, legal, or institutional factors. Rather they are simply the result of the inability of blacks to properly apply themselves to make the most of the opportunities before them. These racialized assumptions, widely held but rarely openly articulated, preclude whites from taking seriously minority demands that inequities be addressed on a structural level.

Here the ethos of evangelical Christianity is almost indistinct from broader American values—freedom, individualism, independence, equality of opportunity—which represent a profound cultural obstacle to genuine racial reconciliation. The merging of "individualist ideals and anti-black sentiments" constitutes a set of norms and expectations that do not allow for structural explanations of racial inequality or for demands by blacks that white evangelicals do something about racial inequities (Tranby and Hartmann 2008, 353–54). As those authors put it:

> American individualism not only blinds white evangelicals to structural inequalities involving race, but it also assigns blame to those who are disadvantaged by race and normalizes and naturalizes cultural practices, beliefs, and norms that privilege white Americans over others. (354)

To be fair, this habit is hardly the exclusive province of white evangelicals; indeed, it coincides with prevailing notions of race and racial inequality in the United States. Evangelicals mirror "the dominant sociocultural factors at the heart of American problems with race and inequality" (Tranby and Hartmann 2008, 345). White evangelical attitudes on race and race relations reflect those issues which lie at the heart of the American race problem in its entirety. In the end, the individualistic views at the core of the dominant white culture preclude the very structural reforms or changes needed to realize meaningful racial progress (Tranby and Hartmann 2008, 354). Ultimately the cultural shaping of evangelicalism specific to black and white evangelicals respectively pushes them in different, nonreconciliatory directions. This chasm in the respective understandings by blacks and whites is undoubtedly a central piece of the race problem, and adds to the entrenchment of a racialized society (Emerson and Smith 2000, 91).

Reinforcing Separation: The Parties, Politics, and Policy Views of Evangelicals

The deep cultural divide between black and white Christians is paralleled in the dominant political, partisan, and policy behaviors of each group. The causal connections between cultural influences, political ideology, and evangelical theology are complex, and well beyond the scope of this essay. Suffice it to say that the cultural rift between black and white evangelicals is very much reflected in and mutually reinforced by the political divide that separates them, thus rendering reconciliation all the more difficult.

Black and white evangelicals are as far apart in their *partisan* affiliations as demographic groups can be. Blacks are easily the most monolithic bloc in the Democratic coalition, with upwards of 95 percent voting Democratic in recent presidential elections. Meanwhile, white evangelicals are the most solid bloc of Republican voters, with over 70 percent voting for the Republican candidate.

These contrasting partisan affiliations are unsurprising, in light of the divergent policy views that flow from black and white racial perceptions. Blacks, with their emphasis on social welfare and economic equality, are far more open to liberal, interventionist social and economic policies (Wadsworth 1997, 346). One would expect them to align with a Democratic Party that favors redistributive economic and social welfare policies, and whose programmatic emphasis is on public solutions to educational access, economic opportunity, health care, and poverty relief.

The white evangelical religious tradition, in contrast, stresses individual morality, traditional values, and a law-and-order criminal justice system. Their individualism generates a natural opposition to the targeting of social and economic policies for the benefit of particular groups. This naturally fosters support for the party of individualism and conservative social values—namely, the Republican Party (McDaniel and Ellison 2008, 183). As McDaniel puts it, "race/ethnicity serve[s] as a prism through which common religious and theological tenets are refracted at sharp angles, yielding divergent values and political allegiances" (Ibid, 189).[3]

Yet something beyond mere policy preferences is at work that makes it difficult to be optimistic about racial reconciliation between black and white evangelicals. It is a deeply fixed distrust based upon each side's perception of the partisan identity of the other. In this sense, the overwhelming identification of black and white evangelicals with their respective parties has been devastating to the cause of racial unity between them.

On one hand, the near-universal support by blacks for the party of the abortion rights orthodoxy is a huge obstacle to many white evangelicals, for whom pro-life concerns trump all else. Meanwhile, majorities of white evangelicals support a party whose history on race has been spotty at best and repressive at worst. Republican resistance to civil rights and its use of thinly veiled racial appeals for partisan benefit—plus its neglect of social justice for blacks—led many to view it as harboring racist elements (Wadsworth 1997, 342). It should not be surprising that conservative Christians who affiliate with that party are tainted by the association. White evangelicals' conservative stances make them appear dismissive of the concerns of the less fortunate, thus validating the suspicions of blacks toward conservatives and Republicans. Republicans' hard line on crime, antipathy toward social welfare, opposition to affirmative action, and general distrust of government reinforce the image of conservative Christians who vote Republican as insensitive to the concerns of minorities (McDaniel and Ellison 2008, 189).[4]

Churches as Reflections of Black/White Evangelical Differences

The social and political differences between black and white evangelicals are inextricably intertwined with the differences in the natures of the predominantly black and white evangelical churches to which they belong. Black and white evangelical churches strongly reinforce, if not shape outright, the attitudes of their congregants on social and political questions.

Black churches have a strong tradition of social outreach, borne out of the great social needs of the large numbers of blacks who migrated north and settled in large urban areas in the mid-twentieth century. Contemporary black evangelical churches are much more likely than their white counterparts to sponsor social programs addressing a variety of societal problems—from after-school and mentoring programs to transitional housing, substance abuse treatment programs, educational alternatives, and more (Greenberg 2000, 392).

White evangelical churches are much less likely to address the social and economic problems of the community. They are less inclined to see their mission as one of social action. Their central focus is on evangelism and the spiritual needs of their congregants (Greenberg 2000, 389). To the extent they address people's material and physical needs it is as a means of reaching them with the message of salvation. While social action is not in conflict with the goal of evangelism, it certainly is secondary (Ibid., 390).

At the same time, these more overtly political churches and their clergy buttress the partisan inclinations of the rank and file. In black churches, explicit political involvement is commonplace. Pastors frequently have strong direct ties to Democratic officeholders and the party. It is routine for Democratic candidates to address congregations from the pulpit on Sunday mornings (Greenberg 2000, 383–84). Indeed, the social activism in black urban churches often gives them strong links to government officials (who, in large metropolitan areas, are typically Democratic). Their prophetic role often translates into an explicit political agenda of economic welfare and social justice concerns for the black community. As a result, black urban churches often end up working with social service agencies and local officials on housing, welfare, police and community relations, and similar issues (Greenberg 2000, 392).

On the flip side, white evangelical churches are likely to support Republican candidates, albeit less openly than their black counterparts. They are places where conservative organizations will circulate their voter guides come election time. They don't necessarily eschew a political agenda, but it is most likely to center on abortion and other socially conservative issues. White churches engaged in social outreach often do so while simultaneously pressing a political agenda that would reduce governmental commitment to social and economic welfare.

By one estimate, at least 90 percent of blacks who attend church do so at exclusively black churches. The percentage of white evangelicals attending predominantly white churches surely is at least that high. The strict racial segregation of Sunday mornings in America, combined with the contrasting messages and missions of these racially segregated places of worship, only amplifies the magnitude of the obstacles to racial reconciliation among evangelical Christians.[5]

RETHINKING RACIAL RECONCILIATION

Despite the often very best intentions of most white American evangelicals, the complex web of factors . . . produce a rather dismal portrait of the realities of and prospects for positive race relations among American Christians in the United States. (Emerson and Smith 2000)

One ought not to overlook the positive contributions by evangelical Christians in the realm of racial reconciliation. Arguably they have laid the foundation for future reconciliation by bringing to the table the one thing that Christians consider essential to true reconciliation—reliance upon the redemptive grace and power of Christ. Reconciliation requires the transformation of hearts, minds, and attitudes—which the evangelical Christian would contend is possible only through the miraculous healing power of Christ the great reconciler. Only then will people be fully equipped to engage and persevere in the long, arduous work of reconciliation (Glynn 1998, 839). Christ's reconciling power gives his followers the motivation and commitment to confront and overcome the wounds that are opened in the process of reconciliation. Without God's grace, the deep resentment and hate from centuries of racism and discrimination seem sure to overwhelm the best of human intentions and efforts.

Moreover, Christ-centered reconciliation is mutual and reciprocal between communities with a common foundational belief. Both sides have access to the reservoir of trust and grace flowing from their shared faith. Black and white evangelicals are uniquely constituted to practice the habits required by reconciliation—humility, repentance, forgiveness, and acceptance. A common faith should engender in whites the capacity to confess and repent, in blacks the complementary capacity to forgive and accept, and in both the strength to build meaningful cross-racial relationships. Thus the evangelical framework imposes a higher standard of conduct and personal engagement than that practiced in the customary secular social and political contexts.

This spiritual dimension—and a grasp of the moral and spiritual aspects of race relations—is missing from purely policy-oriented, structural solutions to inequality. Evangelicals would argue that it is a necessary precondition to genuine racial progress, which is not only about justice, but also about love, grace, and relationships. This may well be a more promising and hopeful first phase of reconciliation than conventional secular approaches (Glynn 1998, 838).

But the evangelical emphasis on the personal and the relational is hardly a sufficient condition for genuine reconciliation. Standing alone, it is sure to fail, given its neglect of the structural barriers to justice and equality for black Americans. White evangelical solutions are too dismissive of societal realities that impact racial groups in highly disparate ways economically, politically, and socially. The inequities between black and white (in access to health care and quality education, their realization of economic success and political power, and their treatment at the hands of the criminal justice system) are too great to ignore.

White evangelicals must escape the cultural constraints which limit their ability to see the impact of race on society. This inability to grasp the structural and societal dimensions of racial problems comes from living in racial isolation. A central piece of the reconciliation puzzle is neither public nor governmental, but rather requires a renewed commitment by white evangelicals to learn what the lives of blacks are like. This requires *authentic social interaction*—worshipping, socializing, living together. It compels a depth of relationship between black and white that goes beyond the merely superficial, and entails a true appreciation for how the other half lives. Only then will white evangelicals truly grasp the reality of our racialized society.

A second piece of a reconstituted approach to racial reconciliation is *intellectual*. The exclusively relational approach reflects what Mark Noll referred to as the scandal of the evangelical mind—the tendency toward action at the expense of reflection.[6] White response in the 1990s to racism and reconciliation was akin to the evangelical impulse on other issues—an intense, energetic, action-oriented agenda to solve the problem. This sense of impatience with the problem and the need for an immediate response, while usually well intended, leaves little space for deeper intellectual reflection. The evangelicals' action-oriented intuition, combined with their shallow cultural understanding of race, yields a one-dimensional remedy for what is undeniably a thoroughly multidimensional challenge (Emerson and Smith 2000, 171). As one would expect, the outcomes are short term in their impact and ultimately ineffectual.

When faced with the complexity of American race relations, evangelicals might refrain from impulsive activism and instead engage in some serious thinking about the issue. That might yield an acknowledgment of the reality for black America. That reality is one in which poverty engulfs one in four blacks, the criminal justice system ensnares one in three black men, and marriage rates are lower and divorce rates higher than for other ethnic groups. It is a reality into which 70 percent of black babies are born without a father present; it includes educational failure of such magnitude in urban schools like Detroit and Chicago that it almost defies comprehension.

A fuller grasp of these realities also might ease the negative stereotypes and perceptions that too many whites hold of blacks. The steep challenges that face so many young blacks from the earliest stages of their lives belie the notion that they somehow have the same opportunities as white America. Their lack of success educationally, financially, or professionally cannot be attributed simply to lack of hard work or effort. Reflection and reason might reveal that so much more is going on by way of institutional and societal factors that contribute substantially to the deep socioeconomic disparities that exist between whites and blacks.

Moreover, even apart from the causes of those inequities, they undeniably raise public policy questions which demand public policy responses. Integrity of the family structure, the alleviation of poverty, a fair and effective criminal justice system, some modicum of access to quality education—these are issues that on some basic level implicate government and compel its involvement. Though few white evangelicals may be impacted personally by these issues, scripture obligates them to pursue remedies on behalf of black Christians and all fellow citizens. All evangelical Christians must be willing to actively engage the public policy apparatus and support policy stances designed to address these problems in a serious way.[7]

Racial reconciliation, however, need not be the tail that wags the dog of politics and policy. It is unlikely, at least in the short term, that conservative Christians will, in the name of better race relations, migrate in droves to the Democratic Party or enthusiastically embrace expansive government. Similarly, black Christians probably will not move in large numbers to the Republican Party just to advance the goal of racial harmony. Yet Christian fraternity should trump partisan opposition. That is, black and white evangelicals must be prophetic voices within their respective parties, calling them to account on matters of mutual concern to Christians within each.[8] For conservative evangelicals, this means serving as the Republican Party's conscience to keep the plight of the poor and working class minorities on the party's agenda. It would include seeking commonsense policy solutions to the hardships that disproportionately plague African Americans. Likewise it would involve calling out those in the party who employ the language of racial division and insensitivity as a tactical tool for partisan advantage.

Blacks must find their voice on abortion and other issues of life, and actively combat the unflinching pro-abortion rights dogma of the Democratic Party. A prophetic presence within the party might also require that they confront those in the Democratic Party who routinely demonize Republicans who prefer private-sector policy solutions or decentralized governmental responses as somehow racist or uncaring about the poor and dispossessed. If each group were to take more seriously the prophetic calling within their parties, it might be a first step toward the restoration of trust between black and white evangelicals, without which reconciliation is a pipedream.

Finally, conservative Christians need to think seriously about a *more activist public policy agenda* which might lay the groundwork for stronger relationships with black evangelicals. That need not equate with the Democratic policy agenda on education, criminal justice, or other issues; conventional Democratic policy approaches have hardly met with stunning success. But the search for effective remedies compels a serious debate over the role of government, best social services practices, the commitment of resources, the need for personal responsibility, and more. There are legitimate policy ideas that span the ideological spectrum, and evangelical Christians, conservative or otherwise, need to be in the midst of the debate.

It is important that the policy specifics advocated by white evangelicals demonstrate an understanding of the structural components of race-based disparity in America. This need not mean wholly dispensing with one's more conservative inclinations with respect to government and politics. Indeed, there are a number of policy approaches that represent a distinctive and serious effort to address obstacles to moving toward greater racial and social equality, and which ought also to be acceptable to those of a more conservative ideological leaning. If white evangelicals are clear about their motives, those policy views might find a more receptive audience among African Americans. For their part, black evangelicals might refrain from assessing the motives of white Christians based upon whether they necessarily buy into standard liberal policy prescriptions for the issues of importance to black Americans. Indeed, blacks also might take a fresh look at the range of public policy alternatives on matters of social justice and economic equality. It is not as if their exclusive loyalties to the Democratic Party have produced dramatic policy successes in the areas of importance to them.

Numerous issue areas have the potential for common ground among black and white evangelicals, regardless of ideology. Several in particular provide a natural starting point for white evangelicals to demonstrate a commitment to addressing social and economic inequities.

* *Faith-based social service delivery.* Upon taking office, President Obama quickly announced his intention to maintain his predecessor's Office of Faith-Based and Community Initiatives (OFBCI). A signature piece of President Bush's domestic agenda, this reform aimed to give faith-based nonprofits the same opportunity as their secular counterparts to participate in publicly funded social welfare programs. Under the Bush administration, the initiative had grown to encompass satellite faith-based offices in virtually every federal department and facilitated involvement by faith-affiliated organizations in programs across the social welfare universe. The initiative had originally been viewed with great promise across ideological and partisan lines, though it eventually came to be viewed with suspicion by many blacks as a politically motivated way to draw black support for President Bush. With the renewal of the initiative by President Obama, the partisan stigma should be gone. Faith-based social services should command the active and energetic support of all evangelicals, given its potential to address a host of social needs that are especially acute in poorer black communities. The faith-based initiative ought not to be an affront to conservative principles, as it funnels public resources through churches, faith-based groups, and grassroots neighborhood organizations.

Without the stigma of Bush (or the perception among blacks that it was a transparent political play to attract black political support), blacks likewise should be amenable to the program, particularly in light of the ability of urban black churches and faith-based organizations to tap into it to serve the surrounding neighborhoods.

- *Criminal justice and punishment.* If evangelical Christians need a model for how to approach criminal justice issues in ways that are consistent both with their faith *and* their conservative policy instincts, they need only examine Chuck Colson's Prison Fellowship Ministry. It is a holistic program that combines overtly religious instruction to address prisoners' spiritual needs with practical training aimed preparing them to successfully reenter society. Colson is no bleeding heart on criminal justice. But he has been an energetic advocate for sentencing reform and alternative modes of punishment for nonviolent offenders. Often aided by public funding, Colson's work is thoroughly infused with a deep compassion for those ensnared in the criminal justice system. His ministry defies easy labeling as conservative or liberal. Rather it embraces creative ways to actually rehabilitate convicted criminals.

- *Education policy.* Surveys indicate substantial support among black Americans for school vouchers and other modes of choice that are the preferred policy mechanism of Christian conservatives. But these will only benefit so many inner-city kids stuck in failing schools. White evangelical Christians need to extend their concern for education beyond their own kids and neighborhoods to include the struggles of public education, especially the steep challenges faced by urban schools. They can serve on public school boards, volunteer in understaffed and under-resourced schools, mentor a public school student, and support their fundraising efforts with their resources. They can enthusiastically support genuine attempts to reform schools. Finally, white evangelicals who support school choice reforms need to strike a less adversarial stance, and forego demonizing the public schools that many minority kids have no choice but to attend.

In these and other policy areas, legitimate policy ideas that defy conservative or liberal labels nevertheless have the potential for consensus support from those across the ideological spectrum. They often include an attractive mix of public and private actors and solutions. They also provide real opportunities for black and white Christians and churches to work together, side by side, to solve important societal problems. They acknowledge the public dimension of the problem while making room for the relational aspect favored by religious conservatives and which may be needed to actually make racial reconciliation stick.

TAKING THE LONG VIEW ON RACIAL RECONCILIATION

The prospect of genuine, lasting reconciliation between black and white evangelical Christians is a distant one, the work of decades rather than months or years. The deep cultural differences between black and white will not recede until they overcome the cultural isolation that blinds whites in particular to the realities of the African American experience in America. There is little in contemporary society to suggest that evangelical Christians are prepared to engage fellow minority believers—through worshipping, living, and working together—sufficiently to overcome the deeply ingrained cultural framework within which they operate. As a result, black and white evangelicals are likely to continue down the divergent political and policy paths that further complicate the goal of reconciliation.

Ironically, finding common ground in the public policy arena might actually serve to quicken the process of establishing mutual trust between black and white evangelicals. Given their dominant cultural standing, it is fair to place the onus primarily on white evangelical Christians, who must cultivate a broader public policy consciousness, one that takes note of the structural impediments to equality for minorities and supports policy initiatives aimed at those structures. To the extent that reconciliation implies the need for mutuality, for black evangelicals that might simply express itself in accepting with a measure of grace and trust the good faith policy strivings of their more conservative white evangelical sisters and brothers. By finding common points of public policy collaboration, black and white evangelicals might be reminded of the theological mandate of a ministry of reconciliation, both through personal relationships and in the pursuit of biblical justice for all.

NOTES

1. This chapter admittedly brushes in very broad strokes. Black and white evangelicals and the churches they attend are not nearly as monolithic as the rhetoric of this chapter might suggest. Space limitations do not permit a more nuanced examination of that variation and divergence. For example, serious fissures have developed within the black church, as isolation has grown between poor urban blacks and the expanding black middle class and middle-class churches.

2. This antipathy to public efforts to alleviate the hardships of minorities is evident in the opposition among white evangelicals to social welfare for the poor, which they contend only fosters dependency and irresponsibility. Some claimed this opposition was the real animating force behind the faith-based initiative that was a signature piece of President Bush's domestic policy program. Advocates of the faith-based initiative were accused of trying to undermine the governmental financial commitment to poverty relief and a variety of social services.

3. White Christians and racial minorities agree on certain issues. Blacks are at least as conservative on key social issues such as abortion, homosexuality, and school prayer. But Republican Party efforts to make inroads with minority voters by emphasizing a family values agenda has been singularly ineffective (McDaniel and Ellison 2008, 189).

4. Ed Gilbreath, a black evangelical who worked for *Christianity Today* for many years, captures this polarizing animosity each group has towards the other's party of choice. That the "evangelical" label has become so bound up with the Republican Party has led many blacks who are clearly evangelical to nevertheless shun the term. They simply do not wish to be associated with the political implications of the term. At the same time, the distaste many white evangelicals harbor for the Democratic Party is a huge obstacle to creating space for black evangelicals in the same church or social tent as white evangelicals. Gilbreath sometimes feels "that some white evangelicals won't consider an African American believer a real Christian unless he or she subscribes to their conservative political views" (Gilbreath 2008, 139).

5. The chasm between white and black worshipping communities was on vivid display in the 2008 presidential campaign story of Barack Obama's pastor, Jeremiah Wright. Wright's controversial preachings were surely shocking to many white evangelicals. Yet, while Wright's articulation of black liberation theology may have been extreme, it was hardly an aberration. On the contrary, his comments reflected a commonly held view among black evangelicals that there can be no real racial healing without black liberation and social transformation.

6. Chris Rice notes the dearth of serious theological work on reconciliation, which lags far behind academic debates, trends, and developments: "In contrast to a mountain of secular books and research, I found not a single twentieth century survey of race and Christianity written in sociology, history, economics or journalism by Christian or secular publishers. The weight of the work is completely anecdotal" (Rice and Perkins 2000, 258).

7. Some take a "glass half full" perspective on the state of racial reconciliation efforts. Chris Rice cites successes by church coalitions and other activists in the areas of education, housing, and employment. These include (1) PromiseKeepers' efforts to get white evangelical males to focus on race relations, (2) the Call to Renewal's interfaith and ecumenical efforts to address poverty across ideological lines, and (3) a Christian Community Development Association that grew from thirty member organizations in 1989 to over five hundred churches and ministries ten years later (Rice and Perkins 2000, 252). Yet it is notable that virtually all of these efforts are private. None really includes the engagement of politics and public policy.

8. See the discussion in the final chapter regarding the cooptation of evangelicals by party and ideology. White evangelicals have especially fallen prey to this, frequently letting party fealty and ideology determine policy views rather than scriptural truth. This has had dire effects for the goal of racial reconciliation and the call for unity and love between fellow believers.

Chapter Twelve

Politics, Evangelicals, and the Unavoidability of Metaphysics

Francis J. Beckwith

Evangelical Protestants have been active participants in American politics since the late 1970s. According to several accounts (Hunter 1991; Liebman and Wuthnow 1983; Hankins 2008), this activism resulted from a number of cultural trends that began taking shape in the 1960s. These trends implicate the state's understanding of human sexuality, human life, the nature of the family, and the meaning of the common good. Several U.S. Supreme Court opinions—including *Griswold v. Connecticut* (1965) and *Roe v. Wade* (1973)—and the ascendancy of libertine views of individual autonomy and privacy, the increasing dissemination and consumption of pornography, and the popular culture's demonization of those who resisted these trends provided a combustible combination. It was one that lit a fire underneath what Richard Nixon called the "silent majority" and Jerry Falwell named "the Moral Majority."

Most of these newly energized citizens and their leaders, often called "the religious right," had very little experience in political activism and most of them received their theological formation in religious traditions that had virtually no identifiable history of thinking very deeply on matters of political or social philosophy. Unlike those in the mainline Protestant denominations, who could easily point to a half dozen predecessors who had produced impressive tomes in support of their political theologies (Dawson 1953; Rauschenbusch 1907), the religious right have had few if any resources that offered a developed social philosophy. For this reason, its leaders would often ready the troops by quoting scripture, appealing to less than reliable accounts of the American Founders' religiosity,[1] and speaking before unbelievers in ways that were ripe for caricature and ridicule by their political adversaries. This has resulted in the strange phenomenon of secular academics and writers exploring evangelical politics and its leadership like amateur anthropologists examining a strange and exotic culture without the benefit of contextualization. Hence, the spate of books over the past decade that have warned us of an impending theocracy engineered by dark forces that want to keep Bob-Jones-University-educated women barefoot and pregnant while home schooling their children in creationism so that they can grow up and shoot abortion doctors.[2]

Within evangelical Protestantism, there has also arisen an "evangelical left," which often agrees with the religious right on some matters (such as abortion and marriage) but parts ways with it on issues such as economic redistribution, social welfare, and just war theory (see Sider 1977; Sider 1987; Gushee 2008).

There are, of course, many evangelicals who are somewhere in between, as well as others who are on the outer fringes of each group. Nevertheless, with rare exceptions, both groups (broadly understood) tend to rely heavily on an appeal to scripture peppered with the deliverances of the social sciences combined with an occasional cherry picking from theological traditions whose resources are rarely plumbed much deeper than is necessary to confirm what the activists already believe.[3]

What I want to suggest in this chapter is that these activists, through their tendency to drift to extrascriptural support for their agendas, have the right intuitions about what is percolating beneath the public policy debates that so animate them. However, I wish to offer a conceptual understanding that better accounts for the deep disagreements in American politics that have energized evangelicals across the political spectrum. This conceptual understanding will clarify some of these contested issues as well as explain why "scripture alone," though an essential doctrine of the Reformation, is inadequate in developing a political vocabulary and grammar that will help evangelicals and their opponents to better grasp what is at stake in what have been called "the culture wars."[4]

It strikes me that it is *a metaphysical question* whose answer dictates the positions of political adversaries in virtually every contested cultural issue: who and what are we, and can we know it? What I mean by *metaphysics* is the area of philosophical inquiry that concerns the ultimate nature of things, both animate and inanimate, and their relationships to one another. Consider this example. Suppose a legal scholar suggests that pre-viable fetuses ought not to be protected by the law because they are not independent beings worthy of moral status. Such a scholar, by employing the viability standard as a legal criterion by which to distinguish beings with moral status from beings without that status, is offering a particular view of human persons in order to support a particular public policy (i.e., abortion rights before viability). Behind the scholar's case is a philosophical anthropology that entails that certain prenatal entities—pre-viable fetuses—are not entitled to protection by the state since they lack a property that, if present, would afford them moral status. This is an instance of the accidental-essential division employed by some metaphysicians when they discuss, defend, or critique a particular philosophical anthropology. J. P. Moreland illustrates, "If something (say Socrates) has an accidental property (e.g., being white), then that thing can lose the property and still exist. For example, Socrates could turn brown and still exist and be Socrates. Essential properties constitute the nature or essence of a thing; and by referring to essential properties, one answers in the most basic way this question: What kind of thing is x?" (Moreland and Rae 2000, 52). So, for the scholar in question, viability is an essential property of beings with moral status, and thus when the unborn lacks that property, it is not a being with moral status. This scholar is, therefore, doing the work of a metaphysician. He or she is attempting, through philosophical reflection and argument, to defend a disputed view of the human person.

"Who and what are we, and can we know it?" is the metaphysical question that seems to me to be behind virtually every issue with which both right-leaning and left-leaning evangelicals have become involved. Whether it is abortion, poverty, marriage, obscenity, racism, religious establishment, the natural environment, or public education, how one answers this metaphysical question will, with virtual certainty, determine what one believes is the correct position on these issues.

Suppose, for example, that one embraces what may be called a secular liberal view of the human person: a human person is a conscious, self-aware, rights-bearing individual whose dignity requires the legal right to make self-regarding choices unencumbered by the demands of spouse, family, church, community, or any other citizen's religious or philosophical vision of the good life. One who holds this view will likely, though not necessarily, support abortion rights, same-sex marriage, no-fault divorce, and consider all religiously motivated policy proposals as a violation of liberal democracy itself, especially if these proposals are intended to limit one's access to pornography or permit the teaching of intelligent design in public schools. The secular liberal, like the Christian liberal, may support a strong welfare state, oppose racism, and care for the environment. But the secular may not do so because he has a rich and deep understanding of other citizens' intrinsic dignity as persons made in the image of God with a certain obligation to be stewards of God's creation. Rather, he embraces these ideas because he believes it to be unfair that some of his fellow citizens do not have the requisite income or social access to acquire the range of personal choices that affluent nonminority citizens presently possess, and that pollution and global warming may harm one's enjoyment of the good life or some romanticized view of nature untouched by the artifices of human civilization. That is, instead of nurturing in the privileged a spirit of charity, one may impart to the marginalized and those less well off the vice of envy as well as the idea that the purpose of political power is to employ one's electoral enfranchisement as a commodity in exchange for the property of those whose lot one has been encouraged to covet.

On the other hand, certain political truths seem to follow if one embraces what Robert P. George calls the Central Tradition (George 1993, 18–47): a human being is by its nature a person-in-community from the moment that person comes into existence, and whose intrinsic value does not depend on present abilities or powers, and that each person has certain natural obligations as a member of his or her community. These obligations are both to one another and to God's creation, and they arise from our roles as mother, father, citizen, child, and so on, and our vocations as minister, banker, baker, or candlestick maker. One who embraces this philosophical anthropology will likely, though not necessarily, oppose abortion and no-fault divorce, support the exclusivity of male-female marriage, hold a stewardship model in regard to the environment, and not be particularly troubled by religiously motivated policies that advance the common good even if these policies may impede the private habits of pornography consumers or suggest to public school students that the belief that the universe and its material properties is the sum total of existing things may not be the only possible deliverance of rational deliberation. One may support some form of the welfare state as well as strongly oppose racism, but not because citizens are entitled to welfare or because racism has bad consequences for its victims who are being denied access to bourgeois indulgences. Rather, one will support the latter and oppose the former because the most fundamental principle of community is charity, which entails loving your neighbor as yourself. One will see justice as requiring a rightly ordered social fabric for the sake of the common good.

Thus, it seems to me that it is a metaphysical question—specifically a question of philosophical anthropology—with differing and contrary answers that is at the root of what has animated evangelical political activism. Fortunately a growing number of evangelicals, especially in the discipline of philosophy,[5] seem to have fully grasped this. Unfortunately, many outside both the evangelical orbit and the wider conversation among orthodox Christians across denominational lines seem to continue to rely on assessments of evangelical politics that are, for lack of a better phrase, so 1988.

In order to better understand this problem and to move forward in correcting it, I will critically look at an issue concerning a metaphysical question over which most evangelicals and their political adversaries strongly disagree: the permissibility and federal funding of embryonic stem cell research.

Stem cells are found in all animals, including human beings. In adults, stem cells serve the function of repairing damaged tissue. For example, "hematopoietic stem cells" are "a type of cell found in the blood" (National

Bioethics Advisory Commission 1999, i). Their purpose is to repair the tissue of a damaged part of the organ of which they are a part, for adult stem cells are differentiated. However, stem cells found in the early embryo (or totipotent cells)—before its cells differentiate into the cells of particular organs—"retain the special ability to develop into nearly any cell type" (Ibid). The embryo's germ cells, "which originate from the primordial reproductive cells of the developing fetus," possess similar properties (Ibid).

Few doubt the potential of human stem cell research and the possibilities it offers for finding cures for numerous diseases such as Parkinson's and Alzheimer's. But the real issue that animates opponents of this research, and raises deep ethical questions, is how these cells are obtained and from what entity they are derived. According to the National Bioethics Advisory Commission, these promising "human stem cells can be derived from" four sources. Embryonic germ cells may be derived from "human fetal tissue following elective abortion," while totipotent embryonic stem cells may be extracted from "human embryos that are created by" in-vitro fertilization "and that are no longer needed by couples being treated for infertility." "[H]uman embryos . . . are created by IVF with gametes [i.e., sperm and egg cells] donated for the sole purpose of providing research material," and "potentially, human (or hybrid) embryos generated asexually by somatic cell nuclear transfer cloning techniques" (Ibid., i, ii). A fifth source could be embryos brought into being by the cloning technique.

With the exception of the first source, extracting the embryo's stem cells can only be accomplished at the cost of killing the embryo itself. This is why most evangelicals oppose both embryonic stem cell research as well as the federal funding of it. According to these citizens, embryos are full-fledged members of the human community, and thus the government at least ought not to underwrite their demise for the sake of another's good. Moreover, these citizens' belief about the nature of embryos is shaped by theological traditions that are the result of a reading of scripture in symbiotic relationship with a particular philosophical anthropology.

For this reason, supporters of embryonic stem cell research have drawn attention to the theological roots of the bioethical views of these citizens and have concluded that their policy proposals are in violation of the First Amendment's establishment clause. Take, for example, the comments of Rutgers law professor, Sherry F. Colb:

> Religious freedom is an essential right in this country. Religion and religious organizations have often provided compassion and support to those in need. Observant members of religious groups have a fundamental constitutional right to practice their respective religions—a right enumerated explicitly in the first amendment. . . . But as strongly as our Constitution protects religion, it forbids our government from becoming a religious one. . . .

> [T]he idea that full-fledged human life begins at conception—is a religious
> notion, and it is one to which some, but not all, religions subscribe.
>
> The idea of "ensoulment" is, of course, a purely religious concept. The notion
> that life begins at conception is counterintuitive if understood in secular terms.
> In a secular world, because an embryo lacks the capacity to think, to experi-
> ence joy, and to suffer pain or distress, it accordingly lacks legal entitlements
> that could possibly trump or even equal the interest in saving lives and curing
> disease through research. A secular perspective, then, would unequivocally
> approve of stem cell research. . . .
>
> Only a religious view would equate a clump of undifferentiated cells the size
> of a pinprick with a fully formed human being—deeming both equivalent
> "life." Proceeding on the basis of this equation . . . wrongfully imposes a
> religious perspective on all citizens, regardless of their religious belief or lack
> thereof. (Colb 2001)

Although the sort of analysis that Professor Colb offers is ubiquitous in both
the professional and popular literature on the subject (see Silver 2006; Dawkins 2007, 294–98; Simmons 2000; Mooney 2005), there are multiple problems with it. I will examine two of them in this essay: (1) she privileges,
without adequate justification, what she calls the secular perspective; and (2)
she mistakenly presents the so called secular and religious perspectives as
two different subjects rather than two different answers about the same subject.

To better understand the first problem—the unjustified privileging of the
secular perspective—I will conscript for my purposes a speech delivered by
then 2008 presidential candidate and senator Barack Obama (D-IL). In a June
28, 2006, keynote address to a group called "Call to Renewal," candidate
Obama offered among his many comments the following thoughts on the
relationship between politics and religion:

> Democracy demands that the religiously motivated translate their concerns
> into universal, rather than religion-specific, values. It requires that their propo-
> sals be subject to argument, and amenable to reason. (Obama 2006)

Elsewhere in his talk, the senator opines on the challenges that face Christian
believers, especially evangelicals, in a society, such as ours, that contains a
variety of different perspectives on a wide range of controversial issues.

> Now this is going to be difficult for some who believe in the inerrancy of the
> Bible, as many evangelicals do. But in a pluralistic democracy, we have no
> choice. Politics depends on our ability to persuade each other of common aims
> based on a common reality. It involves the compromise, the art of what's
> possible. At some fundamental level, religion does not allow for compromise.
> It's the art of the impossible. If God has spoken, then followers are expected to

live up to God's edicts, regardless of the consequences. To base one's life on such uncompromising commitments may be sublime, but to base our policy making on such commitments would be a dangerous thing. (Ibid.)

I would like to make two observations about Mr. Obama's reasoning. First, the first quote is inconsistent with the second one. Mr. Obama states, "Democracy *demands* that the religiously motivated translate their concerns into universal, rather than religion-specific, values." Then he asserts, "At some fundamental level, religion does not allow for compromise. . . . To base one's life on such uncompromising commitments may be sublime, but to base our policy making on such commitments would be a dangerous thing." But Mr. Obama in fact is claiming that his policy is based on the uncompromising commitment of what "Democracy *demands*" of its religious citizens. Thus, Mr. Obama, in his own reasoning, is suggesting a "dangerous thing."

On the other hand, if he is willing to concede that even what he believes about what "democracy demands" may be legitimately called into question by thoughtful religious citizens, then he cannot, on his own grounds, require that these citizens embrace his view unless he can provide to them unassailable reasons. If, according to Mr. Obama, democracy "requires" that the policy proposals of religious citizens "be subject to argument, and amenable to reason," we should expect the same from him. But he does not provide such reasons or arguments. He merely stipulates. Unless he is a prophet or the son of a prophet, that's not good enough.

Second, no Christian should have a quibble with the first quote, if all that Mr. Obama is saying is that religious citizens, if they want to persuade their non-religious neighbors on a particular issue, should, as a matter of prudence and wisdom, offer arguments that the latter may find persuasive. But that's not what the senator seems to be saying. He seems to be telling us that in order for religious citizens to fully participate in our democratic regime they *must* use the language of those who are hostile or indifferent to their faith. Notice that the senator does not say that democracy demands that the secularist translate his policy proposals into the language of theology so that his religious neighbors could be appropriately convinced and thus not be marginalized from the public conversation. For Mr. Obama it is a one-way street; the religious citizen must acquiesce at every turn to the rules imposed upon him by the secularist. And if he objects to this arrangement, he must offer arguments in the language and grammar of the secularist. For Mr. Obama, we should, in the words of Jesus, "give unto Caesar what is Caesar's and give unto God what is God's," but with one small caveat: the authority who has absolute discretion over the two spheres is Caesar, who may only be spoken to in the language of Caesar.

Employing similar reasoning to candidate Obama's, Professor Colb privileges a view of the human person she calls the "secular perspective." But it is not clear what precisely is "secular" about it. After all, Aristotle (1986), whose views many Christians, including St. Thomas Aquinas (1999), have found congenial to their theological projects, offered "secular" theories of ensoulment and philosophical anthropology that relied on empirical observation, philosophical reflection, and arguments to the best explanation that are inconsistent with Professor Colb's "secular perspective." Of course, in an elite culture dominated by Obama's understanding of religion and politics, labeling one's own perspective on embryonic stem cell research "secular" and that of one's opponent as "religious," while bringing the establishment clause to bear on one's case, is strategically savvy. For it means that the lack or presence of either adjective, rather than actual arguments for one's point of view, can do most of the heavy lifting. But the deeper issue that Professor Colb should be engaging is not a matter of vocabulary or grammar, as she inadvertently suggests by her explication of the so-called secular perspective.

She writes that this perspective requires that the law only protect human beings who have interests that arise when certain mental and physical capacities are in place, and because the embryo apparently lacks these capacities, he or she has no interests that the law ought to safeguard. But why should anyone accept that understanding of human beings and their interests? After all, there is a sense in which embryos do have these capacities from the moment they come into being, since the embryo possesses from its genesis basic capacities for the acquisition of certain powers and properties that its being and its constituent parts are intrinsically ordered to work in concert to bring to maturation (see George and Tollefsen 2008; Beckwith 2007). For this reason, Professor Colb is simply mistaken when she describes the embryo as "a clump of undifferentiated cells," for even when the embryo's cells are undifferentiated (i.e., the cells are totipotent and thus have the capacity to develop into any organ), the early embryo, as several scholars have pointed out (George and Tollefsen 2008; Beckwith 2007; Lee 1996; Ashley and Moraczewski 1994; Fisher 1991; McLaren 1982), functions as a substantial unity whose parts work in concert with one another for the growth, development, and continued existence of the whole.[6] According to developmental biologist, Michael Buratovich, "the blastosmeres [the undifferentiated, totipotent, cells of the early embryo] are held together by tight junctions and gap junctions, which allow cells to communicate with each other. . . . By the eight cell stage the cells are very tightly bound to each other. These cells are talking to each other in complex and wonderful ways. They are totipotent because they need to be—how else are they going to make everything from skin to sperm?" (Buratovich, personal communication, June 12, 2003).

With these clarifications, Professor Colb may now want to make the argument that excluding the early embryo from legal protection is still justified, but not because it lacks certain ultimate capacities for the actualization of certain powers, actions, and experiences, for the typical embryo surely does not lack those capacities. Rather, she may want to argue that it is the *present* and *immediate* exercisability of those capacities that distinguishes protectable persons from early embryos, since the latter do indeed lack that power. This is clearly a more defensible position than what Professor Colb offered in her initial salvo. But like that one, this revised one has its sophisticated detractors as well. And this brings me to my second objection to Professor Colb's argument.

She seems to want to turn two different answers to the same questions—what should be the public policy on embryonic stem cell research?—into two different subjects, religious and secular understandings of embryonic human life, about which there is only one answer for public policy: the secular one. Instead of confronting the arguments for the position she labels "religious," she seems to believe that if a position on a policy question can be labeled religious, it is no longer a position that may legitimately have a bearing on the public's deliberation on the issue. But that is putting the cart before the horse. For unless Professor Colb first shows that no argument in principle can provide warrant for a view of embryonic personhood connected to a theological tradition, justice requires that we treat so-called religious and secular understandings of embryonic personhood as different answers to the same question.

After all, Professor Colb in her essay offers an answer to a question of philosophical anthropology to which religious traditions have offered an answer as well. She presents a position—that she calls the secular perspective—in order to justify the killing of early embryos. And she makes her case by suggesting that, because the early embryo lacks certain capacities (or in our revised version of her argument, certain present and immediately exercisable capacities), the early embryo does not have interests that require that the law protect it. But by doing this, Professor Colb is offering an account of the human being, a philosophical anthropology if you will, in order to exclude early embryos from the realm of moral subjects. Not surprisingly, those who oppose Professor Colb's position, mostly Christians, present arguments and counterarguments in order to first show that the early embryo is a moral subject and then from there show that killing that entity in the way that Professor Colb suggests is unjustified. She chooses to call this position "religious," even though its advocates offer real arguments with real conclusions and real reasons (Beckwith 2007; Beckwith 2004; Lee 1996; Lee 2004; Lee and George 2005; Moreland and Rae 2000; George and Tollefsen 2008). Of course, these arguments and the beliefs they support are, for many of their advocates, religious, but they are also offered as deliverances of rational argument. In fact, for many of these believers, there may be no bright line demarcating "faith" and "reason," as if they were incommensurable categories that reside in the same soul side by side while never touching. Rather, these believers may view faith and reason, as St. Augustine viewed them, as natural human faculties designed by God for our acquisition of knowledge. When ordered to the right end, they work together in cooperation for the good of the whole person. As St. Augustine put it, "I believe, in order to understand; and I understand, the better to believe" (quoted in *Catechism* 2000, 158). Nevertheless, the arguments of these believers should be assessed on their merits as *arguments*.

Moreover, neither of the terms "religious" or "secular" is a relevant property of a reason one may offer in support of the strength or soundness of the conclusion that one is advancing. "True," "false," "plausible," "implausible," "good," and "bad" are adjectives that we apply to reasons when we assess the property relevant to its purpose as part of an argument. A *property* is a characteristic had by something. So, for example, one can say, "The dog is brown," which means that the dog has the property of "brownness." However, if one were to say, "The set of all even numbers is brown," one would be saying nonsense, since numerical sets cannot have the property of color. But reasons, like dogs and numerical sets, are things that can only have certain types of properties. Just as a dog cannot have the property of "irrational number" and a numerical set cannot have the property of "blue," "loud," or "tall," a reason cannot be "secular." For "secular," like "tall," "fat," "stinky," or "sexy," has no bearing on the quality of the reason one may offer in an argument to advocate a particular public policy or point of view.

Suppose one believes the conclusion that *unjust killing is morally wrong*, and offers two reasons for it:

1. The Bible forbids unjust killing.
2. The philosopher Immanuel Kant's *categorical imperative* forbids unjust killing.

Most people would call (1) a religious reason and (2) a secular reason, since the first contains the name of a religious book, the Bible, and the second contains a nonreligious principle, the categorical imperative. But how do the terms "religious" and "secular" add to or subtract from our assessment of the quality of these reasons? If one, for example, has good reason to reject the authority of the Bible, then *that good reason* and not the religious nature of the Bible is the real reason why one ought to reject reason (1). On the other hand, suppose that one has good reasons to believe that the Bible is a better guide to moral philosophy than Kant's categorical imperative. In that case, one ought to conclude that (1) is a better reason than (2). But, again, how do the properties of "religious" and "secular" affect such a judgment? At the end of the day, a reason either is weak, strong, true, or false. Thus, "religious" and "secular" are not relevant properties when assessing the quality of reasons a person may offer as part of her argument. This is why the requirement for a secular reason functions as a hindrance to properly understanding the bioethical issues addressed, and the positions held, by most evangelical Christian citizens.

This chapter focuses on the metaphysical questions that percolate beneath the issues concerning the nature of nascent human life. Nevertheless, as I mentioned, though only suggestively, in my introductory comments, this sort of analysis may be extended to numerous other political and moral disputes in which evangelicals and other Christians have become vibrant participants. Although it is certainly true that their political views are formed by a particular reading of scripture and moral theology, that philosophical pedigree by itself is not a sufficient reason to either permanently sequester those views from public consideration or to believe that these are held by advocates without the benefit of rational argument. Because both the evangelical Christian and her political adversary each offer contrary understandings of the human person in order to answer precisely the same political and moral questions, it is in the philosophical subdiscipline of metaphysics where the disagreements rest and not in the contrived dualism of the "secular" versus the "religious."[7]

NOTES

1. Here I am thinking of the popular writer, David Barton. Although some of his work is no doubt accurate and a useful corrective to some mistaken secular accounts of the American Founding (see, for example, Kramnick and Moore 2005), Barton's work is often sloppy and triumphalist, which, unfortunately, tends to cancel out the positive contributions he has made to correcting the anachronisms present in secularist accounts of American history.

2. Okay, that is a bit hyperbolic, but not by much. See, for example, Forrest and Gross (2007), Goldberg (2006), Hedges (2007), and Phillips (2006).

3. Take, for example, Jim Wallis' selective and superficial use of Catholic social thought (CST), from which he only extracts those portions that are consistent with his own political project. See Wallis (2008).

4. I believe that the term "culture wars" was coined by Hunter (1991).

5. J. P. Moreland (Biola University), Dallas Willard (University of Southern California), and Alvin Plantinga (University of Notre Dame) have written and spoken extensively on the issue of thinking of theology as a knowledge tradition, much in the vein of the late John Henry Cardinal Newman (*Idea of the University*). Unfortunately, Moreland, Willard, and Plantinga rarely write or speak of extending their arguments into the political realm. For representative samples of their works, see Plantinga (2000), Moreland (2007), and Willard (2000).

6. An exception to this that is often cited is the phenomenon of monozygotic twinning, which can occur within the first two weeks after conception. But even if every early embryo were to possess an intrinsically directed potential for twinning—this may be triggered by some external stimulus—it would not follow that the early embryo is not a unified organism. It would

only mean that the human being, early in his or her existence, possesses a current capacity that becomes latent after a certain level of development, just as some latent capacities become current later in the human being's existence (e.g., the ability to philosophize).

7. A special thank you to my teaching assistant, Logan Gage (PhD candidate in philosophy, Baylor University), for his assistance in the editing of this chapter.

Chapter Thirteen

The Good Book as Policy Guide: Characteristics, Critiques, and Contributions of Evangelical Public Policy Participation

David K. Ryden

It is clear that the evangelical faith tradition does in fact shape and inform its adherents' approach to public policy in important ways, albeit imperfectly and incompletely. This chapter seeks to clarify the defining attributes of evangelical public policy engagement, as the evangelical consciousness has expanded to include a wide range of issues. It also offers a critical assessment of the nature of evangelical policy activism, in particular examining the dangers of co-optation of evangelicalism by ideology, partisan attachments, and culture. In the end, evangelicals do in fact have something distinctive and worthy to bring to contemporary policy debates, but only if they remain firmly grounded in the theological convictions from which their policy views are ultimately derived. While evangelical policy participation must reflect the complexity of the policy process, it also is imperative to retain the ultimate source of truth, so that evangelicals might embody the hope and optimism that should flow from that realization.

THE BURGEONING POLICY AWARENESS OF EVANGELICALS

In considering the degree to which evangelicals have developed a comprehensive policy agenda, the reviews are decidedly mixed. Clearly the evangelical policy antenna has grown to encompass a range of issues on a much wider scale than typically thought. Yet the evangelical voice has been too soft, if not unheard altogether, on important current policy debates. Moreover, the nature of that evangelical engagement itself is subject to a number of legitimate critiques.

Unsurprisingly, evangelical Christians remain vigilant on culture war issues such as stem cell research, gay marriage, and abortion. But contrary to the caricatured version of evangelicalism, their policy agenda extends well beyond those hot button social issues. In some cases, they are out in front of the policy debate. As the "new internationalists," evangelical Christians have developed a broadly inclusive global mind-set, energetically working to address some of the toughest problems plaguing foreign populations. As a natural outgrowth of their long history of missionary outreach, evangelicals have been at the forefront of efforts to address genocide, global hunger, religious persecution and other human rights violations, and international environmental degradation.

Evangelical Christians also have been active in domestic policy provinces commonly thought to be the exclusive purview of the left. Regarding poverty and other social welfare initiatives, conservative Christian voices have engaged the left, in the process helping to balance the traditional liberal reliance on government aid with a role for intermediate organizations and faith-based nonprofits and carving out a place for personal responsibility. On issues of crime, punishment, and corrections, groups like Charles Colson's Prison Fellowship Ministries represent a faith-based approach that has pushed for prisoner re-entry programs and genuine alternative sentencing reforms.

On still other issues, evangelicals were slow to engage, but eventually responded with seriousness and commitment. Noah Toly's account of evangelical environmental policy involvement shows them to be tardy in coming to the table, but becoming effective participants once they did. Likewise for immigration reform, where the conspicuous silence of the old guard of evangelical leadership has yielded to a vocal, if somewhat fractious, movement for comprehensive reform.

This is not to suggest that the evangelical policy agenda has been complete or exhaustive. On two of the most important policy fronts of the past couple years—health care reform and the financial crisis—evangelicals seemingly had little to say or contribute. Consequently, they missed an opportunity to bring their values to the reshaping of two central pillars of the American economy. But on the whole, serious evangelical thinkers are weighing in on a surprisingly wide range of current policy topics.

As an aside, there is some categorical divergence within evangelicalism that can lead to ambiguity in trying to get a handle on the extent of evangelical involvement in various issues. Evangelical activity can occur on at least four different levels. First there are outspoken or high-profile public evangelical leaders (Dr. James Dobson, Pastor Rick Warren). A second group includes those who are active within government and the policymaking institutions at high levels, and hence wield influence. A third group are scholars and academics who study evangelicalism, such as most of the contributors to this volume. The final category includes rank-and-file evangelicals, those sitting in the pews on Sunday mornings. Clearly the degree of policy activism varies across these levels. Often, the policy work of academics or policy elites understandably may not have found its way down to rank-and-file evangelicals in large numbers. As a result of these differences, there frequently is some imprecision in efforts to gauge the degree to which evangelicals have engaged on a particular issue.

At least on an academic level, the essays in this volume provide a fruitful cross section of the diverse intellectual resources upon which evangelicals might draw. From a methodological standpoint, the essays implement a wide-ranging variety of approaches to exploring the relationship between evangelical Christianity and public policy. Those methods include careful historical analysis (Amstutz), philosophical reflection (Beckwith), careful examination of survey data (Patterson and Lenerville), interviews with policymakers and opinion leaders (Melkonian-Hoover), and reliance upon sociological, economic, and other social science principles (the Ryden essay on race, Bennett). When taken together, the essays provide a rich portrait of the multiple ways in which evangelical Christianity might approach matters of public policy.

IS THERE SUCH A THING AS A DISTINCTIVE EVANGELICAL PUBLIC POLICY FRAMEWORK?

A central inquiry of this book is whether the evangelical faith tradition should inform one's approach to public policy questions, and if so, how. This raises the preliminary question of whether evangelicalism can be associated with anything akin to a discernible or systematic approach to the universe of policy questions. If evangelicalism can be seen as a semi-coherent discernible policy perspective, what are its defining traits?

The short answer to the question is that there is no comprehensive evangelical policy framework to be found, at least in the sense of a perspective akin to liberalism or conservatism that can be relied upon for relatively certain and predictable outcomes to each and every policy question. But if one has a more modest expectation, say, of a common point of reference or prism through which all policy issues can be viewed rather than a magic formula for arriving at easy answers to all questions, evangelical Christianity does, or at least should, provide such a lens. That more modest policy orientation flows out of the defining attributes of evangelicalism itself—an elevated view of scripture, the sinfulness of humanity redeemable only through the saving grace of Christ, and the imperative of sharing the Gospel with the world.

EVANGELICAL POLICY ENGAGEMENT AND SCRIPTURAL AUTHORITY

A key facet of evangelicalism is the fealty to scripture as God's revealed truth. Scripture occupies a special place of authority in the thoughts, actions, and lives of evangelicals. When this exalted view of scripture is melded with the belief that one's faith is relevant to all facets of one's life, scripture is the conclusive source of authority, wisdom, and truth for evangelicals' policy stances and for their activism in pursuit of those goals. Indeed, evangelicals are often criticized for a tendency to reduce policy debates to chapter and verse of the Bible. While there may be something to this claim, the essays in this volume suggest a more complex relationship between policy and Bible.

On the one hand, there undoubtedly are a number of issues where evangelicals are inclined to refer to *explicit scriptural text* in a straightforward manner to arrive at answers to policy questions. The Psalmist's praise to a God who "knew him in his mother's womb" has led evangelicals to stand fast in their opposition to abortion. Similarly specific scriptural passages generate strong opposition to homosexuality in the face of changing societal mores. The countless New Testament references to caring for the poor and marginalized—the "least of these" in our society—have prompted evangelicals to take the social dimension of the gospel to heart, even while they may differ on the specific policy solutions to address those social ills. It is probably fair to say that the more explicit the scriptural reference is, the greater the resolve and certitude of evangelical Christians in the policy stance they derive from it.

In other contexts, however, evangelicals are more likely to apply scriptural authority indirectly, invoking *general biblical values* for guidance in their approach to policy debates. The biblical principle of stewardship shapes the evangelical mind-set on environmental issues, fiscal and budgetary matters, and questions of personal finances. The command to seek justice informs attitudes on crime and punishment, social welfare, and immigration. The dictates to love one's brother and to value all of human life shape evangelical attitudes on issues ranging from abortion and capital punishment to a variety of domestic social welfare programs to global concerns over hunger, disease, and war.

If one were to articulate an overarching biblical point of reference or common analytical framework for policy across the board, it would likely revolve around the understanding of scripture as the revelation of God's creative design for humanity and the world. In other words, the evangelical framework for considering public policy is (or should be) thoroughly grounded in a full understanding of scripture as a detailed description of God's creation, and what the nature of that creation means for mankind. For the evangelical Christian, belief in the biblical account of God's creation and the acceptance of it as constituting the ultimate good for us furnishes a distinct foundation upon which virtually any policy debate can be premised. The aligning of one's policy views with the belief in a revealed transcendent creative design is a leaping-off point for a unique evangelical perspective on the full array of contemporary policy issues.

EVANGELICALS, PUBLIC POLICY, AND THE SPIRIT OF EVANGELISM

A second key definitional component of evangelicalism is the emphasis on evangelism. For evangelicals, Christ's redemptive grace is not just to be received, but is to be shared. Evangelicals are commissioned to go to all corners of the world to spread the Gospel, to seek converts at home and abroad. This evangelizing spirit manifests itself in multifold ways, with important policy ramifications both in terms of style and substance. For instance, Mark Amstutz's fascinating account of the evangelical missionary movement going back two centuries points to a number of indirect policy consequences for American foreign policy. Just the presence of evangelical missionaries in places across the globe helped to inform American foreign policy while contributing to the formation of civil society in those cultures.

More recently, the emergence of a global evangelical policy activism can be attributed to an expanded understanding of what constitutes evangelism. It is no longer confined to preaching the word and proselytizing. A more sophisticated approach stresses servant witness, building relationships, and striving to meet the tangible physical needs of others before attending to their spiritual needs. The practical result has been to place evangelical Christians at the forefront of an array of global policy initiatives—from poverty relief and human rights advocacy to fighting genocide in Darfur and working for the religious liberties of worldwide Christians. That new spirit of evangelism is embodied in World Vision's taking the lead in fighting global hunger. It can be seen in the Bush administration's commitment of resources to combating the AIDS scourge in Africa. It is visible in evangelicals' forceful advocacy of global interests, as they act prophetically to prick the conscience of government and society on a wide range of global problems.

The spirit of evangelism also is evident in evangelical sensibilities as to who bears the ultimate responsibility for addressing problems and crises. Their missionary zeal translates into a sense of personal responsibility and active service, most notably at the international level. Evangelicals are not inclined to sit back, advocate, and await governmental action. Rather, they see it as their responsibility to volunteer, serve, and be a part of the solution to the problem. This action-oriented response is manifested in numerous ways. Students on evangelical college campuses are motivated in large numbers to go on mission trips abroad. Teams from evangelical churches take part in service projects across the world. Evangelicals are among the most generous of charitable givers, during times of international crisis and otherwise. While they may be open to government action, they are less likely simply to bide their time waiting for it to do so.

The focus on evangelism is not only evident in *when* evangelicals are compelled to act. It also means that they cannot ignore the *style of their political participation*—how they "do" politics. For evangelicals called to share Christ with the world, it is imperative that they be sensitive to how they are perceived as a result of their political personae, and to consider whether Christ is visible in their acts and words. They are obliged to pay as careful attention to the tone and manner of their discourse as to the substance of their arguments. This may be one of the greatest challenges for evangelicals involved in the policy process. To capitulate to the contentious, über-partisan, conflict-driven nature of American politics is to risk doing incalculable harm to Christ's cause and His church.

To date, evangelicals' record in this regard has been less than stellar. They have acquired a reputation for stridency in the policy arena that can be traced back to their emergence on the political scene a quarter century ago. That re-entry into politics was stoked in no small part by a deep apprehension over what they saw as a culture in decline. Christian conservative mobilization was defensive in nature, characterized by an "us against them" mentality; it operated as something of a rear guard action to ward off the corrosive influence of the culture. This "culture under attack" mind-set undoubtedly fed a tendency toward conflict and adversarialness that many evangelicals have yet to outgrow.

Evangelicals in the political arena too often continue to be seen as defensive and combative, their behavior thus undermining their witness to the culture and the world. They often are on the attack, perhaps because they see themselves as being under attack. Rather than striving for a more positive and winsome presence, their stance is oppositional and adversarial. While their motives may be sound, their style of political engagement has undermined the evangelistic impulse to win over the world. It has proven more difficult to win souls when one is perceived as angry, intolerant, and judgmental.

The challenge for evangelicals is daunting—to project a more optimistic, loving, and hopeful attitude even when enmeshed in deep differences over controversial policy issues. This does not necessarily mean avoiding tough topics which may provoke broader disapproval; but it does require self-control, civility, and moderation in how issues are addressed. It reinforces the need to address tough issues in a nuanced way, where policy stances are seasoned with well-reasoned arguments and compelling evidence. This is no easy task. Politics is by its nature combative and antagonistic. Policy debates are about differences. Evangelicals certainly cannot expect Christ-like love from their opponents in the midst of animated debates. Yet Christ is to be their model for the substance *and* style of their policy engagement, as they strive to embody God's love for all of His creation. [1]

PUBLIC POLICY AND AN EVANGELICAL THEOLOGY OF THE STATE

In articulating an evangelical policy framework, it is not enough just to consider the proper substantive arguments of a specific policy debate. The resolution of policy debates may well implicate the policymaking processes and institutions themselves. Consequently, evangelical theology might well impact how one views those institutions responsible for making and carrying out policy decisions. In other words, an application of evangelical theology to policy discussions should also include a framework for critically assessing government, its role, and its limits.

Again, the notion of God's created order stands at the center of evangelical views of governmental authority and power, both in the justification for it and in the limits imposed upon it. In both regards, an evangelical theory of government stems from an understanding of the world through the lens of God's creative design and power. It revolves around the Genesis story and the central fact of the marring of creation by human sin. Biblical revelation absolutely demands that evangelicals fully come to grips with the fact of a fallen world and accept the pervasive presence of sin and its consequences for all of creation; all that is in the world bears the consequences of that sinfulness, from the individual to governmental institutions and society at large.

This realization should impact how evangelicals think about policymaking institutions. On an individual level, an awareness of one's own sinfulness and that of others should temper expectations of what can be accomplished through a divinely inspired, but humanly administered, policy agenda. Policy responses must take into account the sinfulness both of the beneficiaries of policies and of those administering the programs; a comprehension of sin counsels that we be wary of human behavior on an individual and collective or institutional scale. Sinfulness does not somehow melt away when we move from the individual to a government bureaucracy or institution. If anything, it is likely to be magnified. The corrosive effect of sinfulness amplified by power is as evident in the workings of institutions as it is individually. A healthy appreciation for the consequences of sin should generate a measure of skepticism as to what politics and government can accomplish.

At the same time, evangelicals understand government to be more than a mere human endeavor or enterprise. It is ordained by God for his purposes, including the legitimate objectives of promoting justice and tending to the common good of society. As Nicholas Wolterstorff states, government represents "God's providential care for us as finite, limited creatures, not just as fallen sinful creatures. Properly functioning government is part of God's providential care for his creation qua creation" (Wolterstorff 2008, 149). Government is not a purely negative institution that exists to control sinful people; it has a positive goal of achieving justice and serving the common good.

Hence we have institutions comprised of fallen individuals, yet ordained by God. This dual realization merits a nuanced attitude toward government. Christians are to accord government proper honor and respect; they should avoid making broadside attacks on government or questioning that it is somehow illegitimate. A thoroughly cynical, anti-government stance is difficult to reconcile with the biblical view of government as God-ordained for His purposes. The proper stance for Christians, it would seem, is to appreciate the appropriate role of government while also valuing the structural means of constraining government as a limited enterprise, as protection against an overreaching state. Thus it is each Christian's duty to respect the state while exercising her prophetic role in holding government to its proper task.

In the end, sin is on every side of the arguments about government and governmental power. Sinful humans, and social institutions made up of sinful humans, require governmental authority to restrict them, toward the end of a well-ordered society. That same sinful nature affects and infects a government of sinful men for whom power may magnify that sinful nature. Government itself is fallen, as are other social institutions. Just as government acts to control the consequences of sin, governmental power must be subject to constraints as well. Thus does the evangelical view of the state align with the Madisonian exhortation to control the governed and the governors.

Clear policy objectives do not necessarily mean clarity on the strategies to use to pursue those objectives. The appropriate role of government varies with the issue and the circumstances. At times the state may be better off prompting or partnering with other policy institutions or actors. In other contexts, the problems are too large and complex for other institutions to realistically address. Sometimes, the dysfunctions of the federal bureaucracy may only impede or complicate the attainment of an efficacious result. In the end, there are no "general principles about the proper role of limited government [that] . . . can replace the necessity of prudential wisdom at every specific moment" (Sider 2005a, 191). Sider nicely captures the need for balance:

> Christians should respect and treasure government as a good gift ordained by God to promote the good and restrain evil. But if it is to be helpful rather than harmful, it must be limited. . . . [S]ociety is much larger than the state and contains many crucial nongovernmental institutions that have their own independence and worth. At the same time, government must act not only to maintain commutative, retributive, and procedural justice, but also to promote distributive justice, especially in order to empower the poor and weak. (192)

PUBLIC POLICY AND THE LIMITS OF THE GOOD BOOK

As has been noted, any overarching policy perspective for evangelical Christians must acknowledge the centrality of scriptural authority—of the Bible as divinely authored and revealing the very mind and nature of the creator. As such, one would expect evangelical Christians to approach scripture as an all-encompassing source of authority and guidance relevant to all aspects of their lives, including evangelical policy discernment. For this reason, the enlarged evangelical policy awareness evident in the foregoing chapters is not surprising. One would expect serious appeal to scriptural authority to broaden evangelicals' policy consciousness. Taking scripture to heart should place upon evangelicals' minds a wide-ranging set of issues, as it in fact has.

Beyond the application of specific biblical passages to particular issues, evangelicals' reading of scripture provides them with an overarching theme in which to ground their policy attitudes generally. The central focus of the Bible—from Genesis forward—is on God's creative design for humanity and the world, God's crafting man and woman in His image, to be in relationship with God himself. God's love of humanity is at the center of the story of His offering of His Son as the sacrificial atonement and redemption for sinful mankind, making relationship with God possible and culminating in salvation and eternal life.

The Bible as God's revealed plan for humanity frames evangelical attitudes in the policy realm writ large. The upshot of seeing people as God's image bearers is to grant to each and every human life an innate worth and value that otherwise would not exist: "Every single person is invited by the almighty Creator to live forever with the living God. That is how immeasurably important and valuable, how full of dignity, every individual person is" (Sider 2005a, 167). Christians who are commanded to love their neighbor as themselves should strive to honor and protect the existence, worth, and value of each human life. This focus on the dignity and well-being of every person has far-reaching policy consequences; it should engender an awareness of the host of factors that impede or interfere with people's realization of lives lived with a dignity and worth derived from their having been created in God's very image. Scripture should plant in each person a rock solid foundational commitment to the care of their fellow man.

An understanding of the innate value of mankind has obvious bearing on issues directly implicating life and death—abortion, capital punishment, the use of force, and matters of war and peace. But the biblical emphasis on human dignity also is relevant on some level to policies that address material well-being—social welfare and poverty, education, immigration, accessibility to heath care, and more. Indeed, it is difficult to find an issue that is not somehow related directly or indirectly to this overarching value.

The belief in a divinely created world raises countless other policy implications for evangelical Christians as well. Man is given dominion over the world, along with the attendant responsibility for the things of the world and stewardship for its care. This is the genesis of the evangelical "creation care" movement addressing environmental issues. The same sense of responsibility for God's world gives rise to a global outlook, in which evangelicals are concerned with issues beyond their own lives or the borders of their own country—human rights, global development and poverty alleviation, and peace.

This scripturally derived framework should orient evangelical thinking on public policy across the gamut of issues. However, that orientation is unlikely to furnish neat, clean answers on specific policy debates as they arise. Nor will it necessarily make it easier for Christians to determine the rightness of policy prescriptions on many policy questions. Indeed, the fact that evangelicals are called to care about an array of issues makes it more imperative that they be sophisticated and thoughtful students of politics, the policy process, and substantive policy arguments.

Understanding scripture as God's revealed plan for humanity serves as the moral framework for policy analysis, even as there are serious limits on its use as a tool for resolving specific policy debates. That one is able to derive from evangelical theology the "correct" value at stake in a policy debate still might fail to produce a conclusive outcome from that debate. A solid grasp of scripture as God's plan for mankind should condition the evangelical's approach to all issues. But it will not magically resolve the tensions between policy questions that implicate God's plan in seemingly conflicting ways. The creation mind-set does not free one from engaging in the hard task of working through issues, prioritizing concerns, or balancing competing creation concerns.

First, agreement on theologically derived ends will not always translate into agreement on the means by which one might hope to best attain those ends. On any number of policy issues, there will be good faith differences over the optimal means of pursuing the agreed upon ends. Jean Bethke Elshtain puts it this way:

> [F]or many issues, clear biblical guidelines are not available, there are not ready-made answers for every situation. This is another way of describing . . . the role of prudential judgments made by political actors in situations where perfect knowledge is never available, where we have to anticipate the reactions to what we are planning to do but can never control them. . . . There is a fog of politics too. We just cannot know everything there is to know. The world of politics is the world of prudential judgments, compromises, and half measures. (Elshtain 2006, 199)

Consider how evangelical Christians might approach questions of socioeconomic and poverty policy. A deeply felt concern for the poor and a desire for economic justice are values that stem from a creation mind-set and the goal of individual worth and dignity that flows from it. But a common commitment to better the condition of the poor may do little to clarify how one should go about trying to accomplish that.

Evangelicals of all stripes hopefully would agree that Christians need to commit themselves to helping those with less, in the name of the innate human value and dignity. But that general agreement hardly ends the conversation over how best to realize it as a matter of policy. Questions abound. To what extent are social and economic justice best achieved by governmental means? Even if government has a significant role, at what level should it occur? Should the federal government be the predominant actor? Or should state and local governments carry more of the burden? How about private actors—individuals, charities, and other intermediate organizations? How much should we work to motivate people to serve in nongovernmental spheres instead—through nonprofit and nongovernmental organizations and churches? Even if one envisions a major role for the federal government in fighting poverty and seeking social justice, how should it do that? What should the policy details look like? How should it be implemented and administered? What best practices ought to be followed? And we haven't even broached the specific programs—be they welfare, job training, homelessness, mental health, or countless other social programs? What will the details of these programs look like? Will governmental agencies avail themselves of faith-based providers? When should the government resort to privatization in the administration of poverty reduction programs?

This is hardly an exhaustive list of questions. In short, one may well agree with Jim Wallis and others that budgets are "moral documents," and still face broad and deep differences—wholly legitimate differences—over the content of that budget and how it is to be carried out. Evangelicals certainly can and often should be a prophetic voice calling the government to account when poverty spending is a pittance and military spending or middle-class entitlements eat up virtually all of the discretionary portion of the budget. But the debate over how to engage public policy processes toward the goal of treating others consistent with God's creative plan and His valuing of all human life leaves a slew of unanswered questions over means, strategies, the relative responsibilities of a host of human institutions, and the contributing role of sinful human behavior.

Or consider the complexities of the debate surrounding health care reform effort of 2009 and 2010. That issue undeniably triggered multiple biblically based values, grounded in the concept of persons created in the image of God and the innate value and dignity of every human life. The highly imperfect health care system as it existed pre-reform certainly threatened these values. It was marred by the absence of health care for millions, poor access to quality care for others, and potential threats to basic financial well-being for those facing a catastrophic health situation. The system's shortcomings should have been enough to make Christians conscious of the issue and generally supportive of some kind of reform to ease its woes.

Moreover, Christians likewise would recognize that the government had a legitimate role to play in reforming health care. The issue raised questions of justice for the poor and marginalized—namely, those least able to access or afford the health care system. The pursuit of justice in these circumstances would seem to be a purpose for which government was ordained. At the same time, the Christian skepticism toward governmental institutions and bureaucracies as marred by human sinfulness would likely make them desirous of some limits on government's role. Human fallibility would likely shape the possible solutions, leading to incentives to motivate individual responsibility and wise health decisions. It also suggests the need for enough of a governmental regulatory presence to ensure responsible behavior by intermediate institutional actors, be they health insurers, employer health care providers, or hospitals.

Finally, the biblical value of stewardship undoubtedly applies to the health care debate. Given spiraling health care costs and the expense of medical treatment, evangelicals might well interpret the biblical command to be wise stewards of our resources to demand reforms that contained serious cost controls. In the end, an evangelical perspective would strive for balance between these biblical values and the sets of interests and responsibilities involved.

From these one can perhaps sketch in the broadest of terms an evangelical health care policy proposal. In the name of human dignity, it would seek to ensure quality access for all citizens and expanded health care coverage. It also would include incentives for personal responsibility and healthy lifestyles, to enhance the dignity of the individual. The evangelical theology of the state would likely mean skepticism toward a single payer plan or another variant that gave too much control to, or required too heavy a presence of, the federal government. It would likely prefer market principles and other incentives where appropriate to accomplish its objectives, subject to sufficient regulation. In the name of stewardship, it would contain serious cost control mechanisms, as well as incentives to reduce waste and inefficiency in the health care delivery system. But beyond these rough parameters, arriving at an acceptable health care bill would entail making a raft of exceeding difficult choices and determinations.

In the health care realm, as in any number of policy contexts, having shared biblical values by no means led to agreed-upon policy outcomes; the complexities of public policy simply leave far too much room for divergent notions of how best to pursue biblical values. More often than not, policy debates demand the exercise of prudential judgments regarding what substantive policy approaches are likely to be more effective. Several important points follow from this. One is that evangelicals must cultivate genuine sophistication as to the workings of policy processes and bureaucracies. They need an in-depth grasp of how the policy process works at a practical level. The other point is that evangelicals ought to bring a sizable measure of humility into complex policy discussions. They should take care not to demonize others who purportedly share their faith but arrive at different policy outcomes.[2]

INVOKING THE GOOD BOOK: NEED EVANGELICALS DO MORE?

There is an important sidebar to the evangelical reliance upon scripture for policy guidance—namely, the extent to which evangelicals rely upon explicitly scripture-based arguments in the context of policy debates. There are questions of real consequence—as a matter of both principle and pragmatic effectiveness—regarding the sufficiency of relying exclusively upon scriptural language to make one's case, or whether one should be expected to offer alternative secular arguments in support of scripturally derived policy stances. Evangelicals have been charged with not utilizing more broadly accessible rhetoric in advancing their policy views. Rather, they have tended to rest their arguments on scripture passages and theological foundations, free of alternative, more universally acceptable terms that might resonate with those outside the evangelical tradition.

The essays provide a range of views on that question. Tim Barnett is at one end of the spectrum. He suggests that evangelicals, at least in the context of economics, are ineffectual precisely because they rarely make the effort to translate biblical principles into the language of secular economics. The failure to transpose the scriptural into the secular is, in his view, at the heart of evangelicals' failure to contest those objectionable economic practices that contributed to the economic crisis of 2008. In other words, the failure to confront egregious economic principles was due partly to a lack of understanding of how scripture applied, precisely because they never sought to convert biblical principles into practical economic policy. In the realm of economics, Barnett sees little tension between biblical values (of righteousness and justice) and secular economic principles (of good will and fairness). Hence a nuanced set of secular arguments to accompany biblical principles can serve both biblical and secular economic ends.

Noah Toly is an articulate spokesman for the opposing view, rejecting what he calls the ethics of necessity; that is, the notion that Christians should be driven by what is pragmatically optimal in a policy debate. Rather he argues for an ethic of freedom, whereby Christians hold fast to their theological foundations and share them unapologetically rather than translating them into worldly views. For Toly, the environmentalist, there is no values-neutral or common vantage point regarding the moral obligations underlying environmental debates. If everyone in a policy debate begins with some predetermined values framework, then evangelicals' one genuine contribution is a clear articulation of the transcendent bases for the stewardship and justice at the center of the environmental movement. Environmental policy engagement on explicitly theological terms—infused with the hope that comes from those religious convictions in the face of seeming intractability on environmental issues—is precisely what evangelicals can offer.

Others are somewhere between these two poles. David Ryden argues that Christians should seek fluency in both secular and theological tongues. They are obligated to pursue parallel modes of argumentation and rhetoric, adhering to the evangelical religious tradition while simultaneously striving for rationales that will engage those outside of evangelical or Christian circles. For Ryden, the Christian witness requires us to be forthright in acknowledging the scriptural foundations for our positions. But in the interests of effectiveness and as a matter of pragmatism and prudence, one also should be able to wield logic, reasoning, social science, and other tools of secular policy discourse—in other words, arguments that will be persuasive in secular circles. The evangelical policy agenda undoubtedly has suffered from rhetorical limitations that impede its making inroads among those who do reject theological sources of authority. Evangelicals have been too easily dismissed out of hand as proof-texting, Bible-thumping anti-intellectuals, due in part to their failure to utilize public (nontheological) rhetoric that is likely to resonate with the nonevangelical world. Until they can do so, their success in the policy arena will be limited at best.

Francis Beckwith agrees that prudence and wisdom may compel Christians to use arguments that non-Christians are likely to find persuasive. But he rejects the view that the secularization of one's policy arguments is somehow the price of entering the public square. He decries what he sees as an artificial distinction between the religious and the secular arguments, and is critical of the presupposition that only secular arguments have public sway, while religious arguments are somehow presumptively illegitimate.

Finally, Mark Amstutz and Zac Calo both suggest that there may not be the same expectation to de-religionize one's activism in the international realm. Evangelicals are freer to openly speak and act out of religious motivation and to tie their policy advocacy to religious impetus. On the global level, the evangelical agenda tends to be more in line with the general direction of policy overall. This differs from many domestic policy issues, where evangelicals stake out positions that contradict nonreligious positions. Globally, evangelicals may face less pressure, and have less of a need, to generate a common, pluralistic voice to engage a broader world that is pursuing a common end.

CRITIQUING EVANGELICAL POLICY PARTICIPATION

Notwithstanding their increasing scope, evangelical thought and action relative to public policy are open to a number of substantive and stylistic criticisms. The first of these has to do with the failure to engage on some key issues. The public policy antenna of evangelical Christians undeniably has grown more sensitive, picking up a host of issues that once were beyond the consciousness of evangelical Christians. Yet that growing policy agenda is not all-inclusive. On some important issues, *evangelical Christians simply have been absent*. On perhaps the two most hotly contested domestic battlegrounds in the past couple years, evangelicals were hardly to be found.

The marathon debate that yielded a historic health care reform bill in the spring of 2010 was heated and controversial, yet it is hard to recall any degree of sustained evangelical engagement. Rather evangelical input was sporadic and inconsequential. The result was an impoverished and polarized debate on a morally weighty issue of long-term significance. Evangelicals were similarly out of the loop on critically important questions of monetary and fiscal policy that thrust us into the economic crisis of 2008–2009. As Tim Barnett notes, evangelicals failed to operationalize biblical values of justice, morality, and righteousness that might have led them to address troubling practices involving the stock and housing bubbles, reckless financial and investment tactics, and more. Instead, their intuitive embrace of the rhetoric of limited government and simplistic anti-regulatory slogans arguably made them complicit in the reckless actions of those responsible for bringing the economy down. Again, their missing voice was a lost opportunity to help curb destructive practices that had deeply felt negative consequences.

Other criticisms go to the effectiveness, or lack thereof, of evangelical policy activism. One such shortcoming is a tendency of evangelicals to deal with specific issues on a *discreet and isolated basis* instead of addressing them within a richer context of cross-cutting considerations that might tangentially impact a variety of issues. For example, evangelicals have mostly treated environmentalism as a freestanding, isolated policy area. Yet environmentalism triggers questions that cut across economics, culture, and sociology. So while evangelicals are to be lauded for taking seriously their role as stewards of God's creation, they—like most other voices in the debate—have neglected the complexities relating to the possible effects of environmental regulations on economics, jobs, and the poor. Noah Toly concludes that sound environmental policy must be less fragmented and more than just about the environment. Another example is the same-sex marriage controversy. Evangelicals who oppose such measures in isolation open themselves up to charges of hypocrisy for their failure to speak to the damages inflicted upon the institutions of marriage and family by heterosexual practices (including evangelical Christians) such as divorce, abuse, adultery, and cohabitation.

A related tendency of evangelicals is to reduce complex policy puzzles to *simplistic slogans and absolutist policy responses*. The complexity that characterizes both scripture and various policy questions means that rarely is a policy prescription easily captured or resolved by a simple answer or principle. On the contrary, issue after issue demands that evangelical Christians develop a carefully measured and nuanced policy approach. Bold pronouncements rarely fit the situation. Typically prudence and modesty caution a humbler approach to the issue at hand.

Tim Barnett's critique of evangelical thinking on economics takes them to task for resorting to simplifications and trite moralistic principles in situations that cry out for extensive reflection on the challenges of modern economics. What was needed—but which was badly lacking—was a deeper understanding of the multifaceted nature of modern capitalism and markets, and a modulated approach to government and its regulatory role in all this.

Instead, evangelicals essentially echoed anti-government, pro-free market platitudes that wholly failed to acknowledge either biblical imperatives or the complex challenges of modern economics. Evangelicals must be savvy and sufficiently learned analysts of policy to make discerning and differentiated policy choices based upon specific circumstances rather than broad generalizations and platitudes.

Debates over education policy reflects something similar. The current education environment touches on a wide range of issues and questions—the need for choice and competition, the wisdom of national standards, values-based education, the role of teachers unions, to countless other reform ideas. Yet much of the evangelical community, when registering their voices on education, are overly obsessed with symbolic cultural markers that arguably have little to do with the actual caliber of education—prayer in schools, the Pledge of Allegiance, and the like.

Another observation regarding evangelical policy involvement is that, by nature, it tends to be *action-oriented and impulsive* rather than reflective and long-sighted. This tendency toward action has its upside, yielding tangible results that have a strong positive short-term impact. But it too often falls short in addressing longer-term concerns. The Amstutz and Calo chapters both identify this entrepreneurial evangelical spirit regarding international matters, though they reach differing conclusions about its effect. Calo views the grassroots activism of evangelicals spurred on by moral indignation as a striking development on the international scene, leading to Nicholas Kristoff's labeling of them as the "new internationalists." Evangelical "boots on the ground" can make a real difference in addressing immediate crises around the globe. But the instinct to act rather than reflect means that longer-term solutions are never formulated and often remain elusive.

Amstutz likewise acknowledges the absence of a coherent moral theory or well-developed philosophical foundation that might serve to frame evangelical policy activism. But he is not inclined to see it as much of a weakness. For Amstutz, the lack of a coherent vision is offset by the entrepreneurial spirit that goes with a decentralized approach. The remarkable ability to mobilize the evangelical troops more than compensates for the absence of a nice, neat theoretical framework for their service.

Finally, much has been written about the *strong spirit of individualism* that imbues evangelical Christianity. This is a prime example of a distinctive element of evangelical Christianity that in turn shapes and informs evangelical policy activism, both substantively and stylistically. Suffice it to say that there is a strong individualistic focus to evangelicalism, which in turn generates an individualistic approach to public policy. The individualistic orientation of evangelical Christianity is at its very center. It begins with the individual act of repentance and commitment of one's life to Christ. It continues with a central focus on an ongoing personal relationship with Christ. It favors individual disciplines of faith—prayer, Bible reading, and devotion. Evangelical worship often emphasizes the experiential and the movement of the Holy Spirit within each individual.

Unsurprisingly this strong individualism is mirrored in evangelical politics and policy preferences. Mark Amstutz notes that the evangelical focus on personal morality and spiritual well-being naturally point to a politics that is likely to tend toward the conservative. It explains why policy issues that raise questions of personal morality and traditional values tend to be a higher priority with evangelicals. Individualistic faith leads to an individualistic, moralistic politics. This can be positive. Amstutz asserts that history confirms that the evangelical emphasis on personal morality has had a profound positive impact on social and political life. The missionary movement and its laserlike focus on conversion also have had far-reaching social, economic, and political benefits.

But it can also have real negative consequences in the context of specific issues. It can prevent evangelicals from striking a more constructive policy balance between individual behavior and institutional solutions. Using the economic realm again as an example, individualism is manifested in an unquestioning faith in limited government, free markets, private property, and self-sufficiency. The result was the lack of appreciation for an institutional regulatory presence that might ensure the maintenance of the biblical interest in economic justice. In the context of race relations, David Ryden explains how white evangelicals' intellectual prism is colored by an individualism that undermined efforts to build better white-black race relations in America. White evangelicals' exclusive focus on individual repentance and building interracial relationships blinded them to the racialized divisions on a broader institutional and societal scale that still negatively impact much of black America. On policies dealing with social welfare, some evangelicals have been far too quick to focus exclusively on individual effort and a philosophy of pull yourself up by your own bootstraps.

The individualism at the heart of evangelicalism also impacts efforts to shape and realize—on the level of implementation rather than substance—a coherent evangelical public policy perspective, one that commands the acceptance of large numbers of lay evangelicals. The individualistic reading and interpretation of scripture gives individuals almost unlimited latitude in discerning for themselves what stances to take on various policies. This individualism also is mirrored on a structural level, in a decentralized faith tradition that values the autonomy of individual congregations and churches above denomination or hierarchy. As a result, evangelicals lack a formal mechanism for arriving at consensus or like-mindedness on issues. Lay Catholics can look to the pronouncements of the U.S. Conference of Catholic Bishops for guidance on current policy controversies. Many other mainline denominations have a public affairs branch office in Washington, D.C., that establishes official denominational policy and lobbies Congress in support of that policy. Evangelicals lack a similar structure that exists to adopt such policy stances and is able to disseminate them to evangelicals sitting in the church pews.

In recent years, there have been increased efforts by evangelicals to speak with a common or institutional voice. Most often, this has entailed the NAE entering the policy fray by drafting and releasing statements on various policy debates and the biblical obligations of Christians on such matters. Those include, most prominently, "For the Health of the Nation" (2004), as well as position papers on the use of torture, global warming and environmental policy, and, more recently, a statement in support of comprehensive immigration reform. On other occasions, a coalition or bloc of high-profile evangelical leaders have issued similar statements, for example "An Evangelical Manifesto" (2008). Yet the decentralized nature of evangelicalism in America prevents those statements from carrying the clout that a similar statement by another denominational body might have. Indeed, statements by the NAE or other self-organized groups of evangelical leaders more often than not provoke a response by other groups of evangelical leaders or pastors who are vocal in their opposition to the statement. Hence they tend not to have much influence with rank-and-file evangelicals.

There is one growing exception to the individualism that is so evident in evangelical public policy views. That is the recent activism of evangelical Christians on the global front. Here evangelicals have grown more accepting of collective action to address global ills, whether through multilateral organizations, formal governmental policy, or NGOs. Necessitated by the lack of geographic proximity and the simple fact that making a difference usually requires working corporately, evangelicals are more inclined to advocate for collective or governmental action to remedy such crises as AIDS, human trafficking, genocide and religious persecution, and international debt relief.

POLICY WITHOUT THEOLOGY: THE PERILS OF CO-OPTATION

> Called to an allegiance higher than party, ideology, and nationality, we Evangelicals see it our duty to engage with politics, but our equal duty never to be completely equated with any party, partisan ideology, economic system, or nationality. ("An Evangelical Manifesto," 15)

A subtext running through the chapters of this book is the search for a more systematic and principled evangelical mode of analysis that can be applied to a broad range of policy questions. The recent developments in evangelical attitudes on public policy, and the potential political repercussions, have upped the ante, making it crucial that evangelicals cultivate a biblical mind-set for analyzing policy. For without the requisite intellectual underpinnings, evangelicals both right- and left-leaning are in danger of falling prey to co-optation of one kind or another—ideological, partisan, or cultural. Whatever its form, co-optation comes at the expense of the integrity of evangelical participation in the policy realm. Evangelicals have proven vulnerable to co-optation in the past, and the danger continues to present itself, though in a number of different forms.

The first variant is *ideological co-optation*. A major challenge to evangel-icals seeking to preserve their faithful convictions in the midst of their politi-cal engagement is the tendency to allow predetermined ideological disposi-tions to drive their understanding of religious authority, rather than the other way around. Too often, the policy agenda of prominent evangelical individu-als and groups is utterly predictable, surely not because of authoritative scrip-tural truths, but rather because the agenda aligns with the political constituen-cies to which that person or group answers or belongs. In short, "[e]vangelicals are . . . particularly susceptible to a kind of worldliness that draws its cues about the political agenda, not from independent Biblical study, but from the community of which they are a part" (Buzzard 1989, 144).

The problem has been most pronounced among conservative evangelical groups. The Christian right has been especially guilty of "projective accom-modation"—adapting scriptural interpretation to fit a predetermined set of political views rather than the opposite (Budziszewski 2006, 20–21). Too often their supposed religiously derived views magically mirror a uniform, unswerving conservative stance across the policy spectrum.

For example, the predisposition of evangelicals toward free markets and limited government almost surely is attributable to ideological commitments rather than theological origins. Moreover, it prevented them from working more energetically to promote biblical principles of economic and social justice. An absolutist ideological commitment to those principles trumped any appreciation for governmental regulations needed to realize biblical val-ues; hence their failure to give voice to scriptural truths regarding greed, covetousness, exploitation, and other casualties of modern capitalism.

Jim Wallis notes that the "religious right has fashioned itself for political power in one utterly predictable ideological guise" (Wallis 2005, 4). Yet the phenomenon exists on the left as well; liberal Christians are often just as predictable, albeit in the opposite direction. Left-leaning evangelicals prac-tice the same habit of selectively reading the Bible to support predetermined ideological commitments. While the right proof texts for abortion and homo-sexuality, the left does so for poverty, war, racism, sexism, and the environ-ment, with each dismissing the other's concerns (Gushee 2008, 59). But to skew one's treatment of scripture to better fit one's ideological preferences is unacceptable, whatever the direction, unless one buys the doubtable proposition that scripture somehow shows a preference for one full-fledged political philosophy or ideology over all others.

A related danger is that of *partisan co-optation*. Party affiliations overlap with ideological predispositions, and have a similar potential to co-opt the honest application of evangelical faith to policy. Evangelical political behavior is similarly open to criticism for having become too enmeshed with the workings and welfare of the major political parties. Mark Noll ended his 1994 work by reflecting on the future of evangelicalism in the public realm. While avoiding firm predictions about the likely direction of evangelicalism in politics, he was prescient in foreseeing the specter of co-optation by the Republican Party of conservative Christians (Noll 1994, 173).

Nothing has generated more searing criticism of the interplay between religion and politics than the perceived marriage between Christian conservatives and the Republican Party. Too many voices to count have lamented the cozy relationship between the religious right and the Republican Party.[3] The severity of the charge is illustrated in theologian Charles Marsh's characterization of what he calls the captivity of the gospel by the Republican exploitation of Christian conservatives. To Marsh, the marriage of conservative Christians and the Republican Party is "the gravest theological crisis of the Christian faith in our time" and "one of the most vivid examples of the church's cultural captivity in its two-thousand-year history" (Marsh 2008, 76).

> As Doctor Faustus sells his soul to Lucifer for twenty-four years of power, so evangelicals have gained much influence in the past decade as a result of their loyalty to conservative politics. But we have achieved access and power at the expense of the integrity of our witness (76) . . . the gospel became so politicized in the United States—and by that I mean identified so closely by white evangelicals with the conservative Right—that the attempt to speak a distinctively Christian word was quite often construed as tendentiously liberal. (77)[4]

Nor is the problem of partisan co-optation exclusive to the Christian right. Just as it has been a solid bloc within the Republican Party, the evangelical left has occupied a similar, albeit much more modest, position in the Democratic Party (Gushee 2008, 83–84). Former Bush speechwriter and evangelical Christian Michael Gerson chastises right and left for "miniaturizing" their faith by too closely following the party platform. Jim Wallis vigorously contends:

> Of course, God is not partisan; God is not a Republican or a Democrat. . . . The best contribution of religion is precisely not to be ideologically predictable nor loyally partisan. Both parties . . . must let the prophetic voice of religion be

heard. Faith must be free to challenge both right and left from a consistent
moral ground. God's politics is therefore never partisan or ideological. (Wallis
2005, xiv–xv)

Whether the co-optation is at the hands of Republicans or Democrats, or in
the name of conservative or liberal principles, the effect is the same—the
shunting aside of the humble submission of one's policy stances to scriptural
authority as the central influence in favor of the false idols of partisanship
and ideology. In functioning as a bloc within a national party, evangelical
Christians give "themselves over to allegiance to a political party . . . [and]
lose the ability to retain their fundamental loyalty to Jesus Christ" (Gushee
2008, 48).

Ultimately, the threat of partisan or ideological co-optation is greatest in
the political vacuum created by the absence of thoughtful in-depth reflection
on what faith and religious conviction mean for substantive policy views.
Partisan planks and political ideology will be determinative of policy views
in the absence of a knowledgeable, intentional scripture-shaped approach.
Allowing party or ideology to trump the good faith application of scripture to
politics is in essence a form of idolatry. As Stephen Monsma says, Christians
cannot let their party loyalty or political instincts be the primary determinant
of their policy views. To do so is to be

> conformed to this world; it means adopting certain policy positions much as a
> secularist would. Evangelicals who have entered the political arena as trans-
> formed Christians and who are truly reflecting the mind of Christ will . . . not
> fit; they will not have a natural home; they will not be assimilated into the
> existing alignment of political forces. (Monsma 1989, 155)

The point is not that Christians must disaffiliate from a party or avoid partisan politics. Given the predominant influence of parties on our politics, it is
not unreasonable to conclude that one may wish to associate with one party
or the other to have some practical influence on politics. But party affiliation
should always be an uneasy alliance, where the evangelical Christian is never
too comfortable with her partisan commitments. It means that religious convictions cannot be bought, used, or accommodated simply for the advance-
ment of a political party or set of ideological ideas. The overriding consideration should be the urgent maintenance of the integrity of one's Christian
witness.

Finally, evangelical Christians face the risk of *cultural capitulation*, the
subordination of theologically grounded thought and action to the dominant
values and ethos of the broader secular culture. Modern evangelical political
activism has had a countercultural flavor to it, especially in the self-perceptions of politically involved evangelicals. The major cultural shifts of the
1960s and 1970s—including the removal of religion in public schools, the

dramatic changes in sexual morays, the drug culture of the 1960s, *Roe v. Wade* and abortion—were what led evangelicals to believe that their traditions were under assault, driving them into the political realm. Indeed, their political action has always seemed more culturally derived than intellectually or theologically driven. The defensive posture of the Dobsons and the Falwells was less about transforming the culture than it was a rear guard defense of traditional morality, normality, and a degree of safety around evangelicals' children, families, schools, neighborhoods, and communities.

Yet it is increasingly difficult to view today's evangelicals as genuinely countercultural. Indeed, the sternest critics of contemporary evangelicalism aim their barbs at what they see as the hypocrisy of evangelicals attacking the culture even as they seemingly have absorbed most of its values. Critics from within and without see an evangelicalism rendered impotent by its adherents' subservience to consumerism and market forces, hyperindividualism, and the dominant societal values fed them through television, movies, music, and other elements of the mass pop culture.

The cultural sway over the lives of Christians is most evident in what Ronald Sider has termed the "scandal of the evangelical conscience"—the reality that the vast majority of born-again Christians live lives seriously at odds with what scripture demands of them (Sider 2005b, 17). According to Sider, a mere 9 percent of adult evangelical Christians live in accordance with a biblical worldview. A recent Barna survey places that figure at 19 percent. While survey results in this area may well raise real methodological problems, the underlying observation seems irrefutable. Whether the behavior at issue involves marriage and divorce, sexual immorality, consumerism and materialism, or racial attitudes, evangelicals are equal-opportunity offenders.[5]

In the end, most evangelicals are one of two things. They are functionally illiterate in their knowledge of scriptural authority or, alternatively, they have become so inured in the broader ways of the culture that their lives are unaffected by biblical truths. Whatever their knowledge of scripture, it is drowned out by the tsunami of popular cultural messages coming at them from all directions. Far from being countercultural, evangelicals have been absorbed by and into the culture. As political scientist and sociologist Alan Wolfe asserts, "American faith has met American culture—and American culture has triumphed" (Lindsay 2008, 129).

EVANGELICALS AND THE ENRICHMENT OF POLICY DEBATE

The conventional wisdom on evangelical involvement in the policy process is that it is largely negative, that evangelicals are rigid and unbending, that they lead to polarization and corrosive politics, and that all they care about is abortion to the exclusion of other significant issues. In fact, most of the chapters in this book offer quite a different take on evangelicals, in which they actually have the potential to foster a healthier and more productive policymaking process. We briefly consider here several of those positive influences that evangelicals might wield, provided they were to take seriously their commitment to advancing the range of biblical imperatives regarding public policy.

The first of those is the possibility of a *more centrist policy approach* that would balance competing considerations and help to span the deep division and polarization that seem to have paralyzed our policymaking institutions. Several of the chapters suggest that, in contrast to the commonly held perception of evangelicals as unbending ideologues, they in fact could help shape policy initiatives that take a new middle way through left and right ideologies. Jennifer Walsh argues that evangelical theological commitments in the area of criminal justice could help to carve out a moderate centrist path that would balance the biblical concepts of justice and mercy for all of God's image bearers, offender and victim alike. It would involve some combination of proportional punishment to ensure the safety of society's vulnerable and sentencing reforms that take rehabilitation seriously and allow for second chances and the possibility of redemption for the offender. Likewise, Steve Monsma's reflections on social welfare policy in the United States similarly envision a middle way between liberal and conservative prescriptions. Here the biblical creation story of people made in the image of God means that they are entitled to the opportunity to meaningful work, to support themselves, and to live lives of dignity. On one hand, this means evangelicals must take an active interest in the poor and advocate for their well-being. But it also elevates the role of civil society and lower levels of government, respectively, in effectively addressing the needs of the poor. The deadening hand of the federal bureaucracy and the dependency its programs tend to engender will just be less effective in providing what the poor often really need to regain their dignity and self-worth. Ruth Melkonian-Hoover sees a similar potential for evangelicals to positively impact the debate on immigration by carving out a centrist policy that borrows from those on both left and right. Melkonian-Hoover sees the possibility of an evangelical plan that would balance respect for the rule of law with considerations of economic justice—for citizen and alien alike.

A second uniquely positive contribution that only evangelicals could make is what Noah Toly calls an "ethic of freedom": it refers to evangelicals reminding us of an alternative foundation for policy considerations—namely, the transcendent one. This perspective is grounded in the evangelical acceptance of God's revelation of His truth for humanity; the value of evangelical contributions to the policy arena lies in their unparalleled ability to articulate transcendent reasons for pursuing policy objectives—these might be mercy in the realm of crime and punishment, stewardship of the environment, generosity in social welfare, prudence and humility in economics, and hospitality in the immigration debate.

This warrants against forcing every argument into a secular paradigm. Indeed, Noah Toly describes as a pathology the "political realism" of whatever works as good. To disengage biblical ends from the Bible and its author as the origin of their obligations and wisdom is a perversion of the good news that evangelicals believe to be true. It is to strip evangelical involvement in policy of the one truly unique thing they can bring to the table, and to simply reduce them to the same sinful engagement of everyone else. Toly exhorts evangelicals to practice the "politics of freedom" whereby they can place their policy input in the Christian context of faith, trust, and hope. Theological truth rather than political necessity is the correct source of moral guidance and right thinking. In this way, evangelical policy engagement is rightly grounded in service to God's kingdom, which is the ultimate end for evangelical Christians.

Moreover, part of the evangelical witness is to advance policy goals as a further reflection of the all-encompassing reach of the good news of the Gospel. Rather than invoking religion to serve the interests of whatever the policy agenda might be, evangelical policy engagement is one more way of serving God's kingdom. Thus does Toly's "ethics of freedom" properly center and ground evangelical engagement.

A third uniquely evangelical contribution grows out of the second; that is a spirit of hope and optimism that stands in stark contrast to the pessimism, cynicism, and fatalism that afflict so much of our politics. In the face of the overwhelming complexities of modern policy questions, many are inclined to throw their hands up in despair. Indeed, far too many evangelicals who are active in the public sphere appear to share this dark view of the future. For evangelicals, there should be comfort in knowing that we cannot solve it all, nor do we have to. Evangelicals should be imbued with a firm realization that policy outcomes and their impact on the world are ultimately in God's hands and not ours. God is the ultimate source of hopefulness, optimism, and humility. Here again, evangelicals should be able to step back and realize the limits of politics, and take solace in its rightful place relative to the Gospel of Christ. Evangelicals need to stand ready to point the world in the right direction, beyond our humble human prospects for success. Ultimately, Christians ought to exhibit a hopefulness and confidence in doing the right thing, doing their very best, and then leaving the outcome to God.

THE EVOLUTION OF EVANGELICAL PARTICIPATION: MATURATION OR CAPITULATION?

We therefore regard reason and faith as allies rather than enemies, and find no contradiction between head and heart, between being fully faithful on the one hand, and fully intellectually critical and contemporary on the other. ("An Evangelical Manifesto" 2008, 10)

[T]he evangelical movement in the United States looks as if it is maturing. That means more social and political influence, not less, as the movement broadens, reaches into the elite, and develops messages with wider appeal. Yet it also means a more pluralistic and less strident movement, more apt to compromise and less likely to be held hostage by a single issue or a single party. The real story of the evangelical political movement today involves neither its death nor its triumph, but rather its slow (and ongoing) shift from insurgent to insider, with all of the moderating effects that transition implies. (Mead 2008, 23)

So what is one to make of the broadening of the evangelical policy mind? Is it a positive sign of evangelical maturation? Or does it signify submission to the dominant cultural values and ethos? Walter Russell Mead undoubtedly is correct in observing that evangelicals are in the midst of an important developmental phase relative to public policy and politics. But whether this in fact reflects genuine intellectual growth and political maturation remains to be seen.

Consider the remarkable shedding of their countercultural ways as evangelicals have moved into the policymaking institutions themselves, at the highest levels and in substantial numbers. In his book, *Faith in the Halls of Power*, Michael Lindsay chronicles the notable gains that evangelicals have made within the media, business, higher education, and—perhaps most noteworthy of all—government. The emergence of a new evangelical elite within government has serious implications for evangelical influences on public policy. It certainly is not easily reconciled with those prophetic images of evangelicals as outsiders standing athwart the dominant centers of political power and culture. Indeed, Lindsay distinguishes these evangelical elites from the rank and file, describing a division between the "cosmopolitan" and the "populist" evangelicals. The former include those elites found at the highest levels of government, the entertainment world, and business. They are put off by the whole evangelical subculture, and even seek to separate themselves from it. Lindsay sees them as

> more interested in their faith being seen as authentic, reasonable, and win-some. . . . They want to have a seat at the table, to be seen as legitimate. They are concerned about what the *New York Times* or *Time* magazine thinks about evangelicals because they are concerned about cultural elites. (Lindsay 2008)

Most tellingly, it is these cosmopolitan evangelicals who Lindsay predicts will be the future face of evangelicals in the public realm.

What Lindsay describes may be a sign of the maturing of evangelicalism; it may demonstrate that they are able to pragmatically engage a pluralistic society and the systems of power without forfeiting their core convictions. Lindsay lauds the "elasticity of [evangelical] convictions" that permits them to collaborate with those who may not share their underlying commitments (Lindsay 2008, 216–17). But others might consider the amplified presence of evangelicals in the halls of power as less benign, coming at the expense of what they see as the integrity of faithful witness in the political world. As such, it is one more example of evangelical capitulation to the broader social and political culture.

The evolving policy views of younger evangelical Christians raise similar questions regarding their standing relative to the popular cultural. A new generation of evangelicals is less susceptible to the partisan or ideological forms of co-optation described above; they are more inclined to deem their faith relevant to a wider range of issues. But it is not clear that their new-found policy awareness is not itself an expression of cultural co-optation. Younger evangelical Christians do not see themselves in the same light as their parents and grandparents. They do not consider themselves alien to the dominant cultural ethos; they have made their peace as full-fledged members of it. Society is not some lost cause or moribund vessel (Kirkpatrick 2008, 11). Indeed, a key piece of their spiritual development is its application to the world; that includes public engagement on issues of poverty, race, and the environment. For them, the biblical imperatives include the betterment of their communities and the world.

These more expansive policy views that are prevalent among young evangelicals are admirable. Yet their sources are not exactly clear, and consequently they present their own perils of co-optation. While older evangelicals have proven susceptible to partisan and political capture, they are to be credited for standing against the culture on important social issues. It remains to be seen whether younger evangelicals can do likewise when circumstances demand it. In becoming so comfortable within the broader culture and all that it entails, have they lost the ability to give prophetic voice to its morally troublesome aspects? The danger is that they never take a stand on anything that might put them in an adversarial stance to the culture. The confluence of Christianity and culture carries with it the temptation to dilute stances considered controversial or retrograde by the broader secular culture, lest one risk its antagonism or derision. Timothy Keller, author of *The Reason for God*, hints at this in describing the commitment to doing good that he has observed among younger Christians. He finds them "philosophically rootless," raised to be leery of the exclusivity of Christianity and conditioned to be tolerant of everything: "They have a deep morality, but they have no idea why" (Gerson 2008).

For the evangelical elites that Linsday describes and for many younger evangelicals, one wonders if they simply are yielding to the inexorable pressure from the outside world to be reasonable, moderate, centrist, forward thinking, and progressive. Both of these subsets of evangelicalism seem to wish to avoid the disapprobation of the world, to avoid being identified as "one of those evangelicals" that the secular world frowns upon. Michael Spencer, writing in the *Christian Science Monitor*, puts it this way:

> We evangelicals have failed to pass on to our young people an orthodox form of faith that can take root and survive the secular onslaught. . . . Our young people have deep beliefs about the culture war, but do not know why they should obey scripture, the essentials of theology, or the experience of spiritual discipline and community. Coming generations of Christians are going to be monumentally ignorant and unprepared for culture-wide pressures. (Spencer 2009)

In contrast to Mead's positive vision of a maturing evangelicalism, Spencer sees it in dire terms—a biblically illiterate evangelicalism ill prepared for an anti-Christian era in which evangelical Christianity is portrayed as hostile to the broader good of society.[6] If evangelicals cannot offer a coherent articulation of the policy implications of scripture, they are unlikely to hold fast in the wake of that hostility.

Consider for a moment the rhetoric employed by the new breed of progressive evangelicals. When asked what is behind the expansion of evangelical policy awareness, Jim Wallis speaks of the "hunger" for social justice, the "yearning" for a moral center and the common good. Faith is the source of hope and personal transformation required for social transformation. But the language of "hunger" and "hope" and "yearning" is as emotional, ephemeral, and intuitive as was the religious right's instinctive and culturally derived focus on traditional values. And those intuitive impulses that represent today's cause can too easily become tomorrow's passé sentiment.

The danger is that policy positions are derived, not from intellectual or doctrinal roots, but from intuition, warm sentiments, and a desire for validation for embracing what is regarded as enlightened by today's secular culture. Unless evangelicals can arrive at a theologically grounded set of reasons for pursuing the new set of issues, they will be no more reflective of God's presence in the world than those obsessed with single-issue politics. It is simply trading in one form of co-optation for another, exchanging the lure of party or ideology for the approval of the secular world.

In the end, perhaps the best model for evangelical policy engagement is "the prophetic tradition itself, with its thorough grounding in a commitment to God's justice and righteousness which touch political, economic, and 'religious' life" (Weeks 2006, 146). But the key to maintaining that prophetic voice—religious people and institutions standing apart and against culture and government when contrary to God's plan and laws—is the anchoring of ideas in their theological commitments.

This then is the rationale for pursuing a more formal evangelical prism through which to view the gamut of policy issues—to strike a path that is loyal to first commitments *and* represents an effective voice in policy debates. In the end, this is the challenge for evangelicals—to bring their understanding of transcendent truth into the political realm with full force, but to do it in ways that are seasoned with the requisite humility and modesty that both faith and politics demand.

NOTES

1. Perhaps nowhere is the need to leaven one's policy rhetoric and activism with modesty, humility, and civility more applicable than when involving interactions between evangelicals of differing policy views. Particularly disturbing is the venom that supposed people of faith on the religious right and left often aim at each other. It is not an overstatement to suggest that policy differences in recent years have sometimes gone so far as to lead the religious right and left to question the very legitimacy of the other's faith commitments. It is difficult to imagine a worse message to share or example to set for the watching world.

2. It should be noted that an expanded evangelical policy agenda heightens the danger of moral equivalence. Scripture may place a long list of issues on the minds of evangelical Christians. But not all issues are of equal magnitude. Just because there is a broad range of issues to which scripture is relevant does not put them all on the same plane of importance. Evangelicals still need to do the hard work of prioritizing and determining to what issues they should commit their resources and energies.

3. The nub of the argument is expressed in a variety of voices and distinctive genres. Someone looking for a cross section might begin with the following: Randall Balmer's *Thy Kingdom Come: An Evangelical's Lament* (2006); Greg Boyd's *The Myth of a Christian Nation: How the Quest for Political Power Is Destroying the Church* (2007); Jimmy Carter's *Our Endangered Values: America's Moral Crisis* (2006); Chris Hedges' *American Fascists: The Christian Right and the War on America* (2007); David Kuo's *Tempting Faith: An Inside Story of Political Seduction* (2006); Kevin Phillips' *American Theocracy: The Peril and Politics of Radical Religion, Oil, and Borrowed Money in the 21st Century* (2006); Andrew Sullivan's *The Conservative Soul: How We Lost It, How to Get It Back* (2006); Jim Wallis' *God's Politics: Why the Right Gets It Wrong and the Left Doesn't Get It* (2005); and Garry Wills' *Under God: Religion and American Politics* (2007).

4. For a more specific example, see Toly's observation in the context of environmental debates that the refusal of some high profile evangelical leaders to engage the issue was likely attributable to their prior political or partisan commitments.

5. The 2008 "Evangelical Manifesto" acknowledged the deep inconsistencies in evangelical beliefs and actions:

> We confess that we Evangelicals have betrayed our beliefs by our behavior . . . we have become known for commercial, diluted, and feel-good gospels of health, wealth, human potential, and religious happy talk, each of which is indistinguishable from the passing fashions of the surrounding world. All too often we have set out high, clear statements of the authority of the Bible, but flouted them with lives and lifestyles that are shaped more by our own sinful preferences and by modern fashions and convenience. . . . [W]e have condoned our own sins, turned a blind eye to our own vices, and lived captive to forces such as materialism and consumerism in ways that contradict our faith. ("An Evangelical Manifesto" 2008, 11–12)

6. Spencer is hardly alone in that view. *Newsweek* editor Jon Meacham garnered much attention with his essay titled "The End of Christian America" (*Newsweek*, April 13, 2009) in which he predicts the end of Christian America. He cited a 10 percent drop in self-identified Christians over the past two decades as evidence of a post-Christian culture, where much of society will be animated by post-Christian values and beliefs.

Bibliography

Abrams, Eliot. "The Christian Lobby." *American Purpose* 2, no. 11 (1997). www.eppc.org/publications/pubID.1795/pub_detail.asp.

Adams, Lawrence. "Foundations for Post-Cold War International Justice: Creation, Polyarchy, and Realism." *Christian Scholar's Review* 28, no. 1 (1997).

Akinola, Peter. "GAFCON: A Rescue Mission." Address delivered June 22, 2008. www .gafcon.org/index.php?option=com_content&task=view&id=57&Itemid=29. Accessed July 23, 2010.

Alumkal, Antony W. "American Evangelicalism in the Post-Civil Rights Era: A Racial Formation Theory Analysis." *Sociology of Religion* 65 (2004): 195–213.

American Friends Service Committee. *Struggle for Justice*. New York: Hill & Wang. 1971.

Amstutz, Mark R. *Christian Ethics and U.S. Foreign Policy*. Grand Rapids, MI: Zondervan, 1987.

Anderson, John. "Does God Matter, and If So Whose God? Religion and Democratization." *Democratization* 11 (2004): 192–217.

———. "A Biblical and Economic Analysis of Jubilee Property Provisions." *ACE Bulletin*, no. 46 (Fall 2005): 25–41.

Anderson, John E., and George Langelett. "Economics and the Evangelical Mind." *ACE Bulletin*, no. 28 (1996): 5–24.

Anderson, Leith. Testimony before US Senate Judiciary Subcommittee on Immigration, Border Security and Refugees. October 8, 2009.

"An Evangelical Manifesto: A Declaration of Evangelical Identity and Public Commitment." May 7, 2008. www.evangelicalmanifesto.com.

Applegate, Brandon K., Francis T. Cullen, Bonnie S. Fisher, and Thomas Vander Ven. "Forgiveness and Fundamentalism: Reconsidering the Relationship between Correctional Attitudes and Religion." *Criminology* 38, no. 3 (2000): 35.

Aristotle. *De Anima (On the Soul)*. Translated by H. Lawson-Tancred. New York: Penguin Putnam. 1986.

Ashley, B., and A. Moraczewski. "Is the Biological Subject of Human Rights Present from Conception?" In *The Fetal Tissue Issue: Medical and Ethical Aspects*. Edited by P. Cataldo and A. Moraczewski. Braintree, MA: Pope John Center. 1994.

Augustine, Sermon 43, 7, 9: PL 38, 257–58.

Baier, Colin J., and Bradley R. E. Wright. "'If You Love Me, Keep My Commandments': A Meta-Analysis of the Effect of Religion on Crime." *Journal of Research in Crime and Delinquency* 38, no. 1 (2001): 3–21.

Balmer, Randall. *Thy Kingdom Come: How the Religious Right Distorts the Faith and Threatens America: An Evangelical's Lament*. New York: Basic Books, 2006.

Banerjee, N. "Southern Baptists Back a Shift on Climate Change." *New York Times*, March 10, 2008.

Barnett, Timothy J. "The Limits of Free Exercise." In *Church-State Issues in America Today: Religion and Government*. Edited by Ann W. Duncan and Steven L. Jones, vol. 1, 257–90. Westport CT: Praeger Publishers, 2008.

———. *Evangelicals and Economic Enlightenment*. Unpublished paper presented at the Annual Conference of the American Political Science Association, 2008.

Bauckham, Richard. "Theology after Hiroshima." *Scottish Journal of Theology* 38 (1985): 583–601.

Beckwith, Francis. J. "The Explanatory Power of the Substance View of Persons." *Christian Bioethics* 10, no. 1 (2004): 33–54.

———. "Legal Neutrality and Same-Sex Marriage." *Philosophia Christi* 7, no. 1 (2005).

———. *Defending Life: A Moral and Legal Case against Abortion Choice*. New York: Cambridge University Press, 2007.

Beisner, E. C., P. K. Driessen, R. McKitrick, and R. W. Spencer. *A Call to Truth, Prudence, and Protection of the Poor: An Evangelical Response to Global Warming*. Cornwall Alliance for the Stewardship of Creation (Report). Available at www.cornwallalliance.org/docs/Call-to-Truth.pdf. 2006.

Bernardin, Joseph Cardinal. "A Consistent Ethic of Life and the Death Penalty in Our Time." In *Capital Punishment: A Reader*, edited by G. H. Stassen. Cleveland, OH: The Pilgrim Press, 1998.

Bernbaum, John, ed. *Economic Justice and the State*. Grand Rapids, MI: Baker Book House, 1986.

Berry, R. J., ed. *The Care of Creation: Focusing Concern and Action*. Downers Grove, IL: IVP, 2000.

———, ed. *Environmental Stewardship: Critical Perspectives, Past and Present*. New York: Continuum International, 2006.

Blank, Rebecca M., and William McGurn. *Is the Market Moral? A Dialogue on Religion, Economics & Justice*. Washington, DC: Brookings Institute Press, 2004.

Blankenhorn, David. "Defining Marriage Down . . . Is No Way to Save It." *Weekly Standard*, April 2, 2007.

Bouma-Prediger, Steve. *The Greening of Theology: The Ecological Models of Rosemary Radford Ruether, Joseph Sittler, and Jurgen Moltmann*. Atlanta: Scholar's Press, 1995.

———. *For the Beauty of the Earth: A Christian Vision for Creation Care*. Grand Rapids, MI: Baker, 2001.

Brennan, Patrick McKinley. "On What Sin (and Grace) Can Teach Crime." *Punishment Society* 5, no. 3 (2003): 347–65.

Brown, William. *Character in Crisis: A Fresh Approach to the Wisdom Literature of the Old Testament*. Eerdmans, 1996.

Brownback, Sam. "Faith in a Winning Message." *Washington Post*, November 12, 2007. A21.

Bruce, Steve. *Politics and Religion*. Cambridge: Polity Press, 2003.

———. "Did Protestantism Create Democracy?" *Democratization* 11, no. 4 (2004): 3–20.

Brueggemann. "Alien Witness." *Christian Century*, March 6, 2007.

Budziszewski, Jay. *Evangelicals in the Public Square: Four Formative Voices on Political Thought and Action*. Grand Rapids, MI: Baker Academic, 2006.

Bumiller, Elisabeth. "Evangelicals Sway White House on Human Rights Issues Abroad." *New York Times*, October 26, 2003.

Buratovich, Michael (developmental biologist). Personal communication with Francis Beckwith, June 12, 2003.

Bureau of Justice Statistics. *Crime and Victim Statistics*. Edited by O. J. Programs: U.S. Department of Justice, 2006.

Buzzard, Lynn. "The 'Coming-Out' of Evangelicals." In *Contemporary Evangelical Political Involvement: An Analysis and Assessment*, edited by Corwin Smidt. New York: University Press of America, 1989.

Byrne, J., L. Glover, and C. Martinez. "The Production of Unequal Nature." In *Environmental Justice: Discourses in International Political Economy and Environmental Policy, Vol. 8*, edited by J. Bryne et al., 230–56. New Brunswick, NJ: Transaction Books, 2002.

Byrne, John, Leigh Glover, and Cecilia Martinez, eds. *Environmental Justice: Discourses in International Political Economy Energy and Environmental Policy, Vol. 8*. New Brunswick, NJ: Transaction Publishers, 2002.

Cancian, Maria, and Sheldon Danziger. "Changing Poverty and Changing Antipoverty Policies." National Poverty Center Working Paper Series #09–06. 2009. Available at www.npc.umich.edu/publications/working_papers/.

Carey, Galen (government affairs director, National Association of Evangelicals). Telephone interview with Ruth Melkonian-Hoover, March 26, 2010.

Carlson-Thies, Stanley W., and James W. Skillen, eds. *Welfare in America: Christian Perspectives on a Policy in Crisis*. Grand Rapids, MI: Eerdmans, 1996.

Carroll, Daniel Rodas (Old Testament professor, Denver Seminary). Personal interview with Ruth Melkonian-Hoover, Littleton, Colorado. April 20, 2010.

———. *Christians at the Border: Immigration, the Church and the Bible*. Grand Rapids, MI: Baker Academic, 2008.

Carson, R. *Silent Spring*. Boston, MA: Houghton Mifflin Company, 1962.

Castree, N. "Environmental Issues: From Policy to Political Economy." *Progress in Human Geography* 26, no. 3 (2002): 357–65.

Catechism of the Catholic Church: Revised in Accordance with the Official Latin Text Promulgated by Pope John Paul II, 2nd ed. Washington, DC: United States Conference of Catholic Bishops, 2000.

Center for Immigration Studies. "Religious Perspectives on Immigration: Panel to Examine Faith-Based Debate." *Center for Immigration Studies*. October 6, 2009. www.cis.org.

Chengappa, Raj, with Rohit Saran and Harinder Baweja, "Will the War Spread?" *India Today*, July 5, 1999.

Chewning, Richard C., John W. Eby, and Shirely J. Roels. *Business through the Eyes of Faith*. San Francisco: HarperSanFranciso, 1990.

"Chicago Declaration of Evangelical Social Concern." November 25, 1973. www.esa-online.org.

Christians for Comprehensive Immigration Reform (CCIR). National Teleconference: "Faithful Perspectives: A Conversation on Immigration and Your Congregation." June 24, 2010.

Churchill, Winston. *The World Crisis: An Abridgement of the Classic Four-Volume History of World War I*. New York: Scribner's, 1931.

Clements, R. E. *Wisdom in Theology*. Grand Rapids, MI: Eerdmans, 1992.

Clemmitt, Marcia. "Protestants Today: Black Churches Cater to Suburban Middle Class." *CQ Researcher* 2007. www.cqpress.com/product/Researcher-Protestants-Today-v17-43.html.

Cohen, S. *Understanding Environmental Policy*. New York: Columbia, 2006.

Colb, S. F. "A Creeping Theocracy: How the U.S. Government Uses Its Power to Enforce Religious Principles." *FindLaw's Writ*, November 21, 2001. Available at http://writ.news.findlaw.com/colb/20011121.html.

Colson, Charles. "What He Could Have Said." *Breakpoint*, June 30, 2008. www.breakpoint.org/listingarticle.asp?ID=8086.

———. "So Much for Tolerance: The Aftermath of Prop 8." *Breakpoint*, November 13, 2008. http://www.breakpoint.org/listingarticle.asp?ID=10520.

Comiskey, Andrew. *The Kingdom of God and The Homosexual*. Anaheim: Desert Stream Press, 2000.

Conant, Eve. "Faith under Fire." *Newsweek*, May 7, 2007.

Cooperman, Alan. "Letter on Immigration Deepens Splits among Evangelicals." *Washington Post*, April 5, 2006.

Cortés, Luis (president, Esperanza USA). Telephone interview with Ruth Melkonian-Hoover, June 25, 2006.

Cox, Dan. "Young White Evangelicals: Less Republican, Still Conservative." *Pew Forum*, September 28, 2007. Available at http://pewforum.org/docsID=250.

Cromartie, Michael. "Religious Conservatives in American Politics 1980-2000: An Assessment," Witherspoon Lecture, given at the Family Research Council, Washington, DC, April 16, 2001.

Crouch, Andy (senior editor, *Christianity Today*). Personal interview with Ruth Melkonian-Hoover, Wenham, Massachusetts, March 25, 2010.

Curry, Dean. *A World without Tyranny: Christian Faith and International Politics*. Wheaton, IL: Crossway, 1990.

Curry, Theodore R. "Conservative Protestantism and the Perceived Wrongfulness of Crimes: A Research Note." *Criminology* 34, no. 3 (1996): 12.

Daggett, Dawn M., Scott D. Camp, Okyun (Karl) Kwon, Sean P. Posenmerkel, and Jody Kelin-Saffran. "Faith-Based Correctional Programming in Federal Prisons: Factors Affecting Program Completion." *Criminal Justice and Behavior* 35 (2008): 848–62.

Daly, Lew. *God's Economy: Faith-Based Initiatives & the Caring State*. Chicago: University of Chicago Press, 2009.

Danchin, Peter. "U.S. Unilateralism and the International Protection of Religious Freedom: The Multilateral Alternative." *Columbia Journal of Transnational Law* 41, no.1 (2002).

Danley, Ian (youth minister, Neighborhood Ministries). Personal interview with Ruth Melkonian-Hoover, May 14, 2010.

Dawkins, Richard. *The God Delusion*. London: Bantam Press, 2007.

Dawson, J. M. *America's Way in Church, State and Society*. New York: Macmillan, 1953.

Delahunty, Robert. "Changing Hearts, Changing Minds: A New Evangelical Politics?" *Journal of Catholic Legal Studies* 47, no. 2 (2008).

DeNavas-Walt, Carmen, Bernadette D. Proctor, and Jessica C. Smith, U.S. Census Bureau, Current Population Reports, P60–235. *Income, Poverty, and Health Insurance Coverage in the United States: 2007*. Washington, DC: U.S. Government Printing Office, 2008.

DeNavas-Walt, Carmen, Bernadette D. Proctor, and Jessica C. Smith, U.S. Census Bureau, Current Population Reports, P60–236. *Income, Poverty, and Health Insurance Coverage in the United States: 2008*. Washington, DC: U.S. Government Printing Office, 2009.

DeYoung, Curtiss. *Coming Together: The Bible's Message in an Age of Diversity*. Valley Forge, PA: Judson Press, 1995.

———. *Reconciliation: Our Greatest Challenge, Our Only Hope*. Valley Forge, PA: Judson Press, 1997.

———. "Tensions in North American Protestantism: An Evangelical Perspective." *Journal of Ecumenical Studies* 35 (1998): 400–404.

DeYoung, Curtiss Paul, Michael O. Emerson, George Yancey, and Karen Chai Kim. *United by Faith: The Multiracial Congregation as an Answer to the Problem of Race*. Oxford University Press, 2003.

Dionne, E. J. "Full Faith." *The New Republic*, March 20, 2008. http://www.tnr.com/toc/story.html?id=980738d9-2967-4749-9b9c-33fd127f865b.

Duff, R. A. "Penance, Punishment and the Limits of Community." *Punishment Society* 5, no. 3 (2003): 295–312.

Dyson, Freeman. *Weapons and Hope*. Harper & Row, 1984.

Eberle, Don. *The Rise of Global Civil Society: Building Communities and Nations from the Bottom Up*. New York: Encounter Books, 2008.

Edgell, Penny, and Eric Tranby. "Religious Influences on Understandings of Racial Equality in the United States." *Social Problems* 54, no. 2 (2007): 263–88.

Edwards, James (policy expert, MITA Group). Personal interview with Ruth Melkonian-Hoover, Washington, DC, February 19, 2010.

———. "Seeking Biblical Principles to Inform Immigration Policy." *Christianity Today*, September 9, 2006.

Ellul, J. *The Ethics of Freedom*. Grand Rapids, MI: Eerdmans, 1976.

———. "Christian Faith and Social Reality." Translated by M. Dawn. In *Sources and Trajectories: Eight Early Articles by Jacques Ellul That Set the Stage*, edited by M. Dawn, 166–183. Grand Rapids, MI: Eerdmans, 1997a.

————. "Political Realism (Problems of Civilization III)." Translated by M. Dawn. In *Sources and Trajectories: Eight Early Articles by Jacques Ellul That Set the Stage*, edited by M. Dawn, 49–91. Grand Rapids, MI: Eerdmans, 1997b.

Elshtain, Jean Bethke. "Afterword." *Evangelicals in the Public Square: Carl F. Henry, Abraham Kuyper, Francis Schaeffer, John Howard Yoder*, edited by J. Budziszewski et al. Grand Rapids, MI: Baker Academic, 2006.

Emens, Elizabeth. "Monogamy's Law: Compulsory Monogamy and Polyamorous Existence." *New York University Review of Law and Social Change* 29 (2004): 2.

Emerson, Michael O., and Christian Smith. *Divided by Faith: Evangelical Religion and the Problem of Race in America*. New York: Oxford University Press, 2000.

Emerson, Michael O., Christian Smith, and David Sikkink. "Equal in Christ, But Not in the World: White Conservative Protestants and Explanations of Black-White Inequality." *Social Problems* 46 (1999): 398–417.

Eskridge, Larry. "Defining Evangelicalism." *Institute for the Study of American Evangelicals*. http://www.wheaton.edu/isae/defining_evangelicalism.html.

Evangelical Climate Initiative. *Climate Change: An Evangelical Call to Action* (Report). Washington, DC, 2006. Available at http://christiansandclimate.org/learn/call-to-action/.

Evans, T. David, Francis T. Cullen, R. Gregory Dunaway, and Velmer S. Burton Jr. "Religion and Crime Reexamined: The Impact of Religion, Secular Controls, and Social Ecology on Adult Criminality." *Criminology* 33, no. 2 (1995): 31.

Farr, Thomas. "The Diplomacy of Religion." *First Things*, May 2006.

Fairbank, John K. "Introduction: The Many Faces of Protestant Missions in China and the United States." In *The Missionary Enterprise in China and America*, edited by John K. Fairbank. Cambridge, MA: Harvard University Press, 1974.

Feder, J. Lester. "The Floral Majority: How the Split between the Creation Care Leaders and Its Grass Roots Activists Is Dictating the Future of the Green Evangelical Movement." *The New Republic*, December 30, 2009. www.tnr.com/article/politics/the-floral-majority.

Fisher, A. "When Did I Begin?" *Linacre Quarterly* 58 (1991).

Fleckenstein, William A. *Greenspan's Bubbles: The Age of Ignorance at the Federal Reserve*. New York: McGraw Hill, 2008.

"For the Health of the Nation: An Evangelical Call to Civic Responsibility." Washington, DC: National Association of Evangelicals, 2004.

Forrest, B., and P. R. Gross. *Creationism's Trojan Horse: The Wedge of Intelligent Design*. New York: Oxford University Press, 2007.

Frankel, Marvin E. *Criminal Sentences: Law without Order*. New York: Hill and Wang, 1972.

Fraser, Albert G., J. Howard Branson, and Curtis A. Williams. "The Church and Crime." *The Prison Journal* 19, no. 3 (1939): 564–66.

Freston, Paul. "Evangelical Protestantism and Democratization in Contemporary Latin America and Asia." *Democratization* 11 (2004): 21–41.

Gagnon, Robert A. "Scriptural Perspectives on Homosexuality and Sexual Identity." *Journal of Psychology and Christianity* 24, no. 4 (2005): 293–303.

Gallagher, Maggie. "What Is Marriage For? The Public Purposes of Marriage Law." *Louisiana Law Review* 62 (2002): 773.

————. "What Marriage Is For: Children Need Mothers and Fathers." *Weekly Standard*, August 4, 2003. www.weeklystandard.com/Content/Public/Articles/000/000/002/939pxiqa.asp.

————. "Banned in Boston: The Coming Conflict between Same-Sex Marriage and Religious Liberty." *Weekly Standard*, May 15, 2006.

————. "If Marriage Is Natural, Why Is Defending It So Hard?" *Ave Maria Law Review* 4 (2006) no. 2.

Galli, Mark. "Blessed Is the Law—Up to a Point." *Christianity Today*. April 7, 2006.

Garvey, Stephen P. "Two Kinds of Criminal Wrongs." *Punishment Society* 5. no. 3 (2003): 279–94.

Gates, Jeff. *Democracy at Risk: Rescuing Main Street from Wall Street*. Cambridge. MA: Perseus Publishing, 2000.

Gatz, Nick. "The Use of Determinate Sentence—An Historical Perspective: A Research Note." *Journal of Criminal Justice* 10 (1982): 323–29.

Geller, Donald. "The India-Pakistan Rivalry: Prospects for War, Prospects for Peace." *The India-Pakistan Conflict: An Enduring Rivalry.* Cambridge: Cambridge University Press, 2005.

George, Robert P. *Making Men Moral: Civil Liberties and Public Morality.* Oxford: Clarendon, 1993.

George, Robert P., and C. Tollefsen. *Embryo: A Defense of Human Life.* New York: Doubleday, 2008.

Gerson, Michael J. "Reasons for Good Friday." *Washington Post,* March 21, 2008, A17.

——— (senior fellow, Institute for Global Engagement). Personal interview with Ruth Melkonian-Hoover, Arlington, Virginia, May 21, 2010.

Gilbreath, Edward. *Reconciliation Blues: A Black Evangelical's Inside View of White Christianity.* Downers Grove, IL: IVP Books, 2008.

Gilgoff, Dan. "Cheat Sheet: Obama's Evangelical Cabinet on Immigration Reform." CNN Belief Blog. www.religion.blogs.cnn.com. July 1, 2010.

Glendon, Mary Ann. *Rights Talk: The Impoverishment of Political Discourse.* New York: Free Press, 1993.

———. "What Happened at Beijing." *First Things* 59 (1996): 30–36.

Glynn, Patrick. "Racial Reconciliation: Can Religion Work Where Politics Has Failed?" *American Behavioral Scientist* 41 (1998): 834–41.

Goldberg, Jeffrey. "Washington Discovers Christian Persecution." *New York Times,* December 21, 1997.

Goldberg, M. *Kingdom Coming: The Rise of Christian Nationalism.* New York: W. W. Norton, 2006.

Goldstein, Laurie. "Obama Made Gains among Younger Evangelical Voters, Data Show." *New York Times,* November 7, 2008, A24.

Griswold v. Connecticut, 381 U.S. 479 (1965).

Gorski, Eric. "Younger Evangelicals Greet Sarah Palin with Excitement—But Also Yawns." *Minneapolis Star Tribune,* September 14, 2008.

Graham, Bradley, and Thomas Ricks. "Military Disparity Add to Uncertainty." *Washington Post,* June 1, 2002.

Graham, Franklin. Informal comments about Samaritan's Purse, delivered at Wheaton College Retreat at the Billy Graham Training Center at the Cove, Ashville, North Carolina, June 13, 2008.

Grainger, Brett. "Will Huckabee's Campaign Encourage Evangelicals to Vote for a Democrat?" *Christian Science Monitor,* February 2, 2008. www.csmonitor.com/2008/0204/p09s02-coop.html.

Grasmick, Harold G., Elizabeth Davenport, Mitchell B. Chamlin, and Robert J. Bursik Jr. "Protestant Fundamentalism and the Retributive Doctrine of Punishment." *Criminology* 30, no. 1 (1992): 26.

Green, John. *The Faith Factor: How Religion Influences American Elections.* Westport, CT: Praeger Publishers, 2007.

Green, John C., Corwin E. Smidt, James L. Guth, and Lyman A. Kellstedt. "The American Religious Landscape and the 2004 Presidential Vote: Increased Polarization." *Pew Forum on Religion and Public Life,* February 3, 2005. Available at http://pewforum.org/newassets/misc/postelection.pdf.

Greenberg, Anna. "The Church and the Revitalization of Politics and Community." *Political Science Quarterly* 115 (2000): 377–94.

Greenberg, Anna, and Jennifer Berktold. "America's Evangelicals: Key Survey Findings." *Religion and Ethics Newsweekly* (May 2004). www.pbs.org/wnet/religionandethics/week733/results.pdf.

Greenberg, Mark. *From Poverty to Prosperity: A National Strategy to Cut Poverty in Half.* Washington, DC: Center for American Progress, 2007. www.americanprogress.org/issues/2007/04/pdf.poverty_report.pdf.

Greenhouse, Steven. "Tire Tariffs Are Cheered by Labor." *New York Times,* September 15, 2009.

Guggenheim, D. *An Inconvenient Truth.* DVD. Directed by Al Gore. Los Angeles: Paramount, 2006.

Gunton, C. *The Christian Faith: An Introduction to Christian Doctrine.* New York: Blackwell, 2002.

Gushee, David P., ed. *Toward a Just and Caring Society: Christian Reponses to Poverty in America.* Grand Rapids, MI: Baker Books, 1999.

———. "Evangelicals and Politics: A Rethinking." *Journal of Law & Religion* 23, no. 1 (2006–2007): 1–14.

———. "The Iraq War Calls for Some Serious Rethinking by Christians." *Christianity Today,* September 26, 2007.

———. *The Future of Faith in American Politics: The Public Witness of the Evangelical Center.* Waco, TX: Baylor University Press, 2008.

———. "Mr. President, We Need More Than Lip Service." *USA Today,* March 16, 2009. http://usatoday.com/oped/2009/03/mr-president-we.html?csp=34.

——— (professor of Christian Ethics, Mercer University). Telephone interview with Ruth Melkonian-Hoover, March 30, 2010.

Gushee, David P., and Dennis P. Hollinger. "Toward an Evangelical Ethical Methodology." In *Toward an Evangelical Public Policy: Political Strategies for the Health of the Nation,* edited by Ronald J. Sider and Diane Knippers. Grand Rapids, MI: Baker Books, 2005.

Guth, James L. "The Bush Administration, American Religious Politics and Middle East Policy: The Evidence from National Surveys." Unpublished paper delivered at the 2004 Annual Meeting of the American Political Science Association, Chicago, Illinois, September 2–5, 2004.

Haas, Richard. "Why Foreign Policy Is Not Pornography." In *Good Judgment in Foreign Policy,* edited by Stanley Renshon and Deborah Welch Larson. Lanham, MD: Rowman & Littlefield Publishers, 2003.

Halteman, James. *Market Capitalism and Christianity.* Grand Rapids, MI: Baker Books, 1988.

———. "Productive Capital and Christian Moral Teaching." *ACE Bulletin,* no. 44 (2004): 26–38.

Hankins, B. *American Evangelicals: A Contemporary History of a Mainstream Religious Movement.* Lanham, MD: Rowman & Littlefield, 2008.

Hansen, Collin. "How Then Shall We Politick?" *Christianity Today,* August 2006. www.christianitytoday.com/ct/2006/august/9.38.html.

Haqqani, Husain. "At The Brink." *San Diego Union Tribune,* June 9, 2002.

Harrill, J. Albert. "The Use of the New Testament in the American Slave Controversy: A Case History in the Hermeneutical Tension between Biblical Criticism and Christian Moral Debate." *Religion and American Culture: A Journal of Interpretation* 10, no. 2 (2000).

Hauerwas, Stanley. *Against the Nations: War and Survival in a Liberal Society.* Harper & Row, 1985.

———. *After Christendom.* Nashville: Abingdon Press, 1991.

Hawken, P. *Blessed Unrest: How the Largest Movement in the World Came into Being and Why No One Saw It Coming.* New York: Viking, 2007.

Hay, Donald. *Economics Today: A Christian Critique.* Leichester: InterVarsity Press, 1989.

Hedges, C. *American Fascists: The Christian Right and the War on America.* New York: Free Press, 2007.

"Henry Institute National Survey on Religious and Public Life." The Henry Institute for the Study of Christianity and Politics, Calvin College, 2008. www.calvin.edu/henry/civic/Civic-RespGrant/Religionand2008Election.doc.

Hertzke, Allen D. *Freeing God's Children: The Unlikely Alliance for Global Human Rights.* Lanham, MD: Rowman & Littlefield, 2004.

———. "The Shame of Darfur." *First Things* 156 (2005): 16–22.

Higham, S., and J. Stephens. "Motivation in Some Abuses Comes to Light." *Concoki Monitor,* May 22, 2004.

Higham, Will. "The Evangelical Crusade." *New Statesman,* August 9, 2004. Available at www.newstatesman.com/200408090010.

Hinojosa, Victor J., and Jerry Z. Park. "Religion and the Paradox of Racial Inequality Attitudes." *Journal for the Scientific Study of Religion* 43 (2004): 229–238.

Hoffmeier, James. *Immigration Crisis: Immigrants, Aliens and the Bible.* Wheaton, IL: Crossway Books, 2009.

——— (Old Testament professor, Trinity Evangelical Divinity Seminary). Personal interview with Ruth Melkonian-Hoover, Wheaton, Illinois, April 6, 2010.

Holzer, Harry J. "Testimony on Income and Poverty in the United States: 2008." Presented before the Joint Economic Committee of the United State Congress. 2009.

———. Testimony before the Massachusetts Senate Committee Studying Gay Marriage. 2003.

Hoynes, Hilary W. "The Employment, Earnings, and Income of Less Skilled Workers over the Business Cycle." In *Finding Jobs: Work and Welfare Reform,* edited by Rebecca Blank and David Card, 23–71. New York: Russell Sage, 2000.

Hoynes, Hilary W., Marianne E. Page, and Ann Huff Stevens. "Poverty in America: Trends and Explanations." *Journal of Economic Perspectives* 20 (2006): 47–68.

Hume, David. *A Treatise of Human Nature,* edited by L. A. Selby-Bigge. London: Oxford University Press, 1965.

Hunter, Joel C. *A New Kind of Conservative.* Ventura, CA: Regal, 2008.

———. Testimony before U.S. Senate Committee on the Judiciary. April 30, 2009.

——— (senior pastor, Northland Church). Personal interview with Ruth Melkonian-Hoover, February 22, 2010.

Hunter, J. D. *Culture Wars: The Struggle to Define America.* New York: Basic Books, 1991.

Huntington, Samuel P. *The Third Wave: Democratization in the Late Twentieth Century.* Norman: University of Oklahoma Press, 1991.

Hutchison, William. *Errand to the World: American Protestant Thought and Foreign Missions.* Chicago: University of Chicago Press, 1987.

Hwang, Jenny (director for advocacy and policy, World Relief). Personal interview with Ruth Melkonian-Hoover, Washington, DC, March 21, 2010.

Hybels, Lynne. Testimony before U.S. Senate Judiciary Subcommittee on Immigration, Border Security and Refugees. October 8, 2009.

Interfaith Stewardship Alliance. "An Open Letter to the Signers of 'Climate Change: An Evangelical Call to Action' and Others Concerned about Global Warming." 2006.

International Crisis Group. "Sudan's Comprehensive Peace Agreement: Beyond the Crisis," March 13, 2008.

James, Scott. "Many Successful Gay Couples Share an Open Secret." *New York Times,* January 28, 2010. www.nytimes.com/2010/01/29/us/29sfmetro.html. Accessed July 21, 2010.

Jenkins, Philip. *The Next Christendom: The Coming of Global Christianity.* New York: Oxford University Press, 2002.

Jelen, Ted G. "Religion and Politics in the United States: Persistence, Limitations and the Prophetic Voice." *Social Compass* 53 (2006): 329–343.

Jobes, K. *I Peter.* Grand Rapids, MI: Baker Academic, 2005.

Johnson, Byron R. "Religiosity and Institutional Deviance: The Impact of Religious Variables upon Inmate Adjustment." *Criminal Justice Review* 12, no. 1 (1987): 21–30.

———. "Religious Programs, Institutional Adjustment, and Recidivism among Former Inmates in Prison Fellowship Programs." *Justice Quarterly* 14, no. 1 (1997): 145–66.

Jones, Robert P., and Daniel Cox. "Religion, Values and Immigration Reform." *Public Religion Research Institute.* www.publicreligion.org. March 23, 2009.

Jones, Stanton L., and Alex W. Kwee. "Scientific Research, Homosexuality, and the Church's Moral Debate: An Update." *Journal of Psychology and Christianity* 24, no. 4 (2005): 304–16.

Jones, Stanton L., and Mark A. Yarhouse. *Homosexuality: The Use of Scientific Research in the Church's Moral Debate.* Downers Grove, IL: InterVarsity Press, 2000.

Kapur, S. Paul. "India and Pakistan's Unstable Peace: Why Nuclear South Asia Is Not Like Cold War Europe." *International Security* 30, no. 2 (2005).

Kennedy, John F. "Remarks at Amherst College upon Receiving an Honorary Degree, October 26, 1963." *Public Papers of the Presidents of the United States, John F. Kennedy,* 815–18. Washington, DC, 1964.

Kirkpatrick, David D. "The Evangelical Crackup." *New York Times*, October 28, 2007.
———. "Huckabee Splits Young Evangelicals and Old Guard." *New York Times*, January 13, 2008. http://nytimes.com/2008/01/13/us/politics/13huckabee.html.
Kottler, Jennifer (director of advocacy and policy). Personal interview with Ruth Melkonian-Hoover, Washington, DC, February 19, 2010.
Kraft, M. E. *Environmental Policy and Politics*, 3rd ed. New York: Pearson Longman, 2004.
Kramnick, I., and R. L. Moore. *The Godless Constitution: A Moral Defense of the Secular State*, 2nd ed. New York: W. W. Norton, 2005.
Kristof, Nicholas. "Following God Abroad." *New York Times*, May, 21, 2002.
———. "Facing Down the Killers." *New York Times*, December 18, 2004.
———. "Evangelicals a Liberal Can Love." *New York Times*, February 3, 2008.
Kullberg, Kelly Monroe. "Justice for the Stranger AND Justice for the Neighbor." *Cross Examinations—Immigration Reform*. May 28, 2010. www.patheos.com.
Kurth, James. "Religion and Globalization." *The Templeton Lecture on Religion and World Affairs*, May 7, 1999.
Kurtz, Stanley N. "What Is Wrong with Gay Marriage." *Commentary* (September 2000), 35–41.
———. "Beyond Gay Marriage: The Road to Polyamory." *Weekly Standard*, August 4, 2003.
Land, Richard. "Immigration Crisis Requires Biblical Response." *The Ethics & Religious Liberty Commission of the Southern Baptist Convention*, April 27, 2006. http://erlc.com/article/immigration-crisis-demands-biblical-response/.
——— (president, Ethics and Religious Liberty Commission, Southern Baptist Convention). Telephone interview with Ruth Melkonian-Hoover, March 19, 2010.
———. "Immigration Crisis Requires a Biblical Response." Interview with Ruth Melkonian-Hoover, April 27, 2010.
Landler, Mark, and Edmund L. Andrews. "For Treasury Dept., Now Comes the Hard Part of Bailout." *New York Times*, October 4, 2008.
Lampman, Jane. "Evangelicals Find the Center." *Christian Science Monitor*. March 18, 2008. www.religionandsocialpolicy.org/newsletters/article_print.cfm?id=7954.
Larson, Heather (director of the Compassion and Justice Ministry, Willow Creek Church). Personal interview with Ruth Melkonian-Hoover, Chicago, Illinois, April 7, 2010.
Latour, B. *We Have Never Been Modern*. Cambridge, MA: Harvard University Press, 1993.
The Lausanne Covenant. 1974. http://www.lausanne.org/covenant. Accessed July 20, 2010.
Lee, P. *Abortion and Unborn Human Life*. Washington, DC: The Catholic University of America Press, 1996.
———. "The Prolife Argument from Substantial Identity: A Defense." *Bioethics* 18, no. 3 (2004):249–63.
Lee, P., and R. P. George. "The Wrong of Abortion." In *Contemporary Debates in Applied Ethics*, edited by Andrew I. Cohen and Christopher Wellman, 13–26. Malden, MA: Blackwell, 2005.
Lee, Thomas (pastor, Boston Chinese Evangelical Church). Personal interview with Ruth Melkonian-Hoover, Boston, Massachusetts, May 11, 2010.
Lewis, C. S. "The Humanitarian Theory of Punishment." In *God in the Dock: Essays on Theology and Ethics*, edited by W. Hooper. Grand Rapids, MI: Erdmans, 1970.
Liao, Enoch (pastor, Boston Chinese Evangelical Church). Personal interview with Ruth Melkonian-Hoover, Boston, May 11, 2010.
Liebman, R. C., and R. Wuthnow, eds. *The New Christian Right: Mobilization and Legitimation*. New York: Aldine Transaction, 1983.
Lienesch, Michael. *Redeeming America: Piety and Politics in the New Christian Right*. Chapel Hill: University of North Carolina Press, 1993.
Lindsay, D. Michael. *Faith in the Halls of Power: How Evangelicals Joined the American Elite*. New York: Oxford University Press, 2008.
Linker, Damon. "Sticking with the Devil They Know." *The New Republic*, November 7, 2008. www.tnr.com/story_print.html?id=36631201-fcf-42a2-84f0-1f956bf5459d.
Logan, James Samuel. *Good Punishment? Christian Moral Practice and U.S. Imprisonment*. Grand Rapids, MI: Eerdmans, 2008.

Long, Ronald E. "In Support of Same-Sex Marriage." *Philosophia Christi* 7, no. 1 (2005). http://homepage.mac.com/francis.beckwith/same-sex.pdf.

Mangalwadi, Vishal and Ruth. *The Legacy of William Carey: A Model for the Transformation of a Culture*. Wheaton, IL: Crossway Books, 1999.

Marsh, Charles. *Wayward Christian Soldiers: Freeing the Gospel from Political Captivity*. New York: Oxford University Press, 2008.

Marshall, Paul. "Human Rights." In *Toward an Evangelical Public Policy*, edited by Ronald J. Sider and Diane Knippers. Grand Rapids, MI: Baker, 2005.

———. Telephone interview with Ruth Melkonian-Hoover, May 20, 2008.

——— (senior fellow, Hudson Institute). Personal interview with Ruth Melkonian-Hoover, Washington, DC, March 22, 2010.

Martin, William. *With God on Our Side: The Rise of the Religious Right in America*. New York: Broadway Books, 1996.

———. "The Christian Right and American Foreign Policy." *Foreign Policy* 114 (1999): 66–80.

Martinson, Robert. "What Works?—Questions and Answers about Prison Reform." *Public Interest* 35 (1974): 22–54.

Marty, Martin E. *Modern American Religion: Under God, Indivisible, 1941–1960*. Chicago: University of Chicago Press, 1999.

McCorkle, Richard C. "Research Note: Punish and Rehabilitate? Public Attitudes toward Six Common Crimes." *Crime Delinquency* 39, no. 2 (1993): 240–52.

McDaniel, Eric L., and Christopher G. Ellison. "God's Party? Race, Religion, and Partisanship over Time." *Political Research Quarterly* 61 (2008): 180–91.

McKelvey, Blake. *American Prisons: A History of Good Intentions*. Montclair, NJ: Patterson Smith, 1977.

McLaren, A. "The Embryo." In *Reproduction in Mammals*, bk. 2, *Embryonic and Fetal Development*, 2nd ed, edited by C. R. Austin and R. V. Short. Cambridge: Cambridge University Press, 1982.

McMahon, Robert. "Christian Evangelicals and U.S. Foreign Policy." *Council on Foreign Relations*, August 23, 2006. www.cfr.org/publication/11341/.

Mead, Walter Russell. *Special Providence: American Foreign Policy and How It Changed the World*. New York: Routledge, 2002.

———. "God's Country?" *Foreign Affairs*, September/October, 2006. http://fullaccess.foreignaffairs.org/20060901faessay85504/walter-russell-mead/god-scountry.html.

———. "Born Again." *The Atlantic*, March 2008, 21–23.

Mensch, Elizabeth. "*Christianity and the Roots of Liberalism*." In *Christian Perspectives on Legal Thought*, edited by Michael W. McConnell et al. New Haven, CT: Yale University Press, 2001.

Messinger, Sheldon L., and Phillip E. Johnson. "California's Determinate Sentencing Statute: History and Issues." In *Determinate Sentencing: Reform or Regression*. Washington, DC: U.S. Government Printing Office, 1978.

Middleton, J. Richard. "Is Creation Theology Inherently Conservative? A Dialogue with Walter Brueggemann." *Harvard Theological Review* 87, no. 3 (1994).

Miller, Lisa. "Our Mutual Joy." *Newsweek*, December 6, 2008.

Miller, Matt, and Barbara Miller. "Keeping the Memory Alive." *Patriot-News*, September 11, 2009. Available at www.pennlive.com.

Minnery, Tom, and Glenn T. Stanton. "Family Integrity." In *Toward an Evangelical Public Policy*, edited by Ronald J. Sider and Diane Knippers. Grand Rapids, MI: Baker Books, 2005.

Moberg, David O. *The Great Reversal: Evangelicalism and Social Concern*. Philadelphia: Lippincott, 1972.

Moltmann, Jurgen. *Theology of Hope*. New York: Harper & Row, 1967.

———. "Political Theology and the Ethics of Peace," *Theology, Politics and Peace*, edited by Theodore Runyon. Maryknoll, NY: Orbis, 1990.

Monsma, Stephen V. "The Promise and Pitfalls of Evangelical Political Involvement." In *Contemporary Evangelical Political Involvement: An Analysis and Assessment,* edited by Corwin Smidt. New York: University Press of America, 1989.

———. *Putting Faith in Partnerships.* Ann Arbor: University of Michigan Press, 2005.

———. "An Effectiveness Perspective." In *Not by Faith or Government Alone: Rethinking the Role of Faith-Based Organizations, 2–4.* Baylor Institute for Studies of Religion, 2008.

Monsma, Stephen V., and J. Christopher Soper. *Faith, Hope and Jobs.* Washington, DC: Georgetown University Press, 2007.

Mooney, Christopher. *The Republican War on Science.* New York: Basic Books, 2005.

Moore, Frank. "A New Light in Prison Life." *The Prison Journal* 4, no. 4 (1924): 3–8.

Moreau, A. Scott. "Putting the Survey in Perspective." In *Mission Handbook: U.S. and Canadian Protestant Ministries Overseas, 2000–2006,* edited by Dotsey Welliver and Minnette Northcutt. Wheaton, IL: Billy Graham Center, Wheaton College, 2004.

Moreland, J. P. *The Kingdom Triangle.* Grand Rapids, MI: Zondervan, 2007.

Moreland, J. P., and S. B. Rae. *Body and Soul: Human Nature and the Crisis in Ethics.* Downers Grove, IL: InterVarsity, 2000.

"Most Evangelical Leaders Still Support Iraq War." *Christianity Today,* February 12, 2008.

Myers, David G., and Letha Dawson Scanzoni. *What God Has Joined Together? A Christian Case for Gay Marriage.* San Francisco: HarperCollins, 2005.

Nash, Ronald H. *Poverty and Wealth: The Christian Debate over Capitalism.* Westchester: Crossway Books, 1986.

National Association of Evangelicals. "Guidelines—Peace Freedom, and Security Studies: A Program of the National Association of Evangelicals." 1986. www.nae.org.

———. "Statement of Conscience concerning Worldwide Religious Persecution." 1996. www.nae.org.

———. "For the Health of the Nation: An Evangelical Call to Civic Responsibility." 2004. www.nae.org.

———. "Immigration 2009." 2009. www.nae.net.

National Bioethics Advisory Commission. "Ethical Issues in Human Stem Cell Research, Volume I," 1999. http://bioethics.georgetown.edu/nbac/stemcell.pdf.

Neff, David (editor in chief, *Christianity Today*). Personal interview with Ruth Melkonian-Hoover, Carol Stream, Illinois, April 7, 2010.

Neill, Stephen. *Colonialism and Christian Missions.* New York: McGraw-Hill, 1966.

Nichols, J. Bruce. *The Uneasy Alliance: Religion, Refugee Work, and U.S. Foreign Policy.* New York: Oxford University Press, 1988.

Niebuhr, Reinhold. *Christian Realism and Political Problems.* New York: The Scribner Press, 1953.

Noell, Edd S. "A Reformed Approach to Economics: Christian Reconstructionism." *ACE Bulletin,* no. 21 (1993): 6–20.

———. "Two Approaches to Fashioning a Christian Perspective on the Liberal Market Order: A Symposium." *ACE Bulletin,* no. 44 (2004): 39–92.

Noll, Mark A. *The Scandal of the Evangelical Mind.* Grand Rapids, MI: Eerdmans, 1994.

———. "Evangelicals in the American Founding and Evangelical Political Mobilization Today." In *Religion and the New Republic: Faith in the Founding of America,* edited by James H. Hutson. Boulder, CO: Rowman & Littlefield Publishers, 2000.

Noll, Mark A., and Luke E. Harlow, eds. *Religion and American Politics: From the Colonial Period to the Present.* New York: Oxford University Press, 2007.

Norris, Pippa, and Ronald Inglehart. *Sacred and Secular: Religion and Politics Worldwide.* Cambridge: Cambridge University Press, 2004.

Northcott, M. S. *The Environment and Christian Ethics.* Cambridge: Cambridge University Press, 1996.

Obama, Barack. Keynote Address. "Call to Renewal." Washington, DC, June 28, 2006. www.barackobama.com/2006/06/28/call_to_renewal_keynote_address.php.

Olasky, Marvin. *The Tragedy of American Compassion.* Washington, DC: Regnery Gateway, 1992.

Ostling, Richard. "The Battle for Latin America's Soul." *Time*, June 24, 2001. www.time.com/time/magazine/article/0,9171,156277,00.html.

Owensby, Walter L. *Economics for Prophets*. Grand Rapids, MI: Eerdmans, 1988.

Pannell, William E. *My Friend, the Enemy*. Waco, TX. Word Books, 1968.

———. *The Coming Race Wars? A Cry for Reconciliation*. Grand Rapids, MI: Zondervan, 1993.

Parker, Kathleen. "Giving Up on God." *Washington Post*, November 19, 2008. Available at www.washingtonpost.com/wpdyn/content/article/2008/11/18/AR2008111802886.html?nav=rss_opinion/columns.

Patterson, Eric. *Latin America's Neo-Reformation: Religion's Influence on Politics*. New York: Routledge, 2005.

Paulson, Henry W. "Fighting the Financial Crisis, One Challenge at a Time." *New York Times*, November 18, 2008.

Pendleton, O. A. "Prison Reform and the Evangelical Churches." *The Prison Journal* 28, no. 2 (1948): 383–97.

Perkins, John, and Thomas Tarrants. *He's My Brother: Former Racial Foes Offer Strategies for Reconciliation*. Grand Rapids, MI: Baker Books, 1994.

Petersen, Douglas. *Not by Might Nor by Power: A Pentecostal Theology of Social Concern in Latin America*. Oxford: Regnum Books International, 1996.

Pew Research Center for the People and the Press and the Pew Hispanic Center. "2006 Immigration Survey." 2006. www.pewresearch.org.

Phillips, Kevin. *American Theocracy: The Peril and Politics of Radical Religion, Oil, and Borrowed Money in the 21st Century*. New York: Viking Adult, 2006.

———. *Bad Money, Reckless Finance, Failed Politics, and the Global Crisis of American Capitalism*. New York: Penguin Group, 2008.

Philpott, Daniel. "Religious Freedom and the Undoing of the Westphalian State." *Michigan Journal of International Law* 25 (2004): 981.

Plantinga, Alvin. *Warranted Christian Belief*. New York: Oxford University Press, 2000.

Pope Pius XII. "Crime and Punishment." In *Contemporary Punishment: Views, Explanations, and Justifications*, edited by R. J. Gerber and P. D. McAnany. Notre Dame, IN: University of Notre Dame, 1972.

Prager, Dennis. "California Decision Will Radically Change Society." *Weekly Standard*, May 20, 2008.

Prison Fellowship Ministries. *About PFM*. www.pfm.org.

Putman, Robert. *Bowling Alone: The Collapse and Revival of American Community*. New York: Simon & Schuster, 2000.

Quinn, Sally. "Worlds Apart." *Washington Post*, August 18, 2008. www.washingtonpost.com/wp-dyn/content/article/2008/08/17/AR2008081702080.html.

Racial Reconciliation Manifesto. www.pctii.org/manifesto.html.

Ramirez, Margaret. "Latinos Courted as Wild Card among Shifting Evangelical Voters." *Chicago Tribune*. January 29, 2008.

Rauschenbusch, W. *Christianity and the Social Crisis*. New York: Macmillan, 1907.

Raush, Jonathan. "Gay Marriage Is Good for America." *Wall Street Journal*, June 21, 2008, A9.

Reed, James. *The Missionary Mind and American East Asia Policy, 1911–1915*. Cambridge, MA: Harvard University Press, 1983.

Reichley, A. J. "Religion and the Future of American Politics." *Political Science Quarterly* 101 (1986): 23–47.

Rice, Chris, and Spencer Perkins. *More Than Equals: Racial Healing for the Sake of the Gospel*. Downers Grove, IL: InterVarsity Press, 2000.

Richter, Paul, and Thomas H. Maugh II. "One Misstep Away from Nuclear War." *Los Angeles Times*, June 1, 2002.

Ricks, Thomas E. *The Gamble: General David Petraeus and the American Military Adventure in Iraq, 2006–2008*. New York: Penguin Press, 2009.

Riley, Naomi Schaefer. "Loyal to the End: Evangelicals Stay the Course." *Wall Street Journal*, November 7, 2008, W11.

Roberts, Julian V. "Public Opinion, Crime, and Criminal Justice." In *Crime and Justice: A Review of Research*, edited by M. Tonry. Chicago: University of Chicago Press, 1992.

Rodriguez, Samuel (president, National Hispanic Christian Leadership Conference). Personal interview with Ruth Melkonian-Hoover, May 13, 2010.

Roe v. Wade, 410 U.S. 113 (1973).

Rothman, David J. "For the Good of All: The Progressive Tradition in Prison Reform." In *History and Crime: Implications for Criminal Justice Policy*, edited by J. A. Inciardi and C. E. Faupel. Beverly Hills, CA: Sage Publications, 1980.

Saad, Lydia. "Americans Evenly Divided on Morality of Homosexuality." *Gallup 2008*. www.gallup.com/poll/108115/americans-evenly-divided-morality-homosexuality.aspx.

Sandys, Marla, and Edmund F. McGarrell. "Beyond the Bible Belt: The Influence (or Lack Thereof) of Religion on Attitudes toward the Death Penalty." *Journal of Crime and Justice* 20, no. 1 (1997): 179–90.

Satinover, Jeffrey. *Homosexuality and the Politics of Truth*. Grand Rapids, MI: Baker, 1996.

———. Testifying before the Massachusetts Senate Committee Studying Gay Marriage, April 28, 2003. National Association for Research & Therapy of Homosexuality. www.narth.com/docs/senatecommittee.html.

Schaefer, Kurt C., and Edd S. Noell. "Contract Theory, Distributive Justice, and the Hebrew Sabbatical." *ACE Bulletin*, no. 45 (2005): 1–19.

Schindler, Jeanne Heffernan, ed. *Christianity and Civil Society: Catholic and Neo-Calvinist Perspectives*. Lanham, MD: Rowman & Littlefield, 2008.

Schlesinger, Arthur, Jr. "The Missionary Enterprise and Theories of Imperialism." In *The Missionary Enterprise in China and America*, edited by John K. Fairbank. Cambridge, MA: Harvard University Press, 1974.

———. *Robert Kennedy and His Times*. New York: Ballantine. 1979

Schlossberg, Herbert, Vinay Samuel, and Ronald J. Sider, eds. *Christianity and Economics in the Post-Cold War Era: The Oxford Declaration and Beyond*. Grand Rapids, MI: Eerdmans, 1994.

Schmidt, Thomas E. *Straight and Narrow? Compassion and Clarity in the Homosexuality Debate*. Downers Grove, IL: InterVarsity Press, 1995.

Schulz, John. "The Matches Are Lit in a Nuclear Power Keg." *San Diego Union Tribune*, June 9, 2002.

Scott, L., ed. *Christians, the Care of Creation, and Global Climate Change*. Eugene, OR: Wipf and Stock, 2008.

Seager, Robert. "Some Denominational Reactions to Chinese Immigration to California. 1856–1892." *Pacific Historical Review* 28 (1959): 49–66.

Shah, Samuel Timothy. "Some Evangelical Views of the State." In *Church, State and Citizen: Christian Approaches to Political Engagement*, edited by Sandra Joireman. New York: Oxford University Press, 2009.

Shapley, Debora. *Promise and Power: The Life and Times of Robert McNamara*. Boston: Little Brown, 1993.

Shattuck, John. "Religion, Rights, and Terrorism." *Harvard Human Rights Journal* 16 (Spring, 2003): 183–88.

Shellenberger, Michael, and Ted Nordhaus. *The Death of Environmentalism: Global Warming Politics in a Post-Environmental World* (Report). 2004. Available at www.thebreakthrough.org/PDF/Death-of-Environmentalism.pdf.

Sherman, Amy L. *The Soul of Development: Biblical Christianity and Economic Transformation in Guatemala*. New York: Oxford University Press, 1997.

Sider, Ronald J. *Rich Christians in an Age of Hunger: A Biblical Study*. Downers Grove, IL: InterVarsity Press, 1977.

———. *Completely Pro-Life: Building a Consistent Stance*. Downers Grove, IL: InterVarsity, 1987.

———. "Justice, Human Rights, and Government: Toward an Evangelical Perspective." In *Toward an Evangelical Public Policy: Political Strategies for the Health of the Nation*, edited by Ronald J. Sider and Diane Knippers. Grand Rapids, MI: Baker Books, 2005a.

————. *The Scandal of The Evangelical Conscience: Why Are Christians Living Just Like the Rest of the World?* Grand Rapids, MI. Baker Books, 2005b.

———— (president, Evangelicals for Social Action). Personal interview with Ruth Melkonian-Hoover, Philadelphia, Pennsylvania, May 4, 2010.

Sider, Ronald J., and Diane Knippers, eds. *Toward an Evangelical Public Policy.* Grand Rapids, MI: Baker Books, 2005.

Sifton, Elisabeth. "Edited Transcripts: The Resurgence of Religion in Politics Series." *Carnegie Council on Ethics and International Affairs.* 2005. http://cceia.org/viewMedia.php/prm TemplateID/8/prmID/5218.

Silver, L. M. *The Clash of Science and Spirituality at the New Frontiers of Life.* New York: Ecco, 2006.

Simmons, P. D. "Religious Liberty and Abortion Policy: *Casey* as 'Catch-22.'" *Journal of Church and State* 42 (2000).

Singer, Peter. "Heavy Petting." *Nerve* (2001). http://www.utilitarian.net/singer/by/2001————.htm.

Singer, Richard G. *Just Deserts: Sentencing Based on Equality and Desert.* Cambridge, MA: Ballinger Publishing Company, 1979.

Smolin, David M. "Will International Human Rights Be Used as a Tool of Cultural Genocide? The Interaction of Human Rights Norms, Religion, Culture and Gender." *Journal of Law and Religion* 12 (1995–96).

Soerens, Matthew (immigration counselor, World Relief). Personal interview with Ruth Melkonian-Hoover, Washington, DC, March 21, 2010.

Southern Baptist Environment and Climate Initiative. "A Southern Baptist Declaration on the Environment and Climate Change." March 10, 2008. Available at www.baptistcreationcare.org/node/1.

"Southern Baptist Leaders Shift Position on Climate Change." *CNN.* March 10, 2008. www.cnn.com/2008/US/03/10/baptist.climate/.

Spencer, Michael. "The Coming Evangelical Collapse." *Christian Science Monitor*, March 10, 2009. www.csmonitor.com/Commentary/Opinion/2009/0310/p09s01-coop.html.

Speth, J. G. *The Bridge at the End of the World: Capitalism, the Environment, and Crossing from Crisis to Sustainability.* New Haven, CT: Yale University Press, 2008.

Stapleford, John E. *Bulls, Bears & Golden Calves: Applying Christian Ethics in Economics.* Downers Grover, IL: InterVarsity Press, 2002.

Stepan, Alfred. "Religion, Democracy, and the 'Twin Tolerations.'" *Journal of Democracy* 11, no. 4 (2000).

Stern, Marc D. "Will Gay Rights Trample Religious Freedom?" *Los Angeles Times*, June 17, 2008. http://latimes.com/news/opinion/la-oe-stern17-2008jun17,0,5628051.story.

Stolberg, Sheryl Gay. "Bush Promotes His Free Trade Initiatives." *New York Times*, January 31, 2007.

Stott, John. *Same-Sex Partnerships? A Christian Perspective.* Grand Rapids, MI: Baker House, 1998.

Strain, Charles R., ed. *Prophetic Visions and Economic Realities: Protestants, Jews, Catholics Confront the Bishop's Letter on the Economy.* Grand Rapids, MI: Eerdmans, 1989.

Strassberg, Maura I. "The Challenge of Postmodern Polygamy: Considering Polyamory." *Capital University Law Review* 31 (2003):139.

Sullivan, Winnifred Fallers. *Prison Religion: Faith-Based Reform and the Constitution.* Princeton, NJ: Princeton University Press, 2009.

Sundt, Jody L., and Francis T. Cullen. "The Correctional Ideology of Prison Chaplains: A National Survey." *Journal of Criminal Justice* 30 (2002).

Swearengen, Jack Clayton. "Arms Control and God's Purpose in History." *Perspectives on Science & the Christian Faith* 44, no. 2 (1992).

Tancredo, Thomas (former congressman, chair, Rocky Mountain Foundation). Personal interview with Ruth Melkonian-Hoover, Littleton, Colorado, April 21, 2010.9

Tapie, Matthew A. "The Retreat and Resurgence of Evangelical Civic Engagement in the Twentieth Century." *Restoration Quarterly* 48, no. 3 (2006): 157–70.

Taylor, Charles. *A Catholic Modernity?* Edited by James Heft. New York: Oxford University Press, 1999.

Taylor, Mark Lewis. *The Executed God: The Way of the Cross in Lockdown America.* Minneapolis: Fortress Press, 2001.

Teague, P. "Foreword." In *The Death of Environmentalism: Global Warming Politics in a Post-Environmental World*, edited by Michael Shellenberger and Ted Nordhaus. Oakland, CA: Breakthrough Insitute, 2004.

Thomas, Jim, and Barbara H. Zaitzow. "Conning or Conversion? The Role of Religion in Prison Coping." *The Prison Journal* 10, no. 4 (1930): 12–23.

Thomas Aquinas. *On Human Nature.* Edited by T. S. Hibbs. Indianapolis: Hackett, 1999.

Toly, Noah J. "Changing the Climate of Christian Internationalism: Global Warming and Human Suffering." *Brandywine Review of Faith and International Affairs* 2, no. 2 (2004): 31–37.

———. "A Tale of Two Regimes: Instrumentality and Commons Access." *Bulletin of Science, Technology, and Society,* 25, no. 1 (2005a).

———. "Climate Change and Climate Change Policy as Human Sacrifice: Artifice, Idolatry, and Environment in a Technological Society." *Christian Scholar's Review* 35, no. 1 (2005b): 63–78.

———. "Are Evangelicals Warming to Global Environmentalism?" *Review of Faith and International Affairs* 4, no. 4 (2007).

———. "Changing the Climate of Religious Internationalism: Global Warming and Human Suffering." In *Handbook of Religion and Politics,* edited by J. Haynes. New York: Routledge, 2008.

Toly, Noah J., and Daniel I. Block. *Keeping God's Earth: Creation Care and the Global Environment in Biblical Perspective.* Downers Grove, IL: IVP Academic, 2010.

Tooley, Mark (president, Institute on Religion and Democracy). Personal interview with Ruth Melkonian-Hoover, Washington, DC, February 19, 2010.

Totten, Mark. "A New Agenda for US Evangelicals." *Christian Science Monitor,* December 16, 2006. www.csmonitor.com/2006/1218/p09s02-coop.html.

Tranby, Eric, and Douglas Hartmann. "Critical Whiteness Theories and the Evangelical 'Race Problem': Extending Emerson and Smith's *Divided by Faith.*" *Journal for the Scientific Study of Religion* 47, no. 3 (2008): 341–59.

Tweedy, Ann E. "Polyamory as a Sexual Orientation." June 29, 2010. Available at SSRN: http://ssrn.com/abstract=1632653.

U.S. Census Bureau, American Fact Finder. "S1501. Educational Attainment, 2006." *American Community Survey.* http://factfinder.census.gov.

U.S. Religious Landscape Survey: Religious Beliefs and Practices: Diverse and Politically Relevant. Pew Forum on Religion and Public Life, June 2008.

Van Bkiema, David. "Who Is Joel Hunter, and Why Is Obama Praying with Him?" *Time,* November 6, 2008. www.time.com/time/politics/article/0,8599,1857140,00.html.

Wadsworth, Nancy D. "Reconciliation Politics: Conservative Evangelicals and the New Race Discourse." *Politics & Society* 25 (1997): 341–76.

Wallis, Jim. *God's Politics: Why the Right Gets It Wrong and the Left Doesn't Get It.* San Francisco: HarperCollins, 2005.

———. *The Great Awakening: Reviving Faith and Politics in a Post-Religious Right America.* New York: HarperOne, 2008.

———. "Afghanistan: A Whole New Approach." *Sojourners: Faith, Politics and Culture. Weblog,* posted October 29, 2009. http://blog.sojo.net/.

Walsh, Jennifer E. *Three Strikes Laws.* Westport, CT: Greenwood Publishing, 2007.

Weeks, David L. "Response." In *Evangelicals in the Public Square: Carl F. Henry, Abraham Kuyper, Francis Schaeffer, John Howard Yoder,* edited by J. Budziszewski et al. Grand Rapids, MI: Baker Academic, 2006.

West Coast Poverty Center. "Changing Labor Markets and Poverty." http://depts.washington.edu/wcpc/LaborMarkets. Accessed July 23, 2010.

Wilbanks, Dana W. *Re-Creating America: The Ethics of US Immigration and Refugee Policy in a Christian Perspective.* Nashville: Abingdon Press, 1996.

Wilcox, Clyde. *Onward Christian Soldiers: The Religious Right in American Politics,* 2nd ed. Boulder, CO: Westview Press, 2000.

Wilcox, W. Bradford. "Need a Long Spoon? Review of *Faith in the Halls of Power,* by D. Michael Lindsay." *Books and Culture* 13 (2007): 33.

Wildmon, Donald., Tony Perkins, James C. Dobson, Gary L. Bauer, Paul Weyrich, J. Daly, et al. Open Letter to Roy Taylor, Chairman of the Board, National Association of Evangelicals. March 1, 2007. Available at www.pauldavidtuff.com/PDF%20Files/NAE%20Letter.pdf. Accessed July 23, 2010.

Willard, D. (2000). "How Reason Can Survive the Modern University: The Moral Foundations of Rationality." Unpublished paper delivered at the American Maritain Association meeting at the University of Notre Dame (19–22 October 2000), retrieved October 10, 2008, from www.dwillard.org/articles/artview.asp?artID=33.

Wilson, James Q. *Thinking about Crime.* New York: Basic Books, 1975.

Wilson, William Julius. *The Truly Disadvantaged: The Inner City, the Underclass, and Public Policy.* Chicago: University of Chicago Press, 1987.

———. "The Political and Economic Forces Shaping Concentrated Poverty." *Political Science Quarterly* 123 (2008–2009): 555–71.

Winter, Roger. "Abyei Aflame: An Update from the Field." Center for American Progress. www.americanprogress.org/issues.

Witte, John, Jr. "Law, Religion and Human Rights." *Columbia Human Rights Law Review* 28, no. 1 (1996): 10.

Wolterstorff, N. *Justice: Rights and Wrongs.* Princeton, NJ: Princeton University Press, 2008.

Wong, Craig (executive director, Grace Urban Ministries). Personal interview with Ruth Melkonian-Hoover, June 9, 2010.

Woodberry, Robert D., and Timothy S. Shah. "Christianity and Democracy: The Pioneering Protestants." *Journal of Democracy* 13 (2004).

World Public Opinion. "WPO Poll Analysis: American Evangelicals Are Divided on International Policy." www.worldpublicopinion.org/incl/printable_version.php?pnt=270.

Wuthnow, Robert, and Valerie Lewis. "Religion and Altruistic U.S. Foreign Policy Goals: Evidence from a National Survey of Church Members." *Journal for the Scientific Study of Religion* 47 (2008): 191–209.

Yale Center for Faith and Culture. "Loving God and Neighbor Together: A Christian Response to 'A Common Word between Us and You.'" www.yale.edu/faith/acw/acw.htm. 2007. Accessed July 20, 2010.

Yarhouse, Mark. *Homosexuality and the Christian: A Guide for Parents, Pastors, and Friends.* Grand Rapids, MI: Baker Books, 2007.

Yuengert, Andrew M. "The Common Good for Economists." *ACE Bulletin,* no. 38 (2001): 1–9.

Zoll, R. "Southern Baptists Fight Climate Change." *Associated Press* (2008).

Zunes, Stephen. "The Influence of the Christian Right in US Middle East Policy." *Middle East Policy* 12 (2005): 73–78.

Zwier, Robert. *Born-Again Politics: The New Christian Right.* Downers Grove, IL: InterVarsity Press, 1982.

Index

About the Contributors

Mark Amstutz is professor of political science at Wheaton College. His scholarly interests are in international affairs and the ethics of global politics. His recent books include *The Rules of the Game: A Primer on International Relations* (2008), International Ethics: Concepts, Theories, and Cases in Global Politics, third edition (2008), *The Healing of Nations: The Promise and Limits of Political Forgiveness* (2004), International Ethics: Concepts, Theories, and Cases in Global Politics (1999), and *International Conflict and Cooperation: An Introduction to World Politics*, second edition (1999). He has written many book chapters and published articles in the *Review of Faith & International Affairs* and the *Journal of State & Church*. Dr. Amstutz has been the recipient of awards on the Wheaton campus both for his teaching and his scholarship. He also has directed a European studies program and twice led shorter study programs to Cuba.

Timothy J. Barnett is assistant professor of political science at Jacksonville State University. He holds degrees in marketing and theology, an MPA from Boise State University, and a PhD in political science from the University of Kansas. He is former president of the Alabama Political Science Association and has written extensively on legislative politics, constitutional federalism, political economy, and religious liberty. Dr. Barnett's recent scholarship examines communitarian values in federalist societies as plausible subsets of individualistic choices, and as such, deserving of the protections commonly afforded to libertarian choices.

Francis J. Beckwith is professor of philosophy and church-state studies, and fellow and faculty associate at the Institute for the Studies of Religion at Baylor University, where he teaches in the departments of philosophy and political science and at the J. M. Dawson Institute for Church-State Studies. He also is the Mary Anne Remick Senior Visiting Fellow at the Notre Dame Center for Ethics and Culture. He holds five earned degrees, including a PhD in philosophy from Fordham University and a Master of Juridical Studies from the Washington University School of Law in St. Louis. He has authored or edited more than fifteen books, including *Confessions of a Vain Philosopher: Reflections on My Return to the Catholic Church* (2008), *Relativism: Feet Firmly Planted in Mid-Air* (1998), *To Everyone An Answer: A Case for the Christian Worldview* (2004), *Law, Darwinism, and Public Education: The Establishment Clause and the Challenge of Intelligent Design* (2003), and *Defending Life: A Moral and Legal Case Against Abortion Choice* (2007). He has published in *Harvard Journal of Law & Public Policy*, *Notre Journal of Law, Ethics & Public Policy*, *Public Affairs Quarterly*, *Journal of Law & Religion*, *Social Theory & Practice*, *Catholic Social Science Review*, *Journal of Medical Ethics*, *Journal of Medicine & Philosophy*, *Journal of the Evangelical Theological Society*, and many others. Dr. Beckwith also was formerly president of the Evangelical Theological Society and board member of both the Society of Christian Philosophers and the Evangelical Philosophical Society.

Zachary R. Calo is assistant professor of law at the Valparaiso University School of Law. He holds a PhD in American religious history from the University of Pennsylvania, has a law degree from the University of Virginia School of Law, and is a doctoral candidate in theological ethics at the University of Virginia. He currently is completing a book on John A. Ryan and twentieth-century American Catholic social thought.

Ron Kirkemo is professor of political science at Point Loma Nazarene University, and holds a PhD in international politics. His research interests lie in the area of Christian influences on American foreign policy. He has authored several books, including *An Introduction to International Law* (1973) and *Between the Eagle and the Dove: The Christian and American Foreign Policy* (1975). He also has published chapters or articles on topics relating to evangelical stances on the strategic implication of the use of nuclear weapons and on teaching as an act of faith.

Jacob Lenerville is a graduate student in political science at California State University, Long Beach.

Ruth Melkonian-Hoover is assistant professor in the political studies department at Gordon College in Wenham, Massachusetts, where she also co-chairs the international affairs major. She received her MA and PhD degrees from Emory University, and her scholarly interests include Latin American politics, immigration, women and politics, and religion and politics. She has published articles in such journals as *Social Science Quarterly*, The Review of Faith & International Affairs, Latin American Perspectives, and *Political Research Quarterly*.

Stephen V. Monsma is a research fellow at the Henry Institute for the Study of Christianity and Politics at Calvin College. He is a professor emeritus of political science at Pepperdine University, where he held the Blanche E. Seaver chair in social science, and a nonresident scholar at the Institute for Studies of Religion at Baylor University. He has published widely on public policy, church-state relations, and faith-based nonprofit organizations. His most recent books include *Healing for a Broken World: Christian Perspectives on Public Policy* (2008), *Faith, Hope and Jobs: Welfare-to-Work in Los Angeles* (2006), Putting Faith in Partnerships: Welfare-to-Work in Four Cities (2004), *The Challenge of Pluralism: Church and State in Five Democracies* (1997, with J. Christopher Soper), *When Sacred and Secular Mix: Religious Nonprofit Organizations and Public Money* (1996), and Positive Neutrality (1993). He has published articles in such journals as the Journal of Church and State, *Policy Studies Review*, and Notre Dame Journal of Law, Ethics, and Public Policy.

Eric Patterson is assistant director of the Berkley Center for Religion, Peace and World Affairs at Georgetown University. He previously was a White House fellow and was on the faculty at Vanguard University in California. From 2005 to 2007 he was a Foster Fellow at the U.S. State Department, where he studied and worked on international illicit trafficking in small arms and light weapons. He is the author or editor of five books, including *Christianity and Power Politics Today* (2008) and *Just War Thinking: Morality and Pragmatism in the Struggle against Contemporary Threats* (2007).

Jeffrey Polet is associate professor of political science at Hope College. He holds an undergraduate degree from Calvin College and a PhD from the Catholic University of America. He coedited, with David Ryden, *Sanctioning Religion? Politics, Law, and Faith-Based Public Services*. Dr. Polet has authored pieces on a broad range of topics, from the constitutionality of term limits to contemporary continental theory. He is currently working on a book on the political philosophy of John Marshall.

David K. Ryden is professor of political science at Hope College. He holds a PhD from the Catholic University of America and a law degree from the University of Minnesota law school. He has authored, coauthored, or edited six books, including *Sanctioning Religion? Politics, Law, and Faith-Based Public Services* (2006), *Of Little Faith: The Politics of George W. Bush's*

Faith-Based Initiatives (2004), *The U.S. Supreme Court and The Electoral Process: Perspectives and Commentaries on Contemporary Cases, Revised and Updated Edition* (2002), and Representation in Crisis: The Constitution, Interest Groups, and Political Parties (1996). He also has authored numerous other articles and chapters on the topics of religion, law, and politics.

Noah J. Toly is assistant professor of politics and international relations and director of urban studies at Wheaton College. He previously served as a policy fellow at the University of Delaware's Center for Energy and Environmental Policy. He is coeditor of *Transforming Power: Energy, Environment, and Society in Conflict* (2006), and he has written several articles on climate change, environmental justice, and urban environments. His interests lie at the intersection of local and global politics, with a focus on cities and global environmentalism.

Jennifer E. Walsh is associate professor of political science at Azusa Pacific University. Her research on how prosecutors and judges use their discretion under the California three-strikes law has been widely disseminated. She most recently published *Three Strike Laws* (2007). She also has served as a consultant to the California District Attorney's Association and has testified before the California state legislature. Professor Walsh also has written on the role of faith-based organizations in providing re-entry services to juvenile delinquents.

Made in the USA
Columbia, SC
28 August 2017